STUDIES IN THE HISTORY OF CHRISTIAN MISSIONS

R. E. Frykenberg
Brian Stanley
General Editors

STUDIES IN THE HISTORY OF CHRISTIAN MISSIONS

Alvyn Austin
China's Millions: The China Inland Mission and Late Qing Society, 1832-1905

Chad M. Bauman
Christian Identity and Dalit Religion in Hindu India, 1868-1947

Michael Bergunder
The South Indian Pentecostal Movement in the Twentieth Century

Judith M. Brown and Robert Eric Frykenberg, *Editors*
Christians, Cultural Interactions, and India's Religious Traditions

John B. Carman and Chilkuri Vasantha Rao
Christians in South Indian Villages, 1959-2009: Decline and Revival in Telangana

Robert Eric Frykenberg
Christians and Missionaries in India:
Cross-Cultural Communication Since 1500

Susan Billington Harper
In the Shadow of the Mahatma: Bishop V. S. Azariah
and the Travails of Christianity in British India

D. Dennis Hudson
Protestant Origins in India: Tamil Evangelical Christians, 1706-1835

Patrick Harries and David Maxwell, *Editors*
The Spiritual in the Secular: Missionaries and Knowledge about Africa

Ogbu U. Kalu, *Editor,* and Alaine M. Low, *Associate Editor*
Interpreting Contemporary Christianity:
Global Processes and Local Identities

Donald M. Lewis, *Editor*
Christianity Reborn: The Global Expansion of Evangelicalism
in the Twentieth Century

Jessie G. Lutz
Opening China: Karl F. A. Gützlaff and Sino-Western Relations, 1827-1852

Stephen S. Maughan
Mighty England Do Good: Culture, Faith, Empire, and World in the Foreign
Missions of the Church of England, 1850-1915

Jon Miller
Missionary Zeal and Institutional Control: Organizational Contradictions in the Basel Mission on the Gold Coast, 1828-1917

Andrew Porter, *Editor*
The Imperial Horizons of British Protestant Missions, 1880-1914

Dana L. Robert, *Editor*
Converting Colonialism: Visions and Realities in Mission History, 1709-1914

Jane Samson
Race and Redemption: British Missionaries Encounter Pacific Peoples, 1797-1920

Wilbert R. Shenk, *Editor*
North American Foreign Missions, 1810-1914: Theology, Theory, and Policy

Brian Stanley
The World Missionary Conference: Edinburgh 1910

Brian Stanley, *Editor*
Christian Missions and the Enlightenment

Brian Stanley, *Editor*
Missions, Nationalism, and the End of Empire

John Stuart
British Missionaries and the End of Empire: East, Central, and Southern Africa, 1939-64

T. Jack Thompson
Light on Darkness? Missionary Photography of Africa in the Nineteenth and Early Twentieth Centuries

Kevin Ward and Brian Stanley, *Editors*
The Church Mission Society and World Christianity, 1799-1999

Timothy Yates
The Conversion of the Māori: Years of Religious and Social Change, 1814-1842

Richard Fox Young, *Editor*
India and the Indianness of Christianity: Essays on Understanding—Historical, Theological, and Bibliographical—in Honor of Robert Eric Frykenberg

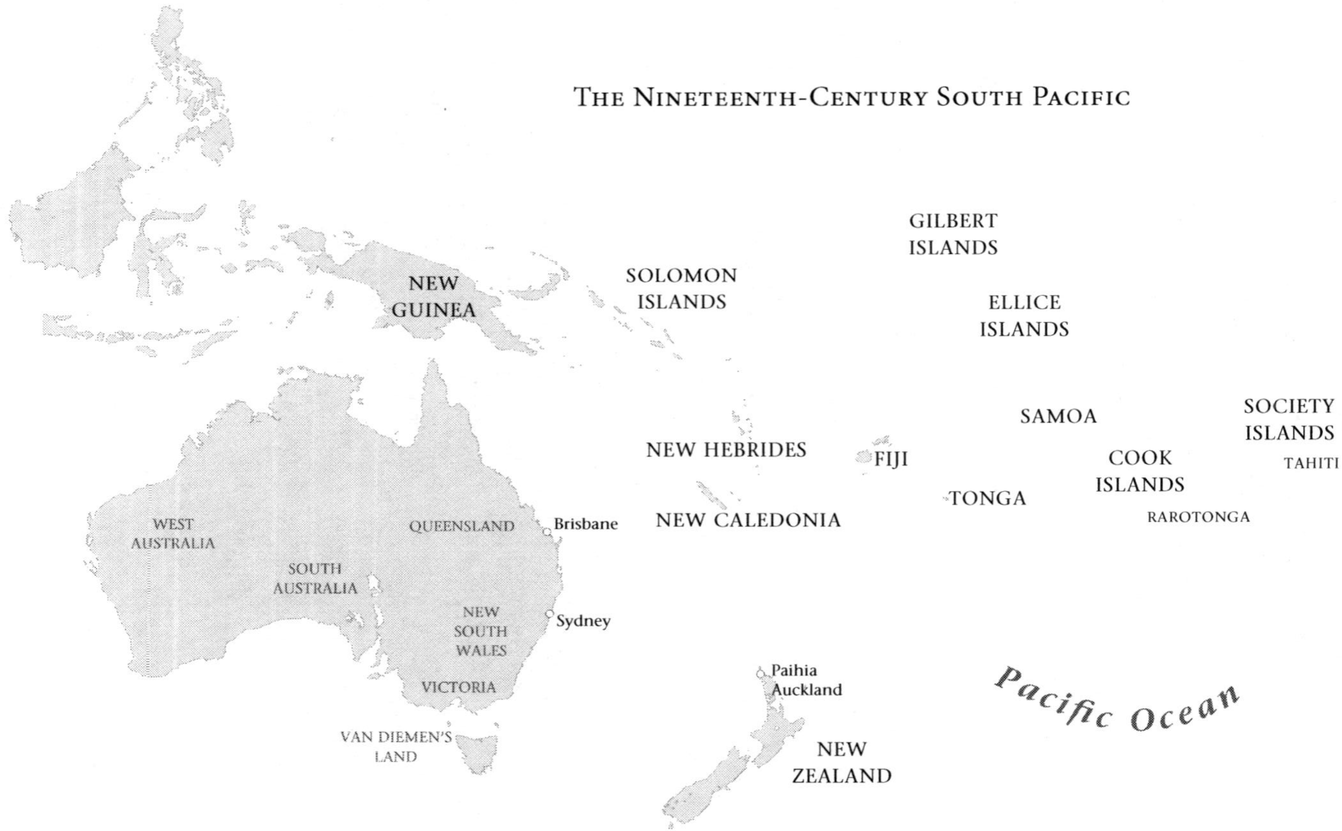

The Nineteenth-Century South Pacific

Race and Redemption

British Missionaries Encounter Pacific Peoples, 1797–1920

Jane Samson

William B. Eerdmans Publishing Company
Grand Rapids, Michigan

Wm. B. Eerdmans Publishing Co.
2140 Oak Industrial Drive NE, Grand Rapids, Michigan 49505
www.eerdmans.com

Published 2017
Printed in the United States of America

26 25 24 23 22 21 20 19 18 17   1 2 3 4 5 6 7 8 9 10

ISBN 978-0-8028-7535-8

Library of Congress Cataloging-in-Publication Data

Names: Samson, Jane, 1962– author.
Title: Race and redemption : British missionaries encounter Pacific peoples, 1790–1920 / Jane Samson.
Description: Grand Rapids, Michigan : William B. Eerdmans Publishing Company, [2017] | Series: Studies in the history of Christian missions | Includes bibliographical references and index.
Identifiers: LCCN 2017026282 | ISBN 9780802875358 (pbk. : alk. paper)
Subjects: LCSH: Missions, British—Islands of the Pacific—History.
Classification: LCC BV3640 .S26 2017 | DDC 266.0099—dc23
LC record available at https://lccn.loc.gov/2017026282

Contents

Preface

Like all books that have taken far too long to write, this one has incurred numerous longstanding debts. My first thanks must go to Brian Stanley for encouraging me to take my research in the direction of missionary studies. Brian's pioneering directorships of the North Atlantic Missiology Project and the Currents in World Christianity program have made a sustained impact on the scholarly study of missions, and his editorship (with Bob Frykenberg) of the "Studies in Christian Mission" series at Eerdmans has given a home to many of the results. I owe Brian and Bob many thanks for their enduring patience, and I am also grateful to anonymous reviewers for many helpful suggestions for improving the manuscript. Any remaining errors are my own.

I must also thank the staff at the Alexander Turnbull Special Collections Library at the National Library of New Zealand, the Church Missionary Society collection at the University of Birmingham, the Hocken Special Collections Library at the University of Otago, the Mitchell Library at the State Library of New South Wales, the Rhodes House Library, and the Special Collections room at the School of Oriental and African Studies. Thanks also to the Australian Board of Missions for permission to consult their archives at the Mitchell. Above all I am grateful to the late Arthur Easton, whose death in 2009 deprived both the Mitchell Library and the scholarly world of his remarkable expertise and kindness. Tony Ballantyne, John Barker, Tolly Bradford, Helen Gardner, John Gascoigne, Brian Gobbett, Thorgeir Kolshus, Michael Scott, Sujit Sivasundaram, and many others have given me invaluable advice at various points in the history of this lengthy project. Because personal circumstances made extensive research in the antipodes or the UK impossible, I must also thank the librarians at my own university for helping me to obtain interloan material.

As usual, I owe special thanks to Sara Joynes, formerly of the Australian Joint Copying Project (AJCP), who has once again provided invaluable expertise and friendship. AJCP and Pacific Manuscripts Bureau (PMB) staff in Australia were also tremendously helpful. A number of students assisted me formally at various stages of the project, and I am grateful to them all: Rebecca Adell, Dawn Berry, Paul Hengstler, David Luesink, and Nathan Lysons. I would also like to thank all members of my senior undergraduate seminars for years of invigorating discussion.

Although the research for this publication began many years earlier, the book was written in the post–9/11 North America. Most of my work up to that point had struggled to recognize those who sought humanity in one another amidst the unequal power relations of the British Empire, especially those who considered themselves to be Christian humanitarians. As phones rang off the hook in religious studies and history departments around North America amid talk of a "clash of civilizations," it was clear that the power of religious identities and their appropriation had never gone away despite the predictions of secularization theorists. Urgent new questions surrounded whether or not these identities inevitably produce an alienated Other or whether there could be grounds for communication and mutual respect.

Speaking of his work on the anthropology of the French missionary Maurice Leenhardt, James Clifford reminds us that if religion and the secular academy are maintained as opposites, "a whole range of political or cultural action *with* others is precluded."[1] Scholars must continue to uncover the relations of power that divide "us" from "them," but we must also explore what it means to desire justice for one another on a shared and vulnerable planet. Religious understandings of the human condition continue to be of global importance, and scholars must take those understandings both critically and seriously.

I dedicate my own contribution to my son Alexander.

1. James Clifford, *Person and Myth: Maurice Leenhardt in the Melanesian World* (Berkeley: University of California Press, 1982), 127.

Introduction

Mission studies has tended to be a highly politicized field. Academics mingle awkwardly (if at all) with retired and serving missionaries at conferences and seminars. Postcolonial sensitivities generate considerable anxiety about the relationship between missions, power, and racism. Scholars feel the need to reassure their readers that they are not being hoodwinked into reading religious apologetics. In some cases, a narrative of progress charts the author's evolution from childhood faith to adult skepticism or hostility, and this classic Enlightenment tale can be found even in the work of scholars dedicated to the postcolonial critique of master narratives.[1]

It is remarkable how long modernism's *othering* of religion has persisted in these postmodern times. As Catherine Bell explained in 1996, secular academics still tended to frame their work in a narrative "of rational and progressively scientific thinking that yielded a 'coherent research tradition' with which to replace the reigning theological paradigm" presumed to be rampant in confessional scholarship.[2] If the modern and the religious are accepted uncritically as separate realms, connections between them will not be explored fully. Edward Said, for example, despite his critique of missionaries (and their texts) as colonizers, praised the Arab Christians who "without exception played an honorable role during the period of the Arab Renaissance."[3] But if missionaries

1. Examples include Rita Kipp, *The Early Years of a Dutch Colonial Mission: The Karo Field* (Ann Arbor: University of Michigan Press, 1990), and Catherine Hall, *Civilising Subjects: Metropole and Colony in the English Imagination, 1830–1867* (Chicago: University of Chicago Press, 2002).

2. Catherine Bell, "Modernism and Postmodernism in the Study of Religion," *Religious Studies Review* 22 (1996): 183.

3. Cited in Jeffrey Cox, *Imperial Fault Lines: Christianity and Colonial Power in India, 1818–*

were colonizers, where did this honorable Christian resistance to colonialism come from? These uneasy intellectual borderlands more often prompted segregation than engagement. Max Quanchi observed of Pacific history that by the 1990s mission and church history was "tending to become restricted within theological colleges, which carries the risk that mission history might become detached from the mainstream of inquiry,"[4] and as my medievalist colleague John Kitchen has pointed out, modernist scholarship has traditionally been "posited on the alterity of the religious belief," enabling academics to create reassuring distance between the deluded religious Other and the realities of race, class, and gender as historical forces. Kitchen diagnosed a fear of apologetics at the heart of this pervasive tendency whereby a serious engagement with religion in history "implies at some level an acceptance of the religious activity or belief under analysis." Kitchen proposed instead a stance, which I also have adopted, from which "we are negotiating, rather than opposing or professing, religion."[5] I have also benefited from the insights of Gauri Viswanathan, especially those concerning how a recovery of the history of religious belief can "begin the search for corrective ways of talking and writing about belief in terms other than 'fundamentalist,' 'premodern,' or 'prehistory.'"[6]

To refuse to categorize the religious believer as fundamentally other has necessitated a refusal to reduce all of their ethnography as othering. Niel Gunson, a pioneering historian of missions in the South Pacific, wrote in 1978 that "although the missionaries were often easily irritated by seeming stupidity or [islander] 'childishness,' most of them regarded the various island peoples as being capable of the same intellectual development as themselves."[7] In *Victorian Anthropology*, George Stocking explained how Methodist missionary Thomas Williams, working in Fiji in the early nineteenth century, "saw a systematic contrast between the natural capacities of the Fijians, and those aspects of their character produced by living 'for many generations, under the uninterrupted

---

1940 (Stanford, CA: Stanford University Press, 2002), 13. Cox's critique of assorted master narratives and of the first-generation postcolonial "unmasking" project about missionaries deserves to be much better known. See Cox, *Christianity and Colonial Power*, 9–19.

4. Max Quanchi, "The Imaging of Pastors in Papua," in *The Covenant Makers: Islander Missionaries in the Pacific*, ed. Doug Munro and Andrew Thornley (Suva: Pacific Theological College and the Institute of Pacific Studies, 1996), 4.

5. John Kitchen, "Going Medieval: Paradigm Shifts and the Phenomenological Tendency in the Contemporary Encounter with Medieval Religion," *Method & Theory in the Study of Religion* 14 (2002): 409.

6. Gauri Viswanathan, *Outside the Fold: Conversion, Modernity, and Belief* (Princeton: Princeton University Press, 1998), xvi.

7. Niel Gunson, *Messengers of Grace: Evangelical Missionaries in the South Seas 1797–1860* (Melbourne: Oxford University Press, 1978), 205–6.

power of influences different from any which we daily feel.'"[8] These earlier insights needed to be recovered in the wake of first-wave postcolonial studies and its tendency to diagnose a monolithic, ahistorical colonial discourse in European texts. Discourse analysis was a healthy corrective to the uncritical, often hagiographical, study of missionaries in earlier periods. Nevertheless, it also called into question the endorsement of indigenous agency being championed by ethnohistory and area studies scholarship since the mid-twentieth century. How could missions have created opportunities for indigenous peoples—opportunities eagerly taken—and at the same time remained instruments of an all-powerful colonialism? Andrew Porter points out that scholars have sought "the elevation of the role played by local Christians," especially in colonial resistance movements, while, at the same time feeling obliged to denounce missionaries as the "forceful and effective agents of empire and colonial control," creating a paradox that was not being addressed, let alone resolved. Porter has called for scholars to build bridges, "however rickety, across the historiographical gulfs that persist."[9]

My own project has been inspired by two recent historiographical trajectories in the study of Pacific missions. In 1992 John Barker wrote of the neglect of Melanesian Christianities by anthropologists, a neglect that he believed was derived, "on the one hand, from a narrow conception of cultural authenticity and, on the other, from a simplistic conception of Christianity as a missionary imposition."[10] In my opinion the roots of this neglect lie in the classical Enlightenment narrative of progress, which traces development from religion to science. Postcolonial sensitivities gave new life to such narratives by focusing on western material and ideological power relations in a new "holy trinity": race, class, and gender. As Bronwen Douglas explains, "Secular anticolonialists, fuelled by moral outrage, often take at face value teleological narratives of a monolithic colonial or mission presence and the attendant suffocation of indigenous agency"—a view, she noted, that provided deeply ironic endorsement for conservative views of history, in which European activities and actors always took center stage.[11] This secular outrage reduced western missionaries to agents

8. Quoted in George Stocking, *Victorian Anthropology* (New York: Macmillan, 1987), 89.

9. Andrew N. Porter, *Religion versus Empire?: British Protestant Missionaries and Overseas Expansion, 1700–1914* (Manchester: Manchester University Press, 2004), 5–7.

10. John Barker, "Christianity in Western Melanesian Ethnography," in *History and Tradition in Melanesian Anthropology*, ed. James G. Carrier (Berkeley: University of California Press, 1992), 145.

11. Bronwen Douglas, "Provocative Readings in Intransigent Archives: Finding Aneityumese Women," *Oceania* 70, no. 2 (1999): 111; see also "Encounters with the Enemy? Academic Readings of Missionary Narratives on Melanesians," *Comparative Studies in Society and History* 43, no. 1 (2001): 37–64.

of colonialism, and their converts to dupes. By 2003 Anna Johnston observed that narratives about monolithic western power could still be found even in "the most cutting-edge postcolonial theory."[12] Recent work on missions in the Pacific and elsewhere has changed this picture considerably, and I too seek to take religion both seriously and critically in order to bring greater nuance to the debate about missionary encounters with indigenous peoples.

The second historiographical intervention to inspire my project has been the recent move to include a consideration of theology in academic historical analysis. Colin Kidd has explained how, in the trinity of race, class, and gender, "race is [only] contextualized alongside issues of status and class, and the social relations of power are, reasonably enough, accorded pride of place in interpretations of the rise of racism."[13] There is nothing wrong with analyzing race in relation to class or gender. Nevertheless, I agree with Kidd's main point that theology remains largely missing in action as an analytical category despite the fact that "scripture has been for much of the early modern and modern eras the primary cultural influence of the forging of races."[14] Here we see a persistent artifact of the traditional separation of the religious and modern realms. More nuanced is Rod Edmond's study of European texts about the Pacific world, which highlights the "contradictory and unstable array of narratives" generated by missionaries who needed to see indigenous peoples simultaneously as savage Others and as potentially redeemable children.[15] Citing Nick Thomas's explanation of these instabilities as functions of "the contradictory colonial objectives of hierarchizing and incorporating," Edmond concluded that missionary ethnography was an "oscillation between science and sermon."[16]

I have wondered whether science and sermon really were such bipolar forces, produced and replicated by colonialism, or whether instead they constituted a symbiosis generated inevitably by the paradoxes of Christian theological anthropology. If so, they long predated European colonialism, and here I take a different lesson than Edmond does from the work of Nicholas Thomas. Thomas has questioned the traditional narrative of progress, which traced a direct route from mutable medieval and early modern discourses about pagan Others to modern, fixed distinctions of race. He wondered whether modern

12. Anna Johnston, *Missionary Writing and Empire, 1800–1860* (Cambridge: Cambridge University Press, 2003), 10.

13. Colin Kidd, *The Forging of Races: Race and Scripture in the Protestant Atlantic World, 1600–2000* (Cambridge: Cambridge University Press, 2006), 19.

14. Kidd, *Forging of Races*, 19.

15. Rod Edmond, *Representing the South Pacific: Colonial Discourse from Cook to Gauguin* (Cambridge: Cambridge University Press, 1997), 111.

16. Edmond, *Representing the South Pacific*, 108.

missionaries might have retained earlier notions about a mutable Other, one who could be converted and incorporated, and therefore "whether differences between missionary and secular projects were manifested at the fundamental level of their conceptions of otherness."[17] I prefer this complex picture and its freedom from binaries or teleological assumptions, but I identify its origins in a much earlier era.

Modern missionaries had not retained medieval or early modern approaches to the Other; instead, all of these approaches came from the same source: the ancient and necessarily paradoxical theological anthropology of Christian missions. This theology did not come from the rise and fall of empires, important as those were in giving (or denying) power to Christian missionaries. It was not necessarily linked with the modern scholarly discipline of anthropology either, although this book will discuss points where modern anthropological theories were useful for missionaries, and where they themselves contributed to anthropological journals and debates. The reason they could do this easily, even eagerly, is not because they were oscillating between the religious and scientific realms. Instead, they were bringing all available resources to bear as they struggled to live out the paradox of what I call *othering and brothering.*

Sara Sohmer has called for "a consideration of developments in Victorian intellectual life," which "can prove useful in any attempt to analyze the complex patterns of identity and tension that characterized missionaries' interaction with indigenous peoples and with anthropologists."[18] A new generation of Pacific historians has taken up this challenge in recent years: a collection of papers published in 2008 by the University of Melbourne introduced new research on missions with a rejection of the traditional reductionist analysis of missionaries as agents of colonialism and of Christianity as an alien imposition. Instead, Peter Sherlock made an eloquent plea for seeing how "resistance and accommodation were possible, and in the midst of the violence implicit in colonialism, humanity—the exercise of choice and compassion—was an historic possibility."[19] The social, political, educational, and economic dimensions of British missionary work, steeped in the gendered cultural conceptions of the day, could both accommodate and undermine imperial power.

17. Nicholas Thomas, *Colonialism's Culture: Anthropology, Travel and Government* (Cambridge: Polity Press, 1994), 125.

18. Sara Sohmer, "The Melanesian Mission and Victorian Anthropology: A Study in Symbiosis," in *Darwin's Laboratory: Evolutionary Theory and Natural History in the Pacific,* ed. Roy MacLeod and Philip F. Rehbock (Honolulu: University of Hawai'i Press, 1994), 317.

19. Peter Sherlock, "Missions, Colonialism and the Politics of Agency," in *Evangelists of Empire? Missionaries and Colonial History,* ed. Amanda Berry et al., History Conference and Seminar Series 18 (Melbourne: eScholarship Research Centre, 2008), 19.

Some of the insights of postcolonial theological anthropology should also be noted here. In a pioneering application of Mikhail Bakhtin's theory of dialogic relationships, Bo-Myung Seo has questioned the traditional focus of both theological and philosophical anthropology "as the question of the self rather than the question of the other," asking instead what could happen if the order of priority was reversed. For Seo, Otherness is central to the teachings of Jesus, to the relationship of God with humanity, and to the interactions of human beings with one another.[20] Bakhtin's dialogic approach is familiar to scholars in many fields of study, and Seo's point is that the Bible's emphasis on strangers and neighbors presumes a self-or-other dialogue, generating "a liberative theological anthropology as the anthropology of the Other."[21] Seo is reacting to a common misconception about mission history, one that he repeats uncritically, saying that "the receiving of the gospel had to be complemented by the receiving of Western cultures and ideals."[22] The situation was much more complicated than that, and Marc Cortez is more helpful when he explains that "theological anthropology has always participated in such dialogue with the surrounding culture based on its conviction that, if God is the creator of all reality, we should not reject truth wherever it might be found. The modern situation differs only in the range and complexity of available dialogue partners, including the modern social sciences."[23]

Here there is no polarization of engagement and alienation, of pre-modern and modern, or of religion and science. Both Seo and Cortez are highlighting an inevitably paradoxical theological challenge that Christian missionaries have struggled to meet since the earliest days. An early second-century text makes the point nicely: "For the Christians are distinguished from other men neither by country, nor language, nor the customs which they observe" but instead, whether inhabiting Greek or "barbarian" lands, they followed "the customs of the natives in respect to clothing, food, and the rest of their ordinary conduct." Under Roman imperial rule "they dwell in their own countries, but simply as sojourners. As citizens, they share in all things with others, and yet endure all things as if foreigners. Every foreign land is to them as their native country, and every land of their birth as a land of strangers."[24] They were borderland people,

20. Bo-Myung Seo, *A Critique of Western Theological Anthropology* (New York: Edwin Mellen Press, 2005), i.

21. Seo, *Critique of Western Theological Anthropology,* 97; see also Caryl Emerson, *The First Hundred Years of Mikhail Bakhtin* (Princeton: Princeton University Press, 2000).

22. Seo, *Critique of Western Theological Anthropology*, 100.

23. Marc Cortez, *Theological Anthropology: A Guide for the Perplexed* (London: T&T Clark, 2010), 6.

24. *Epistle of Mathetes to Diognetus,* chapter 5; http://www.earlychristianwritings.com/text

liminal, who had to accommodate themselves to their surroundings in order to perform their duty of gospel witness effectively. As we will see, missionaries to the Pacific sometimes became so converted to their new homes that they found Britain increasingly alien. Sometimes the conversion was so complete that they preferred indigenous ways and beliefs to their own.

The main question is no longer whether or not missionaries were entangled with colonial power relations: I will be taking that entanglement for granted. From the late eighteenth to the twentieth century and beyond, missionary activity took place amid growing western influence and colonization. Late eighteenth-century British settlements in Australia were accompanied by a growing number of free settlers from Britain and elsewhere. Growing British trade in the Pacific generated the establishment of whaling stations and commercial depots. European beachcombers, explorers, and naturalists arrived in the islands while indigenous sailors, laborers, adventurers, and interpreters departed. In the nineteenth century, British missionaries came to Australia as Britain gradually laid claim to the continent. The first missions to New Zealand were created then as well. By the twentieth century, collaborations between missions, churches, and governments in Australia would produce destructive assimilation projects, including the forcible adoption of Aboriginal children by white families. At the same time missionaries contributed to the preservation of Aboriginal languages and supported indigenous land rights.

In New Zealand, British missionary activity predated formal colonization, and missionaries could be found both criticizing and facilitating the Treaty of Waitangi, by which New Zealand became a British colony in 1840. Elsewhere in the South Pacific there was a similar picture: some missionaries called for colonization, even naval bombardments, to support their efforts. Others were deeply critical of rising imperial intervention. Meanwhile, the introduction of foreign foods and diseases, along with new forms of social and gender relations, was transforming indigenous bodies and cultures. The resulting disruption to indigenous lifeways made it easier for missionaries and churches to work with colonial governments and anthropologists to introduce new systems of labor, education, and medical care. As the "scramble for the Pacific" intensified in the later nineteenth century, Britain's Pacific colonies multiplied.

Some missionaries welcomed these developments while others wondered whether a greater segregation of the indigenous population would be the best way to protect them against the obvious ravages of disease, alcohol, and cultural

/diognetus-roberts.html (accessed 31 March 2014). Written during the later second century, this apology was composed during a persecution of local Christians, possibly under emperors Valerian or Diocletian. The author is unknown.

dislocation. In the early twentieth century, Australia and New Zealand began to administer colonies of their own: often in areas under previous German control, but also in places like Papua New Guinea, where Australia had a long-standing influence and which it eventually took from Britain in 1906. In all cases missionaries held a wide range of opinions about western impact on Pacific peoples. Their views were sometimes deeply inconsistent: they could sincerely lament the loss of life to newly-introduced diseases, for example, while at the same time introducing profound social changes that were both psychologically and culturally deadly. Some articulated these moral dilemmas; others seemed oblivious to them.

During the twentieth century, mission societies themselves undertook increasingly vigorous internal critiques concerning race relations and Aboriginal policies, and by the time of the formation of the World Council of Churches in 1948, a vocal generation of local church leaders and theologians, many of them female, were making pointed recommendations about enriching the relationship between Christianity, missions, and social justice. By the 1960s missions and churches were closing the residential schools they had staffed since the nineteenth century and beginning processes of repentance and reconciliation that continue today. Churches and missions worked alongside Aboriginal activists to achieve federal voting rights in Australia and Canada. The power of non-elite interventions, such as black theology, feminism, and liberation theology, sharpened these processes further as the number of practicing Christians in the western world continued to decline. Today, non-western Christians are often the face of Christian missions.[25] The relationship between missions and colonialism is clear enough but it cannot, without remainder, capture the complex interactions and apparent contradictions of western Christianity's encounter with indigenous peoples.

At the heart of each of the following chapters of this book is the fundamental paradox in missionary accounts of Pacific peoples: the symbiotic relationship between othering and brothering. This integrated phrase is intended to challenge the idea that only one or the other is the real story, making missionary ethnography shuttle between the two poles. Othering is impossible without brothering, they are mutually dependent. A spatial metaphor might be useful here: rather than picturing the two concepts as binary opposites, I see them as two axes on a grid. Othering can be seen as a vertical axis, employed by missionaries (and many others) to rank the world's peoples higher or lower according to various scales of civilization, progress, or evolution. The horizon-

25. Gwinyai Henry Muzorewa, *An African Theology of Mission* (Lewiston, NY: Edwin Mellen Press, 1990).

tal axis, brothering, required missionaries as a matter of faith to believe in the unity and equality of human beings in a story stretching from the perfection of creation to the final judgment when all things would be made new. Over space and time, missionaries plotted onto this grid their complex ethnographies and contradictory projects.

Although this is not a study of indigenous Christianities—that would have made the project unmanageably large—I am very mindful of the growing literature on the complexities of non-western religious conversion, especially in the context of colonialism. As Steven Kaplan notes, essential elements of Christianity necessarily complicated mission encounters. "Lacking either a stated code of laws such as Jewish Halachah or Islamic Sharia, or a single holy language such as Hebrew or Arabic, Christianity repeatedly absorbed elements from the cultures it entered, and thus numerous local or national Christianities emerged."[26] Pacific peoples were not merely the targets of missionary enterprise; they were also teachers, friends, family members, and clergy. Unfortunately, the stereotype of a monolithic mission intolerance has proved remarkably durable. We can compare Kaplan's view above with that of David Hanlon, who has characterized missionary activity in terms of struggle "against an island people and way of life they did not love, like or much understand."[27] I hope to demonstrate how missionaries sought engagement as well as othering, and I will be including discussions of how indigenous informants and colleagues made their own contributions to this process.

The gender-exclusiveness of my phrase "othering and brothering" is intentional, pointing as it does to unfinished business that wracks Christian communities around the world. In terms of church leadership, the barriers of class and race were overcome relatively quickly when compared with those of gender and sexuality. Female and LGBTQ Christians, to a greater or lesser extent, remain othered in most Christian denominations. Opponents of their leadership (or sometimes even their membership) have easily crossed racial, geographical, and social boundaries to make common cause against "women and gays." In the history of Christianity there is little evidence of equality among the members of the trinity of race, class, and gender. Gender (and sexuality) trumps the other two every time. This, not race, is the final frontier.

A thematic rather than a chronological approach proved useful in organizing my research findings, enabling me to underline the ongoing symbiosis of

26. Steven Kaplan, ed., *Indigenous Reponses to Western Christianity* (New York: New York University Press, 1995), 2–3.

27. David Hanlon, "Converting Pasts and Presents: Reflections on Histories of Missionary Enterprises in the Pacific," in *Pacific Lives, Pacific Places*, ed. Lal and Hempenstall (Canberra: Journal of Pacific History, 2001), 114.

othering and brothering across a broad range of themes, concluding with that of gender to show how the symbiosis was baffled by alterities too profound to embrace or, at times, even to comprehend. Each chapter therefore draws on ethnography, material culture, and other sources of analysis produced by a variety of mission societies, time periods, locations, and individuals. This book is therefore not a comprehensive history of missionary ethnography in any one time or place, and its coverage is inevitably uneven. Some of the individuals I discuss have attracted scholarly interest before; others have been almost completely neglected. Many more could have been included, and I hope that others will explore the extensive archival materials available. Meanwhile, I have brought together Pacific material from the late-eighteenth-century era of pioneer missions to the interwar period, during which academic anthropology strengthened its hold on the moral and scientific high ground in Pacific ethnography. Much more work remains to be done, especially on the twentieth century.

The lack of a chronological narrative and the absence of attempts to compare or contrast different missions might strike readers as puzzling. After all, metropolitan theories about missiology changed over time, as did the education of missionaries and their ability to access scholarly publications from remote stations. I will sketch some general trends in the next chapter, but my goal is not to present a narrative of progress concerning growing enlightenment in mission encounters with indigenous peoples over time. On the contrary, my work challenges such a narrative. Early missionaries could be intellectually and spiritually generous; later and better-educated ones could be bigots. Missionaries did not necessarily reflect the metropolitan policies of their denominational group, nor were their well-known denominational rivalries necessarily carried over into their scholarship concerning Pacific peoples. As Patricia Grimshaw and Andrew May point out in their collection on missions, indigenous peoples, and cultural exchanges, "we do not deny that we are talking about individual missions at particular times and in specific places," but these activities were "dynamic and spectacularly unpredictable, serving to break down the notion of 'mission' as a unitary category."[28] A scientific ecu-

28. Patricia Grimshaw and Andrew May, eds., *Missionaries, Indigenous Peoples and Cultural Exchange* (Brighton: Sussex Academic Press, 2010), 3. Reconsidering the "missionary position" has benefited extensively from two studies of opposite ends of the Pacific world: Brett Christophers, *Positioning the Missionary: John Booth Good and the Confluence of Cultures in Nineteenth-Century British Columbia* (Vancouver: University of British Columbia Press, 1998), and Vicente M. Diaz, *Repositioning the Missionary: Rewriting the Histories of Colonialism, Native Catholicism, and Indigeneity in Guam* (Honolulu: University of Hawai'i Press, 2010). Sadly, due to the great divorce between north and South Pacific area studies, these two fine scholars seem unaware of one another's work.

menism was common, prompted perhaps by the realization that those in the field had more in common with each other than they did with their distant metropolitan superiors.

Even so, the story of missionary influence on anthropology is not the main theme of this book. In some cases, missionary ethnography and philology strongly resisted the leading scientific theories of the day, and this evidence of resistance is as interesting as its opposite. Theological anthropology drove the agenda, not the emerging social sciences. As Norman Etherington has observed, "the most striking feature of missions is *diversity*."[29] Some missionaries were interested in contemporary anthropological debates; others were not. All, however, were necessarily interested in how to engage with the Other. Amid this bricolage lies our theme of othering and brothering: a persistent tension amidst a diversity of personalities, circumstances, and official policies. The central focus of this book is the provocative richness of that tension.

29. Norman Etherington, ed., *Missions and Empire* (Oxford: Oxford University Press, 2005), 15.

Part One

CHAPTER 1

Anthropologies

One of the most defining moments in my research for this project occurred when I encountered the mid-twentieth-century journal *Practical Anthropology*. A Christian publication aimed primarily at missionaries and their supporters, the journal obviously saw nothing contradictory in relating academic anthropology directly to missiology or vice versa. Its 1954 inaugural issue revealed a deep entanglement between science and religion, declaring its aim to be "a medium for the orientation of thinking Christians toward a cross-cultural view, toward an understanding of culture which is not bound to the narrow experience of the West, but which is molded by a respectful recognition of the way of life of people everywhere."[1] The struggle to obtain anthropological training for missionaries had already been a prolonged one: "To many [missionaries] there is no apparent connection between anthropology and the Christian ministry," admitted the editors.[2] We will see that for many anthropologists there was no apparent connection either. The journal's relatively brief existence under its original title underscores the main point of this chapter: the distance, even hostility, between missionaries and anthropologists was neither natural nor inevitable, yet it developed and persisted.[3] In response to a puzzled missionary in the field, who was wondering how to start developing an anthropological approach, the editor of *Practical Anthropology* suggested learning "to ask the

1. Frontispiece, *Practical Anthropology* 1, no. 1 (1953): n/p.

2. "Editorial Statement," *Practical Anthropology* 1, no. 1 (1953): 1–2.

3. The journal joined with *Missiology* under the latter's title from 1973. The first editor of the combined journal was the Reverend Alan Tippett, former Methodist missionary in Fiji and holder of graduate degrees in both anthropology and history; see Gerald H. Anderson, "Introducing Missiology," *Missiology* 1, no. 3 (1973): 4.

right questions *of ourselves*" (emphasis original). This type of reflexivity was an important part of the ancient discipline of *theological* anthropology, a concept that must be carefully distinguished from the academic anthropology that developed in the later nineteenth century. They both share an intellectual quest for theories of the nature of the human person, but to speak of anthropology in a theological context can encompass scholarly work from the second century CE to the present day. The story of the emergence of modern anthropology is well known, as is the variety of Christian interactions with its secular theories.[4] For our purposes, however, the most important feature of theological anthropology is its emphasis from the earliest days on the unity of humanity. All people were made in the divine image and in relationship both with God and with one another. Every non-Christian Other was also a brother.

What to do about this was another matter. Missionary activity had not always been an essential feature of Christianity. Interest in missions waxed and waned over time and varied between denominations. Nevertheless, where there was missionary expansion, the paradoxical relationship between othering and brothering emerged, even in Christianity's earliest days when the Jewish Christian norm was challenged by others—Samaritans, Gentiles—who were Other.[5] The Book of Acts tells of a vision experienced by the apostle Peter in which he was commanded to abandon ritual purity in order to preach the gospel to non-Jews (Acts 11:1–10).[6] This was also the approach of the most famous of the early missionary apostles, Paul. In the scriptural account of Paul's activities, he articulated a "one blood" anthropology in support of his mission to the Gentiles, explaining how God "hath made of one blood all nations of men for to dwell on all the face of the earth. . . . That they should seek the Lord, if haply they might feel after him, and find him, though he be not far from every one of us" (Acts 17:26–27). Even during periods of persecution, sometimes very severe, Christian anthropology of one blood continued to envision a humanity united by a common origin and destiny.

4. For a general overview see Stocking, *Victorian Anthropology*. For discussions of the importance of the Pacific world to the development of modern western racial science see Bronwen Douglas, *Sciences, Voyages, and Encounters in Oceania 1511–1850* (Houndsmills, UK: Palgrave Macmillan, 2014), and John Gascoigne, *Encountering the Pacific in the Age of the Enlightenment* (Cambridge: Cambridge University Press, 2014).

5. For an introduction to the postcolonial study of Christian Scripture see Anna Runesson, *Exegesis in the Making: Postcolonialism and New Testament Studies* (Leiden: Brill, 2010), and R. S. Sugirtharajah, *Exploring Postcolonial Biblical Criticism: History, Method, Practice* (Malden: John Wiley & Sons, 2011). See also Victor Kiernan, *The Lords of Human Kind: European Attitudes to Other Cultures in the Imperial Age*, 2nd ed. (London: Serif, 1995), 15 and Paul Goodman's *Of One Blood: Abolitionism and the Origins of Racial Equality* (Berkeley: University of California Press, 1998).

6. All scriptural references are to the King James (Authorized) version, the standard English-language Bible before the mid-twentieth century.

Centuries later, when Christian European powers began building empires of their own, this theological universalism was challenged by many different factors including what we now conceptualize as "race." The universalism of one blood stood in opposition to othering on a global scale, even as the concept of race was being invented and reinforced by imperial power.

This tangle confronted all missionaries taking up the biblical Great Commission and its simultaneous othering and brothering of non-Christians. In the Gospel of Matthew, Jesus orders his disciples to go and "teach all nations, baptizing them in the name of the Father, and of the Son, and of the Holy Ghost" (Matt. 28:19). Those in need of baptism were fundamentally Other according to this theological anthropology, but they must simultaneously be kindred of one blood, or the gospel could be neither preached nor received. Some sort of genuine engagement had to be possible. After Spain's discovery of the Americas, some Roman Catholic missionaries began calling for debate about the humanity and integrity of indigenous peoples. Conversion was the ultimate goal, to be sure, but the beginnings of a concept of human rights can also be traced to this period, and especially to the arguments of Bartolomé de las Casas and other theologians at Salamanca in the sixteenth century.[7] The conviction that indigenous peoples were fully human produced some sensitive observations of their cultures, leading some scholars to identify the sixteenth-century mendicant friars of New Spain as the first modern ethnographers.[8]

The British undertook some evangelization of Native Americans in their settler colonies during the early modern period, but the Reformation had raised questions about mission work. Some Protestant theologies denounced the presumption of the idea that Christians could do anything at all about the salvation of others. They asserted that looking to one's own spiritual interests and leaving the rest to God is all we are called to do. These quietist convictions were strong among Calvinists, and they affected the newly emerged Church of England and remained present among Presbyterians and other dissenting denominations in the British Isles.[9] Both Anglican and Protestant interest in missions was limited as a result.

7. Ivan Hannaford, *Race: The History of an Idea in the West* (Baltimore: Johns Hopkins University Press, 1996), 149–50. Compare with Rupert Costo and Jeanette Henry Costo, *The Missions of California: A Legacy of Genocide* (San Francisco: The Indian Historian Press, 1987).

8. Leonard Plotnicov, Paula Brown, and Vinson Sutlive, eds., "Introduction" to *Anthropology's Debt to Missionaries* (Pittsburgh: University of Pittsburgh Press, 2007), xi and in the same volume Hugh G. Nutini, "The Contributions of Mendicant Friars to Mesoamerican Ethnography," 23–30.

9. Particularly useful on this point is Michael D. Robinson, *The Storms of Providence: Navigating the Waters of Calvinism, Arminianism, and Open Theism* (Dallas: University Press of America, 2003).

When an evangelical revival began in Britain in the early eighteenth century, the outcome for missions was far from clear. Two areas of society that generally looked upon each other with mistrust joined forces as the lower-class constituents of revival movements (especially Methodism) allied with elites who were skeptical of evangelical political loyalty. The lack of procedures for appointing Church of England bishops overseas hampered the growth of Anglican missions as well.[10] Anglican chaplains abroad concentrated mostly on the spiritual welfare of British settlers, military personnel, and commercial staff. In territory ruled by the East India Company there was open hostility to any attempt to convert Indians to Christianity, and British missionaries had to be forced on the Company through acts of Parliament in the early nineteenth century.[11]

Nevertheless, the expansion of British rule in North America and Asia, the growth of British overseas commercial enterprise, including the transatlantic slave trade, the rising respectability of evangelicalism, and the impact of Enlightenment notions of progress all played a role in fostering a more favorable attitude toward missions in Britain by the nineteenth century. Norman Etherington warns that "not only is it difficult to point to any one cause of missionary enthusiasm, but different causes predominated at different times."[12] The influence of Moravian missiology, however, was one of the most critical factors. Moravian missions had been operating in British territory for some time, notably in what is now the Canadian North, and it was at a Moravian chapel in London that John Wesley, the founder of the Methodist movement, first experienced the emotional response to faith that would characterize his evangelicalism.[13] Stuart Piggin's neglected study of mission theology and training outlines the Moravian theological position: its highlight was a modification of Calvin's notion of predestination in order to permit a preaching of the gospel "which invited all men to receive the mercy of a loving God."[14] This moderated Calvinism, together with the Arminianism of John Wesley, generated a missiology that emphasized human universality. So successful were these theological

10. Norman Etherington, "Introduction," in *Missions and Empire,* ed. Norman Etherington (Oxford: Oxford University Press, 2005), 15.

11. Penny Carson, "The British Raj and the Awakening of the Evangelical Conscience," in *Christian Missions and the Enlightenment,* ed. Brian Stanley (Grand Rapids: Eerdmans, 2001), 45–70.

12. Etherington, "Introduction," 17.

13. Colin Podmore, *The Moravian Church in England 1728–1760* (Oxford: Clarendon Press, 1998), and John Mason, *The Moravian Church and the Missionary Awakening in England, 1760–1800* (Suffolk: The Boydell Press for the Royal Historical Society, 2001).

14. Stuart Piggin, *Making Evangelical Missionaries 1789–1858* (Appleford, UK: Sutton Courtenay Press, 1984), 81.

arguments that by the later eighteenth century "to an extent perhaps unequalled in British ecclesiastical history before or since, the Church, whether conceived of in narrow denominational terms, or as embracing all believers, was thought of as a *missionary* Church."[15] Although some later Pacific missions had a more catholic or high-church Anglican origin, for the first fifty years they were dominated by the evangelical efforts of various denominations, and their missiology was grounded in individual passion: the passion with which the classic evangelical experience of conversion was embraced.

This intensity of religious experience and the urgent evangelical call to salvation generated prominent debates about eschatology, especially those concerning the nature and timing of the anticipated second coming of Christ. By the early nineteenth century, millennial prophets and theologies had become popular, even fashionable. Some had diagnosed the end times in such events as the rise and defeat of Napoleon, the globalization of European influence, and the social dislocations of the industrial revolution. Views differed about whether or not mission activity was desirable in the end times: a reflection of longstanding Protestant quietism. One of the most popular eschatologists of the day, Edward Irving, taught a form of pre-millennialism that sought to "hasten the return of Christ by a policy of rapid evangelistic expansion" since "Christ could not return until every nation had had an opportunity of responding to the gospel."[16] The vast majority of evangelical Christians, however, believed that sustained spiritual, intellectual, and financial efforts were needed more than apocalyptic visions. Still, the popularity of preachers like Irving helped to boost the development of new mission societies in the late eighteenth and nineteenth centuries.

The first of these to focus on the Pacific field was a mainly Congregationalist society founded in 1795 and known from 1818 as the London Missionary Society (LMS). The LMS chose Tahiti for its first mission in response to Captain Cook's accounts of Pacific peoples. Stories of human sacrifice and cannibalism, set amid tropical beauty, were compelling motivations for missionary service. So too was the growing British dominance at sea. After defeating Napoleon in 1815, Britain would remain a naval superpower for most of the nineteenth century, and missionaries were conscious of the role of naval power in their ability to undertake distant missions. "To this diffusion of light and truth the naval greatness of Britain eminently contributes," declared LMS founder Thomas Haweis in 1812, "facilitating conveyance into all lands, and the most distant isles of the

15. Piggin, *Making Evangelical Missionaries*, 115.

16. Brian Stanley, *The Bible and the Flag: Protestant Missions and British Imperialism in the Nineteenth and Twentieth Centuries* (Leicester: Apollos, 1990), 76.

sea."[17] Maritime routes carried the empire's ideas, emigrants, trade, and troops around the world. In the vast Pacific the role of the Royal Navy was simply crucial, and it was significant that so many navy officers and crew members in the early and mid-nineteenth century were enthusiastically Christian. Missionaries enjoyed special privileges: regular visits to their stations by passing warships, mail services, transportation between islands, and, on controversial occasions, armed support.[18] Assisted by enthusiastic sponsors at home, aided by the reliable maps now readily available from the Admiralty, other mission societies began their own Pacific ventures in the wake of the LMS pioneers. In 1814, the evangelical Anglican Church Missionary Society (CMS) began operations in New Zealand and, a little later, in Australia. In 1822, the Wesleyan Methodist Missionary Society (WMMS) settled in the Tongan islands and spread, by means of auxiliary missions, to Samoa, Fiji, and the western Pacific. In 1848, Presbyterian missionaries from the Canadian colonies formed the New Hebrides Mission.[19]

British missionaries were not always evangelical Christians, however, and the emphasis on incarnational theology in catholic Anglicanism must also be considered. Here a focus on the incarnation of God invited all Christians, including missionaries, to represent Christ to others. This approach underlined the significance of the sacraments in Christian life, especially the Eucharist. The incarnational theological principles were central to the Oxford Movement of the early and mid-nineteenth century, and to the Anglo-Catholic revivals of the late-nineteenth and early-twentieth centuries. Some of the leading figures of these movements cut their teeth in the Pacific mission field.[20]

The return of the LMS missionary David Livingstone from Africa prompted the formation of the Universities Mission to Central Africa in 1860. Based on Oxford Movement principles, this mission became a model for others, such as

17. Thomas Haweis, *A View of the Present State of Evangelical Religion throughout the World with a View to Promote Missionary Exertions* (London: Williams & Son, 1812), 15.

18. See Jane Samson, *Imperial Benevolence: Making British Authority in the South Pacific* (Honolulu: University of Hawai'i Press, 1998); Richard Blake, *Evangelicals in the Royal Navy, 1775–1815: Blue Lights and Psalm-Singers* (Woodbridge, UK: Boydell and Brewer, 2008); and Helen Gardner, *Gathering for God: George Brown in Oceania* (Dunedin: Otago University Press, 2006), 67–84.

19. The best introduction to British evangelical missions in the South Pacific remains Gunson, *Messengers of Grace*.

20. See Steven Maughan, "An Archbishop for Greater Britain: Bishop Montgomery, Missionary Imperialism, and the SPG, 1897–1915," in *Three Centuries of Mission: The United Society for the Propagation of the Gospel 1701–2000*, ed. Daniel O'Connor (London: Bloomsbury, 2000), 358–70, and the award-winning travel account by Montgomery's Canadian great-grandson Charles Montgomery, *The Last Heathen: Encounters with Ghosts and Ancestors in Melanesia* (London: HarperCollins, 2004).

the Melanesian Mission and New Guinea Mission in the southwest Pacific.[21] The pioneering role of bishops in these missions distinguished them from their earlier evangelical Anglican counterparts and from those of the British Protestant denominations. Colonial bishops were first consecrated in the later eighteenth century, but debate continued about the desirability and legal means of consecrating missionary bishops for operations outside British territory. George Selwyn, the Bishop of New Zealand, was the first of a new breed. He was consecrated in 1841 with a diocese whose boundaries stretched (thanks to clerical error) far beyond New Zealand waters into Melanesia. His efforts produced the Melanesian Mission in 1849 with its own bishop, John Coleridge Patteson, whom Selwyn consecrated in 1861. The New Guinea Mission was founded in 1891, also under its own bishop. Later, when the mission territories became formal dioceses, these island endeavors, combined with Anglican Australian missions, were organized as the Australian Board of Missions.

High Church missions sought to regenerate the universal church through the gifts that Melanesians and Papuans would bring. Part of this theological package involved what would later become known as fulfillment theology—the belief that God had already made himself known to all human beings. By implication, all human cultures already contained the basic building blocks of the Christian faith. Advocates of this position found inspiration in the story of the apostle Paul's activities at Athens. Accused of introducing a foreign god, Paul praised the piety of the Athenians, whose many temples included an altar with the inscription "To an unknown god." He announced, "What therefore you worship as unknown, this I proclaim to you," adding the one blood anthropology we have already considered. He concluded that God is not far from each one of us and quoted a line from Greek poetry: "For we too are his offspring" (Acts 17:22–28). The legacy of this universalist anthropology had also influenced early Jesuit missionaries to the Americas, where they accepted, "at least provisionally, some analogies between native beliefs and Christian doctrine."[22]

An early push to ordain indigenous clergy in the Melanesian Mission was characteristic of this approach; George Sarawia was ordained deacon in 1868, only seven years after the consecration of John Coleridge Patteson as the mission's first bishop. A priest by 1873, Sarawia represented the fruits of Patteson's vision of a Melanesian church, as opposed to a British church transplanted to

21. For general introductions to these missions see David Hilliard, *God's Gentlemen: A History of the Melanesian Mission 1849–1942* (St. Lucia: University of Queensland Press, 1978), and David Wetherell, *Reluctant Mission: The Anglican Church in Papua New Guinea 1891–1942* (St. Lucia: University of Queensland Press, 1977).

22. Eliga H. Gould, "Prelude: The Christianizing of British America," in *Missions and Empire*, ed. Etherington (Oxford: Oxford University Press, 2005) 21.

Melanesia. Patteson had been influenced by two prominent Anglican theologians, Richard Hooker and Joseph Butler, who "both taught that a knowledge of natural law, representing the divinely ordained moral law, was common to all peoples."[23] Missionaries therefore needed "to identify the points of contact—'the element of faith'—in Melanesian religion and to build on these."[24] Such identification required anthropological fieldwork. It also involved a reflexivity about western culture that could generate romantic idealism: "The bell was ringing for Evening prayers as we went ashore," recalled a visitor to the parish of indigenous priest Henry Tagalad at Ra, "and we slipped into the little Church as Henry was reading the Confession."[25] The Melanesian village and its church was upheld as a source of authentically human life, reproaching the social chaos of the urbanized western world. By the twentieth century, fulfillment theology was dominating missiological debate across denominations, as revealed by the 1910 interdenominational world conference on missions in Edinburgh.[26]

This book will focus mainly on the British missionaries who engaged directly with metropolitan scientific debates in order to promote a universalized Christian anthropology, but it is important to note that it was Pacific peoples themselves who undertook the most widespread, intensive, and dangerous work of missions. Often marginalized by their European contemporaries, indigenous teachers, clergy, and congregations were the most effective agents of Christianization in the Pacific world.[27] Most missions placed an early emphasis on educating indigenous male teachers to carry the gospel to other areas

23. David Hilliard, "The God of the Melanesian Mission," in *Vision and Reality in Pacific Religion*, ed. Phyllis Herda, Michael Reilly, and David Hilliard (Christchurch: Macmillan Brown Centre for Pacific Studies, 2005), 198. See Robert Ottley, *The Doctrine of the Incarnation* (London: Methuen & Co., 1896).

24. Hilliard, "The God of the Melanesian Mission," 200.

25. Quoted in David Hilliard, *God's Gentlemen*, 96.

26. Brian Stanley, *The World Missionary Conference, Edinburgh 1910* (Grand Rapids: Eerdmans, 2009), 206. See missionary J. N. Farquhar's *The Crown of Hinduism* (Oxford: Oxford University Press, 1913). For a mid-twentieth-century example, see Eric J. Sharpe, *Not to Destroy, But to Fulfil* (Uppsala: Gleerup, 1965).

27. This neglected topic is beginning to receive increased academic attention; see Ron and Marjorie Crocombe, eds., *Polynesian Missions in Melanesia: From Samoa, Cook Islands and Tonga to Papua New Guinea and New Caledonia* (Suva: University of the South Pacific, 1982); Doug Munro and Andrew Thornley, eds., *The Covenant Makers: Islander Missionaries in the Pacific* (Suva: Pacific Theological College and the Institute of Pacific Studies at the University of the South Pacific, 1996); Peggy Brock, "Setting the Record Straight: New Christians and Mission Christianity," in *Indigenous Peoples and Religious Change*, ed. Peggy Brock (Leiden: Brill, 2005), 107–28; Tolly Bradford, *Prophetic Identities: Indigenous Missionaries on British Colonial Frontiers, 1850–75* (Vancouver: University of British Columbia Press Press, 2012).

or island groups, although some societies were quicker than others to ordain these men to formal ministry. In 1848 the WMMS approved four Fijian men for ordination, and there were already Tongan Methodist ministers. John Geddie began ordaining indigenous deacons for the New Hebrides Mission in 1855, and the first Melanesian Anglican clergyman, George Sarawia, was ordained priest in 1873.

However, the process of indigenization was too slow for some critics. J. W. Burton believed that by the turn of the twentieth century the existing Methodist training institute in Fiji had become an absurdity. By the time a Fijian man went through the required stages of village teacher, catechist, senior teacher, and native minister, he was often a grandfather before being granted "full connexion" with the church. As a result of internal Methodist critique, a special theological institute was set up in 1908 to provide a fast track for the brightest graduates of the training institute, and the skills of the resulting generation of Fijian ministers "proved conclusively that the Fijian has qualities that fit him for fuller responsibilities."[28] This assessment was deeply paternalist: Burton believed that some European ministers were still required in Fiji to help "withstand the influence of the evil side of civilization," but if it was not for that, "we could probably displace more of our present Australian staff by well trained Fijian ministers."[29] The development of fully independent island churches was another story. Even the Melanesian Mission, with its early indigenization of the deaconate and priesthood, did not ordain its first indigenous bishops until 1963.[30] Nevertheless, neither race nor rank proved to be durable barriers for long, unlike gender: only men were considered to possess unique and permanent markers of fitness for mission or church leadership. Metropolitan debates about women's ministry had waxed and waned in some denominations since the Reformation, and they would intensify during the twentieth century. Only then would the gender-related question of sexual orientation be addressed directly, and the limits of traditional theological anthropology would be shaken to their foundations.[31] Meanwhile, most Pacific mission leadership would remain exclusively, unreflectively, and heterosexually male.

28. J. W. Burton, *A Hundred Years in Fiji* (London: Epworth Press, 1936), 92.

29. Burton, *A Hundred Years in Fiji*, 92.

30. Darrell L. Whiteman, *Melanesians and Missionaries: An Ethnohistorical Study of Social and Religious Change in the Southwest Pacific* (Pasadena: William Carey Library, 1983), 427.

31. Recent examples often draw on a combination of feminist and postcolonial analysis. See Elizabeth Johnston, *She Who Is: The Mystery of God in Feminist Theological Discourse* (New York: Crossroad, 1992); April De Conick, *Holy Misogyny: Why the Sex and Gender Conflicts in the Early Church Still Matter* (New York: Continuum, 2011); C. Norman Kraus, *On Being Human: Sexual Orientation and the Image of God* (Eugene, OR: Cascade Books, 2011); Hwa-Young Chong,

Missionaries to the South Pacific were drawn to that particular field of service for reasons they often recalled later on. One important factor was the embodied presence of Pacific Islanders in Britain.[32] The visit of "Prince Lee Boo" of the Pelew Islands (now the Republic of Belau) was particularly notable. The East India Company trading vessel *Antelope* was shipwrecked at Belau, and a narrative of the subsequent events was published by the captain's son Henry Wilson in 1788. Wilson had left one of his sailors behind while Lee Boo, second son of the local ruler, went to England with several other islanders. The first generation of missionaries offering themselves for Pacific service often referred to boyhood glimpses of Lee Boo, and they read eagerly about his journey to Britain. He learned to read on the voyage to England and, while there, gave accounts of his religious beliefs that were interpreted by Wilson and others as evidence of an indigenous belief in the immortality of the soul.[33] His intelligence and eagerness to learn were taken as evidence of indigenous malleability. Wilson had intended to inoculate Lee Boo against smallpox as soon as he was able to understand and consent to the procedure, but the young man died of the disease before he could be vaccinated. These tragic circumstances enhanced LMS interest in the South Pacific. Writing about Lee Boo's brief visit, the Reverend John Hockin declared:

> Judging from the mild and tractable disposition displayed by the natives of these islands, and their attachment to the English nation . . . let me indulge a hope that the time is not far distant, when the dayspring from on high, which hath visited them faintly, will break forth with glory; and the light of the Gospel will be propagated with more assurance of success in those mild regions, and still milder inhabitants, than in less genial climates, where the minds of the people as yet seem to be scarcely awake to the contemplation of the Almighty.[34]

In Search of God's Power in Broken Bodies: A Theology of Maum (New York: Palgrave Macmillan, 2013); and Eboni Turman, *Toward a Womanist Ethic of Incarnation: Black Bodies, the Black Church, and the Council of Chalcedon* (New York: Palgrave Macmillan, 2013).

32. See Vanessa Smith, "Banks, Tupaia, and Mai: Cross-cultural Exchanges and Friendship in the Pacific," *Parergon* 26, no. 2 (2009): 139–60.

33. George Keate, *An Account of the Pelew Island, situated in the Western Part of the Pacific Ocean. Composed from the Journals and Communications of Captain Henry Wilson, and Some of His Officers, who, in August 1783, were there Shipwrecked in the Antelope, a Packet Belonging to the Honourable East India Company* (London: G. Nicol, 1788), 328.

34. John Pearce Hockin, *A Supplement to the Account of the Pelew Islands; compiled from the journals of the Panther and Endeavour, two vessels sent by the Honourable East India Company to those Islands in the Year 1790 and from the Oral Communications of Captain H. Wilson* (London: W. Bulmer and Co., 1803), 59.

Pacific peoples were presumed to be ready and waiting for the gospel, a tribute to the powerful impressions (and distortions) generated by Lee Boo.[35]

An intense process of self-scrutiny preceded the interview and selection process for missionaries. Interior, vocational questions can be difficult to analyze, not helped by the tendency for missionaries to formulate their calling differently for mission officials than for family, friends, or academic colleagues. Their motives were "usually both mixed and complex; most missionaries may have been motivated by a combination of factors, and to dissect them for the purposes of analysis might be to rob the organism of its life."[36] This journey of personal discernment was accompanied by educational and institutional qualifications that varied according to denomination and could change over time. The LMS initially preferred single men with practical skills whose artisan background would suit them for the challenges of mission-building and enable them to marry into indigenous families. After its first mission to Tahiti failed, it recruited married men and placed an increased emphasis on education. Some missions, notably the Melanesian Mission, preferred university men from the start. By the later nineteenth century, some denominations were accepting applications from women to formal missionary posts as nurses or teachers. Missionary wives had frequently carried out these duties on an informal basis as "helpmeets" for their husbands.[37]

Amid this diversity and historical change, the unresolvable tension between othering and brothering remained. How much othering was too much, rendering mission work pointless? How much brothering might suggest that salvation may lie along non-Christian paths? In their inevitable engagement with these dilemmas, missionaries also engaged with island languages and cultures. To be effective, they had to do fieldwork, a word we normally associate with professional anthropology. This would suggest a ready partnership between modern missions and the developing social sciences, yet this relationship was anything but straightforward. By the later nineteenth century, growing hostility toward

35. Lee Boo continues to fascinate us. The church where he is buried has done extensive research on his visit. See http://www.stmaryrotherhithe.org/index.php?option=com_content&view=article&id=14&Itemid=14 (accessed 6 November 2013). And there is a video of relevant sites in London made recently by a Belauan visitor to London. See http://www.youtube.com/watch?v=ABaN2xcRnvY (accessed 6 November 2013).

36. Piggin, *Making Evangelical Missionaries*, 125.

37. Pioneering work in this area includes Diane Langmore, *Missionary Lives: Papua, 1874–1914* (Honolulu: University of Hawai'i Press, 1989); Patricia Grimshaw, *Paths of Duty: American Missionary Wives in Nineteenth-Century Hawai'i* (Honolulu: University of Hawai'i Press, 1989); and Margaret Jolly and Martha Macintyre, eds., *Family and Gender in the Pacific: Domestic Contradictions and the Colonial Impact* (Cambridge: Cambridge University Press, 1989).

missionaries was related in part to the rising influence of "salvage" models of anthropology that, as John Barker explains, attempted "to understand indigenous cultural and social systems before they were swept way by the forces of modernization."[38] Meanwhile, increased scientific specialization in Europe was creating fault lines and boundaries between those who would become professional scientists and the so-called amateurs. Numerous new scientific organizations arose, such as the Royal Geographical Society and the British Association for the Advancement of Science in Britain, and battles began for the introduction of science courses to university curricula. Comparing this picture with the eighteenth-century world of polymaths like Joseph Banks, who coordinated global scientific networks from their well-appointed homes, Felix Driver points out that the rise of specialist, professional science "signaled not so much the creation of a new public sphere for science as its proliferation and fragmentation."[39] In this fracturing intellectual world, specialists competed for credibility and resources. The role of the overseas amateur, such as the missionary, became an increasingly marginalized one.

A concerted attempt by anthropologists to generate more scientific anthropological data of their own is usually traced to Bronislaw Malinowski's *Argonauts of the Western Pacific* (1922) and its recommendation that anthropologists undertake their own fieldwork. One reason for doing this was the assumption that ethnography by "the average practical man, whether admnistrator, missionary, or trader," was fatally biased and "strongly repulsive to a mind striving after the objective, scientific view of things."[40] Although Malinowski was prepared to make a small number of exceptions, his frustration, even contempt, for non-academic ethnography was clear:

> The habit of treating with a self-satisfied frivolity what is really serious to the ethnographer; the cheap rating of what to him is a scientific treasure, that is to say, the native's cultural and mental peculiarities and independence—these features, so well known in the inferior amateur's writing, I found in the tone of the majority of white residents.[41]

38. John Barker, "Christianity in Oceanic Societies," in *Christianity in Oceania*, ed. John Barker (New York: University Press of America, 1990), 7.

39. Felix Driver, *Geography Militant: Cultures of Exploration and Empire* (Oxford: Blackwell, 2001), 32.

40. Bronislaw Malinowski, *Argonauts of the Western Pacific: An Account of Native Enterprise and Adventure in the Archipelagoes of Melanesian New Guinea* (Long Grove, IL: Waveland Press, 1922), 5–6, http://anth.alexanderstreet.com.login.ezproxy.library.ualberta.ca/View/1669184 (accessed 7 November 2013), 5–6.

41. Malinowski, *Argonauts of the Western Pacific*, 6.

Malinowski's views did not spring from nowhere, however; in 1913, the British psychologist and anthropologist W. H. R. Rivers had recommended "work in which trained investigators can give their whole attention to ethnological work" as compared with the amateur efforts of missionaries and others.[42] What is clear is that by the early twentieth century, professional anthropologists were already claiming moral and scientific high ground over the amateur efforts of missionaries in the South Pacific and elsewhere, even though they often depended heavily on earlier missionary fieldwork and on existing mission resources such as transportation and translation services. The growing popularity of functionalist theories of culture contributed to this process of alienation. Functionalism's teleology presumed that "a society in perfect equilibrium is considered the ideal, and change, particularly change introduced by contact with some external agent, is harmful."[43] It is easy to see how this view of culture would collide with theories of mission. By the 1960s, amidst debate concerning the relevance of theological anthropology in light of the apparent triumph of secular functionalism, James Gustafson wrote that "where the functionalist stops is but a station in the Christian interpretation of man: God's work is done through the orders of preservation, the establishment of justice, the fulfillment of human potentialities."[44] An article in the 1966 volumes of *Practical Anthropology* noted that missionaries were increasingly reluctant to ask advice of anthropologists not only because of frequent hostility toward missionary activity but also because "perhaps without quite realizing it, many anthropologists are devotees of the cult of the exotic."[45] There was also widespread resentment about being pumped for information and resources in return for the promise of shared research results, only to find that rarely did the anthropologists hold up their end of the bargain.[46] Better anthropological training for missionaries had been encouraged by mission societies themselves from the late nineteenth century onward, as we will see in the next chapter, but the two solitudes re-

42. Cited in James Urry, "'Notes and Queries on Anthropology' and the Development of Field Methods in British Anthropology, 1870–1920," *Proceedings of the Royal Anthropological Institute of Great Britain and Ireland* (1972): 50. See also Thorgeir S. Kolshus, "House upon Pacific Sand: W. H. R. Rivers and His 1908 Ethnographic 'Survey Work,'" in *The Ethnographic Experiment: A. M. Hocart and W. H. R. Rivers in Island Melanesia, 1908*, ed. Edvard Hviding and Cato Berg (Oxford: Berghahn, 2014).

43. Daniel T. Hughes, "Mutual Biases of Anthropologists and Missionaries," in *Mission, Church, and Sect in Oceania*, ed. James A. Boutilier, Daniel T. Hughes, and Sharon W. Tiffany (Ann Arbor: University of Michigan Press, 1978), 78.

44. James M. Gustafson, "Man—In Light of Social Science and Christian Faith," in *Conflicting Images of Man*, ed. William Nicholls (New York: The Seabury Press, 1966), 51–70.

45. Eugene A. Nida, "Missionaries and Anthropologists," *Practical Anthropology* 13 (1966): 273.

46. Nida, "Missionaries and Anthropologists," 274.

mained in divergence. Commenting on the persistent hostility between these two groups into the 1970s, Daniel Hughes noted ruefully that upon "reflecting on the many anthropologists and missionaries I have seen become close and lasting friends, I find that one party often refers to the other somewhat as an American middle-class white boasts that 'some of my best friends are black.'"[47]

Meanwhile, the views of missionaries themselves revealed their growing marginalization. A telling comparison can be made between the self-identification of a Victorian Methodist missionary, Lorimer Fison, and that of an early twentieth-century member of the Anglican New Guinea Mission, Copland King. Fison never doubted that he was the expert: distant armchair anthropologists were both dependent on his fieldwork and, in many cases, inferior in their scientific analysis. He was deeply skeptical about the observations of naval officers, gentlemen travelers, and other transients who lacked the linguistic skills and local connections to conduct proper fieldwork. He even wrote a brief satirical skit for his research collaborator A. W. Howitt, starring their favorite whipping boy Sir John Lubbock, called here a "scientific traveler." Lubbock, notorious for his somewhat indiscriminate use of observations made by transient visitors, is attempting to interview a "benighted heathen" in order to determine the extent of devil worship among the indigenous people:

> **Scientific traveler** 'Hi Johnny! What name that fellow? That fellow debolo [devil] &c'
>
> **Benighted heathen** nods & replies 'All right. That fellow all the same debolo. You got bacca [tobacco], eh?'
>
> **S.T.** (imparts the noxious weed) 'What fellow that fish, Johnny? Fish that fellow debolo, eh?'
>
> **B.H.** nods & grins still more cheerfully, being pleasantly conscious of the tobacco wh. he has stuck behind his ear.[48]

Besides illustrating Fison's wonderful sense of humor, this sketch has a number of deeper meanings. It demonstrates the superiority felt by missionaries over distant theorists who lacked the means to gather, understand, or interpret field data. Proper fieldworkers (i.e., missionaries) were the real experts. While

47. Hughes, "Mutual Biases," 65.

48. Lorimer Fison to A. W. Howitt, 21 June 1878, Lorimer Fison Project, Letterbook No. 6, PMB 1039, reel 4.

compiling their book, Fison and Howitt praised one another's expertise highly, to the point that Howitt had wondered whether their "mutual admiration society" might make readers doubt their professionalism. Fison understood the position in terms of relative debt. He was in Howitt's debt, he wrote, insisting that Howitt had nothing to thank him for. Mr. Morgan, on the other hand, "is under obligation to me for I have done much work for him."[49] Fison was reveling in the dependent position of this distinguished American anthropologist.

A frequent critic of the misguided theories of Lubbock and others, Fison wrote to Howitt that he thought "it needs the special training of these inquiries of ours to prepare the most accurate scholar to perceive the drift of allusions to the intersexual organizations" and other research topics.[50] Fison claimed his place in this specially-trained academic elite without hesitation. Even his relationship with the American anthropologist Lewis Henry Morgan, whom Fison greatly admired, featured the assumption that the field expert was always superior to the distant metropolitan theorist.[51] A remarkable book, *Southern Anthropology*, was published in 2015 by Helen Gardner and Patrick McConvell. It is an exploration of Fison and Howitt's main publication on Australian anthropology and a wonderful example of the fruitfulness of a multidisciplinary approach that includes historical theology. I regret that this book appeared too late for me to incorporate more fully into my analysis, especially because of its sensitivity to "the intensely local sites of praxis where the universal and wide-ranging theorist of human difference of the period met the reality of human experience."[52]

Many antipodean missionaries and clergy held similar views, such as Charles Bullock, whose reading of the Reverend Richard Davis's missionary work in New Zealand prompted him to contrast "Christian facts" with "asopho-philosophical 'day-dreams.'"[53] By the early twentieth century, however, the rising professionalism of anthropology was having an impact not only on

49. Lorimer Fison to A. W. Howitt, 12 October 1878, Lorimer Fison Project, Letterbook No. 6, PMB 1039, reel 4.

50. Lorimer Fison to A. W. Howitt, 17 January 1879, Lorimer Fison Project, Letterbook No. 6, PMB 1039, reel 4.

51. For a detailed analysis of the Fison/Morgan relationship see Helen Bethea Gardner, "The Origin of Kinship in Oceania: Lewis Henry Morgan and Lorimer Fison," *Oceania* 78, no. 2 (2008): 137–50 and "'By the Facts We Add to Our Store': Lorimer Fison, Lewis Henry Morgan and the Spread of Kinship Studies," *Oceania* 79, no. 3 (2009): 280–92.

52. Helen Bethea Gardner and Patrick McConvell, *Southern Anthropology—a History of Fison and Howitt's* Kamilaroi and Kurnai (London: Palgrave, 2015), 9.

53. Charles Bullock, *Missionaries and Anthropologists; or, Christian facts versus asopho-philosophical 'day-dreams.' The success of missionary enterprise in New Zealand illustrated from the biography of the Rev. Richard Davis* (London: William Macintosh, 1865).

anthropologists' views of missionary ethnographers but also the self-confidence of the missionaries themselves. The Reverend Copland King sent a manuscript article titled "Native Life in North East British New Guinea" to his mentor, the Cambridge anthropologist Alfred Cort Haddon. Haddon had established the study of anthropology at Cambridge as Lecturer in ethnology in 1900 and Reader in 1909. He made three research trips to New Guinea, a sign of the new interest in personal fieldwork by professional scholars. One of the pioneers of the New Guinea Mission, King proudly counted the number of years that he lived in New Guinea, underlining the authoritative nature of his observations. He added, however, that he had "tried to confine myself to what I know, and whenever I do propound any theories, I want them to be taken as those of an amateur."[54] Another of Haddon's missionary collaborators, John Henry Holmes of the LMS mission in New Guinea, was delighted when Haddon showed some of his work to the Cambridge classicist and anthropologist James George Frazer:

> I am intensely pleased with Dr. Frasers [*sic*] comment, not because I set undue value on the Notes so much as the encouragement I derive from a word of cheer from such an authority; I am intensely interested in the study of the Gulf of Papua natives, it has been my delight to observe their customs in detail, but in days gone by I have needed experts like you and Dr. Fraser to guide me.[55]

The generational gap between Fison and King reveals what amounts to a role reversal: those who had been the amateurs were now the professionals, while former experts with special training in the field were now presenting themselves as humble and grateful assistants.

There is no need to rehearse here the well-known postmodern and postcolonial critiques of the objectivity that Malinoswki and other early and mid-twentieth-century anthropologists took for granted. Critique of the "bad missionary" stereotype soon followed. In 1980 Claude Stipe warned that anthropology's prejudices against missionaries had been based not only on academic theories but also on an unexamined secularism.[56] By 1990 Sjaak van der Geest was observing something deeply ironic in anthropology's hostility toward missionaries: "If, however, anthropologists take ethnocentrism and the impo-

54. Copland King, "Native Life in North East British New Guinea," A. C. Haddon Papers, Envelope 2021, Cambridge University Library, Cambridge, UK.

55. John Henry Holmes to Haddon, 1 July 1902, A. C. Haddon Papers, Envelope 2068, Cambridge University Library, Cambridge, UK.

56. Claude E. Stipe, "Anthropologists versus Missionaries: The Influence of Presuppositions," *Current Anthropology* 21, no. 2 (1980): 165–79.

sition of alien premises as characteristics of the missionary, they also define themselves as missionaries."[57] At the beginning of the twenty-first century, Ad Borsboom and Jean Kommers felt the need to call on both groups to recognize that "competition and antagonism have become outdated discourses based on the rather arrogant assumption that there is a dominant center that knows what is best for the poorer peripheries of the world."[58] There was no sanitizing boundary between objective university anthropologists and their tainted amateur predecessors. Professional anthropology had emerged from complex historical circumstances, including relationships with colonial governments, Christian missions, military expeditions, and many other aspects of western expansion. Postcolonial mission studies have revealed similar entanglements, meaning that the "inferior amateur's writing" can now be investigated with as much interest as the ethnographies of professional anthropologists.

One of the first attempts to organize data from the field was made by ethnologist James Cowles Prichard, whose efforts helped to produce a questionnaire first published by the British Association for the Advancement of Science in 1839.[59] The Royal Navy followed suit with the Admiralty's *Manual of Scientific Inquiry* from 1849; Prichard wrote the ethnological chapter just before his death.[60] The Royal Geographical Society's *Hints to Travellers* appeared in 1854. James Urry has concluded that the various editions of *Notes and Queries*, published from 1874 into the 1920s, "show the gradual development of field methods and the ideas which, culminating in Malinowski, were to have a lasting effect on British anthropology."[61] Missionary ethnographers and others interested in a more rigorous, scientific approach had several sets of guidelines available by the mid-nineteenth century, and they sometimes created their own questionnaires

57. Sjaak van der Geest, "Anthropologists and Missionaries: Brothers Under the Skin," *Man* 25, no. 4 (1990): 591. For a similar observation about "fundamentalism" in both professions, see Philip Gibbs, "Culture and Faith: The Contribution of the Melanesian Institute, Papua New Guinea," in *Anthropology's Debt to Missionaries*, ed. Plotnicov, Brown, and Sultive (Pittsburgh: University of Pittsburgh Press, 2007), 123. For a lament about the lack of systematic investigation of the issue, see Peter Pels, "Anthropology and Mission: Towards a Historical Analysis of Professional Identity," in *The Ambiguity of Rapprochement: Reflections of Anthropologists on Their Controversial Relationship with Missionaries*, ed. R. Bonsen, H. Marks, and J. Miedema (Nijmegen: Focaal, 1990), 81.

58. "Introduction" to *Anthropologists and the Missionary Endeavour: Experiences and Reflections*, ed. Ad Borsboom and Jean Kommers (Saarbrüken: Verlag für Entwicklungspolitik Saarbrüken GmbH, 2000), 10.

59. Also see George Stocking, *Victorian Anthropology* (New York: The Free Press, 1991), 79, and Driver, *Geography Militant*, 51.

60. Samson, *Imperial Benevolence*, 12–13.

61. James Urry, "'Notes and Queries on Anthropology,'" 45. See also Gardner, *Gathering for God*, 112–14.

for circulation or forwarded those of their academic partners. They also engaged with the aspects of scientific theory that were congenial to their theological anthropology while rejecting others, as we will see in the following chapters. Along the way, they made substantial contributions of their own to the development of those theories, as well as providing the fieldwork data that sustained them.

Ironically, one of the most powerful tributes to missionary anthropology was paid by Malinowski himself in the preface to William James Viritahitemauvai Saville's *In Unknown New Guinea* (1926) when he acknowledged how "the superiority of the long-time resident becomes obvious," admitting that he "had not even discovered the existence of initiation" before Saville and members at the LMS mission had drawn it to his attention.[62] When missionaries sent out questionnaires of their own, trying to obtain comparative data, they began to understand the frustration of anthropologists in Europe and the United States who sometimes appealed to the mission societies for research assistance. Responding to Howitt's complaints about the lack of response to his latest questionnaire, Fison declared, "Your correspondents are treating you just as mine treated me, & as men who do our work must expect to be treated." Only when he had begun conducting his own comparative inquiries, he said, did he come to understand Lewis Henry Morgan's "fervour of gratitude" after their collaboration began. It had seemed "the most natural thing on earth to go zealously into such an inquiry for the sake of increasing the world's stock of knowledge when one was in a position to do it," but after his own researches began, he "was looked upon by [his] own familiar friends as being affected with a harmless craze . . . & on one occasion [he] was even solemnly rebuked by an Elder who looked upon [his] work as a sinful waste of time."[63]

Scholars still struggle to find appropriate terminology with which to distinguish between different types of anthropologists in the nineteenth and early twentieth centuries. Lynette Turner's essay on the academic partnership between A. W. Howitt and the Reverend Lorimer Fison is a case in point. Fison was conducting research on Aboriginal Australian kinship systems when he met the colonial administrator A. W. Howitt, and the two men began an enduring scientific collaboration. Turner, however, explains that she cannot call them scientists, preferring the ambivalent phrase "transitional figures," because neither man held a university post.[64] A 1988 biographical dictionary edited

62. William James Viritahitemauvai Saville, *In Unknown New Guinea* (London: Seeley Service & Co., 1926), 10.

63. Lorimer Fison to A. W. Howitt, 21 June 1878, Lorimer Fison Project, Letterbook No. 6, PMB 1039, reel 4.

64. Lynette Turner, "Alfred W. Howitt and Lorimer Fison: 'Victorian' ethnography and the gendered 'primitive,'" in *Writing and Race*, ed. Tim Youngs (London: Longman, 1997), 220.

by Thomas L. Mann attempted to include everyone who had contributed to modern anthropology, breaking down a total of 3,485 entries into categories including professional anthropologists (over 700), missionaries (106), and priests (138). It is not clear why "missionary" and "priest" were considered exclusive categories, nor why the well-known Anglican priest and missionary Robert Codrington was listed only under "anthropologist."[65] The point here is not to single out individual scholars for particular criticism but rather to underline a persistent problem with professional categorization and value judgments concerning missionary ethnography.

Some missionary observations were strikingly sophisticated, revealing an awareness of what would become known as cultural contamination. William Colenso of the CMS in New Zealand underlined his expertise in familiar terms, emphasizing his extensive knowledge of the Maori "before the country became settled," having "traveled so very much among them," often "in parts where no white man had ever been before me."

He was worried about recording practices of alleged antiquity that, in fact, he knew had come from western contact. He therefore emphasized that his fieldwork was done "at a period in their history when *they had no extraneous foreign matter to trouble them or to talk about.*"[66] Colenso was assuming that the absence of settlers meant a lack of contamination, and that was not necessarily the case, but the main point here is that he was aware of a problem that academic theorists in Europe or the United States were overlooking. His reflections on ethnographic methodology also included a remarkable degree of reflexivity, using the theological concept of *kenosis*. Introduced in a first-generation Christian hymn quoted by St. Paul in his letter to the Philippians, *kenosis* was the original Greek term for the willing self-emptying of Christ in his incarnation as a human being: "Who, being in the form of God, thought it not robbery to be equal with God: But made himself of no reputation [the concept of *kenosis*], and took upon him the form of a servant, and was made in the likeness of men: And being found in fashion as a man, he humbled himself, and became obedient unto death, even the death of the cross" (Phil. 2:5–8). In modern English, *kenosis* is usually translated as "emptying." Colenso recommended *kenosis* to all would-be anthropologists in New Zealand: "happy was that missionary or teacher, who could empty himself, as it were, of his foreign ideas and ways, and thus go with [the Maori] after their manner in seeking to impart truth: all

65. Thomas L. Mann, ed., *Biographical Dictionary of Anthropologists Born before 1920* (New York and London: Garland Publishing, 1988).

66. Colenso, "On the Colour Sense," 49. Emphasis original.

such always found willing hearers."[67] No godlike being, the ethnographer should humble himself, like Christ, and accommodate himself to the people he would serve. This is not a secular academic methodology, but nevertheless Colenso saw it as the best route to scientific objectivity.

He was convinced that anthropological ignorance had directly contributed to the dwindling Maori population. The decline of Maori power and influence was not simply a mechanical consequence of disease or warfare; instead, it had cultural roots. Aware of the dilemmas of culture change, he did not shrink from the responsibilities borne by missionaries like himself:

> The sudden termination of polygamy, slavery, and the taboo system, without anything to replace the last two, has been the chief cause of their decline *as a people* in *status* and influence. Had some comprehensive mind early arrived in New Zealand, to point out to the *first* missionaries the sure consequence of the utter and sudden removal of what then upheld the tribes and nation, unless renewed with something equally strong and equally suitable, more cautious and better adapted means for preserving them might have been used. However distasteful these three things might be to an European and Christian, they were the life of the New Zealander.[68]

It is obvious that Colenso hoped for the eventual disappearance of polygamy, slavery, and *tapu*. He was no moral relativist. Nevertheless, his critique of the early New Zealand missions and their negative impact was based on an intense reflexivity about Christian history and Scripture:

> Slavery (though an ugly word) might have been ameliorated in New Zealand, where its form was mild compared with what it was in ancient Rome, even as it was both there and in Asia Minor by Paul. Polygamy might have been far better dealt with, for the time, according to the lenient dealings of God with the Jewish fathers, and with New Testament teaching, than according to ecclesiastical dogmas. And much of the taboo might have been softened and altered, and borne with too for a time, until a better and not altogether distinct scheme, suited to uphold and expand the moral character of the neophyte Maori Christian, had been got ready.[69]

67. Colenso, "On the Colour Sense," 70.

68. William Colenso, "On the Maori Races of New Zealand," written for the New Zealand Exhibition 1865 and published in *Transactions and Proceedings of the New Zealand Institute* 1 (1875): 418–19.

69. Colenso, "On the Maori Races," 419.

Other missionaries also reflected on their own biases and responsibilities. William Saville of the LMS mission to New Guinea wrote of observations of local women that described them as "beasts of burden" due to the ability to carry heavy loads on their heads. However, after observing how often the less heavily-laden men had to defend their women from attack, Saville noted that it was merely a European cultural prejudice that deemed carrying loads on the head to be bestial. The European practice of lugging bags by hand seemed absurdly inefficient to New Guinea islanders of both sexes, and thus, said Saville, "If we smile at the tyranny of custom among a savage people, the savage has the same liberty to smile at the tyranny of custom among us civilized beings, hide-bound in conventionalities."[70]

For Daniel Macdonald of the Presbyterian mission in the New Hebrides the whole concept of savagery was problematic. The Efatese among whom he lived and worked were "mild and gentle in speech and manner. . . . They are hospitable and generous. They live according to strict laws and customs handed down to them from their forefathers. In their way, or according to their lights, they are pious and religious." To be sure, they were also "cannibals, addicted to witchcraft, and infanticide, and licentiousness, and to treachery in war, and apt, or used to be apt, to kill castaways from ships or canoes." Here is the othering and brothering pattern with a sharply reflexive edge. Macdonald reminded his readers

> that there were 'wreckers' not so long ago in Cornwall, and that people were burned alive not so long ago for witchcraft in England and America, and that infanticide and licentiousness can be found nearer home than the South Sea Islands; and that in England, in the present day, there are advocates of the practice of putting to death the aged and the hopelessly diseased.[71]

For Macdonald, labeling indigenous cultural practices wicked was completely to misunderstand the situation: "there are wicked men among the savages, according to their own standard, just as among us according to ours. But wickedness of this kind is different from the wickedness that is sanctioned by public opinion, and not considered as blameworthy—such, for instance, as the worship of idols, and cannibalism, or polygamy."[72] In Macdonald's work, as in

70. Saville, *In Unknown New Guinea*, 74.

71. Daniel Macdonald, *Oceania: Linguistic and Anthropological* (Melbourne: M. L. Hutchinson, 1880), 196.

72. Macdonald, *Oceania*, 196.

that of many other missionary ethnographers, we will find the working out of an intellectual politics very different from the traditional stereotype. Like Colenso and Saville, Macdonald refused to privilege his own European cultural background as somehow free of traditional constraints, hypocrisy, or socially sanctioned behavior that should be morally condemned. William Colenso went even further: "The writer of this essay has seen a chief,—a lineal descendant of ancient kings,—whose nod yesterday was life or death, who had several wives, many fine children, and a number of slaves; whose home was fully of merry laughing faces, food, and hospitality," he wrote, but he had also seen him later as

> a baptized man, without servants or helpers, with little food and less clothing, ashamed and vexed at not having the means to be hospitable; with one weak wife (soon brought to be so through extra daily labor) and three children, for whom he himself had daily to work very hard, and yet could *not* procure for them the fish and birds and pork of former days; while any one of his late slaves was far better off than he.[73]

Colenso wrote of his grief at seeing this change for the worse:

> and he has asked Christianity, 'Was there really a necessity for all this?' Very likely, had those notable Maori kings been only gradually altered, and not so suddenly and rudely abolished, and had fitting *short* Christian services obtained instead of wearisome long ones, the principal chiefs, heads of tribes, would have kept their *status*, order would have prevailed, the rising generation would have both known and kept their proper place, and decrease in their numbers would have been considerably less, they would have confidence in the Government, missionaries, and settlers, instead of suspicion; in all probability there would have been now no war with the Government, and the degrading fanaticism which now obtains would never have found support. *Fuit Ilium!* Cook found the New Zealanders healthy, happy, and contented in the midst of all their wars and poverty;—*are they so now?*[74]

Colenso insisted on connecting mission work to the broader issue of colonialism, even if the relationship between the two was a more complex one than he and his contemporaries realized. Something so profound as religious change could not have somehow taken place in the "right" way, avoiding all

73. Colenso, "On the Maori Races," 419.
74. Colenso, "On the Maori Races," 418–19.

negative social, cultural, or political consequences. Nevertheless, missionaries like Colenso did not have to wait for professional anthropologists to point out the tragedies of too-rapid change, nor did they lack the capacity to criticize their own beliefs and practices where necessary. Recent scholarship has recognized that "all ethnographers observe 'the field' differently and experience different senses of emotional reflexivity in relation to their background ideologies, both religious and political."[75]

Missionary ethnography was as empirical as any other science of the day. They wanted to get the facts right. Referring to his recent anthropological publications, Charles Fox of the Melanesian Mission thanked a friend for his constructive criticism during the drafting process "because there *the one thing* is to get at the truth. Criticism is the very breath of science. I rejoice in the severest criticism of my own work."[76] John Henry Holmes of New Guinea, writing to A. C. Haddon in 1907, thanked the anthropologist for sending along Volume Five of the published proceedings of the Cambridge Torres Straits Expedition, sheepishly confessing that he had little intention of reading it. "I am not reading anything in it on totemism at all studiously," he explained, "I want to keep my mind open to study the totemism of these Elema tribes & at the same time avoid the possibility of being influenced by the recorded studies of the totemism of other tribes & peoples."[77] He did not want to begin with a theory and make his research fit into it. This was the sting in the tail of Holmes's deference to Haddon in other contexts. Holmes recognized the rising importance of professional anthropology, but by describing his methodology in this way he was underlining his durable credentials as an empirical scientist.[78]

75. Andrew Strathern and Pamela J. Stewart, "Ethnographic Records from the Western Highlands of Papua New Guinea: Missionary-Linguists, Missionary-Ethnographers," in *Anthropology's Debt to Missionaries,* ed. Plotnicov, Brown and Sutlive (Pittsburgh: University of Pittsburgh Press, 2007), 151–60. See also J. Abbink, "Anthropology and the Missions: A Critical Epistemological Perspective," *Methodology and Science* 18 (1985): 253–69 and E. Brandwie, "Ethnology and Missionaries: The Case of the Anthropos Institute and Wilhelm Schmidt," in *Missionaries, Anthropologists and Cultural Change,* ed. D. L. Whiteman (Williamsburg: College of William and Mary, 1985).

76. Charles Elliot Fox, "A Missionary in Melanesia," 29, MS-Papers-1171–02, Alexander Turnbull Library, Wellington, NZ. Emphasis original.

77. John Henry Holmes to A. C. Haddon, 31 October [1907], A. C. Haddon Papers, Envelope 2068, Cambridge University Library, Cambridge, UK.

78. For more on Holmes, see R. E. Reid, "John Henry Holmes in Papua. Changing Missionary Perspectives on Indigenous Cultures, 1890–1914," *Journal of Pacific History* 13, no. 3 (1978): 73–87. Compare the allegedly "accidental [missionary] ethnographers" in Linda Colley, *Captives: Britain, Empire and the World, 1600–1850* (London: Jonathan Cape, 2002), or those in Jean Michaud, "Missionary ethnographers in Upper-Tonkin: the early years, 1895–1920," *Asian Ethnicity* 5, no. 2 (2004): 179–94.

This ongoing quest for academic credibility explains the educational bonds between anthropologists and missionaries that arose despite the rising antagonism between these two groups generally. A growing emphasis on quality missionary education during the nineteenth century had prompted the founding of several training institutions, some of them combining general ministerial training with advanced education specifically aimed at preparation for mission work. There was no universal model. As Niel Gunson has pointed out,

> The Calvinistic Methodist directors of the LMS, like their Wesleyan counterparts, placed much more emphasis on qualifications in zeal and piety. The Puritan tradition, on the other hand, emphasized the value of learning, and it was the Independent [Congregationalist] and Presbyterian directors who urged the need for a systematized education of missionaries.[79]

The eventual dominance of these Puritan views led to the establishment in 1801 of a college at Gosport that provided both missionary and seminary training. At Gosport, and later at Hoxton after the college moved there in 1826, there was an emphasis on catechesis, book publication, school management, and grammatical training (largely from the classics) designed to assist in translation work. Sometimes a visiting or retired missionary would provide tutoring in specific languages such as Tahitian, but this special training could not be provided regularly. Of special note, however, was the emphasis on the need to train indigenous ministers to lead missions and churches among their own people. In keeping with their notions of cultural hierarchy, seminary leaders such as the Reverend Dr. David Bogue believed that it would be easier to do this in Asia than in Africa or the Pacific. Stuart Piggin noted the deep tension in Bogue's views when he "charged his students with the duty of putting natives in charge of church affairs as quickly as possible, and to guard against lording it over them" but at the same time emphasizing "that missionaries should act as overseers of the churches which they planted and should have greater authority over them than anyone else."[80] The pattern of othering and brothering was established well before missionaries even left for the South Pacific.

Little, if anything, in their domestic curriculum prepared missionaries for their encounters with alien and sometimes incomprehensible cultures. A college at Cheshunt, established by the evangelical Countess of Huntingdon, offered a preaching-centered curriculum for Calvinists. Several other colleges

79. Gunson, *Messengers of Grace*, 64.

80. Piggin, *Making Evangelical Missionaries*, 178.

also provided training from a variety of denominational perspectives. We also need to note the establishment in 1824 of the South Sea Academy on Moorea in the Society Islands, founded to educate the wives and sons of missionaries. Niel Gunson gives us the contents of an examination it gave to the teenaged Samuel Wilson in 1826. Following the usual training method of memorization and repetition, Wilson learned *précis* of the following by heart for his exam:

> The epistle to the Hebrews; and also the Epistle of James; thirty-one hymns; fifty-one pages of Ayliffe's Catechism on Divine Revelation; the whole of the Missionary hymns; Murray's Grammar to the end of Syntax; ten chapters of Pinnock's Catechism on Geography; twenty-two chapters of ditto on Chronology; the whole of the Assembly's Catechism with the proofs; twenty-nine pages of a Catechism on the Arts and Sciences; seven chapters of Pinnock's Catechism on Rhetoric.[81]

By the middle of the nineteenth century, the expansion of missions in increasingly British-ruled South Asia was making its presence felt, and Sanskrit now usually joined Greek, Latin, and Hebrew in the language curriculum. An awareness of what we call culture was developing, which prompted the Anglican missionary college of St. Augustine's, Canterbury "to form a Museum, which may illustrate the habits and customs of those parts of the British Empire to which the Students are destined."[82] Missionary museums were not new, but teaching museums aimed at illuminating culture were. St. Augustine's collections included a feather cloak and helmet donated by King Kamehameha IV of Hawaii and brought to Britain by Queen Emma during her visit in 1865.[83] At St. Augustine's there was to be a well-rounded program including

> a knowledge of Oriental languages, and those of the Southern Seas, together with their many dialects; a familiar acquaintance with the histories, religions, usages, and traditions of the Heathen nations, and, as in the case of the Hindoos, with their sciences and metaphysics: for want of which it has hitherto often befallen a Missionary to spend the first and most vigorous years of his enterprise in learning on the spot things which should have been intimately known before he set foot on his field of labor.[84]

81. Gunson, *Messengers of Grace*, 77.

82. *Calendar of the Missionary College of St. Augustine, Canterbury* (London: H. Ward, 1851), 29.

83. R. J. E. Boggis, *A History of St. Augustine's College, Canterbury* (Canterbury: Cross & Jackman, 1907), 151.

84. Boggis, *A History of St. Augustine's College*, 151.

To receive this detailed knowledge, the college turned to the published ethnography of missionary researchers around the world, including Pacific pioneers such as William Ellis, John Williams, and Richard Taylor for use in courses on comparative religion and the history of religion. At the Calvinistic Methodist or Welsh Presbyterian Theological College, the focus was primarily on India, and teaching in comparative religion was largely confined to discussions of relationships between classical Mediterranean religions and Hinduism. This reflects the anthropological preoccupations of the time, including the marginalization of Islam when compared with the very detailed study given to Sanskrit and the ancient "Aryan" Hindu texts. It also reflects the expansion of the British empire. By the end of the nineteenth century Buddhism was being introduced to the curriculum, but although the college was sponsoring a mission in Africa from 1896, it did not study African languages or religious beliefs.[85] As Stuart Piggin noted:

> preachers had to be well educated men, who had studied to present themselves as workmen who need not be ashamed. There is, accordingly, a large body of evidence showing that the typical missionary in our period prosecuted his studies with a diligence remarkable even in an age when aspiring youths were noted for their studious habits. He was not afraid of the intellect and he was determined to make full use of 'reason' in the pursuit of his aims.[86]

In 1912 an article in *The Daily News and Leader* proclaimed: "The time is long past when the public view of the missionary was of a monument of misdirected zeal and incapacity. The modern missionary is quite a different person. He is usually a highly trained man of intellect and character, who when he goes forward distinguishes himself by his courage and initiative."[87]

It is by no means clear that all outsiders had abandoned the traditional view of "misdirected zeal." Anthropologists were growing increasingly critical of missions by the turn of the twentieth century, but some were also eager to help, especially in the wake of the 1910 Edinburgh missionary conference. The conference declared that mission work was of direct scientific value: "In exploration, scores of missionaries have been pioneers; in sociology, their observations have contributed a mass of material of the highest value"; and "their

85. *Calendar of the Calvinistic Methodist or Welsh Presbyterian Theological College* (Wrexham: Hughes & Son, 1897).

86. Piggin, *Making Evangelical Missionaries*, 71.

87. "The Making of a Missionary," *Daily News and Leader*, 31 May 1912, A. C. Haddon Papers, Envelope 4067, Cambridge University Library, Cambridge, UK.

study of developed languages has enriched philology and all human culture."[88] This was all very well, but formal missionary education reflected little of this pride in scientific achievement, not least because of steadily declining funds.[89] The problem was extensively discussed at the Edinburgh 1910 conference, although to date scholars have mainly concentrated on the outcomes for female missionaries training for service in Asia and Africa. For our purposes, its most important features involve "the fertile dialogue between serving missionaries and scholars" that had emerged by the end of the conference and had inspired the establishment of the *International Review of Missions* in 1912.[90] The conference's Commission V, dedicated to "the preparation of missionaries," had observed that the European and American mission societies were far in advance of Britain in terms of providing field-specific language and cultural instruction.[91] It pleaded with British society boards "that theological curricula would be enriched for all students by a fuller treatment of missionary subjects, even if that involves some revision of the traditional curriculum."[92] Encapsulating othering and brothering in a nutshell, it observed that "a missionary is powerless to help a people whom he cannot love."[93] In this case, anthropology and love should go hand in hand to counter the arrogantly lax preparation in the past:

> Time was when it seemed easy to put men who had little more than an elementary education behind them, through two or three years of Bible study, a little Christian doctrine, some instruction in English composition and in sermon making, perhaps a smattering of New Testament Greek, and launch them out to preach the Gospel to the heathen.[94]

Outlining what should replace this unsatisfactory situation, the Commission prioritized five areas: science and history of missions, religions of the world, sociology, pedagogy, and the science of languages, including the relevant field languages. Anthropology does not appear on the list, but it quickly becomes clear that the Commission conceptualized sociology as the study of

88. World Missionary Conference, *Report of Commission VII: Missions and Governments* (Edinburgh and London: Oliphant, Anderson & Ferrier, 1910), 96.

89. Stanley, *World Missionary Conference*, 200.

90. Stanley, *World Missionary Conference*, 200.

91. World Missionary Conference, *Report of Commission V: The Preparation of Missionaries* (Edinburgh: Oliphant, Anderson & Ferrier, 1910), 51; Internet Archive, Scholars Portal Books, books1.scholarsportal.info/viewdoc.html?id=158388 (accessed 8 October 2013).

92. World Missionary Conference, *Report of Commission V*, 80.

93. World Missionary Conference, *Report of Commission V*, 104.

94. World Missionary Conference, *Report of Commission V*, 107.

culture and culture contact. Earlier generations "did not foresee all the strange consequences that inevitably arose from the cross-currents of commerce and politics" in indigenous societies, requiring missionaries to be familiar with "social science" generally.[95]

The expansion of the University of London in the service of empire produced developments that were very helpful for missionary societies wondering how to meet these clearly articulated but poorly funded goals. The government's Treasury department had recently published its "Report on the Organisation of Oriental Studies in London," proposing the establishment of a new College of Oriental Studies (later the School of Oriental and African Studies) for the preparation of colonial officials and civil servants. Best of all, the proposal had been made "by public men of wide experience, not in relation to Missions, but in a general enquiry as to the social and civil influence of Europeans upon Oriental civilization."[96] Perhaps missionaries could study at the new College, or at other institutions while in England before their departure or while on furlough leave, and a board of missionary studies was set up in order to assist the various mission societies with their programs.

The Pacific world had been all but invisible at the Edinburgh conference, but the British Board of Study for the Preparation of Missionaries was well aware of its high profile in anthropological research, and some Pacific anthropologists were sympathetic to the board's activities. A. C. Haddon, for example, taught anthropology courses at the LMS's Cheshunt College and elsewhere, and several years later one of his former missionary students wrote to say, "Your lectures gave me an interest in Anthropological & kindred subjects, & I have prepared & read two or three papers on Magic, Fetishism, Folklore, &c" but it was often difficult for him to obtain copies of scientific literature.[97] Another former student, this time from the Anglican college of St. Augustine's in Canterbury, recalled attending Haddon's lectures purely out of interest; he was a parish priest at the time. "I went to the lectures to encourage others—as well as for my own interest. Halfway through the term I was amazed by a call to go out to Burma as Bishop of Rangoon. . . ."[98] Now Warden of St. Augustine's, he wanted to tell Haddon what an impact the course had on him: "Your lectures saved me from any danger that might have existed, of lightly estimating native customs etc.—of

95. Dudley Kidd, "Kaffir Socialism and Missions," *The East and the West* (April 1909); quoted in World Missionary Conference, *Report of Commission V*, 169.

96. World Missionary Conference, *Report of Commission V*, 185.

97. Herbert Crouch to A. C. Haddon, 20 December 1911, A. C. Haddon Papers, Envelope 4067, Cambridge University Library, Cambridge, UK.

98. Arthur M. Knight to A. C. Haddon, 21 September 1911, A. C. Haddon Papers, Envelope 4067, Cambridge University Library, Cambridge, UK.

failing to give them attention and respect." He was grateful to have been set "on the right lines—and so helped to set those whom I had to lead, on the right lines also—and now that I am at a Missionary College I am still feeling the benefit."[99]

An extended correspondence between Haddon and Canon H.U. Weitbrecht, head of the British Board of Study for the Preparation of Missionaries, reveals both opportunities and challenges in meeting the Edinburgh conference's recommendations. Weitbrecht, a former CMS missionary to India, approached Haddon in 1911 for advice about a possible vacation school in ethnology and sociology at Cambridge for outgoing missionaries: "How much time would be needed to 'get a practical grasp' of these subjects, given that the students already had a university degree?"[100] Haddon responded in such detail that a discouraged Weitbrecht thought that the course would need to be pondered not as a real prospect but "rather as an ideal."[101] Haddon was frustrated by this response, regarding anthropological training as

> more essential as a preparation for mission work than anything else. It is very important to have a general and sympathetic knowledge of the institutions of less advanced societies, as the new ideals inculcated by most missionaries are at first incompatible with the stability of native institutions. . . . It is not sufficiently recognized that most natives have a very rigid system of ethics which makes for social solidarity, and any weakening of this is liable to entail disastrous results.[102]

Haddon's sympathy for missionary work is clear in his correspondence with Weitbrecht: "Is it not our duty gently to lead the tender flock through this difficult country and thereby follow in the footsteps of the Almighty Himself who has gradually educated mankind through diverse dispensations?" Perhaps for that reason he became sarcastic about the prospects for this course: "I will send you shortly a rough scheme of the work which I consider suitable for the sixteen hours which appear to be all that your students can give to the subject. . . ."[103]

99. Arthur M. Knight to A. C. Haddon, 21 September 1911, A. C. Haddon Papers, Envelope 4067, Cambridge University Library, Cambridge, UK.

100. Canon Weitbrecht to A. C. Haddon, 16 November 1911, A. C. Haddon Papers, Envelope 4067, Cambridge University Library, Cambridge, UK.

101. Canon Weitbrecht to A. C. Haddon, 18 December 1911, A. C. Haddon Papers, Envelope 4067, Cambridge University Library, Cambridge, UK.

102. A. C. Haddon to Canon Weitbrecht, 19 December 1911, A. C. Haddon Papers, Envelope 4067, Cambridge University Library, Cambridge, UK.

103. A. C. Haddon to Canon Weitbrecht, 19 December 1911, A. C. Haddon Papers, Envelope 4067, Cambridge University Library, Cambridge, UK.

In this case the professional anthropologist wished to be of greater service to mission education than circumstances would permit.

Canon Weitbrecht managed to organize eighteen hours of lectures on ethnology and sociology for a vacation course at Oxford for departing missionaries, and Haddon generously suggested possible lecturers and reading lists. Soon a similar course was run at Cambridge for missionaries on furlough: a key recommendation at Edinburgh. A sample syllabus from the Cambridge course reveals the scope of the topics covered: phonetics, education, sociology, African languages, Hinduism, voice production, linguistics, the religions of China and Korea, Islam, history of linguistics, anthropology, Buddhism, missionary method, and history of missions.[104] Priorities and axiologies become clear in this program: Africans were represented only by the study of their languages; African religions and culture were subsumed into the "anthropology" section while Asian religions got specific lecture courses of their own.[105] Haddon himself lectured on the Pacific within the sociology section of the course. Apparently African and Pacific peoples did not yet possess "religions" for academic purposes, despite the best efforts of Pacific missionary anthropologists like Robert Codrington.

After the Second World War, such training (official or unofficial) was considered essential, but there was now a debate about what kind of anthropology should be taught. In *The Missionary and Anthropology* (1945), Gordon Hedderly Smith urged his American audience to consider the merits of formal training in cultural anthropology, adding that "general religious systems of belief in the study of the primitive and comparative religions" was now standard fare at missionary colleges.[106] It seems that the study of religion was considered separate from the study of other elements of culture. Confusion lay in the current "vast scope" of anthropological inquiry, including social and physical anthropology, and in complex debates about anthropological theory. Nevertheless, Smith was convinced that in addition to the skills of "the linguist, the explorer, the evangelist, the translator, the mechanic, the doctor, the architect, and the teacher, should be added the anthropologist."[107] He added that "many great missionaries were anthropologists. They were obliged to be by the very nature

104. "Board of Study's Vacation Course," August 1913; A. C. Haddon Papers, Envelope 4067, Cambridge University Library, Cambridge, UK.

105. Brian Stanley, "Africa through European Christian Eyes: The World Missionary Conference, Edinburgh 1910," in *African Identities and Global Christianity in the Twentieth Century*, ed. Klaus Korschorke (Wiesbaden: Harrassowitz Verlag, 2005), 165–80.

106. Gordon Hedderly Smith, *The Missionary and Anthropology: An Introduction to the Study of Primitive Man for Missionaries* (Chicago: Moody Press, 1945), 5.

107. Smith, *The Missionary and Anthropology*, 21.

of their pioneer task. They brought to bear their intellect and practical forces on the problems before them and history is replete with their achievements," citing Robert Codrington of the Melanesian Mission as his prime example.[108] By this time, however, the network of intellectual relationships between missionaries and anthropologists, with its roots in the eighteenth century, had been largely severed. Missionaries seeking guidance for practical anthropology would need to do so on their own terms.

108. Smith, *The Missionary and Anthropology*, 24.

CHAPTER 2

Networks

The age of steam accelerated global communications in the nineteenth century, but many Pacific missionaries still felt isolated. Letters to one another and to distant friends were full of laments about missing mail, delayed deliveries, and the frustration experienced by those who wished they could be more reliably connected to academic centers of learning and debate. Face-to-face meetings between missionaries and anthropologists were rare before the twentieth century, but occasionally there was personal contact, sometimes through family connections. One delightful example involved a surprise meeting in Oxford. On his first trip to England, Lewis Henry Morgan arrived at the university armed with a letter of introduction to "a certain gentleman at Oxford," one Mr. Walker. While visiting the Walker home, Morgan grew eloquent in his praise of his missionary friend and research partner Lorimer Fison. Mrs. Walker and her sister listened, smiling, until Morgan paused for breath, at which point Mrs. Walker said, "You can't think what pleasure you have given us, Mr. Morgan. You have been speaking of our own brother." Overcome with delight, Morgan "leaped from his chair & literally rushed about the room," and his sister's account of this serendipitous meeting gave Fison great pleasure when she wrote to Fiji to tell him about it.[1]

The nurturing of correspondence and the exchange of books and manuscripts demonstrated friendship and intellectual partnership, providing a substitute for conversations that might never take place in person. Fison collaborated with Howitt in distant Australia by asking, via Morgan, for Howitt's

1. Lorimer Fison to A. W. Howitt, 21 June 1878, Lorimer Fison Project, Letterbook No. 6, PMB 1039, reel 4.

rough copy to be "paged as your American copy is paged" so that Fison could create notes for insertion. He would send the resulting compilation back to Morgan in Rochester, New York, and Morgan would collate the material for the resulting book, in addition to facilitating matters at the press.[2] To help another missionary colleague, Robert Codrington of the Melanesian Mission, Fison sent a manuscript to the Cambridge anthropologist E. B. Tylor with his own notes on it, interleaved with Codrington's material.[3] This was the only sensible way to proceed when inter-island communications remained slower than the intellectual pace of those who prided themselves on their locally-grounded expertise, yet longed to engage with metropolitan debates.

Missionaries could afford few books and were glad of sympathetic friends in the book trade. George Robertson of Melbourne was one of these, offering his services at a discounted rate for Methodist missionaries in the field. Lorimer Fison heard of Robertson from his colleague George Brown and wrote to him often, ordering books on subjects ranging from theology to microscopy. Writing from Fiji in 1877, Fison asked for the new edition of John Ferguson McLennan's *Studies in Ancient History* since "the old editions . . . will not serve my purpose."[4] The limitations of island postal delivery were frustrating, and a letter from Fison to Howitt reveals how important second-hand information from friends and reviewers was in keeping up with the pace of metropolitan publication. Fison's sister had told him of the recent appearance of Henry Maine's *Ancient Law & Institutions*. She promised to send him a copy, along with other books, but the package never arrived. Fison subscribed to scientific journals, and friends sent him cuttings of reviews, so he had been able to get the gist of Maine's work second hand. This was also how he had heard about the new edition of McLennan's *Primitive Marriage*: "The subject is attracting much attention now & I wish we could get into print. I am stopped for want of books for which I have sent to George Robertson. Both Lubbock & Herbert Spenser, says the Spectator, have been writing on Communal Marriage of late, & it is necessary to know what they have said."[5]

Despite these logistical challenges, considerable intellectual networking was also taking place among missionary ethnographers themselves, thanks not

2. Lorimer Fison to A. W. Howitt, 12 October 1878, Lorimer Fison Project, Letterbook No. 6, PMB 1039, reel 4.

3. Lorimer Fison to E. B. Tyler, 30 March 1881, Papers of Sir Edward Burnett Tyler, Box 11A, Pitt Rivers Museum, Oxford, UK.

4. Lormer Fison to George Robertson, 19 November 1877, Lorimer Fison Project, Letterbook No. 6, PMB 1039, reel 4.

5. Lorimer Fison to A. W. Howitt, 27 November 1877, Lorimer Fison Project, Letterbook No. 6, PMB 1039, reel 4.

only to booksellers and mutual academic collaborators but also to a striking degree of scientific ecumenism. Robert Codrington of the Anglican Melanesian Mission had been telling Fison about his own research and mentioned sending a draft article to England for publication. In a letter placing other orders for books, Fison asked Robertson to keep an eye out for a new article by Codrington: "I cannot give you its title, but if it have [*sic*] made its appearance, you will be sure to know, & I should be glad of a copy."[6] It was more efficient to write to Robertson in Melbourne than to ask Codrington himself; there were regular mail steamers to the Australian colonies whereas a letter to Norfolk Island would have to be forwarded on from some other port. In the meantime, having seen another piece by Codrington, Fison could forward the information to fellow missionary George Brown, explaining that "inasmuch as some of their customs are remarkably like those of your own natives . . . I am sure that I shall be more than glad to have your remarks upon them."[7]

To expedite his growing correspondence with Codrington, Fison urged him not to wait for a vessel bound for Fiji, but instead to send letters care of the Methodist General Secretary in Sydney. From there they would be forwarded to Fiji at Methodist expense, saving Codrington and the Anglican mission time and money. Transnational scientific collaboration had been possible before, even in time of war, but the creation of ecumenical scientific networks so far in advance of the twentieth century ecumenical movement is an equally important example of scientific border-crossing. Not until the Edinburgh Missionary Conference of 1910 would Protestant and Anglican mission societies gather formally together to discuss the need for greater communication and collaboration in the mission field, and only after the Second Vatican Council were Roman Catholics permitted to pursue formal ecumenical dialogue or to worship with their fellow Christians. Meanwhile, enthusiasm for anthropology and other scientific pursuits had already been bringing members of different denominations together in the Pacific world. It is certainly true that "the withdrawal of expatriate missionaries and changes in attitudes to and interpretations of indigenous ways of life" would accelerate the sharing of resources across denominational lines, but those expatriate missionaries had already been sharing resources in ways that have been underestimated in work on Pacific ecumenism.[8]

Meanwhile the dangers of plagiarism loomed for missionary anthropologists with regard to their research findings. They frequently encouraged one

6. Lorimer Fison to George Robertson, 19 November 1877, Lorimer Fison Project, Letterbook No. 6, PMB 1039, reel 4.

7. Lorimer Fison to George Brown, 23 November 1877, Letterbook No. 6, PMB 1039, reel 4.

8. Kerry James and Akuila Yabaki, eds., *Religious Cooperation in the Pacific Islands* (Suva: Institute of Pacific Studies, University of the South Pacific, 1989), ix.

another to "publish under your own name" rather than by means of anonymous research notes or word lists in scientific journals. When Codrington mentioned that his material on Melanesian religious beliefs was being published anonymously, Fison warned him about "the coolness with which some people will abstract other folks' property," telling of one striking case of academic plagiarism which was "as dishonest as it would have been to steal the poor man's money . . . & I could give you other instances of a like kind within my own experiences."[9] Fison himself was scrupulous concerning material from his fellow missionary ethnographers, advising his Methodist colleague George Brown to send him his ethnographic materials "& you shall have the full credit of them," or to send them directly "to the Anthrop'l Soc'y, or in some other way get them into the hands of competent men." He declared "I work at these things for the love of the work itself, & don't care very much about any kudos belonging to it. Let us only get the work done. That is the main thing."[10] This is not what other letters reveal, however; Fison was very attentive to the difference between the use of his materials by fellow laborers in the field and the (often unattributed) citation of his research by metropolitan anthropologists.

European and American university anthropologists were often crucial publication advisors and assistants. Fison, Howitt, and Morgan's collaboration is one example. Another is the partnership between Professor Edward Winslow Gifford of the University of California and the Methodist missionary to Tonga, E. E. V. Collocott. They exchanged offprints and research notes for decades after Gifford visited Tonga on a Bishop Museum–sponsored research expedition in 1920–21. A largely self-taught anthropologist, Gifford was eager to help his missionary friend get his own research results into print:

> Did J.P.S. accept your 'Experiment in Tongan History'? If not I can run it for you in the American Anthropologist of which I am now the acting editor. Have you any other Tongan paper you care to submit? What about reviewing my Place Names and Myths for the Anthropologist? Be as caustic as you like, for I shall not exercise my editorial prerogatives.[11]

9. Lorimer Fison to Robert Codrington, 19 June 1878, Lorimer Fison Project, Letterbook No. 6, PMB 1039, reel 4.

10. Lorimer Fison to George Brown, 23 November 1877, Lorimer Fison Project, Letterbook No. 6, PMB 1039, reel 4.

11. E. W. Gifford to E. E. V. Collocott, 29 May 1924, Rev. Dr. E. E. V. Collocott Correspondence, PMB MS 28 and Wilhelm G. Solheim, "Edward Winslow Gifford, 1887–1959," *Journal of the Polynesian Society* 68, no. 3 (1959): 177–80, http://www.jps.auckland.ac.nz/document/?wid=2985 (accessed 12 November 2013).

Collocott also received offers of help from the Bishop Museum (now the Bernice Pauahi Bishop Museum) in Honolulu. The museum published a number of his papers over the years, and by the mid-1920s its director, Herbert Gregory, felt that the museum should be giving a higher priority to salvage anthropology. Writing to W. H. Skinner, editor of the *Journal of the Polynesian Society*, Gregory confessed that "the Bishop Museum has been negligent in this regard and as atonement for its sins has adopted a policy which assigns its income to men and printers ink."[12] The beneficiaries were established missionary fieldworkers such as Collocott, to whom Gregory wrote that

> it is of urgent importance to record Polynesian ideas before it is too late. . . . I therefore welcome your proposal to make translations accompanied by notes on customs and language. . . . Please go ahead. With a view to getting advice, you may send on to Honolulu a synopsis, if you like; but you are the Tongan authority and your previous work shows that it is safe for the Museum to do about what you think should be done.[13]

The intellectual networks of two LMS linguists provide snapshots of both the challenges and the rewards of scientific collaboration in the Pacific world. Samuel Ella completed a Samoan translation of the Bible in 1857, after consulting the Presbyterian missionary John Geddie of the New Hebrides Mission. Ella sent a copy of the published results to Geddie's station on Aneityum, and the two continued to exchange letters about the challenges of translation and printing work.[14] Retired LMS missionary Samuel Whitmee asked the Methodist Lorimer Fison for help with a comparative dictionary of Polynesian languages. Fison eagerly awaited the proof sheets in order to send "the completed portion of my share in the work which I shall of course be very glad to do." He wondered whether Whitmee's plan included the Melanesian islands, and, if so, he thought "the [Anglican] Rev. R. H. Codrington, M.D. of Norfolk Island would willingly give you the language of the Banks Group."[15] A spirit of shared scientific enterprise allowed these missionaries to transcend the sectarian boundaries that were so frequently present elsewhere in the mission field.

12. Herbert Gregory to W. H. Skinner, 9 July 1924, Rev. Dr. E. E. V. Collocott Correspondence, PMB MS 28.

13. Herbert Gregory to W. H. Skinner, 19 January 1925, Rev. Dr. E. E. V. Collocott Correspondence, PMB MS 28.

14. John Geddie to Samuel Ella, 17 September [1868], Rev. Samuel Ella Correspondence, 1836–1858, ML A202, CY Reel 2974, State Library of New South Wales, Sydney, Australia.

15. Lorimer Fison to Samuel Whitmee, 29 June 1878, Lorimer Fison Project, Letterbook No. 6, PMB reel 4. The "M.D." is an error: Codrington held a D.D.

Missionaries could also exploit metropolitan scientific rivalries for their own purposes. Angry about J. F. McLennan's sharp critique of his mentor Lewis Henry Morgan, Lorimer Fison told his research partner A. W. Howitt about a rejoinder that he hoped to publish. Confessing that he was embracing the scriptural "wisdom of the serpent," Fison reckoned that "Morgan's sympathies will gush forth towards it & even the bowels of the Smithsonian will yearn towards the supporters of an American who has been ill treated by a Britisher."[16] This might make it easier for two Britishers such as Fison and Howitt to have their work published by the prestigious Smithsonian press.

Collaboration between theorists at home and missionaries abroad had begun early in the Pacific context, bringing religion and science together in a way that has puzzled some historians. W. Patrick Strauss identified a "strange relationship" between the nonconformist LMS and the British government that was brokered by Sir Joseph Banks. Approached by the Reverend Thomas Haweis, one of the founders of the LMS, for "some hints, how persons, who may be left at Otaheite [Tahiti] may be serviceably employed, whilst instructing the natives, in any attempt that may be of use to ourselves, & future navigators who may call there," Banks obliged and began to receive a steady stream of publications, letters, and journals from missionaries in the Pacific and elsewhere.[17] He sometimes forwarded this material to statesmen, and he sponsored the LMS request to dedicate the first issue of their Pacific missionary journals to the King. Banks gained permission for the LMS to send a mission to the Cape Colony in South Africa, and a few years later he enabled them to enter Ceylon [Sri Lanka] as well. In return for this generous patronage, Banks received a regular supply of botanical and ethnographic specimens from the society's missions in Africa and the Pacific. Strauss declared that these developments represented "an accommodation of thought between the Newtonian rationalists of the late eighteenth century and the militant evangelical missionary societies of that period and the immediately successive ones,"[18] but these intellectual networks were an outcome of intellectual affinity rather than a forced "accommodation." The expanding British empire provided what Felix Driver calls "an infrastructure for scientific exploration, or a means of its legitimation,"[19] and, as we have seen, theology also provided an infrastructure for both missionary and anthropological work. Of special importance here is the recent historiography that has so

16. Lorimer Fison to A. W. Howitt, 10 August 1878, Lorimer Fison Project, Letterbook No. 6, PMB 1039, reel 4.

17. Cited in W. Patrick Strauss, "Paradoxical Cooperation: Sir Joseph Banks and the London Missionary Society," *Historical Studies: Australia and New Zealand* 11 (1964): 246.

18. Strauss, "Paradoxical Cooperation," 252.

19. Driver, *Geography Militant*, 39.

decisively overturned the old modernist assumptions about incompatibility between religion and science. It was this presumed incompatibility that informed Strauss's assumption that "accommodation" was needed in order for "militant" missionaries to interact with science. Instead, we should presume an affinity between missionaries and science and proceed from there.[20]

There is little evidence from studying history in the South Pacific to support the notion of a fundamental incompatibility between religion and science, and no need to restate the well-known importance of the Pacific world to European science as "a crucial testing ground" that by the nineteenth century had become "central in the key debates that transformed understanding of the very shape of human development and universal history."[21] John Douglas, editor of Captain Cook's third-voyage journals, observed that the Pacific Islands were "fit soil" for judging how far unassisted human nature will be apt to degenerate; and in what respects it can ever be able to excel."[22] We will see for how long various forms of degeneration theory lingered in missionary ethnography, and why. Meanwhile, physical anthropology and biologically-based racism were developing alongside a theological anthropology that stressed human universality. This complex development was given new urgency by the appearance of Charles Darwin's theory of natural selection.[23] Generations of modernist historians have assumed that Darwin dealt a fatal blow to religion in the nineteenth century. It is true that missionary ethnographers preferred universalist theories for theological reasons, and although Darwin's own theory underlined the unity of the human species, later social evolutionists suggested exclusively natural laws at the heart of human society and culture.[24] It was not evolutionism as such that

20. For example, see James R. Moore, *The Post-Darwinian Controversies: A Study of the Protestant Struggle to Come to Terms with Darwin in Great Britain and America, 1870–1900* (Cambridge: Cambridge University Press, 1979), and John Hedley Brooke, *Science and Religion: Some Historical Perspectives* (Cambridge: Cambridge University Press, 1991), revised recently as Thomas Dixon, Geoffrey Cantor, and Stephen Pumfrey, eds., *Science and Religion: New Historical Perspectives* (Cambridge: Cambridge University Press, 2010). See also Timothy Larsen, *Crisis of Doubt: Honest Faith in Nineteenth-Century England* (Oxford: Oxford University Press, 2006).

21. Tony Ballantyne, "Introduction" to *Science, Empire and the European Exploration of the Pacific* (Aldershot: Ashgate, 2004), xv.

22. Cited in P. J. Marshall and Glyndwr Williams, *The Great Map of Mankind: British Perceptions of the World in the Age of Enlightenment* (London: J. M. Dent & Sons, 1982), 259.

23. Bronwen Douglas, "Climate to Crania: Science and the Racialization of Human Difference," in *Foreign Bodies: Oceania and the Science of Race 1750–1940*, ed. Bronwen Douglas and Chris Ballard (Canberra: ANU e-Press, 2008), 72.

24. Roy MacLeod and Philip F. Rehbock, eds., *Darwin's Laboratory: Evolutionary Theory and Natural History in the Pacific* (Honolulu: University of Hawai'i Press, 1994), and Helen Gardner, "The 'Faculty of Faith': Evangelical Missionaries, Social Anthropologists, and the Claim for Human Unity in the 19th Century," in *Foreign Bodies*, ed. Douglas and Ballard, 259–82.

bothered missionary ethnographers, it was the omission of faith from the list of evolutionary drivers. As usual, they felt that their empirical findings were more convincing than metropolitan theories, believing that their research would ultimately prove the case for the role of faith in human development.[25]

Concerning Darwin, some missionary scientists were openly critical of the narrow-mindedness of their wider religious communities. George Brown had been relatively uninterested in ethnography until he went to New Britain with several Fijian colleagues to found a new Methodist mission in 1875. His colleague Fison, already a keen ethnographer, was delighted by Brown's new interests, reporting that "we are fortunate in having on that [New Britain] station one of our Missionaries who is an indefatigable worker for science as well as for the Gospel, & it is a great pity that the two works do not more frequently go together."[26] This was not necessarily the view of the Methodist community in Australia. By 1877 Sydney was ablaze with rumors that Brown had given a hearing to islanders' stories about men with tails. Missionaries in the western Pacific began comparing notes. "Have you any tradition about tailed men?" Fison asked Codrington:

> when Brown was here [in Fiji] last June I could not get him to commit himself to a negative on the matter. . . . He would not say that he had found any proof, but on the other hand he would not say that he had found none. "You shall hear from me as soon as I have ascertained the facts he said, & that was all I could get out of him. It really seemed as if he had met with evidence that staggered him, but he is too cautious a man to commit himself.[27]

Fison wondered whether or not these tails might turn out to consist of decorative clothing or other personal accoutrements, but he saw no prima facie case for dismissing the existence of real tails "inasmuch as it would be easy enough to produce a tail by means of a very simple surgical operation & we know that not a few tribes are in the habit of performing much more complicated & painful

25. For a fuller discussion of missionary ethnography's complex relationship with Darwinian theory see Helen Bethea Gardner, "The Origin of Kinship in Oceania: Lewis Henry Morgan and Lorimer Fison," *Oceania* 78, no. 2 (2008): 137–50 and "'By the Facts We Add to Our Store': Lorimer Fison, Lewis Henry Morgan and the Spread of Kinship Studies in Australia," *Oceania* 79, no. 3 (2009): 280–92.

26. Lorimer Fison to Robert Codrington [1879], Lorimer Fison Project, Letterbook No. 6, PMB 1039, reel 4.

27. Lorimer Fison to Robert Codrington [1877], Lorimer Fison Project, Letterbook No. 6, PMB 1039, reel 4.

operations to produce what appears to us to be horrible disfigurement."[28] He added that stories of "wild men" were common around the world, particularly as told by coastal people about a relatively inaccessible interior.

For our purposes, the most important point concerns Brown's response to his Methodist critics. Darwin's *Origin of Species* had long been in print, and *Descent of Man* had appeared in 1871, generating further controversy. It was provocative for a Methodist missionary to refuse to dismiss stories of men with tails. On his next visit to Sydney, Brown was accosted by a devout man who told him that even if the existence of tailed men could be verified, the evidence should be concealed in the interests of religion because "the evolutionists would make such a pernicious use of it!" Fison shared his colleague's indignation: "The faith saved by the concealment of truth! A wrathful man was my friend Brown on that occasion. 'If I can get hold of one' he cried in his wrath, 'I'll bottle him up in spirit of wine, tail & all, & send him to the biggest Darwinian of the day with my compliments.'"[29]

At about the same time, W. G. Lawes of the LMS was publishing reports of "tailed men" in New Guinea. The Australian newspaper the *Echo*, having published Lawes's account, was later forced to publish an editorial disclaimer. Even though Lawes himself had been skeptical about the scientific truth of the stories, the *Echo* felt obliged to distance itself from him. "It is to be regretted," it declared, "that missionaries should lend themselves to retail the cock-and-bull stories of a lot of mendacious savages."[30] Clearly the paper's management was aware how many readers might be lost if they appeared to support Darwin's theory of the evolution of humans from ancestral apes.

In Brown's case, a mischievous sense of humor accompanied his devotion to empirical science as well as his desire to take indigenous knowledge seriously. Why should the stories of "savages" be automatically dismissed? Science would either prove or disprove their claims, so why not investigate them? Neither Brown nor Lawes had insisted that the stories were true; what both missionaries emphasized was the remarkable consistency and detail of the stories, and the need for their scientific investigation. It is significant that tempers ran higher in Sydney than on the mission stations. Scientifically-minded missionaries con-

28. Lorimer Fison to Robert Codrington, 19 June 1878, Lorimer Fison Project, Letterbook No. 6, PMB 1039, reel 4.

29. Lorimer Fison to Robert Codrington [1877], Lorimer Fison Project, Letterbook No. 6, PMB 1039, reel 4.

30. "Notes of the Day," *Echo*, 9 March 1877. For a detailed discussion of the alleged contrast between indigenous stories and scientific facts, see Clive Barnett, "Impure and Worldly Geography: The Africanist Discourse of the Royal Geographical Society, 1831–73," *Transactions of the Institute of British Geographers* 23, no. 2 (1998): 239–51.

firm historian John Garrett's verdict that Pacific missionaries were "people who combined gripping awareness of a divine call with scientific curiosity and a passion for the eternal welfare of the human race."[31] This passion invited them to listen to what their indigenous informants had to say. It also invited them to disrupt what Clive Barnett and others have termed "the discursive structures of written networks of knowledge" that usually set "confused and chaotic oral testimony" against superior European findings.[32] For all their privileging of European science, missionaries could not afford to believe that indigenous information was always confused and chaotic. How else could they acquire linguistic and cultural literacy if it was? These entanglements take us a long way from traditional exclusionist views of religion and science. As Stuart Piggin has noted,

> preachers had to be well educated men, who had studied to present themselves as workmen who need not be ashamed. There is, accordingly, a large body of evidence showing that the typical missionary in our period prosecuted his studies with a diligence remarkable even in an age when aspiring youths were noted for their studious habits. He was not afraid of the intellect and he was determined to make full use of 'reason' in the pursuit of his aims.[33]

Thus missionaries could be found contributing to a range of scientific disciplines, not only to anthropology.[34]

Metropolitan theorists were interested in field data from a wide variety of sources, and this magpie tendency is readily visible in the archive of Darwin himself. Like Joseph Banks and others, Darwin cultivated a global network of informants and gatherers, including missionaries. He had a longstanding interest in the civilizing activities of missions, and so he read their anthropological work with particular interest. In one case, he seems to have read more generously than one of the period's most famous anthropologists, J. F. McLennan. McLennan was locked in combat with the American anthropologist Lewis Henry Morgan in a story that we will revisit later. Darwin thought that McLennan should read the work of Lorimer Fison, who had recently published *Kamilaroi and Kurnai* with his research partner Howitt in 1880. McLennan was

31. John Garrett, *To Live Amongst the Stars: Christian Origins in Oceania* (Fiji: World Council of Churches, 1982), 10.

32. Barnett, "Impure and Worldly Geography," 244.

33. Piggin, *Making Evangelical Missionaries*, 71.

34. Niel Gunson, "British Missionaries and Their Contribution to Science in the Pacific Islands," in *Darwin's Laboratory*, ed. MacLeod and Rehbock, 283–316.

most grateful for the reference, admitting that he had not yet read the book, and wondered whether he could borrow Darwin's own copy![35] The point here is not to valorize Darwin, but rather to underline how intertwined the worlds of science and religion were, generating a pragmatism whereby each could recognize scientific value in the work of the other. Far from "accidental ethnographers," missionaries were, as Sujit Sivasundaram explains, "at the forefront of the intellectual encounters of the British empire."[36]

This dynamic relationship between science and religion helps to explain the lack of a monolithic missionary view of academic anthropological theory. The connection between missions and governments concerning Aboriginal policy, for example, has been studied extensively by historians.[37] However, missionaries held widely divergent views about scientific theories of race, especially those of the later nineteenth and early twentieth centuries that emphasized the inevitability of Aboriginal extinction. In his recent study of the Aborigines Protection Society, James Heartfield has proposed that "the missionary view of the threat of extinction, that it was an evil to be avoided, was at least as strong as the other view, that it was a fact of life to be accepted."[38] The "missionary view" actually varied widely. Missionaries welcomed the way Darwin's theory stressed the unity of humanity as a single species: an apparent scientific endorsement of ancient one blood theological anthropology. But what about scientific theories that proposed the inevitable extinction of indigenous humans? How were missionaries who believed fundamentally in one blood able, at the same time, to support anthropologies of vanishing races? In 1907, Archdeacon Philip Walsh gave a paper to the Auckland Institute that

35. J. F. McLennan to Charles Darwin, 30 November 1880, DAR 171, item 26, Cambridge University Library, Cambridge, UK.

36. Sujit Sivasundaram, "A Global History of Science and Religion," in *Science and Religion: New Historical Perspectives*, ed. Thomas Dixon, Geoffrey Cantor, and Stephen Pumfrey (Cambridge: Cambridge University Press, 2010), 177. For a detailed analysis of the Pacific context, see his *Nature and Godly Empire: Science and Evangelical Mission in the Pacific, 1795–1850* (Cambridge: Cambridge University Press, 2005).

37. For example, Warwick Anderson, *The Cultivation of Whiteness: Science, Health and Racial Destiny in Australia* (Carleton: Melbourne University Press, 2002); Andrew Armitage, *Comparing the Policy of Aboriginal Assimilation: Australia, Canada and New Zealand* (Vancouver: University of British Columbia Press, 1995); John J. Cove, *What the Bones Say: Tasmanian Aborigines, Science and Domination* (Ottawa: Carleton University Press, 1995); Andrew Markus, *Governing Savages* (Sydney: Allen & Unwin, 1990); Patrick Wolfe, *Settler Colonialism and the Transformation of Anthropology: The Politics and Poetics of an Ethnographic Event* (London: Cassel, 1999).

38. James Heartfield, *The Aborigines' Protection Society: Humanitarian Imperialism in Australia, New Zealand, Fiji, Canada, South Africa, and the Congo, 1836–1909* (London: Hurst & Co., 2011), 76.

summarized his long ministry among the Maori and addressed the issue of their population decline since the mid-nineteenth century. So determined was Walsh to follow the fashionable dying race theory that he forced contradictory evidence to fit it:

> In spite of various statements, based on census returns and on local personal observation, that the Maori is holding his own, or even increasing in numbers, the fact is patent that, taking it as a whole, the race is fast dying out, and that, if the decay continues at the present rate, a comparatively short time will witness its extinction. . . .[39]

He explained away the *rising* population revealed by official statistics as a function of greater accuracy in the returns, certain that future censuses would prove that the population was in terminal decline. He criticized those who claimed that the Maori were already in decline before Captain Cook encountered them, focusing instead on the devastation produced by European contact, including mission policy. Missionary efforts to introduce European-style agriculture had been disastrous. European firearms and diseases, along with the widespread seizure of Maori lands after the wars of the mid-nineteenth century, had accelerated the process of decline. Native schools aggravated racial distinctions and failed to prepare Maori children for the kinds of work they would encounter as adults; instead of finding professional work, young Maori men were doing manual labor regardless of their level of education. "The Maori has lost heart and abandoned hope," concluded Walsh, quoting with approval the views of the German scientist Dr. Ferdinand Hochstetter that "compared with the fresh and full vigor with which the Anglo-Saxon race is spreading and increasing, the Maori is the weaker party, and thus he is the loser in the endless 'struggle for existence.'"[40]

Christine Weir has suggested that a frustration with the slow pace of conversion, or with backsliding, prompted some missionaries to become more sympathetic to racialized explanations of inferiority.[41] Nevertheless, this relationship with science "remained interwoven with descriptions of particular societies and individuals with unique value and potentiality in the sight of God."[42] I would add that a keen awareness of the devastation of colonialism must be included,

39. Archdeacon Walsh, "The Passing of the Maori: An Inquiry into the Principal Causes of the Decay of the Race," *Transactions and Proceedings of the New Zealand Institute* 40 (1907): 154.

40. Quoted in Walsh, "The Passing of the Maori," 172.

41. Weir, "'White Man's Burden,' 'White Man's Privilege': Christian Humanism and Racial Determinism in Oceania, 1890–1930," in *Foreign Bodies*, ed. Douglas and Ballard, 286–88.

42. Weir, "'White Man's Burden,'" 287.

even if today we disapprove of the policies created in response to this awareness. Only a few years after Walsh had expressed his views in New Zealand, the Australian Board of Mission (ABM) denounced the readiness of missionaries to accept such views. It believed that "respect and sympathy" should greet the view "that the natives must be cared for, especially in sickness and in regard to material comfort, and possibly morally," disavowing the claim "that the natives must die out, and that it will be best for them, and especially for the white man, that they should die out." This attitude, it was felt,

> may be classed under the heading 'Humanitarian,' but it cannot be under 'Christian.' Because (1) it is wrong to assume of any race that they are going to die out; further, a study of the statistics of Aboriginal Missions in North Queensland and in the islands of Torres Straits does not back up the assumption. (2) The primary need of the Aboriginal race is a spiritual need.

The ABM report concluded: "We deplore the use by Christians of the phrase, 'the smoothing of the pillow of a dying race,' in regard to Aboriginal Mission work. We say that it is wrong to regard the passing of this race as inevitable. . . ."[43] Debate would continue into the mid-twentieth century, by which time indigenous population growth in Australia, New Zealand, and elsewhere would finally discredit theories about vanishing races.

Another way of uncovering the complexity of the missionary view is to consider missionary contributions to periodicals such as the *Australasian Anthropological Journal*. Dedicated from the beginning to an exploration of racial degeneration, anthropometrics, and other classic Social Darwinist modes of inquiry, the journal was sponsored by the Australasian Anthropological Society after its founding in 1895. The Society's general council included the Reverend John Hargrave and the Reverend W. Ridley, and articles by missionaries appeared in the journal from the first year of publication. The Reverend Hargrave took a particularly warm interest in promoting the journal, lending his "magic lantern machine"—a projector—and offering to find venues where society members could give papers.[44] The Reverend Carr-Smith of St. James's in Sydney joined him in publicizing lectures to his Anglican congregation.[45] Under a new title, *Science of Man*, the journal continued to call for salvage ethnography to be done before it was too late. The inevitable extinction of indigenous populations was

43. "Aboriginal Missions: The Church's Attitude," *ABM Review* (1 February 1914): 190.

44. "The Month's Proceedings," *Australasian Anthropological Journal* 5 (1897): n/p.

45. "Notice of recent proceedings," *Science of Man* 1 (1898): n/p.

presumed. Hargrave became secretary of the ABM in 1897, finding no contradiction between his leadership roles in a major mission society and the Anthropological Society, despite the latter's pessimism concerning the future of Aboriginal Australians. He seems to have embraced the vocabulary and methodology of late nineteenth-century social engineering while simultaneously maintaining the traditional missionary belief in the ultimate thriving of indigenous peoples.

At the first meeting of the Anthropological Society, Hargrave moved a resolution to bring about "the practical Application of the Science of Anthropology," expressing the hope that both the Aboriginal and European races in Australia could be advanced and developed "so as to prevent either of these degenerating, and to arrest by proper measures the progressive increase of organic, and neurotic, affectious, or insanity, and crime, with other forms of degeneration."[46] Thus did Hargrave reveal his interest in eugenics among other muscular forms of "the practical Application" of anthropology. Extracts from Galton's writings on eugenics were read aloud at subsequent meetings, yet Hargrave never abandoned his idea of a multiracial Australia. He exemplified the constant border-crossing between science and religion or between religious outlooks and modern ones—something that was typical of missionary ethnography. From our postcolonial standpoint, Hargrave was no better than the terminally pessimistic social Darwinists; after all, his approach would be typical of those who were laying the foundations of devastating Aboriginal assimilation policies in Australia and elsewhere. The point is that missions and churches were able and willing to work with governments on assimilation policies precisely because they did not have a monolithic or hostile view of evolutionary theories and their implications. Indeed, there was plenty of interaction between a selective reception of the scientific assumptions of the day and the traditional missionary belief in a universal humanity; in other words, between othering and brothering.

Meanwhile, the number of missionary contributors to *Science of Man* escalated at the turn of the century and some pointed ironies arose, especially in the frequent contributions of the Reverend Daniel Macdonald of the New Hebrides Mission. A Presbyterian linguist, Macdonald was perhaps the last and most determined advocate of a Semitic-centered theory of indigenous Pacific settlement and culture. In numerous publications he promoted the theory (by now thoroughly discredited by other Victorian linguists) "that the Semitic relationship of the Oceanic family of languages will be fully established in the opening years of the 20th century, just as the inter-relationship of the Indo-

46. "Minutes of Anthropological Society meetings," 5 December 1895, Anthropological Society of Australasia, ML 1296/00, Box 1, f. 8, State Library of New South Wales, Sydney, Australia.

European languages was established in the opening years of the 19th."[47] Nothing could have been further from the truth, yet the journal published Macdonald's intensely old-fashioned philology while, for his part, he ignored its views on the struggle for survival. This is a salutary warning for historians that writing for such journals did not always indicate sympathy with the parent society's aims.

Sometimes attitudes varied between individual members of the same mission, and attitudes also changed over time. The Anglican missionary C. E. Fox, reflecting in the 1940s on earlier Melanesian Mission reports, noted that Bishop Cecil Wilson had said at the turn of the twentieth century that missionaries were "like nurses in a hospital tending a dying patient." Fox added drily: "No-one would dream of writing that now, 50 years later."[48] He was also critical of the current discourse of development, which he found equally racist. He pointed out that Bishop Patteson, the first bishop of the mission, had been especially revered by Melanesians because he lived out the Christian belief there is "neither white nor brown"—a paraphrase of Gal. 3:28: "There is neither Jew nor Greek, there is neither bond nor free, there is neither male nor female: for ye are all one in Jesus Christ." Patteson "was their friend and never despised them or condescended to them," wrote Fox. "When people talk of them as 'niggers' there is always contempt. But what is even more galling is the condescension which talks of them as a child race. . . . There is something of the same when we call them 'boys' or 'natives.' Patteson called them friends."[49] Writing after the Second World War, Fox was rejecting two secular theories: social Darwinist talk of inevitable extinction and the more recent and allegedly progressive humanitarian discourse about development and protection. Fox's views take us outside the scope of the present study and into the interesting question of how two horrific wars with European origins had undermined the whole concept of "Christian civilization" and its alleged benefits.[50]

In his incisive study of the recent "Darwin wars," Andrew Brown notes

47. Daniel Macdonald, "Grammatical Relationship of the Oceanic Family of Languages: Their Formative Terminations," *Science of Man* 5, no. 3 (1902): 43–54.

48. Charles Elliot Fox, "A Missionary in Melanesia," 73, MS-Papers-1171–03, Alexander Turnbull Library, Wellington, NZ.

49. Fox, "A Missionary in Melanesia," 77. For more on friendship between missionaries and islanders in the Melanesian Mission, see Helen Bethea Gardner, "Defending Friends: Robert Codrington, George Sarawia and Edward Wogale," in *The Atlantic World in the Antipodes: Effects and Transformations since the Eighteenth Century*, ed. K. Fullagar (Newcastle, UK: Cambridge Scholars Publishing, 2012), 146–66.

50. Brian Stanley, *The World Missionary Conference, Edinburgh 1910* (Grand Rapids: Eerdmans, 2009), 305; see also Keith Robbins, "Britain, 1940 and 'Christian civilization,'" in *History, Society and the Churches: Essays in Honour of Owen Chadwick*, ed. Derek Beales and Geoffrey Best (Cambridge: Cambridge University Press, 1985), 279–99.

that for all the diversity of theories of evolution, they "are agreed on one thing: that there is a human nature, and the study of our evolution can help us discover how we ought to live."[51] Although it was not his intention to study the intersection of religion and science, he noted that many prominent writers about evolutionary theory were zealously policing the traditional separation of science from religion. For Richard Dawkins, author of *The Selfish Gene* and other bestselling works, "the world appears as bright islands of scientific enlightenment surrounded by a ravening darkness of ignorance and religion."[52] Even the seasoned myth-buster Steven Weinberg wrote recently in the *Times Literary Supplement* that "given the battering that traditional religion has taken from the theory of evolution, it is fitting that the most energetic, eloquent and uncompromising modern adversaries of religion are biologists. . . ."[53] It is unclear what is meant here by "traditional religion" when, as we saw in the case of George Brown, even Victorian missionaries did not necessarily take a "battering" from evolutionary theory.

Some theories were more congenial to theological anthropology than others, as we have seen in the case of Daniel Macdonald's philology and the allegedly Semitic Pacific. Macdonald's orientalist scholarship might appear to be of purely academic interest in our postcolonial times, but in a recent essay the late Edward Said, who had once pronounced that philology had died before the early nineteenth century, explained why he now believed that its revival would have potentially liberating aspects. "The abiding basis for all humanistic practice," he wrote, was "philological, that is, a detailed, patient scrutiny of and a lifelong attentiveness to the words and rhetorics by which language is used by human beings who exist in history."[54] Our missionary ethnographers could not have put it better. While the orientalism of missionary philology inevitably Others its indigenous objects, it also affirms a humanistic, universal approach to human unity.[55]

Another example involves diffusion theory. In addition to filling out scientific questionnaires and corresponding with metropolitan theorists, the globalizing networks of British science enabled Pacific-based missionaries to

51. Andrew Brown, *The Darwin Wars* (London: Simon & Schuster, 2000), x.

52. Brown, *The Darwin Wars*, 25.

53. Steven Weinberg, "On God, Christianity and Islam," *The Times Literary Supplement* (17 January 2007): 5.

54. Edward W. Said, "The Return to Philology," in *Humanism and Democratic Criticism*, ed. Edward W. Said (New York: Columbia University Press, 2004), 61.

55. If people are connected by webs of linguistic history and meaning, they can create forms of communication that transcend the boundaries of race or culture, as Said himself affirmed when he created the West-Eastern Divan Orchestra with Jewish conductor Daniel Barenboim in 1999.

engage with current debates about Indian history and anthropology. Although geographically distant, India was intellectually present through theories about "Aryan" language and culture. As Tony Ballantyne has noted of New Zealand missionary ethnographers:

> This tendency to view the Pacific as an Asian frontier was extended and consolidated during the nineteenth century, especially in New Zealand where there was a sustained and enthusiastic engagement with Jonesian philology and Prichardian ethnology. New Zealand was charted, described and settled in a world that was fundamentally shaped by the 'Oriental renaissance' and this powerful thread in the intellectual life of the young colony moulded understandings of Maori language and history.[56]

As we have seen in the case of Macdonald's Semitic Pacific, missionaries shared this interest well beyond New Zealand, orientalizing the whole Pacific world. They were also aware of academic disputes about theories of Aryan diffusion. Samuel Ella of the LMS Samoan mission supplied linguist Sidney Ray with information on Samoan languages and orthography, helping him to obtain the works of an older generation of missionary translators in Samoa as well as his own current research.[57] In return, Ray sent offprints of articles on Oceanic language relationships to Ella, warning the missionary of his opposition to Aryan theories: "I do not agree with Dr. Fraser's [*sic*] attempts to connect those [Samoan] myths with Aryan ones of the Sun &c. I maintain that we are not yet in a position to attempt the comparison of the Oceanic languages with those of other linguistic families. . . ."[58]

Ella also exchanged research material and publications with the New Zealand surveyor and ethnologist S. Percy Smith, whose diffusionist theories were more congenial than Ray's skepticism. Smith wrote to Ella in 1898 that he had "come to the conclusion that we must look for the home of the Polynesians in inland India,"[59] thanking the missionary for the research he had done to support this theory, noting especially Ella's "Relationship of the Polynesian Languages with the Malay," which he believed would "shew comprehensively

56. Tony Ballantyne, *Orientalism and Race: Aryanism in the British Empire* (New York: Palgrave Macmillan, 2006), 57.

57. Sidney Ray to Samuel Ella, 12 September 1895, 27 December 1895, and 16 June 1896; Samuel Ella Correspondence 1895–1899, ML A211, Mitchell Library, Sydney, Australia.

58. Sidney Ray to Samuel Ella, 27 December 1895, Samuel Ella Correspondence 1895–1899, ML A211, Mitchell Library, Sydney, Australia.

59. Percy Smith to Samuel Ella, 17 March 1898, Samuel Ella Correpondence 1895–1899, ML A211, Mitchell Library, Sydney, Australia.

what the Malays have borrowed from the Polynesians, for I agree with Dr Fraser [*sic*] that this appears to be the correct view, not vice versa."[60] This paper of Ella's was not subsequently published in the *Journal of the Polynesian Society* as he had hoped, so he read part of it at the Australasian Association for the Advancement of Science (AAAS) meeting in 1898. To Ella's delight, he met there the well-known missionary ethnographers George Brown and Lorimer Fison who "most warmly commended" Ella on his paper.[61] Ella and Fison were already prominent members of the anthropology section of the AAAS, and Ella became the section president in 1893. He later published another paper that makes his debt to oriental diffusionism clear. His work on comparative Polynesian grammar demonstrated "a close affinity and agreement between the several dialects of these people, spread over a very extensive portion of the Pacific" that, despite local variations, "point distinctly to a common origin."[62] In the now familiar way, Ella underlined his scientific credentials while, at the same time, acknowledging the growing authority of metropolitan academics:

> I have cautiously abstained from putting forth any theory founded upon mere conjecture, or weak premises, and I earnestly solicit close and searching investigation from all available sources; and that the facts and evidences obtained may be placed before competent philologues and ethnologists.[63]

In the 1920s, Grafton Elliot Smith's theory of Egyptian influence brought new life and popularity to diffusionism. Smith, by then Professor of Anatomy at University College London, was proposing that Egypt was the source of all human civilization. Despite "decay and degradation," he asserted that Egyptian influences had reached the Pacific through the great prehistoric migrations of the Polynesians. These influences assumed "strangely exotic forms" and later, cut off from their source by time and distance, they "rapidly deteriorated."[64] Smith wrote the preface to Charles Fox's *The Threshold of the*

60. S. Percy Smith to Samuel Ella, 17 March 1898, Samuel Ella Correpondence 1895–1899, ML A211, Mitchell Library, Sydney, Australia.

61. Samuel Ella to Sidney Ray, 26 September 1898, Samuel Ella Correpondence 1895–1899, ML A211, Mitchell Library, Sydney, Australia.

62. Samuel Ella, "Dialect Changes in the Polynesian Languages," *Journal of the Anthropological Institute of Great Britain and Ireland* 29, no. 1/2 (1899): 165.

63. Ella, "Dialect Changes," 166.

64. Grafton Elliot Smith, *The Ancient Egyptians and the Origin of Civilization* (London: Harper, 1923), 200, cited in K. R. Howe, *The Quest for Origins: Who First Discovered and Settled the Pacific Islands?* (Auckland: Penguin, 2003), 53–54.

Pacific (1924) in which Fox, among other things, included the illustration of an ancient Egyptian ocean-going canoe in comparison with one from San Cristoval.[65] Although Fox was not convinced by all of Smith's arguments, he agreed that San Cristoval culture bore traces of influence from a "seafaring people of the archaic civilization, who set outwards before cremation had reached the coast of India, and that their civilization is mainly Egyptian."[66] In his preface, Smith pointed proudly to the findings of psychologist and ethnographer W. H. R. Rivers, whose knowledge of Fox's research had converted him to the Egyptian diffusion theory.[67] This orientalization of the Pacific world built bridges of blood and culture kinship between Pacific peoples and the familiar lands of the ancient Mediterranean.

The globalized intellectual networks of the British empire were enhanced by the activities and publications of scientific expeditions. By the late nineteenth century academic anthropologists were visiting the Pacific world in person. For the most part these expeditions encountered missionaries at their stations, but occasionally missionaries themselves were invited to join as part of the scientific staff. Writing to Robert Codrington in 1877, Lorimer Fison noted plans for a two-year American voyage around the world to be directed by James Woodruff. "The offer made me is a liberal one," he told his friend. "I should visit many places where valuable information is to be obtained as to the speciality which I follow."[68] He hoped to meet Codrington in person (for the first time) when the expedition called at Norfolk Island. In a letter to George Brown, Fison noted that the expedition featured "quite an army of professors on board, & agents of colleges & learned societies without number, including a number of ladies. No expense has been spared. . . ."[69] Fison was excited by the opportunity to conduct his research on kinship systems on a much wider scale than before, and he hoped he would be able to return to England for two months during the course of the expedition (by the 1870s, missionary furloughs were usually spent in Australia or New Zealand). He was sorely tempted by "an opportunity of seeing once more kinsfolk & friends whom, failing this chance, I shall never

65. C. E. Fox, *The Threshold of the Pacific. An Account of the Social Organization, Magic and Religion of the People of San Cristoval in the Solomon Islands* (London: Kegan Paul, Trench, Trubner & Co, 1924), figures 4 and 4a.

66. Fox, *Threshold of the Pacific*, 364.

67. G. Elliot Smith, preface to *Threshold of the Pacific*, by C. E. Fox, v-viii.

68. Lorimer Fison to Robert Codrington [1877], Lorimer Fison Project, Letterbook No. 6, PMB 1039, reel 4.

69. Lorimer Fison to George Brown, 23 November 1877, Lorimer Fison Project, Letterbook No. 6, PMB 1039, reel 4.

see again."[70] Despite these enticements, he felt that his duty to the mission was paramount, and he turned the invitation down. In the end, the expedition never sailed; it was cancelled in 1879 after the death of its patron.

Visiting scholars were grateful for the intellectual and material support of missions. In *The History of Melanesian Society* (1914), W. H. R. Rivers presented the fruits of research conducted during the Percy Sladen Trust Expedition to Melanesia. After thanking a number of his professional colleagues, Rivers drew attention to the crucial role of the Melanesian Mission, and we have already noted his relationship with the work of Charles Fox. Several missionaries were named in his text,

> but I owe so much to one that I cannot pass over his name in silence. No one who studies the part taken in my theoretical scheme by the facts collected from the Banks Islands and Tikopia can fail to recognize how this scheme would have suffered if this part of my work had not been done, or had been done less fully. Not only would the collection of this material have been impossible without the help of the Rev. W. J. Durrad, but large sections of the evidence consist of information, collected by Mr. Durrad after I had left the islands, which he allows me to record side by side with that we obtained when working together on the *Southern Cross*.[71]

Thanks to advances in transportation technology, but also to the expansion of mission activity in the western Pacific, scientific expeditions could now connect more easily with local expertise. Rivers's emphasis on fieldwork methodology anticipated that of Malinowski, although his optimistic view of the reliability and authenticity of his Christian-indigenous sources would draw fire in later years.[72]

In 1920–21 the Bishop Museum funded a two-year expedition to Tonga that introduced Methodist missionary E. E. V. Collocott to Professor E. W. Gifford of the University of California. The two men corresponded for many years afterward, as we know, and Gifford helped to publish Collocott's Tongan ethnography in *The Anthropologist*. They exchanged offprints of one another's articles and encouraged each other through the challenges of ill health, writers' block, and demanding teaching loads. Collocott seems to have never written a paper jointly with his collaborator, perhaps because Gifford found it so difficult to find time to

70. Lorimer Fison to Robert Codrington [1877], Lorimer Fison Project, Letterbook No. 6, PMB 1039, reel 4.

71. W. H. R. Rivers, *The History of Melanesian Society*, vol. 1 (Oosterhout, Netherlands: Anthropological Publications, 1968), viii.

72. See Kolshus, "House upon Pacific Sand."

write up his Tongan material, but there is also some intriguing evidence of diplomatic foot-work in areas of shared interest. Collocott wanted to write a paper on the Fahu (the relationship of a man to his sister's children and his father's sister's children) and Gifford agreed that "it is one of the fundamental institutions of Tongan society," which he had "made a special effort" to document on his visit to Tonga. "I see nothing to prevent your writing a paper upon it if you desire to, only I fear that I shall have to cover the same ground again. . . . you will have the paper in print long before I can possibly get my big paper on Tongan society ready for the press; so the supplication would be on my part, not yours."[73] He had already "practically given up the notion of an exhaustive paper on Tongan religion" because Collocott had "so thoroughly covered the ground with [your] papers that are already published and with the paper that is shortly to be published in America in which you include Murley's materials, that it hardly seems worth while for me to attempt anything. You have stated the general principles and the most that I could do is to add a few more details."[74] In this case, as late as 1922, it was the missionary who was still leading the way while the professional anthropologist, mired in administrative and teaching commitments, worried about how to make a distinctive contribution to the field.

The Collocott/Gifford correspondence also reveals a transnational migration of anthropologists during this seminal time for the discipline. The University of Sydney developed its own anthropology program, an initiative reflecting both the importance of the South Pacific to anthropology and an antipodean desire to host a local academic center of expertise. Gifford told his missionary friend that these developments were drawing two important scholars to the area, one being Grafton Elliot Smith. A native of Sydney, Smith was leaving the University of London for Australia, courtesy of the Rockefeller Institute, and "his mission will be to try to induce the Australian Universities to establish departments of anthropology in order to rescue for science what is left [of] Australian aboriginal culture, language, and racial facts."[75] Even more exciting was the rumor "that our mutual friend A.R. Brown will be given the leadership if everything goes right. This, please, is all sub-rosa."[76] The Cambridge-trained Radcliffe-Brown had already taken a post at Cape Town and was appointed to the first chair in

73. E. W. Gifford to E. E. V. Collocott, 20 March 1922, Rev. Dr. E. E. V. Collocott Correspondence, PMB MS 28.

74. E. W. Gifford to E. E. V. Collocott, 20 March 1922, Rev. Dr. E. E. V. Collocott Correspondence, PMB MS 28.

75. E. W. Gifford to E. E. V. Collocott, 29 May 1924, Rev. Dr. E. E. V. Collocott Correspondence, PMB MS 28.

76. E. W. Gifford to E. E. V. Collocott, 29 May 1924, Rev. Dr. E. E. V. Collocott Correspondence, PMB MS 28.

anthropology at Sydney in 1925. Gifford's department was becoming something of a clearing house for anthropologists en route for fieldwork or academic appointments in the South Pacific. A report to Collocott on the 1926–27 academic year was a case in point. "This coming year promises to be an interesting one for us," he told his friend. "A. R. Brown is coming through in March on his way to Sydney" and "B. Malinowski is coming to teach in summer session."[77]

Sometimes missionaries themselves were involved with these exciting developments. Robert Codrington of the Melanesian Mission worked out a complete scheme for the enhancement of Australian academic anthropology, which he shared with his old friend Lorimer Fison in 1893. Particularly interesting is Codrington's assumption that missionaries qualified for university professorship alongside their academic colleagues. Having encountered Sidney Ray at the recent Oriental Congress in England, Codrington agreed with Fison

> that as you say the Colonies ought to provide for research in these [western Pacific] tongues. Some one should found a professorship at Melbourne for you, and some one else another at Sydney for Mr. Ray. . . . It is an extraordinary thing that an under master in a Bethnal Green Board School should be an European authority on Island languages. I wish I could do something for him, but there is nothing in my power beyond advertising him, which I do on all occasions when possible.[78]

On a recent visit to New Zealand and the islands, Codrington had shared his views with ethnographer and philologist Basil Thompson who, in turn, was in touch with Lorimer Fison on the subject of Fijian philology and other matters of mutual interest. Thompson wrote to Fison to "agree with Dr. Codrington that it is the solemn duty of one of the Australian Governments (in better times) to found a traveling fellowship for Pacific Anthropology."[79]

Academics urged some of their missionary friends to secure formal academic recognition for their anthropological work. Herbert Gregory, director of the Bishop Museum in Honolulu, wrote to Collocott with thanks for a paper on Tongan myths and poems. "Melbourne University will do well if they recognize your work by a Doctor's degree," he suggested, and "perhaps Gifford or Gregory might be appointed one of the readers. If Melbourne doesn't come across, why

77. E. W. Gifford to E. E. V. Collocott, 8 February 1926, Rev. Dr. E. E. V. Collocott Correspondence, PMB MS 28.

78. Robert Codrington to Lorimer Fison, 22 November 1893, "Rev. Lorimer Fison: Articles, Letters & misc. papers, 1873–1907," Lorimer Fison Project, PMB 1042.

79. Basil Thompson to Lorimer Fison, 5 August 1893, "Rev. Lorimer Fison: Articles, Letters & misc. papers, 1873–1907," Lorimer Fison Project, PMB 1042.

not try Sydney University, which is now developing anthropology?"[80] In the end it was Melbourne who came across, granting Collocott a Litt. D. in 1928 in recognition of his extensive contribution to the field.

None of this means that the older missionaries were free of snobbery concerning "colonial" scholarship. Codrington agreed with Fison that

> it is as you remark a great calamity that in Australia and N. Zealand alike the people who wrote and read papers are not really competent. They get the reputation, and are puffed by their fellow colonists, being themselves quite unconscious of their ignorance. They want someone among their own set who will learn—outsiders they despise. This is not colonial as such: it is proverbial that the 'local antiquary' in England is a perfectly untrustworthy authority who enjoys the greatest reputation in his own place.[81]

He might have believed that it was "not colonial as such," but the parallel with local antiquaries is telling in terms of Codrington's view of relative scholarly prestige. Collocott's correspondence from Tonga also underlined the centrifugal forces still being exerted on Pacific scholarship by the Atlantic world well into the early twentieth century. Collocott initially published virtually all of his work in American or European journals, with the exception of the Bishop Museum press in Honolulu. When approached by Percy Smith of the New Zealand–based Polynesian Society, Collocott replied that he could "do nothing for this Society," and Smith replied heatedly, "It seems to me that sending your contributions to Europe and America, is rather a mistake, when we have on this side of the world a publication which is devoted especially to Polynesian matters."[82] Noting Collocott's questions about the availability of various dictionaries of Polynesian languages, most of them long out of print, Smith remarked that he was "the happy possessor of I think, all that has been published on the subject, and these books are now very valuable." He added that

> As to your want of a Niue dictionary, if you send five shillings to the Govt. Printer, Wellington, you will get a far more complete one than that of Mr. Williams, compiled by Mr. Tregear from the Scriptures, and from my

80. Herbert Gregory to E. E. V. Collocott, 4 September 1926, Rev. Dr. E. E. V. Collocott Correspondence, PMB MS 28.

81. Robert Codrington to Lorimer Fison, 22 November 1893, "Rev. Lorimer Fison: Articles, Letters & misc. papers, 1873–1907," Lorimer Fison Project, PMB 1042.

82. Percy Smith to E. E. V. Collocott, 19 February 1921, Rev. Dr. E. E. V. Collocott Correspondence, PMB MS 28.

> collection made in the island itself in 1902. Our 'Journal' also published all the traditions I could collect in that island, with the native texts.[83]

The lure of expert information proved irresistible and Collocott decided that the Polynesian Society was worthy of notice after all. He applied for membership by return of post and sent in a paper the following year.[84] By 1923 he had registered the Methodist Tubou College in Tonga for membership, and had been offered an associate editorship of the *Journal*.[85]

83. Percy Smith to E. E. V. Collocott, 19 February 1921, Rev. Dr. E. E. V. Collocott Correspondence, PMB MS 28.

84. Percy Smith to E. E. V. Collocott, 27 April 1921; and W. H. Skinner to E. E. V. Collocott, 30 October 1922, Rev. Dr. E. E. V. Collocott Correspondence, PMB MS 28.

85. Herbert E. Gregory to W. H. Skinner, 9 July 1924; and W. H. Skinner to E. E. V. Collocott, 28 July 1924, Rev. Dr. E. E. V. Collocott Correspondence, PMB MS 28.

CHAPTER 3

Othering and Brothering

Although this book focuses on British missionaries, it is vital to note the crucial role played by indigenous peoples whose part was sometimes occluded in missionary accounts. Especially in published ethnography, missionaries often presented information using the scientific third person voice without any indication of the role of others in the research and analysis or of any reflexivity about the facts.[1] A classic example of this disjunction can be found in CMS missionary William Yate's popular volume *An Account of New Zealand* (1835).[2] A lengthy chapter titled "Customs of New Zealand" contains neither reflexive language nor any acknowledgment of indigenous assistance, yet letters between Yate and Maori correspondents are appended. Yate would have included the letters as evidence of his soundly empirical, scientific methodology in gathering the facts, but they are also evidence of his dependence on (and friendship with) indigenous informants.

In a recent study of indigenous Christian leadership in the Pacific, Raeburn Lange has rejected postcolonial generalizations about the occlusion of indigenous voices. He points to books by missionaries William Gill, A. W. Murray, Robert Steel, and others that give credit to indigenous knowledge, assistance, and (sometimes) research in its own right. Patii, the Ma'ohi pastor on Raivavae, provided the early LMS mission with linguistic anthropological information; Patii was only one of the "priests and bards and other learned natives" upon whom J. M. Orsmond and other missionary ethnographers relied.[3] The Poly-

1. Gardner, *Gathering for God*, 16.

2. William Yate, *Account of New Zealand* (Shannon: Irish University Press, 1970).

3. Raeburn Lange, *Island Ministers: Indigenous Leadership in Nineteenth Century Pacific Islands Christianity* (Canberra: Pandanus Books, 2005), 4–35.

nesian teachers Apolo of Aitutaki and Tairi of Ngatangiia wrote accounts of the people of Manihiki and Rakahanga in the northern Cook Islands. Mamae's ministry on Mangaia included the production of historical accounts of the island, and W. W. Gill's published ethnographical works were dependent on information that Mamae provided. Lange does not deal extensively with Gill's *Gems from the Coral Islands* (1855) even though it was perhaps the most revealing of his works in this respect. Its introduction made the author's perspective clear:

> Every island gained to Christianity and civilization, westward of the Tahitian group, has been gained through the labor of Native Missionaries; and many stations in the Hervey, Samoa, Penrhyn, New Hebrides, and New Caledonia groups, are now suitably occupied and efficiently worked by Native Teachers and Pastors.[4]

Language difficulties were overcome by these pioneering missionaries and teachers, who were also the ones to develop a written form of these languages "and invariably [were] the pundits of the first European missionaries who resided among these tribes."[5]

The word "pundit" reminds us of the networks of empire. As Christopher Bayly has shown, the British government's information network of local experts, from political secretaries to spies, was central to its empire-building in India.[6] The ubiquitous word "pundit" is ancient, from the Sanskrit for "learned man," and yet it is also modern, becoming a common reference under the British Raj for Indians employed as religious or legal advisors, surveyors, and teachers. A title both of respect and subordination, its use expanded to Africa, the Pacific, and elsewhere. Used here by Gill to describe LMS indigenous teachers, its double-edged meaning is revealed. Gill genuinely respected his indigenous colleagues and friends, naming them in his published texts as he did with his "friend and assistant" Tairi.[7] He collected their letters for publication (in translation) in their own words. As Lange notes,

4. W. Wyatt Gill, *Gems from the Coral Islands* (Philadelphia: Presbyterian Board of Publication, 1855), iii.

5. Gill, *Gems from the Coral Islands*, 18.

6. C. A. Bayly, *Empire and Information: Intelligence Gathering and Social Communication in India, 1780–1870* (Cambridge: Cambridge University Press, 1996).

7. For example, "Letters from the Rarotonga Missionaries at New Guinea to Rev. W. W. Gill" (1878–1880), MSS Micro SO1815, University of Hawai'i at Manoa, Manoa, USA. Also see the translation of a Mamae narrative in Michael Reilly, "A Political Succession Text from Mangaia," *Journal of Pacific Studies* 102, no. 1 (1993): 70–98.

> The training of [indigenous] ministers was more formal than that of religious specialists in pre-Christian times, and it was based on written rather than oral knowledge, but they inherited the respect traditionally given to the guardians of sacred lore and ritual. Sometimes they had expertise in traditional as well as scriptural knowledge: a number of them were valued ethnographical informants.[8]

Nevertheless, both missionaries and their indigenous partners were working within a framework of modern, western scientific investigation and publication. Indigenous testimony was mediated accordingly, including the translation, selection, and organization of information from indigenous sources.

First impressions of the extreme alterity of Pacific peoples needed to be set into context. In June 1840 the newly arrived the Reverend John Smithies traveled up to Perth, Western Australia, in a small boat rowed by two Aboriginal boys, "who were greased and wilged all over the head and face and but very partially covered with the last remains of a Kangaroo skin."[9] This was Smithies's first glimpse of his mission's Aboriginal inhabitants, and it shocked him. He immediately sought to ground himself in the conception of human unity, reminding himself of the universalized imperatives of his mission: "My visions and feelings were arrested, my sympathies excited, and my fears only allayed by the remembrance 'That of one blood hath God made and that for these my Saviour died.'"[10] In a moment of intense emotional affect, Smithies used Scripture to help him to achieve the theologically correct response to the strangeness he encountered. The result reflects Stuart Piggin's argument that "missionary paternalism could have been reinforced by the practice, as exemplified by St. Paul, the missionary who was the model for so many of them, of regarding converts as children to be disciplined as well as brothers to be respected as equals."[11] Othering and brothering was not merely a feature of the modern missionary enterprise in its entanglement with colonialism and racism. It was also a basic feature of Christian discourse, hence the "children" so frequently addressed by Paul in the New Testament; children who at first included fellow Jews, fellow Greek-speakers, and sometimes fellow Roman citizens. Paul's children were not necessarily racial, social, or spiritual Others, yet they were not fully brothers either. Younger in the faith, they were on a different level of a paternal hierarchy

8. Lange, *Island Ministers*, 326.

9. William McNair and Hilary Rumley, *Pioneer Aboriginal Mission: The Work of Wesleyan Missionary John Smithies in the Swan River Colony, 1840–1855* (Nedlands, WA: University of Western Australia, 1981), 35.

10. McNair and Rumley, *Pioneer Aboriginal Mission*, 35.

11. Piggin, *Making Evangelical Missionaries*, 131.

whose echoes we still find in Christian leadership designations such as "elder" or "father."

Into this longstanding tension between equality and hierarchy came Christianity's encounters with a wider world and, eventually, its inevitable entanglement with race in its modern sense. By the later eighteenth century, Montesquieu and other social theorists had added historical and environmental stages, along with a global comparative scope, to traditional notions of cycles of development and degeneration in human societies. A belief in human progress began to characterize ethnological speculation about the relationship between different peoples and their relative level of civilization. Expanding imperial frontiers allowed European theorists to gather global data to support stadial theories of development that placed western civilization at the top, South African and Australian subsistence cultures at the bottom, and Asian civilizations somewhere in the middle. As George Stocking points out, "eighteenth-century anthropology did not seriously question the basic unity of all the diverse groups who had been contacted in the age of discovery—a unity which was also the heritage of the Christian tradition."[12] The Bible compelled Christians to regard all humanity as of one blood not only because of texts from the New Testament but also because of the Genesis story of a single human pair—Adam and Eve—from whom all human beings descended. This emphasis on monogenesis was traditionally Christian, but it also became part of a developing academic debate that featured secular as well as theological theories.

In early nineteenth-century Britain the main advocate of monogenist social theory was James Cowles Prichard, a devout Christian who was horrified by the polygenist approach of theorists like Lord Kames, James Hunt, and Robert Knox. Inspired in part by the developing science of comparative anatomy, Kames and others had proposed that Africans, Native Americans, and other non-Europeans were members of distinct species. These early anthropologists often shared significant interests, such as philology, with monogenist theorists like Prichard, and both groups employed increasingly scientific techniques such as comparative anatomy.[13] The line of demarcation between the two groups is therefore not a straight one. Prichard's early work employed concepts of physical change and development that to some extent foreshadowed evolutionary theory, although they never went so far as to propose the evolution of humanity from another species. Prichard's later work, however, used environmental determinism to explain biological differences between the world's peoples. He was also interested in more recent events, particularly the historical process by

12. Stocking, *Victorian Anthropology*, 17.
13. Stocking, *Victorian Anthropology*, 49.

which humans had spread out across the globe from the biblical lands. This did not free his work from stadial assumptions about a scale of civilization by which "savage" people could (in theory) progress toward the European heights. As George Stocking explains, "Prichard's ethnology was fundamentally diffusionist rather than developmentalist, because diffusion (in a broader sense which included both the migration of peoples and the diffusion of culture) was a better means for linking separated nations to a single source: if one could not prove identity, one could at least establish contact."[14] Here lay its attractiveness for othering and brothering. Peoples separated by time, distance, and culture were still fundamentally one; therefore missionaries could establish contact and preach the gospel. Prichard's influence on ethnography was considerable, not only in terms of his published scientific work, but also his contribution to a widely-disseminated scientific questionnaire for naval officers.[15] The fields of ethnology and philology generally were heavily influenced by Europe's relatively recent discovery of the Pacific world, and they benefited from the rapid expansion of Pacific commerce and colonization.[16]

Douglas Lorimer warns that polygenist theories drew more contemporary attention than their scientific credibility warranted. Infuriated monogenists engaged so vigorously with them not because of some religious hostility to science per se (as they were themselves scientists) but because they found polygenist theories theologically offensive, for polygenesis contradicted Scripture. For Lorimer, the polygenists were "an eccentric group of extremists," who had little impact on the dominant humanitarian, abolitionist, paternalist approach to colonial race relations. A postcolonial mythology about the supposed hardening of racial attitudes after about 1870 has meant that "Hunt probably has had more readers among researchers in the last thirty years than among Victorians in the last three decades of the nineteenth century."[17] For example, Bronwen Douglas has found that

14. Stocking, *Victorian Anthropology*, 51.

15. Prichard's best-known works were the various editions of *Researches into the physical history of man*, first published in 1813 and retitled in its fourth edition to *The Natural History of Man* (London: H. Bailliere, 1855). He also contributed a chapter titled "Ethnology" to J. W. Herschel's *A manual of scientific enquiry, prepared for the use of Her Majesty's Navy and adapted for travelers* (London: John Murray, 1849), 423–40.

16. Bronwen Douglas, "'*Novus Orbis Australis*': Oceania in the Science of Race, 1750–1850," in *Foreign Bodies: Oceania and the Science of Race 1750–1940*, ed. Bronwen Douglas and Chris Ballard (Canberra: ANU e-Press, 2008), 99–155; John Gascoigne, *Encountering the Pacific in the Age of the Enlightenment* (Cambridge: Cambridge University Press, 2014); and Marshall and Williams, *The Great Map of Mankind.*

17. Douglas Lorimer, "From Victorian Values to White Virtues: Assimilation and Exclusion in British Racial Discourse, c. 1870–1914," in *Rediscovering the British World*, ed. Phillip Alfred

"racial opinions congruent to Knox's were common intellectual currency, including amongst the (mostly) scientifically respectable, politically liberal or radical Darwinians."[18] This debate cannot be resolved here, but when considering missionary writings—not normally the focus of debate—we find general consistency among missionary views of race across the conventional boundary-line of 1870. The ethnographers among them paid attention to the metropolitan theorists, engaging, for example, with some aspects of social evoluntionary theory, but not with others. They adopted some of the language of late nineteenth-century social Darwinism in some cases, while vigorously rejecting the idea of dying races elsewhere. They sometimes clung tenaciously to philological theories such as diffusionism long after these had been discredited by academic linguists. What remained consistent was the radical universalism of their theological anthropology.

James Hunt and The Cannibal Club conducted business using a gavel featuring a carved African head, and placed a "savage" skeleton in the front window of their office opposite the Christian Union. Nevertheless, anthropologists and "ethnologicals" had always shared some intellectual interests, and by the later nineteenth century these included anthropometrics. Some missionary ethnographers, such as George Brown at the Methodist mission on New Britain, sent human remains to interested friends, and Brown's collecting practices are a good example of the ambivalent engagement of missionaries with metropolitan scientific theories. Scholars have struggled to label Brown's collecting practices as either scientific or religious in motivation; for example, Richard Eves does not deny "that the churches did not also take up many of the scientific views of the time, particularly on race, or that artifacts did not confirm such views," but his main point is that "on the whole, collecting was subsidiary to evangelism."[19] My examination of missionary interactions with Pacific peoples has deliberately avoided this traditional, polarized approach in favor of an analysis that recognizes the deep entanglement of religion with science. Brown was a noted zoologist as well as a missionary anthropologist, and, as Helen Gardner has shown, his transactions with islanders were intended to build relationships as well as acquire specimens or objects. His artifacts were used for a wide range of purposes from gifts to friends to items specially requested by museums. He

---

Buckner and R. Douglas Francis (Calgary: University of Calgary Press, 2005), 133. Compare Douglas, "Climate to Crania," 64.

18. Compare Douglas, "Climate to Crania," 64.

19. Richard Eves, "Dr. Brown's Study: Methodist Missionaries and the Collection of Material Culture in the Pacific," *Museum Anthropology* 24, no. 1 (2000): 31. Compare Paula G. Rubel and Abraham Rosman, "George Brown, Pioneer Missionary and Collector," *Museum Anthropology* 20, no. 1 (1996): 60–68.

also collected skulls and other human remains for both scientific and religious purposes, and without prejudice to his fundamental belief in human unity: "While Brown purchased bodies in the service of his missionary work and collected skulls and skeletons for friends and scientists, he remained unmoved by the arguments of physical anthropology."[20]

Other missionaries remained similarly unmoved, clashing with aspects of polygenism that proved remarkably durable. In the pages of *The Science of Man* (the official publication of The Anthropological Society of Australasia) debate continued into the twentieth century about one of the oldest claims of the polygenists: that interracial sex would produce either direct sterility, or sterile offspring. A letter signed by "Aboriginal" declared "that it is an accepted fact that aboriginal women will not bear children to an aboriginal husband after having borne children to a European."[21] The Anglican missionary E. R. Gribble wrote from his station at Yarrabah to object. Aboriginal women at his mission had married Aboriginal men after having had children with European men and their marriages had been fruitful. "Another interesting fact is that here, where half-castes have married, children have been born," he added.[22] Gribble mentioned this because analogies involving cross-breeding between horses and donkeys (producing sterile mules) had been used for generations to claim that sex between different human races, if fruitful at all, would produce sterile offspring. It seems incredible to see the sterility question still being debated in a scientific periodical at this late date. Gribble noted that the writer's claims were being used to support conclusions about the inevitable extinction of Aboriginal Australians; he added, "Our experience here explodes the theory [of depopulation] advanced by 'Aboriginal.'" He invited the writer to visit the mission station where "he would find much food for thought and also change, considerably, his present opinions. The birth-rate, during the last two years has been above the death-rate considerably."[23] This was meant to undercut popular talk of a dying Aboriginal race and the lingering influence of polygenist claims about hybridity and sterility. It was also a paternalist and assimilationist argument for the segregation of Aboriginal populations. It was *not* proof that Gribble was straightforwardly "a Social Darwinist in attitude."[24]

20. Gardner, *Gathering for God*, 145.

21. Cited in E. R. Gribble, "A Reply to 'Aboriginal,'" *Science of Man* (1 October 1908): 89.

22. Gribble, "A Reply to 'Aboriginal,'" 89.

23. Gribble, "A Reply to 'Aboriginal,'" 89.

24. Christine Halse, "Gribble, Ernest Richard Bulmer," in *Australian Dictionary of Biography*, vol. 14 (Melbourne: Melbourne University Press, 1996); http://adb.anu.edu.au.login.ezproxy.library.ualberta.ca/biography/gribble-ernest-richard-bulmer-ernie-10367/text18363 (accessed 15 April 2014).

The term "race" held multiple and contradictory meanings well into the later nineteenth century. Writing in New Zealand in 1870, CMS missionary Richard Taylor countered polygenist John Crawfurd by speaking of all humanity as "our race" in its shared descent from Adam and Eve. He also cited Darwin to demonstrate that in the theory of natural selection there was "nothing to invalidate the scriptural account of man's creation."[25] Darwin himself had said that there was "no essential distinction between species and varieties" of animals, and had predicted that "the dispute between the monogenists and the polygenists will die a silent and unobserved death."[26] However, his quarrel with Crawfurd seems rather forced. A philologist, Crawfurd had actually been a supporter of Prichard's against Hunt and the Cannibal Club, but had disagreed with him about whether or not linguistic differences pointed to distinctly different races in Polynesia and elsewhere.[27] This is a valuable reminder of the porous boundaries between anthropologists and the Prichardian ethnologists.

The systematic collecting of material artifacts was also characteristic of nineteenth-century anthropologies. It is not difficult to find examples of dismissive, even contemptuous attitudes toward Pacific material culture in missionary writings, especially when the objects concerned were of religious significance. The early LMS missionary John Williams was presented with fourteen "idols" at Raratonga that he dismissed as "carved with rude imitations of the human head at one end, and with an obscene figure at the other," wrapped in *tapa* cloth and decorated. "Some of these idols were torn to pieces before our eyes," Williams wrote with satisfaction, "others were reserved to decorate the rafters of the chapel we proposed to erect; and one was kept to be sent to England, which is now in the Missionary Museum."[28] Adrienne Kaeppler's pioneering work on Captain Cook's ethnographical collections has been enhanced by re-

25. Richard Taylor, *Te Ika a Maui* (London: W. Macintosh, 1870), 66.

26. Charles Darwin, *Origin of Species* (London: John Murray, 1859), 288 and Charles Darwin, *Descent of Man* (London: John Murray, 1871), 280. For an introduction to the relationship between miscegenation and colonialism see Robert J. C. Young, *Colonial Desire: Hybridity in Theory, Culture and Race* (London: Routledge, 1995).

27. Stocking, *Victorian Anthropology*, 100; also see Gareth Knapman, "Race, Empire and Liberalism: Interpreting John Crawfurd's History of the Indian Archipelago" (paper presented to the 17th Biennial Conference of the Asian Studies Association of Australia in Melbourne, July 1–3, 2008), available at artsonline.monash.edu.au/mai/files/2012/07/garethknapman.pdf (accessed 25 November 2013); and David N. Livingstone, *Adam's Ancestors: Race, Religion, and the Politics of Human Origins* (Baltimore: Johns Hopkins University Press, 2008), 112–14.

28. John Williams, *A Narrative of Missionary Enterprises in the South Sea Islands* (London: John Snow, 1841), 30. For more on this museum and its collection of "trophies" from the South Pacific and elsewhere, see Rosemary Seton, "Reconstructing the Museum of the London Missionary Society," *Material Religion* 8, no. 1 (2012): 98–102.

cent studies in the theory of museum acquisition and display, many of which emphasize the connection between collection and colonialism.[29] However, as Annie Coombes has noted, the objects presented by missionary museums (or donated by missionaries to other museums) can "be seen as the site of production of a tacit consent for some of the tenets of the imperial project," but at the same time they also offer "the possibility of their disruption."[30]

Robert Codrington of the Melanesian Mission was part of a process of intellectual networking that allowed him to bring Oxford to the islands, and the islands to Oxford. This process included the substantial donations he made to the Pitt Rivers Museum after his retirement to England. In letters to his brother Tom written during the 1870s, Codrington described his growing interest in anthropology and his developing relationship with the Blackmore Museum in Salisbury, England; this museum influenced the Devizes Museum and others in arranging their collections according to the Four-Age System of Palaeolithic, Neolithic, Bronze, and Iron. It also gathered contemporary material in order to illustrate the cultural as well as chronological location of the Stone Age. The great watchword of the museum was "progress," and this was readily compatible with Codrington's fulfillment missiology.[31] As Niel Gunson has noted: "For these 'Christian evolutionists' the so-called primitive religions were not perversions of old cultures or even the inferior off-castings of cultural evolution but religions to be respected for their place in preparing humankind for higher religion."[32] A proud field researcher, Codrington deplored the haphazard use made by theorists of missionary ethnography. He sent copies of his journals to his brother Tom, but insisted that they not be published, worrying that his jottings might generate the sort of "random extract" that "is quite enough for an Anthropologist to quote in proof of some theory of savage life."[33] The jottings

29. Adrienne L. Kaeppler, *"Artificial Curiosities": Being an Exposition of Native Manufactures Collected on the Three Pacific Voyages of Captain James Cook, RN, at the Bernice Pauahi Bishop Museum, January 18, 1978-August 31, 1978, on the Occasion of the Bicentennial of the European Discovery of the Hawaiian Islands by Captain Cook, January 18, 1778* (Honolulu: Bishop Museum Press, 1978); Susan M. Pearce, *Museums, Objects, and Collections: A Cultural Study* (Leicester: Leicester University Press, 1992); Annie E. Coombes, *Reinventing Africa: Museums, Material Culture and Popular Imagination in Late Victorian and Edwardian England* (New Haven, CT: Yale University Press, 1994); Tim Barringer and Tom Flynn, eds., *Colonialism and the Object: Empire, Material Culture and the Museum* (London: Routledge, 1998).

30. Coombes, *Reinventing Africa*, 161.

31. Edward T. Stevens, *Flint Chips. A Guide to Pre-Historic Archaeology, as Illustrated by the Collection in the Blackmore Museum, Salisbury* (London: Bell and Daldy, 1870), x.

32. Niel Gunson, "British Missionaries," 303.

33. Robert Codrington to Thomas Codrington, 7 August 1869, "Robert Codrington: Journals and Letters," Melanesian Mission MSS; School of Oriental and African Studies, London, UK.

reveal that he would furnish his colleagues with trade goods for each mission tour of the islands and send them out with copies of lists of desiderata compiled by Edward Stevens, curator of the Blackmore Museum.[34] His colleagues did not always get the artifacts that either Stevens or Codrington wanted, and, even if they did, the objects could be interpreted in contradictory ways. Stevens was interested in contemporary savage culture as a parallel to prehistoric culture, but Codrington had other interests. His observations of rapid historical change in the islands, added to evidence of such change before European contact, made him doubt current theories about arrested or retarded development.[35] Melanesians made decisions for practical reasons and sought practical alternatives to discarded objects or forms of production:

> I am anxious to get a very fine kind of dress made—Banks I. & worn by certain persons at feasts only. It is really well made & with good design. The value of it is that the [islanders] go stark naked, & this is the only garment worn. I can't find evidence of decadence on the part of those people for it is inconceivable that people could rise into good work with nothing of an inferior sort. The amazing speed with wh [*sic*] the Melanesians lose arts ought to be set as against the now fashionable theory. We lately learnt that the great island of S. Cristoval or part of it, has lost the art of canoe making in historical times . . . I have some facts about the matter collected and will endeavor to get more.[36]

For Codrington, ethnography was about building connections as well as interpreting cultural distance. After a lengthy list of the types of material culture that he observed (and collected) among the islands, he remarked: "So long a catalogue of their arts of life shews that Melanesians do not take a very low place among the backward peoples of the world" and "in these matters there is much value in what natives say about themselves."[37]

His willingness to listen helped him to understand the significance of one of the South Pacific's most iconic objects: poisoned arrows. It was the European conception of them that was poisoned, not the arrows themselves.[38] A

34. Robert Codrington to Thomas Codrington, 22 September 1869, "Codrington Journals and Letters."

35. Compare Stevens, *Flint Chips*, x.

36. Robert Codrington to Thomas Codrington, 29 July 1870, "Codrington Journals and Letters."

37. Robert Codrington, *The Melanesians* (New Haven, CT: HRAF Press, 1957), 290.

38. Compare with Michael O'Hanlon's analysis of the macabre speculation surrounding New Guinea "man-catchers" in "'Mostly Harmless'? Missionaries, Administrators and Material Cul-

substantial collection of Codrington's Melanesian material was bequeathed to the Pitt Rivers Museum in Oxford after his death, including numerous arrows. As he had explained, "the Melanesian weapons, however, which demand more attention, and require most explanation, are the poisoned arrows, as yet so little understood. The belief in the deadly virulence of the poison used, and in the hideous methods of preparing it, is too firmly fixed to readily give way."[39] After the death from tetanus of Commodore James Goodenough in 1875 following an attack on his landing party by Santa Cruz (Nendö) islanders, so persistent was the "poisoned arrow" mythology in the Royal Navy that the Admiralty authorized the publication of a medical paper refuting the presence of poison in Melanesian arrows, and warning against the hysteria produced by unfounded assumptions.[40]

Codrington invites us to consider the objects in a more Melanesian way. Islanders were not interested in the materiality of arrow wounds, or in the secondary effects of tetanus. The power of the arrows was real, but not in the way Europeans assumed: "The point is of a dead man's bone, and has therefore *mana*, it has been tied on with powerful *mana* charms, and has been smeared with stuff hot and burning, as the wound is meant to be, prepared and applied with charms; that is what they mean by what we, not they, call poisoned arrows."[41] Codrington described a conversation he had with a young naval officer who insisted that he had seen decomposing flesh attached to the heads of island arrows, but "when asked whether he had taken one into his hand to examine it, he replied with disgust that he would not have the thing near him. He probably to this day believes that he has the witness of his own eyes to the truth of the common belief."[42] Christianized islanders were less likely to die from arrow wounds than their unconverted neighbors because "the absence of alarm and distress" aided recovery, and in one case Codrington recalled a recovering man's assertion: "My mind is easy, I have heard from the Bishop."[43] *Mana* was now on the bishop's side, and therefore on his. We can

ture on the Coast of British New Guinea," *Journal of the Royal Anthropological Institute* 99, no. 5 (1999): 377–95.

39. Codrington, *The Melanesians*, 306.

40. A. B. Messer, *Continuation of an enquiry into the reputed poisonous nature of the arrows of the South Sea Islanders* (London: Government Printer for The Admiralty, 1876). For more on constructions of the death of Goodenough and his shipmates see Jane Samson, "Hero, Fool, or Martyr? The Many Deaths of Commodore Goodenough," *Journal for Maritime Research* 10, no. 1 (2008): 1–22.

41. Codrington, *The Melanesians*, 308.

42. Codrington, *The Melanesians*, 311.

43. Codrington, *The Melanesians*, 307. For a more detailed discussion of Melanesian "poisoned" arrows, see Jane Samson, "Poisoned Arrows and Poisoned Ethnographies from Victorian

find evidence of othering and brothering in Codrington's analysis as a key to what Nicholas Thomas calls "the ambiguity of curiosity."[44] Missionaries could not afford to cut off opportunities for contact and mutual understanding, no matter how alien indigenous cultural practices might be.

Cannibalism posed a particularly striking challenge to brothering. Sir George Rose, a Member of Parliament, opened his address to the Wesleyan Methodist annual meeting in London in 1840 with a familiar evangelical denunciation of the French *philosophes* and their idealized view of natural man. "The Wesleyan Missionaries did not go amongst those 'children of nature' with such views," boomed Sir George. "They did not venture amongst them because they believed them to be virtuous and good. They knew that the inhabitants of Feejee were monsters in depravity and cruelty; but they fearlessly landed on their inhospitable shores, in the spirit of Him who came to seek and to save that which was lost."[45] Descriptions of cannibalism were already prominent in explorers' accounts of Fiji when the Methodist mission was first established there. John Hunt and his colleague Richard Lyth had feared for their lives, and those of their families, after the bodies of about thirty men, women, and children were piled at the door of their mission house the year before Sir George's speech in London. They believed that these people had been killed by a local chief, Tui Cakau, in revenge for the death of one of his men, and they described in lurid detail what happened to the bodies. Here the demands of theological anthropology intruded and Hunt wrote of his relief at finding he felt no hostility towards the perpetrators: "I can love these my enemies most cordially and heartily, so that if they will only allow us to live, I will spend my strength for their welfare."[46]

Lyth's analysis was more scholarly, attempting to locate cannibalism in the biblical world of ancient Palestine. The following note on cannibalism from "Feejee: Island of Somosomo, Sayings & Customs" is characteristic: "Offering human sacrifices. Such are their Baolas, or human bodies for food. Before eaten they are presented to their gods. Tuiilaila said 'Our god is an angry god, if we do not give him the Baola to eat he will kill us.' See Deut. XII. 31 & note in Bagster."[47]

Melanesia," in *The Victorians and the Pacific: Encounters at Home and Abroad*, ed. Amy Woodson-Boulton, Richard Fulton, and Peter Hoffenberg (forthcoming).

44. Nicholas Thomas, *Entangled Objects: Exchange, Material Culture, and Colonialism in the Pacific* (Cambridge, MA: Harvard University Press, 1991).

45. Wesleyan Methodist Missionary Society, *The Wesleyan Missionary Notices Relating Principally to the Foreign Missions*, new series 1, no. 18/19 (1840): 302.

46. Quoted in Andrew Thornley, *The Inheritance of Hope: John Hunt, Apostle of Fiji* (Suva: Institute of Pacific Studies, 2000), 131.

47. Richard Burdsall Lyth, "Feejee: Island of Somosomo, Sayings & Customs," ff. 16–17, ML B548, CY Reel 207, Mitchell Library, Sydney, Australia. "Bagster" refers to editions of the Septu-

The quotation to which Lyth refers is "Thou shalt not do so unto the Lord thy God; for every abomination to the Lord, which he hateth, have they done unto their gods; for even their sons and their daughters they have burnt in the fire to their gods" (Deut. 12:31).

However frighteningly alien they might be, Fijians and their cultural practices could be incorporated into the biblical narrative, and therefore into the story of salvation. This was the approach taken by other early missionaries to the Pacific, such as Thomas Kendall of the CMS mission to New Zealand. In an impassioned letter to directors of the society in 1822, Kendall begged them not to exaggerate the practice of cannibalism or to presume that members of the mission were in danger from it. "What is the use of us continually harping upon the word *cannibalism*," he fumed, "when the origin of it arises from the notion of sacrifices after Men at first became subject to error and death?"[48]

By the later nineteenth century, a greater awareness of the disruptive impact of European contact was providing additional material for missionaries eager to provide historical and cultural justification for cannibalism. In the Melanesian Mission, Robert Codrington was adamant that it had never been practiced in the Banks or Santa Cruz Islands. Rare in the Solomon Islands, it had increased in recent years due to the increased interaction between islands prompted by European activities in the region. Younger men from the western Solomons were now eating the bodies of defeated enemies, to the shock and disapproval of their elders. In this "they have followed the custom of men from the eastern coast who have lived with them, and of the Bauro men of San Cristoval whom they have visited."[49] At San Cristoval this battle-flesh was sometimes traded. Nevertheless, according to Codrington, "to kill for the purpose of eating human flesh, though not unknown, is rare, and is a thing which marks the man who has done it. This is a subject on which stories which come from traders are not very trustworthy."[50]

Later, the sensational topic of cannibalism became of great interest to academic anthropologists and ethnohistorians, and more recently in postcolonial studies, generating impassioned debate about whether or not Pacific peoples had really been cannibals, or whether such allegations were really just a feature of colonial discourse. I am less interested in what really happened than in exploring the features of missionary observations about cannibalism, but it is

---

agint (the ancient Greek translation of the Hebrew scriptures) by the London publisher Samuel Bagster & Sons. For the reference to which Lyth refers see *The Septuagint Version of the Old Testament* (London: Samuel Bagster and Sons, 1844), note to 249.

48. Thomas Kendall to CMS Secretary, 28 December 1822, "Thomas Kendall Letters etc. (CMS)," ARC 0031, MS 0071, Hocken Library, Wellington, NZ.

49. Codrington, *The Melanesians*, 344.

50. Codrington, *The Melanesians*, 344.

worth noting the main outlines of the current debate. Indignant about what they considered to be racist calumny, some ethnohistorians argued that precontact cannibalism never existed.[51] Anthropologist Gananath Obeyesekere agreed that after contact with western colonialism "there developed a form of pronounced anthropophagy that must be seen in terms of the European presence."[52] For Marshall Sahlins, on the other hand, "the concept of power is a theoretical black box on the way to becoming a black hole—into which cultural curiosities of all kinds, unfortunately including the curiosity of anthropologists, are being sucked."[53] Not only anthropologists were curious; ever since the 1990 publication of Maggie Kilgour's seminal study *From Communion to Cannibalism: An Anatomy of Metaphors of Incorporation*, literary scholars have discussed cannibalism as an identity marker in the service of multiple discourses of colonialism, racism, and gendered subjectivity.[54] Sahlins pointed out, however, that much postcolonial scholarship on cannibalism presumed that the voluminous missionary testimony on its practice should be automatically discounted "on the grounds of evangelical conspiracy" with colonialism, yet this "would be to fly in the face of [missionary] status among specialists as remarkably attentive observers of Fijian cultural practices of all kinds."[55]

As challenging as cannibalism or headhunting might be to the theological requirements of brothering, it was in the realm of supposedly universal nat-

51. For example, W. Arens, *The Man-Eating Myth: Anthropology and Anthropophagy* (Oxford: Oxford University Press, 1979).

52. Gananath Obeyesekere, *Cannibal Talk: The Man-eating Myth and Human Sacrifice in the South Seas* (Berkeley: University of California Press, 2005), 151. But not only Europeans were involved: numerous indigenous teachers and clergy were also active in the islands and made their own observations of cannibalism; for example, see Maretu, *Cannibals and Converts: Radical Change in the Cook Islands*, trans. and ed. Marjorie Crocombe (Suva: Institute of Pacific Studies, University of the South Pacific, 1983), 33–34.

53. Marshall Sahlins, "Artificially Maintained Controversies: Global Warming and Fijian Cannibalism," *Anthropology Today* 19, no. 3 (2003): 3.

54. Maggie Kilgour, *From Communion to Cannibalism: An Anatomy of Metaphors of Incorporation* (Princeton: Princeton University Press, 1990); also see Frank Lestringant, *Cannibals: The Discovery and Representation of the Cannibal from Columbus to Jules Verne* (Berkeley: University of California Press, 1997), and Kristen Guest, ed., *Eating Their Words: Cannibalism and the Boundaries of Cultural Identity* (Albany: State University of New York Press, 2001).

55. Sahlins, "Artificially Maintained Controversies," 4, n. 4. Postcolonial literary specialist Patrick Brantlinger agrees in *Taming Cannibals: Race and the Victorians* (Ithaca, NY: Cornell University Press, 2011), 45. Headhunting has a similar historiographical legacy; see James Axtell and William C. Sturtevant, "The Unkindest Cut, or Who Invented Scalping?" *The William and Mary Quarterly* 37, no. 3 (1980): 451–472 and compare Ricardo Roque, *Headhunting and Colonialism: Anthropology and the Circulation of Human Skulls in the Portuguese Empire, 1870–1930* (New York: Palgrave Macmillan, 2010).

ural affections that missionary ethnography became particularly fraught with tension. Assumptions about the universalism of parental care for children, for example, were often challenged. From the late eighteenth-century Marquesas, William Pascoe Crook reported little affection between husbands and wives and therefore "it is natural to suppose that Paternal Affection, likewise, cannot be very strong."[56] He was careful to note exceptions to the rule, however: "Fathers often treat their nominal Children very harshly; yet they seem to place a pride in having a numerous family; and Children are, not uncommonly, much fondled."[57] Still, "As they grow up, little care however is taken, even as to their necessary sustenance. The Children are early inured to the most barbarous spectacles; & amuse themselves by playing with the mangled limbs, & private parts, of naked bleeding corpses."[58] Later, from the Presbyterian New Hebrides Mission, the Reverend M. Frater also wanted to make a case for the culpability of parental corruption of a presumed childhood innocence:

> These little children have their times of pain and suffering and trouble, as have the children in all lands. But the thing which impresses one everywhere, more especially in the Christian villages where they have little or no fear of enemies, is the fun—the real pleasure of living enjoyed by these dark-skinned youngsters. In many ways they are very much like the boys and girls of Home Lands, only they show their happiness in somewhat different ways.[59]

Frater blamed indigenous mothers for failing to discipline their children:

> In heathen villages the chances from the very first seem all against the child living. Indeed, it is a wonder so many survive. There is little cleanliness in the home, and outside of it an utter neglect of all sanitary laws. The mothers, in many cases, are too young to know how to take care of their little ones. Mothers, whether old or young, have no idea of training, and the little ones soon become master. Every baby invariably gets what it cries for, if only it cries long enough.[60]

56. William Pascoe Crook, "Account of Marquesas Islands" (1799), 100, ML C111, Mitchell Library, Sydney, Australia. Crook's manuscript has been published, see *William Pascoe Crook, An Account of the Marquesas Islands, 1797–1799*, ed. Greg Dening (Papeete, Tahiti: Haere Po, 2007).

57. Crook, "Account of Marquesas Islands," 100.

58. Crook, "Account of Marquesas Islands," 100–101.

59. M. Frater, "Child-Life in the New Hebrides," *The New Hebrides Magazine*, October 1908, 8.

60. Frater, "Child-Life in the New Hebrides," 8.

Parental neglect alternates with over-indulgence in this confused account, demonstrating the challenge posed by universalist assumptions and recalling middle-class debates in Britain about disarray in working-class households. Some missionaries were anxious to demonstrate that their islanders were more naturally virtuous in this respect than others, and they used biblical references to underline the universality of child care practices. William Wyatt Gill of the LMS mission to Mangaia wrote approvingly of the way that "a single child is universally carried astride on the hip of the mother," reflecting (he believed) an Old Testament prediction: "'Thy daughters shall be nursed at thy side' (Isaiah, lx.4)."[61] From among the Toaripi people of New Guinea, the pioneering LMS missionary James Chalmers reported that "the father frequently nurses the child. . . . Children are lovingly cared for by parents and relatives. . . . There is no betrothal in infancy."[62] The Anglicans in New Guinea proudly asserted that

> The Papuan is distinguished by strong domestic affections, which show themselves in numberless ways. A short time ago a native was working on the roof of one of the buildings being erected by the Mission at the headquarters, Dogura, and very nearly fell from his elevated position. His first words, as he realized the danger he had escaped, were: —'Had I been killed, who would look after my wife and child!' Perhaps it is the possession of this redeeming trait of character, which makes pictures of the Crucifixion appeal so strongly to the natives of New Guinea.[63]

When this redeeming trait seemed elusive, missionaries struggled to make sense of their observations. Some noted the practice of infanticide and abortion, as in A. S. Webb's account of the island of Aoba in the New Hebrides Mission. Webb attempted to explain these practices in practical terms. "There was this to be said for infanticide," said Webb, "that when a mother died in child-birth or leaving a very young baby, the child would, if not killed, die of starvation, since artificial feeding or wet nurses were not available." He added that "nowadays one seldom hears of infanticide," a revealing observation that suggests that either there had been a remarkably rapid and extensive abandonment of traditional practice, or that infanticide was not as common or little thought of as he claimed. He did note, however, that "abortion or prevention is as regularly

61. W. Wyatt Gill, *Cook Islands Customs* (Suva: University of the South Pacific, 1979), 2.

62. James Chalmers, "New Guinea. Toaripi and Koiari Tribes," in *Report of the Second Meeting of the Australasian Association for the Advancement of Science* (Sydney: AAAS, 1890), 314.

63. New Guinea Mission, "New Guinea Notes," *Report of the New Guinea Mission* (Sydney: W. A. Pepperday & Co., 1905), 40.

practiced as among white folk," an ambiguous statement to say the least.[64] William Bromilow, reporting on the 'Edugaula people of southeast New Guinea, noted that the motives for infanticide were the mother's death, the birth of twins ("because of the great trouble in nursing"), illegitimate children, children born after a forced marriage disagreeable to the woman, lack of breast milk, an unfaithful husband, or because of a husband's taking a second wife during the pregnancy of the first wife.[65] For Ernest Gribble in Australia, there were scientific explanations for the practice of abortion and infanticide by indigenous peoples, such as when "a balance was struck between the scanty food supply and the population by such practices as abortion, infanticide, certain rites, and ceremonies."[66]

The point of these intellectual struggles was to maintain human universalism in the face of diverse and sometimes deeply alienating cultural practices. Sometimes the struggle seemed pointless. The Reverend Thomas Jaggar, an early Methodist missionary to Fiji, observed that

> Last Sunday week a young woman was bitten by a shark whilst bathing in the river, and then buried alive. From her grave she entreated a draught of water, but no. They stamped the earth on her with more violence. Without natural affection. Unmerciful.[67]

However, on one of his earliest cruises among the western Pacific islands, the Anglican bishop George Selwyn denounced the tendency to generalize about the morality of whole societies from individual anecdotes, especially when it served the cause of racism:

> The character of a people ought to be judged by the unpremeditated acts of single individuals rather than by those of large bodies. In the absence of any means of oral communication the individual character remains almost unknown. If a murder is committed, it is said to be committed by 'the natives'; if a war breaks out 'the natives' are said to be in rebellion; and by the force of this habitual error of language the whole race is condemned for the acts of a few, till the domineering Anglo Saxon unconsciously

64. A. S. Webb, "The People of Aoba, New Hebrides," reprinted in *Mankind* 2, no. 4 (1937): 77.

65. W. E. Bromilow, "Some Manners and Customs of the Dobuans of S. E. Papua," *Report of the Meeting of the Australasian Association for the Advancement of Science* 12 (1909), 482–83.

66. E. R. Gribble, *A Despised Race: The Vanishing Aboriginals of Australia* (Sydney: Australian Board of Missions, 1933), 1.

67. T. J. Jaggar to Richard Burdsall Lyth [1840], in Richard Burdsall Lyth, "Feejee: Island of Somosomo, Sayings and Customs," ML B548, Mitchell Library, Sydney, Australia.

> follows Nero, in wishing that the whole native race had but one neck that he might cut it off at one blow.[68]

Any analysis of natural affection is as difficult as that of domestic life or the family across cultural and temporal boundaries. As Margaret Jolly and Martha McIntyre have observed, such labels derived "not only from the residential forms but from the activities which at first may appear as similar to Western or European patterns" but might "not accord with Western models at all."[69] We can extend this critique wider to include such activities as music. Often presumed to be a universal language, music is central to Christian liturgy. As hymnody, it was believed to establish a two-way communication between worshipers and God, lifting their voices and hearts, and conveying grace in return. The idea persists: reviewing evangelical hymn-writing in various mission contexts in Europe, North America, and beyond, historian Mark Noll concludes that racial difference "is not intractable enough to completely stifle the gospel ecumenicity of evangelical hymnody."[70]

In the Pacific world, some missionaries denigrated the debased indigenous music of the islands, attempting to replace it with what they presumed to be the purer traditions of their own hymnody, while others extolled island musicality as evidence of a common human nature. David Hazlewood, an early Methodist missionary to Fiji, noted "a humdrum kind of chant" with which Fijians chanted poetry, concluding that "they have nothing while in their heathen state that bears any resemblance to our mode of singing" and "it will be a long time before they will appear to advantage in this refined art; if indeed their voices will ever be capable of it at all."[71] This discouraging view seemed to be grounded in a technical assessment of rhyming meter. Monosyllabic words were rare in Fijian and few words accented the final syllable, explaining why Hazlewood's views of Fijian music were published in the context of his grammatical work on the Fijian language and dialects. Creating a Fijian hymnody for religious worship was a challenge since iambic meter and regular feet were so difficult to achieve. Hazlewood discovered, however, that the trochaic meter was well suited to Fijian and, conveniently, this was also the measure "in which most of our sacred poetry is written."[72]

68. George Selwyn to William Selwyn, 15 [August] 1850, Selwyn MSS, Selwyn College, Cambridge, UK.

69. Margaret Jolly and Martha Macintyre, "Introduction" to *Family and Gender in the Pacific: Domestic Contradictions and the Colonial Impact* (Cambridge: Cambridge University Press, 1989), 2.

70. Mark A. Noll, "We Are What We Sing," *Christianity Today* 43, no. 8 (1999): 40.

71. David Hazlewood, *A Compendious Grammar of the Feejeean Language, with Examples of Native Idioms* (Vewa: Wesleyan Mission Press, 1850), 66.

72. Hazlewood, *Compendious Grammar*, 68.

Robert Codrington reported from the Melanesian Mission that music and poetry were inextricably related in the western Pacific: "There is no conception of poetry without a tune, though tunes without words are not unknown. In songs certain words or forms of expression, which are not used in common speech, are everywhere thought poetical and appropriate, and words are lengthened or shortened to fit what must be called the meter."[73] He noted that in the Banks Islands there existed a distinct song-dialect and makes a very revealing comparison: "the song-language is so different from that of ordinary speech that the two have the appearance of two dialects, as completely as in the Dialogue and Chorus of a Greek play."[74] Just as some missionaries compared island practices with those of Old Testament times, so Codrington created kinship by drawing parallels with ancient Greece, the "cradle of civilisation."[75] On the island of Aurora, Codrington observed bamboo rods pierced with holes and fastened to the tops of trees to catch the wind and so to "contrive an Æolian Flute, such as those mentioned by Dr. Tylor in his 'Early History of Mankind.'"[76] Although skeptical about Tylor's theory of animism in primitive religion, as we will see, Codrington was happy to use Tylor's work to create a universalist picture of musical technology with diffusionist overtones.[77] Vanessa Agnew has concluded that European observations about indigenous music performed a functional purpose when they "categorized and hierarchically ordered people according to their musical practices," although she also discusses how musical information gathered on Cook's voyages, notes of Tongan and Maori part-singing for example, came as a surprise to scientists because Europe was presumed to be the leader of musical invention. This, along with unexpected resonances such as the Tahitian love for bagpipes, "destabilized a number of intellectual edifices, including the hierarchical ordering of uncultivated peoples."[78] As we have seen, missionary observations achieved a related but different purpose: the reinforcement of humanity's shared spiritual destiny. Their destabilizing evidence of musical brotherhood suited this purpose well.

73. Codrington, *The Melanesians*, 334.

74. Codrington, *The Melanesians*, 334. For more on hymn culture in Melanesia during this era, see Michael Webb, "Heart, Spirit and Understanding: Protestant Hymnody as an Agent of Transformation in Melanesia, 1840s–1940s," *Journal of Pacific History* 50, no. 3 (2015): 275–303. Webb believes that hymnody could serve "as an agent in establishing, mediating and transforming relationships between Islanders and outsiders, and among Islanders themselves" (277).

75. On the widespread fascination with Greece in the nineteenth century see Richard Jenkins, *The Victorians and Ancient Greece* (Oxford: Blackwell, 1980).

76. Codrington, *The Melanesians*, 340.

77. Also see George Stocking, *After Tylor: British Social Anthropology 1888–1951* (Madison: University of Wisconsin Press, 1995), 44.

78. Vanessa Agnew, *Enlightenment Orpheus* (Oxford: Oxford University Press, 2008), 99.

Missionaries assumed that the Bible was of universal human relevance and devoted much energy to developing translations that could transcend cultural difference, as we will see in the next chapter. There was one other text, however, that missionaries translated and published with almost as much enthusiasm as the Bible: John Bunyan's *The Pilgrim's Progress*. Originally published in 1678, Bunyan's iconic work was embraced by eighteenth- and nineteenth-century British Christians as a timeless account of the trials and rewards of the journey of faith.[79] Despite its incomprehensibility for Pacific Islanders, missionaries doggedly translated this complex allegorical narrative into a wide range of Pacific languages. Niel Gunson notes Tahitian, Rarotongan, Tongan, and Fijian versions and there are many more, including Samoan.[80] The effort of translating this work must have brought its own rewards, for it was of little use in proselytism. "One Tahitian is said to have regarded the book as a literal account of the religious life and went seeking earnestly for Apollyon to kill him," notes Gunson.[81] He also quotes from the journal of LMS missionary George Charter of Raiatea who, writing in 1848, clearly did not understand the difficulties presented by cultural difference, preferring instead to rely on a child race model of pedagogy:

> At our meeting today the people expressed their inability to understand what they had read in the Pilgrim's progress. They said 'it is a very dark book'. . . . Titabu came to me and stated he felt very much ashamed yesterday because he could not understand the portion of the pilgrim upon which we conversed in the chapel . . . . I reminded him that a child did not become a man in a day.[82]

Gunson is right about this extract's evidence for the limited horizon of sympathy for the islanders' puzzlement, but there is more to it than that. What we find here is a clear example of othering and brothering rather than a straightforward lack of communication. Charter saw Titabu as a child, and his people as morally handicapped:

79. Isabel Hofmeyr, *The Portable Bunyan: A Transnational History of The Pilgrim's Progress* (Princeton: Princeton University Press, 2004), and David N. Dixon, "The Second Text: Missionary Publishing and Bunyan's Pilgrim's Progress," *International Bulletin of Missionary Research* 36, no. 2 (2012): 86–90.

80. For other examples see John Bunyan, *O le Malaga a le maumausolo nai le olga nei I le olaga atali: ua fa'atusaina male miti, na tusia e Ioane Paniani* (Samoa: LMS Press, 1846), and John Bunyan, *Pilgrim's Progress: Translated into Mukawan, Eastern Papua* (Sydney: Pacific Christian Literature Society, 1950).

81. Gunson, *Messengers of Grace*, 193.

82. Quoted in Gunson, *Messengers of Grace*, 193.

> Poor creatures they had no idea what Bunyan intends to convey, nor of the weapons he mentions. . . . They appear destitute of such doubts and fears, and probably it is not possible in their state of ignorance, so lately emerged from barbarism, to experience, to any great degree such emotions and conflicts. They cannot view sin in its true light, nor feel its burden.[83]

The othering here is clear enough. The motives for Charter's persistence are much less clear, but involves the necessity of brothering. British Christians grew up with the Pilgrim and, in adulthood, continued to find it a deeply meaningful and inspiring text. Surely such inspiration would be universal among Christians, regardless of race or culture? It was not so simple, but missionaries were necessarily optimistic about human universals, and generations of them labored around the world to translate Bunyan for their bemused and baffled flocks. In a protest published in the international press in 1900, Malietoa Tanus denounced the European-led partition of Samoa, accusing the LMS missionaries there with collecting vast sums of money from Samoans "in return for which they only received a Bible, a Prayer Book, or a 'Pilgrim's Progress.'"[84]

We have already seen how the idea of an oriental Pacific, by which language and culture were presumed to have been diffused outward to the Pacific from the ancient biblical lands, performed a crucial role in missionary assumptions about human universals. If philology could not necessarily prove physical human unity, as Crawfurd and others had contended, perhaps other aspects of culture would provide the connection. A Semitic Pacific was gradually, though not completely, replaced by an Aryan Pacific in missionary ethnology during the nineteenth century. Tony Ballantyne's work on CMS missionary Richard Taylor shows how his work shifted in its focus on the center of universal cultural diffusion. At first Taylor had sought Semitic roots for Maori and other Pacific languages, working with the biblical story of the creation of humanity in the ancient Near and Middle East. He then moved on to the study of comparative religion, concluding that there was a "remarkable resemblance of many of their [Maori] customs to those of the Jews [which] would almost entitle us to suppose they were connected with the lost tribes of Israel."[85] As a people connected not only to the world of the Bible but also directly to God's covenant with the Israelites, a Semitic Maori could be invited by missionaries to rejoin a story of salvation that had always been theirs, interrupted only

83. Quoted in Gunson, *Messengers of Grace*, 193.

84. "Malietoa Enters a Protest," *New York Times*, 13 January 1900.

85. Quoted in Ballantyne, *Orientalism and Race*, 61.

for a while by time and space before they were reminded of it by European missionaries.[86]

Nevertheless, Taylor's research, and his familiarity with the increasingly popular Aryan theories of his day, prompted him to give increasing prominence to a possible Maori connection with India. Taylor and a fellow missionary, Octavius Hadfield, began to document supposedly Sanskrit features in Maori. After drawing religious, social, and material culture parallels, Taylor concluded that "the affinity between Sanscrit and Maori is much closer" than that between Maori and Semitic languages and cultures, and "the widow sacrificing her life at the husband's death is a [particularly] remarkable agreement. The figures sculptured on the caves of Ellora and Salsette bear a singular resemblance to the Maori *hei tiki* in their form."[87] However, because of the ongoing theological and anthropological power of the Semitic connection, Taylor eventually settled on a compromise, promoting the idea of a migration of Semitic peoples (possibly one of the "lost tribes" of Israel) via India to the Pacific. The main point was that

> This speculative history firmly asserted the unity of humanity: even if Taylor was somewhat uncertain about the Semitic origins of Maori, he had no doubt they were part of God's Creation. This unity was borne out in language. . . . his vocabulary compared Maori words to Hebrew, Greek, Latin, Sanskrit, French, Gothic, Turkish, Malay, Tongan, Scottish and Teutonic.[88]

The scientific unsustainability of this exercise was already apparent by the later nineteenth century, but that was not the point of Taylor's research. I would go further than Ballantyne to suggest that Taylor's theory of a Maori/Semitic/Aryan link was making a more detailed point than the general unity of humanity. The brothering in his work is clear enough but, even amid his quest for the broadest possible linguistic affinities, it was *certain* affinities that mattered more than others. Whatever comparisons might be made with European languages, the real meat of Taylor's analysis lay in identifying the point of ultimate origin: Semitic or Aryan? Hebrew or Sanskrit? An affinity in those directions could carry both theological meaning and an affirmation

86. He was also writing with the probable approval of his Maori colleagues and friends; Ballantyne notes the Maori preference, under some circumstances, for an identification with Jews rather than Aryans; Ballantyne, *Orientalism and Race*, 165–68. On the recent revival of diffusionist theories in New Age popular speculation about Maori origins, see K. R. Howe, *The Quest for Origins: Who First Discovered and Settled New Zealand and the Pacific Islands?* (Auckland: Penguin, 2003).

87. Ballantyne, *Orientalism and Race*, 64.

88. Ballantyne, *Orientalism and Race*, 65.

of cultural ties between the Pacific and Indo-European worlds. Taylor did not look for affinities with African languages. Instead, he privileged the Semitic and the Aryan because other affinities would have been of lesser theological importance, and a relationship with Africans would not have underlined brotherhood with civilized Europe. This reveals how brothering did not necessarily imply equality. Taylor's Maori flock might have been his kindred, but, by linking them with the cultures of ancient Eurasia, Taylor was constructing them as contemporary ancestors left behind by time. Chapter five will take up this issue in greater detail.

The demands of theological anthropology prompted missionary ethnographers to favor diffusionist theories about Semitic or Aryan languages long after such theories had been discredited by professional linguists. One of the best examples is the little-known missionary philologist from the Presbyterian New Hebrides Mission, Daniel Macdonald. One of the most persistent supporters of Prichardian Semitic diffusionism, Macdonald published a book-length study of his theory in 1880, arguing that the Pacific was "homogeneous as to language, and substantially also as to religion, manners, and customs," despite being variable in physical type.[89] The point was to undermine those who sought to separate Pacific peoples into different biological races. For Macdonald, there were only "modifications of the Oceania race, caused by its intermixture with or absorption of African Negroes on the one hand and Asiatic Mongols on the other."[90] Macdonald claimed that his intent was to counter the crude notions of Crawfurd and other polygenists, but Crawfurd had been dead for nearly twenty years.[91] I would argue that theological anthropology was the main driving force.

For Macdonald, unity of language and culture proved unity of blood. This does not mean that his ethnological scheme was free of othering. Macdonald's theory of diffusion from an Old World center of civilization, like that espoused by Richard Taylor in New Zealand, was based on the assumption that the initial human foray into the Pacific had been followed by a process of degeneration. While Europe had forged ahead, the Pacific world had declined. "The race is fundamentally possessed with the trading and navigating instinct, and I have no doubt that it was that instinct that led their fathers into the island world," Macdonald wrote, consulting Smith's *Bible Dictionary* for supporting data about ancient Phoenecian, Chaldean, and Arabian commercial networks.[92] The good

89. Daniel Macdonald, *Oceania: Linguistic and Anthropological* (Melbourne: M. L. Hutchinson, 1880), 1.

90. Macdonald, *Oceania*, 1.

91. Macdonald, *Oceania*, 5.

92. Macdonald, *Oceania*, 213.

news was that Pacific peoples were the descendants of these energetic forebears; the bad news was that

> they are, and always have been, a part of the 'unchanging East.' No doubt many portions of the race in the more outlying parts have sunk considerably, though even they have not sunk so much as we might have expected. If some of the Oceanians have lost such arts as pottery-making, cloth-weaving, and writing, others seem to have invented the outrigger canoe, and the making of a kind of cloth out of the bark of trees.[93]

This is a prime example of how Ballantyne's analysis of the "Oriental Maori" can be extended outward into the Melanesian context and beyond.

The Reverend John Mathew, a prolific researcher of Australian Aboriginal culture and language, insisted that it was South Asian Dravidian that was the ancestor of Aboriginal languages. His study was traditional ethnology, presuming that all linguistic and cultural similarities proved a direct relationship. Perhaps the most entertaining of these equations was his study of boomerangs. After conceding that returning boomerangs were unique to Australia, he noted that non-returning ones were found in India. "We search the Malay and Papuan armories in vain for any trace of it and are therefore obliged to credit some other race with its introduction to Australia, unless we unnecessarily assume that it was invented here independently."[94] Diffusionism explained everything by "taking it for granted that the cradle of the human race was in Asia whence all the nations have radiated like successive swarms from a parent hive. . . ."[95] In other cases, missionary ethnographers did not use a specific scientific theory to anchor their observations, preferring a generalized child race discourse linked to vaguely Eastern origins, mentality, and culture. These observations can sharply underline the othering involved in the search for kinship. The Anglican bishop of New Guinea, Montagu Stone-Wigg, wrote in 1912 that the Papuan should be understood as

> a child—a child with the passions of a man. He quickly passes from one mood to another. He is excitable, demonstrative in joy and grief, passionate and fickle. He lives in the present and thinks of little beyond the limits

93. Macdonald, *Oceania*, 213.

94. John Mathew, "The Australian Aborigines," *Journal and Proceedings of the Royal Society of New South Wales* 23 (1889): 375. This prizewinning essay was the basis for his 1899 book *Eaglehawk and Crow: A Study of the Australian Aborigines, Including an Inquiry into their Origin and a Survey of Australian Languages* (London: Nutt, 1899).

95. Mathew, "The Australian Aborigines," 382.

of the passing day; also he is essentially Eastern in thought and ways, and must not be measured by Western standards.[96]

To conclude this general discussion of the othering and brothering symbiosis, we should note F. A. Campbell's recollections of his island flock in the Presbyterian mission to the New Hebrides. "If we believed that they were less than men, we would not feel that we had any serious duty toward them," he wrote, but because they were "included in the Kingdom of Christ," it necessarily followed that "of whatever character or condition they may be—lovely or unlovely—a noble race or a very contemptible one—because Christ does not despise them, we dare not."[97] There is no question about the vertical othering present elsewhere in his observations: Pacific peoples, in his opinion, "have no history" and "can not be expected to take any rank among the kingdoms of the world."[98] Nevertheless, the main point of his summary was to underline their essential humanity and, therefore, the mission's duty toward them: a horizontal process of brothering. Based on ancient one blood theological anthropology, Campbell's statement presents a cultural hierarchy together with the means of its undoing. "The point with the Melanesians," explained Robert Codrington, "was not to turn them into Englishmen but to make them Christians; and, as a first step, to convince them that, in the sight of God who made them, and redeemed them, Englishmen and Melanesians were alike equal."[99] Here we have a theological anthropology that was vertical and exclusive, distinguishing Christians from non-Christians, but also horizontal and inclusive, aspiring to equality. "A leading principle was to banish all idea of inferiority of race," noted an early history of the Melanesian Mission's activities, explaining that "self-respect, manliness, and conscientiousness" were "qualities which belong by right of creation to both races alike."[100] We should note the importance of a shared manliness here. The intent might have been to banish racism, but unexamined boundaries of gender remained intact.

96. Montagu Stone-Wigg, *The Papuans: A People of the South Pacific* (Melbourne: The Shipping Newspapers for the Association for Missionary Services, 1912), 33.

97. F. A. Campbell, *A Year in the New Hebrides, Loyalty Islands, and New Caledonia* (Geelong: George Mercer, 1873), 5.

98. Campbell, *A Year in the New Hebrides*, 5. For a pioneering discussion of related issues see Eric Wolf, *Europe and the People Without History* (Berkeley: University of California Press, 1982).

99. Quoted in Campbell, *A Year in the New Hebrides*, 83.

100. E. S. Armstrong, *The History of the Melanesian Mission* (London: Isbister and Co., 1900), 82, 83.

Part Two

CHAPTER 4

Translations

After arriving on Fiji in December 1838, the Reverend Thomas Jaggar was overwhelmed by the physical demands of pioneering mission work. Resources and energy were scarce during the heat of the "sickly season" as Jaggar and his family unloaded stores, including a precious printing press, and struggled to build a house while succumbing in turns to debilitating illness. Despite these significant challenges, by January 12 Jaggar was proudly working on the beginning of an English-Fijian vocabulary, a project at which he labored consistently, taking brief breaks only when suffering from severe eye inflammation. He would need to preach competently in the indigenous language, something that would require careful preparation. As Niel Gunson observed, early mission pioneers were particularly prone to unintentional gaffes: "Stories of wrongly used or wrongly pronounced words in missionary sermons are legion," such as "the Wesleyan missionary who informed his congregation that 'the time of woman was now come,'" who had less reason to be embarrassed than some of his colleagues.[1] The importance of preaching in the Methodist tradition required linguistic competence.

Just as important was the printing press that arrived with Jaggar, the means by which "words where by we may be saved might speedily be placed in the hand of every Feejeean."[2] Like most Protestant missionaries, Jaggar assumed that literacy and access to a translated Bible would be the gateway to religious

1. Gunson, *Messengers of Grace*, 257.

2. Thomas James Jaggar, *Unto the Perfect Day: The Journal of Thomas James Jaggar, Feejee 1838–1845*, ed. Esther and William Keesing-Styles (Auckland: Solent Publishing, 1988), 5.

conversion. Islanders had their own agendas, valuing books and writing for reasons of their own, including prestige and rivalry.[3]

The compulsion to translate Scripture would require a deep engagement with indigenous cultures, and the act of translation itself was an affirmation of human unity. However Other islanders might seem, missionaries believed that the translated word would speak to them, and in the early years of missionary work everyone (linguistically talented or not) was needed to assist with the rapid translation and promulgation of Scripture and other materials. They approached their work with less arrogance than some scholars have suggested. Christopher Herbert has proposed that the LMS "selected the South Seas for proselytizing largely from a belief that the 'primitive' Polynesian languages could readily be mastered in a few weeks' time."[4] In the field, however, "the missionaries were profoundly impressed by the discovery of the complexity of these languages, which taxed their intellects nearly to the breaking point." If their initial bigotry softened with time and experience, "the alteration was in good measure unconscious and never caused them to abandon the rhetoric of 'unbridled passions.'"[5] Here we encounter again the academic construct of accidental, even unwilling ethnographers.

Rather than presenting a monolithic discourse of othering, missionary translation work and philology features a complex interplay between alterity and universalism.[6] The primary question was not whether Pacific languages were complex or not, but whether they were Semitic, Aryan, or otherwise intimately linked with the Holy Land or Europe.[7] The goal, as ever, was to build connections while describing cultural distance. The briefly held assumption about the primitive state of Polynesian languages did not even originate with missionaries. Captain William Bligh met with LMS director Thomas Haweis after returning to England following the *Bounty* mutiny. The two men attempted to recruit missionaries to depart for Tahiti on Bligh's second voyage, but without success.[8] It was Bligh who assured Haweis that Tahitian would be easy to learn

3. Vanessa Smith, *Literary Culture and the Pacific: Nineteenth-Century Textual Encounters* (Cambridge: Cambridge University Press, 1998), 53–100.

4. Christopher Herbert, *Culture and Anomie: Ethnographic Imagination in the Nineteenth Century* (Chicago: University of Chicago Press, 1991), 185.

5. Herbert, *Culture and Anomie*, 185.

6. For more, see Jane Samson, "Translation Teams: Missionaries, Islanders, and the Reduction of Language in the Pacific," in *Missionaries, Indigenous Peoples and Cultural Exchange*, ed. Patricia Grimshaw and Andrew May (Brighton: Sussex Academic Press, 2010), 96–109.

7. Gunson, *Messengers of Grace*, 207.

8. The plan was thwarted when the missionaries demanded (and were refused) ordination before departure; Davies, *The History of the Tahitian Mission 1799–1830*, ed. Colin Newbury (Cambridge: Cambridge University Press, 1961), xxviii.

and, in supposed evidence of this, he provided Haweis with a Tahitian word list that he had compiled.[9]

When the first LMS missionaries eventually arrived at Tahiti, they realized at once that their leaders had been badly misled. Recovering in NSW after the forced evacuation of the first group of missionaries, William Shelley wrote that the Tahitian language was

> not as easily attained as is generally imagined. It is true a person may in five or six months gain such a knowledge of it as to be able to ask a question or give an answer & the natives adapting themselves to their mode of speech thay imagine thay have attained a greater knowledge of it than thay have but the farther thay advanse in knowledge the more thay see of their Ignorance. After a close application of two years & nine months I did not account myself to have half attained it [original spelling retained].[10]

Criticism of what they had been told before departure is clear here, and similar views were repeated after the re-establishment of the mission by John Jefferson, who made enough progress with the language to emphasize that it is "a copious language, and not a barren one . . . it is sufficient to teach any Doctrine taught in the Bible."[11] It was a sophisticated language, "even more [extensive] than any navigator who has given specimens of it was aware of."[12] This was a dig at Bligh and his misleading word list. The spelling and grammar of these two men's reports tells its own story: the first LMS missionaries were chosen for hardiness and practical skills rather than academic qualities. Nevertheless they acknowledged the importance of engaging with the Tahitian language on its own terms. The Roman alphabet could be used successfully only by giving "each of the consonants such names as could be pronounced by the natives, who cannot pronounce a word or syllable ending in a consonant," and as a result "the English names of *f, h, m, n,* and *r* would not suit them."[13]

There is no doubt that presumptions about European superiority were widespread in Britain and elsewhere, but missionaries were challenging some of those presumptions. The early mission reports from Tahiti reflect views that can also be found in the much later writings of James ("Bob") Love of the Presbyte-

9. Davies, *History of the Tahitian Mission*, xxix.

10. William Shelley to LMS, 30 April 1800, M1/SSJ, Box 1, Council of World Mission Archives, School of Oriental and African Studies, London, UK.

11. Cited in Gunson, *Messengers of Grace*, 255.

12. Davies, *History of the Tahitian Mission*, xliv.

13. Davies, *History of the Tahitian Mission*, 77.

rian Kunmunya mission at Port George IV in Western Australia. Conscious of popular prejudice against so-called primitive Aboriginal culture, Love praised the "amazing complexity" of the Warora language and the "beautiful regularity of the grammatical construction."[14] Perhaps the most eloquent description of delight comes from William Colenso, one of the early CMS missionaries to New Zealand. "The more I have seen and known of the works of the Ancient New Zealander," he wrote,

> the more I have been struck with the many indications of their superior mind,—of their fine perception of the beautiful, the regular, and symmetrical; of their desire and labor after the beautiful; of their prompt and genuine, open and fearless criticisms,—in a word, of their great Ideality. And this high faculty of theirs which they possessed in an eminent degree, will probably be better known and understood hereafter than it is at present.[15]

As evidence of this, he listed various cultural attributes including language: "its great grammatical precision, its double duals and double plurals, its euphony, its rhythm, and its brevity, and its many exquisite particles and reduplications, both singular and plural, all highly pregnant with meaning, which almost defy translation into English."[16]

In Fiji, the Methodist missionary Thomas Williams found that Fijian was much more precise and expressive than English, noting its pronominal system with regard to personal and possessive pronouns. Most languages have only two numbers, singular and plural, but Fijian had four, adding a dual and triad. The word "our" in English was crude by comparison. Fijian also multiplied the forms of possessive pronouns according to whether the thing being described was edible, drinkable, or neither:

> Let the Englishman who wishes to say, 'My house, my cheese, and my cider,' be required by the laws of his language to use a separate form of the 'my' in each of these three combinations, because cider is something to be drunk, cheese something to be eaten, and house neither the one nor the other; he will express himself with the nicety on which the Fijian insists in this respect.[17]

14. McKenzie, *Road to Mowanjum* (Sydney: Angus and Robertson, 1969), 48.

15. William Colenso, "Contributions towards a Better Knowledge of the Maori Race," *Transactions of the Royal Society of New Zealand* 11 (1879): 80.

16. Colenso, "Contributions," 82.

17. Thomas Williams, *The Islands and their Inhabitants*, ed. George Stringer Rowe, vol. 1 of *Fiji and the Fijians* (London: Alexander Heylin, 1858), 260.

Williams went beyond this positive comparison with English. Ancient Greek, one of the foundations of classical and biblical scholarship, was the gold standard of linguistic sophistication. Williams noted the prolific use of expletives in Fijian "or, as they are called by the natives, 'the ornaments of speech' . . ." because "it is a piece of Fijian affectation to crowd as many of them as possible into sentences. Greek itself is often out-Greeked by these dainty word-worshippers of the Southern Seas."[18] He also noted how

> The Greek and other cultivated tongues have different words for 'to wash,' according as the operation has reference to the body, or to clothes and the like; and, where the body is spoken of, their synonyms will sometimes define the limb or part which is the subject of the action. The Fijian leaves these languages far behind; for it can avail itself of separate terms to express the washing process, according as it may happen to affect the head, face, hands, feet, and body of an individual, or his apparel, his dishes, or his floor.[19]

The comparison with Greek allowed Williams to underline the language's ability to express advanced philosophical and theological concepts: "The expression of thought in Malayo-Polynesian is simple, inartificial, flowing, and vigorous; and, as a vehicle of Christian truth, whether by word of mouth or by writing, the languages of this family will admit of comparison with the capabilities of much more polished tongues."[20] This type of observation was common; made for obvious missiological reasons. Williams wished to underline Fijian intellectual and cultural capabilities, claiming that missionary activity among a people "so strong-minded, so enterprising, and so versatile" meant that there was "no reason why Fijian literature should not by and by take rank with the noblest cultures, to which the Gospel is at present shaping the genius and heart of so many heathen populations of our globe."[21] Far from believing that indigenous languages were innately inferior, missionaries were required by their own theological imperatives to think otherwise.

Walter Ivens, one of the Melanesian Mission's finest linguists and ethnographers, reflected on the assumptions, made by non-missionaries, about "the so-called jargons of savages" and the alleged problem of translating the Bible into languages lacking exact equivalents to English vocabulary. Like many, he

18. Williams, *Islands and their Inhabitants*, 263.
19. Williams, *Islands and their Inhabitants*, 265.
20. Williams, *Islands and their Inhabitants*, 256.
21. Williams, *Islands and their Inhabitants*, 266.

reminded his readers that the inhabitants of Britain were, in their time, the heathen Other: "To question whether the Gospels can be translated, *e.g.*, into one of the languages of Malaita . . . is to forget the history of our own language. One has only to look at Coverdale's Bible, to say nothing of the Douai Bible, to see the immense number of foreign words expressive of religious ideas that have been imported bodily into English from the classical languages." He noted that no existing language was uniquely sacred; Jesus of Nazareth spoke Aramaic and knew Hebrew, yet the New Testament accounts of his life and teachings were in Greek. Ever since the day of Pentecost, wrote Ivens, "no one language is above another in this respect, and that every man has a right to look on his own language as God-inspired."[22]

Pacific languages had never taken written form, and missionaries needed to create orthographies and grammars as aids to translating biblical and liturgical material. In 1818, Cambridge was treated to the sight of CMS missionary Thomas Kendall in company with two Maori chiefs, Hongi and Waikato, from New Zealand, walking to and fro among the colleges to consult with specialist linguists. Hongi and Waikato also accompanied Kendall to London, although it should be noted that both of them (especially Hongi) were far more interested in London's armories than in Kendall's translation work. Kendall's view, however, was that this joint visit was "for the purpose of settling the orthography and, as far as possible, of reducing the language itself of New Zealand to the rules of Grammar, with a view to the furtherance of the Mission sent out to that country."[23] Anyone researching Victorian linguistics will have noted a frequent use of the word "reduced" in connection with the introduction of literacy to oral cultures. To postcolonial eyes, there is at first something disturbing about the concept of reduction or rendering in this context, with its overtones of diminishment at the hands of some outside force. Agreeing with Claude Lévi-Strauss's diagnosis of "organized tyranny," Christopher Herbert has declared that missionary literacy projects in the Pacific involved "covert violence" aimed at "'reducing' the wild Polynesian libido by imposing a system of restraint upon it."[24] Teaching islanders to read and write was primarily "a means of reordering the mind itself and putting it in thrall to new institutions."[25] He contrasts bigoted missionary ethnography with the "disinterested cultural study" of modern times, concluding that any real study of culture was "ruled out beyond recall"

22. Walter G. Ivens, *Dictionary and Grammar of the Language of Sa'a and Ulawa, Solomon Islands* (Washington: Carnegie Institution, 1918), 164.

23. Thomas Kendall, *A Grammar and Vocabulary of the Language of New Zealand* (London: Church Missionary Society, 1820), preface, n/p.

24. Herbert, *Culture and Anomie*, 167.

25. Herbert, *Culture and Anomie*, 167.

for missionaries because of "the divine authority of [their] own religion and [their] own 'civilized' society."[26] Recent endorsements of Herbert's work by Pacific specialists requires an investigation of these assumptions.[27]

The *Oxford English Dictionary*'s earliest definition of the verb "to reduce" is useful: "To bring back, recall (a thing or person) *to* one's memory, mind, etc."[28] A process of engagement, rather than tyranny, is suggested. Consider again Kendall's visit to England with his two Maori patrons. I say patrons because Kendall and the rest of the CMS mission in New Zealand were completely dependent upon support from sponsoring chiefs; so much so, that they had been forced to trade firearms and ammunition for food to keep themselves and their families alive. It was not the first time that Maori chiefs had visited England. Tui and Titere had arrived two years earlier and spent some time at Cambridge with Professor Lee at the urging of the CMS Committee, where there was suspicion about Kendall's translation methods.[29] Incensed, Kendall planned his own trip and brought his own Maori supporters. His modesty concerning his own knowledge of their language is striking. Writing aboard ship en route to England, he informed the CMS that Maori was "a matter of such importance that I cannot allow myself to be a competent judge," adding later that he was indebted to Pankhurst's Hebrew Lexicon "for much of my little knowledge of the true idiom of the New Zealand Language" because the Hebrew placement of suffixes and affixes was helpful to him, whereas English grammar was not.[30]

The influence of the language and people on Kendall himself is clear. His biographer Judith Binney notes that Kendall based his new Maori orthography on the "Italian" open-vowel system because it was an appropriate fit with spoken Maori, while his critics believed that Maori should be forced to conform to English symbols.[31] A process of mutual conversion had taken place between Kendall and his Maori colleagues: "The intense and constant study of words,

26. Herbert, *Culture and Anomie*, 167.

27. For example, Rod Edmond, *Representing the South Pacific: Colonial Discourse from Cook to Gauguin* (Cambridge: Cambridge University Press, 1997); Vanessa Smith, *Literary Culture;* and Anna Johnston, "The Strange Career of William Ellis," *Victorian Studies* 49, no. 3 (2007): 491–501. All three present nuanced historical research at odds with their deference to Herbert's theory of translation-as-violence.

28. *The Oxford English Dictionary Online* (accessed 16 June 2013).

29. Judith Binney, *The Legacy of Guilt: A Life of Thomas Kendall* (Auckland: Oxford University Press, 1968), 50.

30. Thomas Kendall to CMS, 3 July 1820, "Thomas Kendall Letters etc. (CMS)," MS 0071, Hocken Library, Dunedin, NZ. The *Lexicon* to which he refers had already been published in several editions, ed. John Pankhurst, *An Hebrew and English Lexicon without Points* (London: T. Davison, 1807).

31. Binney, *Legacy of Guilt*, 62.

and of ideas expressed in those words, to which Kendall had devoted himself, had created a sympathetic attitude towards the complexities and implications of a language of which understanding is gained only through knowledge of the traditions of the people."[32] Binney's insight is similar to that described later by Vicente Rafael in his pioneering book *Contracting Colonialism* (1993), where he proposed that "translation and conversion produce[d] the vernacular as that which simultaneously institutes *and* subverts colonial rule."[33] This complexity resonates well with the othering and brothering symbiosis in theological anthropology.

Translation involved making choices concerning which dialect of a language to translate or which of many languages to use for teaching at a mission station. Thomas Williams noted that some Fijian dialects were similar in vocabulary while others were strikingly different. At first, the mission resolved to translate at least some Scripture into all of the dialects, and the mission press issued various runs in Bauan, Rewan, and Lakeba. The Lakeba people had hosted the earliest mission station, and they were annoyed when the missionaries began to prefer the Bauan language (today's "Standard Fijian") because of Bau's increasing political influence. Hymns continued to be printed in Lakeban for a time, to conciliate them.[34] The reasons for favoring Bauan reveal an interesting combination of philological argument and political opportunism. Missionary James Calvert declared (without explanation) that Bauan was "evidently the purest" of the Fijian dialects, adding that "the rising power of Mbau" had "caused its forms of language to be more widely known than any other, and gave evident tokens of at last superseding every other."[35] The mission's fortunes had become increasingly tied to Bau and its ambitious chiefs. Thomas Williams invoked images of ancient empires when he declared that "Mbau, however, is at once the Athens and the Rome of Fiji; and it is the language as spoken there, into which the Scriptures have been translated. . . ."[36] This remarkable statement linked the histories of Fiji and Europe together. Just as Athens and Rome had been cradles of civilization and centers of political and religious leadership for Europe, so Bau, the missionaries hoped, would lead the whole Fijian archipelago to Christianity. That both were examples of empires is also significant; the "rising power of Mbau" was being strongly resisted in other parts of Fiji.

32. Binney, *Legacy of Guilt*, 62.

33. Vicente L. Rafael, *Contracting Colonialism: Translation and Christian Conversion in Tagalog Society*, 2nd ed. (Durham and London: Duke University Press, 1993), xv.

34. James Calvert, *Mission History*, ed. George Stringer Rowe, vol. 2 of *Fiji and the Fijians* (Suva: Fiji Museum, 1985), 224.

35. Calvert, *Mission History*, 224.

36. Williams, *Islands and their Inhabitants*, 257.

In the Anglican New Guinea Mission, the decision to work with the Wedauan language at the first mission station was implemented by a diocesan committee appointed "to select suitable material for translation and publication" in addition to raising funds for a printing press.[37] New Guinea was rich in languages, and each new station presented a fresh dilemma. Missionary Copland King recalled his move to a new coastal station at Ambasi: "The language spoken at my present station, Ambasi, is not quite the same as the Binandere. I have decided to consider the Binandere as the standard, and therefore I do not use any words or phrases unless I can get them tested first on the river."[38] Decisions made by distant committees, or even by mission pioneers on the ground, did not necessarily stand the test of time. In New Guinea and elsewhere in the western Pacific, where linguistic diversity was the greatest in the world and there were fewer indigenous empire-builders than in Fiji and Polynesia, missions usually abandoned the quest for a single indigenous lingua franca, working instead in various local languages or, by the twentieth century, in English.

The Melanesian Mission was a notable exception. From its beginnings in the 1840s, the mission had brought young men from various islands to a central mission school located first in New Zealand, then on Norfolk Island, and eventually at Pawa on Uki ni Masi in the Solomon Islands. The mission eventually chose the language of Mota (an island of the Banks group in the New Hebrides) to be the official language of the mission, but this decision was not initiated by either of its earliest bishops. Later, missionary Charles Fox recalled that Bishop Patteson, fluent in eight languages and functional in many more, had been happy to teach different groups of boys in their own languages. Assisting him at the mission school, however, was the irascible Reverend Lonsdale Pritt: "a harsh master, waspish to his colleagues, always complaining about lax discipline."[39] Pritt, Fox tells us, was the one to introduce the idea of a mission lingua franca. Unable to match Patteson's linguistic talents, Pritt declared "that he only knew one language, the language of Mota," and "if he were to be in charge of the school, that must be the language for all the boys; and so, as it were by accident, Mota became the common language."[40] Pritt left the mission in 1867 after students complained of severe beatings, but his linguistic legacy was momentous. Only in 1916, under pressure from islanders themselves, would the mission reluctantly abandon Mota in favor of English as its language of instruction. "English is a foreign language," lamented missionary Walter Ivens,

37. New Guinea Mission, *Occasional Paper* (1932): 2–3.

38. *ABM Review* (February 1914): 187.

39. Hilliard, *God's Gentlemen*, 33.

40. Charles Elliot Fox, "A Missionary in Melanesia," MS-Papers-1171–03, Alexander Turnbull Library, Wellington, NZ.

and "one does contend strongly for the principle that the Melanesian should be taught Christianity through the medium of one of his own languages."[41]

How had Pritt known Mota? In his autobiography, the first Melanesian Anglican priest, George Sarawia, recalled how he had taught the language to Patteson in 1857 during a mission visit to his home island.[42] It is significant that the mission's knowledge of Mota first came from a Melanesian man's gift of his time and expertise. Sarawia recalled the first visit of the mission ship, and how fear and confusion wrestled with curiosity as he decided to go on board. He, Bishop Selwyn, and John Patteson sat down in the stern "and they asked me the name of the island, and the names of people. I told them and they wrote them down in a book, but I did not know then what a book was."[43] Nervously, Sarawia continued the lesson when "they wrote down some other words too, the words for you, he, you (plural), we two, I, all of us . . . they wrote down a few words of Mota that day, and we were astonished that they understood so quickly a little Mota and could speak it properly."[44] Here an islander nicely turns the tables, astonished that Europeans were capable of understanding his language.

The role of George Sarawia in teaching Mota to the first Bishop of Melanesia highlights the occlusion, in many missionary accounts, of the voices and roles of indigenous informants. Some simply omitted any mention of indigenous assistance in the work of translation, especially in their published accounts. George Brown transformed first-person, past tense journal entries into third person and the present tense in his published work, including accounts of cannibalism. Helen Gardner observes that this grammatical alteration "removed the action from real time, making it [cannibalism] an abstract possibility and thus eliminating his Christian responsibility to intercede in the events."[45] These important points about person and tense in missionary texts can be expanded. Missionaries often wrote in the passive voice, obscuring the identity of the actors involved in translation work or other joint activities. We read that the gospel "was translated" or the Bible "was rendered" into the language of the people without learning who had done the actual work.

In other cases they made their debt to indigenous informants clear. In the early years of the LMS mission to Tahiti and the Society Islands, Pomare II played a direct role in translation work. He corrected the missionaries' drafts, provided them with new words, and explained nuances and usage: "Davies

41. Ivens, *Dictionary and Grammar*, 171.

42. George Sarawia, *They Came to My Island* (Siota: St. Peter's College, 1968), ii.

43. Sarawia, *They Came to My Island*, 2.

44. Sarawia, *They Came to My Island*, 2.

45. Gardner, *Gathering for God*, 16.

would give Pomare the manuscript and he would mark every place where he thought the language was faulty."[46] Working conditions were more Tahitian than British; Crook reported how his colleague Nott had to avert his eyes during Pomare's sexual attentions to his favorite *mahu*.[47] Reporting on his progress in translating the New Testament into Aneityumese (Anejom), the Canadian Presbyterian missionary John Inglis acknowledged the assistance of the Reverend T. W. Meller, the rector of Woodbridge in Suffolk. Meller was editorial superintendent of the British and Foreign Bible Society and had somehow learned enough Aneityumese to impress Inglis. "How he has acquired it I do not know," reported Inglis, "but that is of little consequence."[48] After praising Meller, Inglis also acknowledged the assistance of Williamu, a convert whose brief account of himself had been translated by Inglis. Appended to Inglis's report, it declared that Williamu had "lived here [Aneityum] a long time with Mr. And Mrs. Inglis,"[49] and had "thrown his whole heart into the work in which we are engaged."[50] Whatever his other duties might have been in the Inglis household, Williamu had been a full partner in the translation work.

Sometimes a missionary's views changed over time concerning his indebtedness to indigenous expertise. The Reverend J. E. Newell of the LMS mission to Samoa reviewed E. Schultz's *Sprichwortliche Redensarten der Samoaner* (1906), noting his use of indigenous assistants:

> What inexhaustible patience was required in interviewing the thirty natives whose aid Dr. Schultz enlisted for his work, only those who have endeavored to fathom the irregularities and peculiarities of this style of speech can truly estimate. Such knowledge as the author was in search of is a severe demand on the native intelligence, and implies a mental training and an appreciation of our European eagerness to know the reasons and usages of exceptional phraseology which very few (hardly any) natives possess.[51]

46. Gunson, *Messengers of Grace*, 258.

47. Gunson, *Messengers of Grace*, 258.

48. J. Inglis to Reformed Presbyterian Synod, n/d, *The Home and Foreign Missionary Record* (October 1862): 274.

49. "Williamu's Address," in J. Inglis to Reformed Presbyterian Synod, n/d, *The Home and Foreign Missionary Record* (October 1862): 277.

50. "Williamu's Address," 276.

51. J. E. Newell, "Dr. Schultz on Samoan proverbial sayings and figures of speech: a criticism and appreciation by the Rev. J. E. Newell, London Missionary Society," J. E. Newell Papers, Box 9 "Anthropological," n/p, South Seas Personal-Special, Council of World Mission Archives, School of Oriental and African Studies, London, UK.

The colonial discourse analysis writes itself: Newell's stolid lack of reflexivity and his racist conceptions are clear. Newell himself, however, points the way to another reading. Later in his review he praises the miscellaneous section of Schultz's book "because it gives us expressions and similes quoted from the folklore which is alas! almost a sealed book to us, notwithstanding the labors of Powell, Pratt, Dr. Kramer, Dr. Stuebel and others."[52] The fact that Samoan folklore remained a sealed book to outsiders, despite the alleged superiority of European intelligence and academic training, points to an alternative hermeneutic. Perhaps, despite the efforts of the thirty Samoans who did their best for Dr. Schultz, the demands on European intelligence and mental training were simply too great for Schultz to grasp the meaning or significance of what they were telling him!

Later in his career, Newell's attitude toward native intelligence was very different. His papers shed light on the neglected career of Timoteo, one of two Samoan mission teachers dispatched to Papua with their wives by the LMS in 1884.[53] He comes to life in a makeshift notebook titled "Timoteo's notes on Kabadi translated by Newell 1895." A letter by Newell to the Polynesian Society explained that Timoteo, "a friend and correspondent," had sent him extensive notes on the language and customs of the Kabadi people of New Guinea. "Unfortunately Pastor Timoteo does not know English and our extensive correspondence during the 12 years has been in Samoan," but Timoteo had published Samoan-language articles on the Kabadi for *Sulu Samoa*, a periodical edited by Newell. Recognizing the anthropological value of Timoteo's work, Newell was translating portions of it into English for submission to the Society's journal. He added that Timoteo had recently sent him a grammatical outline of the Kabadi language, saying, "So far as I am aware Timoteo is the only living authority on this dialect. He is the only Native Teacher in [Rabade] who is capable of classifying his knowledge, as he is the only man possessing adequate knowledge of the dialect for philological purposes."[54] There had been a dramatic shift in Newell's opinion of the intellectual capacity and partnership of Pacific Islanders. Years earlier, he had declared Samoans to be inherently incapable of language classification work, but by 1895 he believed that a Samoan was the *only* person capable

52. Newell, "Dr. Schultz on Samoan proverbial sayings," n/p.

53. Sione Lātūkefu and Ruta Sinclair, "Pacific Islanders as International Missionaries. Papua New Guinea and Solomon Islands," in *Polynesian Missions in Melanesia: From Samoa, Cook Islands and Tonga to Papua New Guinea and New Caledonia*, ed. Ron and Marjorie Crocombe (Suva: Institute of Pacific Studies, University of the South Pacific, 1982), 2.

54. Timoteo, "Timoteo's notes on Kabadi translated by Newell 1895," J. E. Newell Papers, Box 9 "Anthropological," folder 2, n/p, South Seas Personal-Special, Council of World Mission Archives, School of Oriental and African Studies, London, UK.

of such work because he was the man who had done the fieldwork. Timoteo was now a friend, correspondent, fellow pastor, and scientific authority to whom Newell openly deferred in the context of formal scientific correspondence.[55]

Along with his growing respect for the intellectual capacity of Pacific Islanders, Newell had also learned to reflect on his own limitations. A manuscript titled "Notes: chiefly ethnological of the Tokelau, Ellice and Some of the Gilbert or Kingsmill Islands" tells us that Newell visited these islands in 1885 and 1894 and was now writing some "brief and discursive and partial" accounts of the anthropological information he gathered. He added that "the writer's Samoan experience & the limits of his knowledge of other South Sea peoples & ignorance of Western Polynesia will no doubt have coloured his views as to the origin of the peoples embraced in this survey."[56] The point here is to take seriously the impact of Pacific peoples themselves on the views of outsiders like Newell, challenging preconceived notions, breaking down barriers, and provoking self-reflection.

In the manuscript of William Pascoe Crook, the first missionary to the Marquesas Islands, we find some early reflections on such perspectives and biases. Written in 1799, the manuscript describes Crook's attempts to learn the local language. He had met with unexpected difficulties because

> having no idea of any language but their own, they seemed wholly incapable of returning intelligent answers to enquiries about the meaning of their words. If asked the name of anything, they would reply 'a maia havea,' a thing, to be sure. Wishing to find out a term for 'adrift,' Mr. C. described a Canoe in that situation, & enquired how they called it. They replied, 'A Canoe,' & cried that they never heard of such a thing; expressing their surprise that Gods could not talk as men did.[57]

No wonder that historian Greg Dening, editor of the Crook manuscript, observed that "Crook's perceptions were changed more than Enata's."[58] John

55. The notes were published as "Notes on the Kabadi Dialect of New Guinea, Pastor Timoteo. Translated by the Rev. J. E. Newell," *Journal of the Polynesian Society* 6, no. 24 (1897): 201–8.

56. J. E. Newell, "Notes: chiefly ethnological of the Tokelau, Ellice and some of the Gilbert or Kingsmill Islands," J. E. Newell Papers, Box 9 "Anthropological," folder 2, n/p, South Seas Personal-Special, Council for World Mission Archives, School of Oriental and African Studies, London, UK. The notes were published as an article of the same name in the Australasian Association for the Advancement of Science's *Proceedings*, section F, Report 6 (1895): 603–12.

57. William Pascoe Crook, "An Account of Marquesas Islands, 1799," 165–66, ML CY Reel 329, Mitchell Library, Sydney, Australia.

58. Greg Dening, *Islands and Beaches: Discourse on a Silent Land. Marquesas 1774–1880* (Honolulu: University of Hawai'i Press, 1980), 142.

Hunt of the Methodist mission, one of the earliest translators in Fiji, devoted himself to the work of preparing a New Testament in Fijian. His colleague James Calvert reported that Hunt "found that the language was best learned by constant intercourse with the people,"[59] and Hunt has left us a detailed account of his methodology in his own words:

> 1. To read over the chapter for translating in the Greek Testament, and examine particuarly any word of which I have any doubt as to its meaning. I read Bloomfield's Notes and Campbell's translation and any other books that I have to assist me to ascertain the meaning of the text. 2. After having mastered the chapters as I think, I commence translating and I use as my standards for the text the Greek and the English translations and for the translation not any man exclusively, but myself, all the Natives I can have access to, and the translations that have already been made.

Hunt was sensitive to the differences between the Fijian dialects, although he would later promote Bauan as a Fijian lingua franca by claiming (wrongly) that most Fijians already understood it in addition to their own local dialects. He realized too late that this view was incorrect.[60] Meanwhile, at his Somosomo station he had been working closely with Noa, a convert who later accompanied him to Viwa when the mission was relocated there. They worked together on a Viwa dialect translation of the Wesleyan catechism, but after it was printed in 1843 some of the other missionaries objected to the liberties Hunt had taken with the original English version. Hunt's greatest defender was Noa who declared that "the new catechism was using the Viwa language as it had been before missionaries came while the older catechism was the language of the Lotu people since the introduction of Christianity."[61] Noa appreciated the cultural specificities of the old English version and praised efforts to create a Fijian version that was attentive to Fiji's very different cultural context.

Hunt's biographer notes that there was a demonstrable focus on indigenous-driven translation work at Hunt's station: he and his wife began teaching English at Viwa in order to enable Fijians to undertake their own translation of literary and scientific works in English.[62] Hunt himself could not have made his debts more clear: "I have the most important assistance that can be desired,

59. Calvert, *Mission History*, 222.
60. Thornley, *Inheritance of Hope*, 250, 266.
61. Quoted in Thornley, *Inheritance of Hope*, 4.
62. Thornley, *Inheritance of Hope*, 232.

in a very intelligent native, who has been with me three years, and has become an excellent preacher. I have him by me when translating, and make him the judge of the work, so far as the Fijian is concerned."[63] A similar attentiveness prompted David Cargill, one of Hunt's colleagues, to create a special orthography for Fijian, including the English "d" for the Fijian "nd" and "b" for "mb."[64] Cargill believed that the Roman alphabet would suffice as long as a distinctive Fijian orthography was respected. Despite all of this, later generations sometimes occluded the debts that earlier missionaries had openly acknowledged. Reflecting on the centenary of the Fijian mission, Methodist superintendent J. W. Burton discussed the co-operative process of translation, but only as a collaboration between English missionaries. He made no mention at all of Fijian participation.[65]

The Reverend Copland King of the Anglican New Guinea Mission provided one of the most detailed explanations we have of the teamwork involved in translation work. When the white staff at the up-river mission station were recalled in 1900 due to illness, most of the boarders there were sent to Dogura (at Wedau). There the young men finished school, some were baptized, and some would teach at Dogura themselves. King recalled

> I started one of these boys, Edmund Dudu, after he had been at Dogura for six years, and back in the district as pupil teacher for two, at translation work. He took the Wedau Gospel, and wrote it out in Binandere. As he did so, I read over his translation with him, making corrections as necessary, then typed it, made him read it over with me, and then typed it again. Several other boys, who in their turn came from Dogura, read it over with me. Every revision involved numberless discussions on the meaning of the original, the force of the words chosen, and other matters. It was my business to keep my eye on the Analytical Concordance. The boys had to tell me of anything which sounded strange or hard or wrong; then we could discuss how it could be amended.[66]

Readers at the Binandere services used drafts of the new translation in their readings, welcoming help from the congregation in clarifying meanings and

63. Calvert, *Mission History*, 225.

64. David Cargill, "A Brief Essay on the Feejeean Language," *Report of the Wesleyan Methodist Missionary Society* (1840): 132–43. Missionaries elsewhere in the world had found the Roman alphabet completely inadequate, creating their own syllabic systems, e.g. John MacLean, *James Evans, inventor of the syllabic system of the Cree language* (Toronto, ON: Methodist Mission Rooms, 1890).

65. J. W. Burton, *A Hundred Years in Fiji* (London: Epworth Press, 1936), 63.

66. *ABM Review* (February 1914): 187–88.

syntax. King was clear about his position of dependency—"I have to take the natives' opinion on trust"—and he was happy to do so because "they were working, not to satisfy the Missionary, but to enlighten their own people."[67] The stenciled copies were used by local readers at church services, further revisions were made, and only then was a final copy typed for the printer.

In Western Australia in the 1920s, the Presbyterian mission at Kunmunya had a self-described translating team that gathered around Bob Love to begin the translation of the gospel of Mark, and who continued to assist him when work began on the Hebrew scriptures. Love's partners were "Ernie (whom Bob addressed by his native name, Njimandum . . .), Albert Barunga . . . and Wondoonmoi, quite an old man now, the native who had tried twice to kill [Love] in 1914, but who had since become his friend."[68] Every day, the group met on the verandah of Love's house, sitting together around a cane table. Sharing daily life with Aboriginal people sometimes solved tricky translation problems; the great man did not simply come up with ideas and then call for indigenous responses. Love told a story about his difficulty with the word "beginning," a serious drawback when attempting to translate the first chapter of Genesis. The problem plagued his team for a considerable length of time. Out pigeon hunting one day, Love and some Aboriginal friends traced a stream of water to its source in a spring:

> Next language day I told my team what we had done, in following a stream to its beginning. I sketched a map of the stream, naming the place, and following up the course to the place where it sprang from under the rock. I asked, What is this? Quick as a flash, Wondoonmoi put his finger on the source of the stream and said "Wundjanguru." He then ran his finger along the course of the stream till, at the place where it debouched into the sea, he said "Umindjunguru." A great discovery! Alpha and Omega, the beginning and the end![69]

A similarly deep sense of obligation was expressed by the early twentieth-century Anglican missionary Charles Eliot Fox as he recalled his work on the Arosi language of San Cristoval in Solomon Islands. He performed *haimarahuda* with his friend Martin Taki, exchanging names and possessions, and beginning a new life as the member of a San Cristoval family. Living and working with his new relatives, he felt that "the main thing was to listen to them and to imitate them." Often he and the other men of the village would wake in the

67. *ABM Review* (February 1914): 188.
68. McKenzie, *Road to Mowanjum*, 89.
69. McKenzie, *Road to Mowanjum*, 90.

night to replenish their fire and there was a particular candor to these midnight conversations when "the people would speak very freely, and you could listen to what they were saying and pick up a great number of new words and phrases, writing them down later on."[70] Eventually he learned enough to create a dictionary and grammar, and to begin work on an Arosi translation of the New Testament. Fox denied himself primary agency in this project:

> The real work of translation is done by the Melanesians, and not by the white men. We speak of Codrington translating the New Testament into Mota, but really he did the explaining of the meaning to Edward Wogale, who was a native of Mota, and Wogale did the actual phrasing of the translation in the native idiom, and this has been so in all the translations of the Mission. The Melanesians have not really got the credit that they deserved for these translations, which are spoken of as having been done by the white men.[71]

Of interest here is the difference between how missionaries like Fox or Codrington actually lived and worked and how their activities might be reported by others in missionary periodicals and other venues. Fox shows a consciousness of the process by which a missionary's best efforts to credit indigenous expertise could be thwarted. Codrington himself would have been the first to acknowledge his obligations to islanders. Late in his life, hard at work on translating the prophetic books of the Hebrew scriptures into Mota, Codrington declared, "I am not altogether in favor of translating obscure passages & parts of the scripture until a fair number of natives can make something out of them," meaning that the triumph of completing some translation or other should take a distant second place to the needs of the audience.[72]

Some translators were also careful to respect the cultural context of their translation work, as when Bob Love of the Kunmunya mission described the difficulties presented by English idiom. There was no attempt to privilege the English context here; on the contrary, English was dealt with reflexively, as the expression of a particular culture:

> To speak of the heart as the seat of the emotions would not convey sense to a Worora man. Like Hebrew, which speaks of "bowels of compassion,"

70. Charles Elliot Fox, "A Missionary in Melanesia," MS-Papers-1171–02, Alexander Turnbull Library, Wellington, NZ.

71. Fox, "A Missionary in Melanesia."

72. Cited in Allan Davidson, "The Legacy of Robert Henry Codrington," *International Bulletin of Missionary Research* 27, no. 4 (2003): 174.

> Worora speaks of the belly as the seat of gentle affections. A man of good disposition has a good belly. If he is righteously indignant, his belly is hot. The pancreas is regarded as the seat of anger, and the nodules in the mesentery are supposed to be the seat of laughter. The ear is the home of the intellect, and one does not lay up memories in the heart, but in the ear.[73]

Others missionaries seemed tone-deaf to cultural context, universalizing their assumptions about language to a point that rendered Fijian almost impossibly alien. Joseph Waterhouse noted its niceties and complexities, but also what he regarded as a fatal absence:

> The Fijian can describe all his sensations and desires, and has a most copious vocabulary describing things within his knowledge and for ideas derived from his senses, but for spiritual things, and indeed for many matters of ordinary virtue, he has no words. He has no name for "continence" or "gratitude," for "conscience" or "ingratitude," for "justice" or "holiness." The word used for "god" is also employed to express anything superlative, whether good or bad.[74]

Waterhouse was suspiciously confident about the lack of words for important concepts, perhaps because he interpreted Fijian information in English terms. "Some of the chiefs pretend an innocent conceit," he claimed, "asserting the non-existence in their social circles of certain words. Thus, a man of great rank assured a missionary that there was no such word as 'anxiety' in his dialect."[75] There was probably nothing innocent about a high-ranking chief's interest in denying that he knew anything about fear or anxiety.

Nevertheless, cultural distance posed problems for even the most sensitive missionaries anxious to translate complex theological and moral concepts into the indigenous language. Sometimes no amount of local assistance was enough. The linguistically-minded daughter of Lorimer Fison, in a long letter to her father's friend George Brown, noted that

> As for forgiveness the Fijian has neither the word for it in his language nor the knowledge of it in his heart. Our missionaries had to render "Forgive

73. McKenzie, *Road to Mowanjum*, 48.

74. Joseph Waterhouse, *King and People of Fiji* (London: Wesleyan Conference Office, 1866), 245.

75. Waterhouse, *King and People of Fiji*, 245.

> us our trespasses" by "Punish us not for our trespasses" & I need not point out to you how far "Punishment" falls short of "Forgive us."[76]

Two available words might "be redeemed by having the meaning of forgiveness put into them" including *buluta* (to bury), sometimes used to indicate the overlooking of past offences, "though indeed this burying is but the burying of the Indian warhatchet, to be dug up again at a future day." The second word, *vakalecalecava*, indicated the killing of a member of an enemy group for the purpose of revenge. She noted that "this word had been adopted by the R. C. Priests in their version of the Lord's Prayer & is fully capable of taking to itself the new & better meaning, having indeed a beautiful fitness for it—the death of Christ being the Valecava [the victim whose death satisfies the demands of vengeance] whereby the Just God can be strictly just & yet Vakalecalecava our sins."[77]

More worrying was the absence of any Fijian equivalent for "peace" except for words indicating the absence of war, or others indicating a plentiful food supply. She concluded:

> None but they who have had the work to do, can form any just estimate of the extreme difficulty of setting forth the Gospel truths in a language such as this. For the message of wrath, for the warnings & the threatenings, we find its vocabulary amply sufficient. But the glorious words of promise, the offer of mercy, the breathings of infinite love & tenderness—when we would set forth these, there are we straitened indeed.[78]

Copland King faced similar difficulties in the Anglican New Guinea Mission: "In some countries the chest is the seat of the emotions; here it is the throat. Bad throat means sorrow; a throaty man is a wise man; to take the throat is to love, in some languages it is to be loved. Anger, however, is a biting of the liver. In S. Luke vii. 45. 'Thou gavest me no kiss,' is translated, 'Thou didst not smell my nose.'"[79] At least in these cases there were existing words or phrases that could convey the desired meaning. Finding names for Middle Eastern plants and animals was more difficult. "Grapes and fig-trees can be represented by other fruit. The native fig dos not cast its leaves, but other trees do," King wrote, but "foxes and wolves

76. M. C. Fison to George Brown, 2 May 1913, Methodist Overseas Mission, George Brown Correpondence, CY Reel 3405, Mitchell Library, Sydney, Australia.

77. M. C. Fison to George Brown, 2 May 1913, Methodist Overseas Mission, George Brown Correpondence, CY Reel 3405, Mitchell Library, Sydney, Australia.

78. M. C. Fison to George Brown, 2 May 1913, Methodist Overseas Mission, George Brown Correpondence, CY Reel 3405, Mitchell Library, Sydney, Australia.

79. *ABM Review* (February 1914), 188.

have no native equivalent, and unfortunately both these words are awkward to translate from the English, so we turn to the Greek for help."[80]

Like the Methodists in Fiji, King struggled for words to convey "the theological words distinctive of Christianity," and, also like them, he wrote to Robert Codrington of the Anglican Melanesian Mission for help. King was using indigenous words for "forget" or "do not punish" but remained dissatisfied with the results. Codrington told him

> that Bishop Patteson had invented certain compounds, which were in use practically all over that Mission. The compound for "forgive" means "to determine to leave one, to think away." I translated this into Binandere, and the Christian boys, who knew what forgiveness was, said that it would do. It does not answer, however, in the other dialects that we have tried. I may mention that the different Missions in New Guinea are at present attempting a united inquiry into such words as these. We are comparing our difficulties, in the hope that others' experience may be useful to us. We have a list of over sixty of these words already, and each correspondent adds more. Often it is impossible to invent a native compound word, and some term has to be introduced from another language, and then its meaning taught.[81]

Sometimes the outcome of this difficult process was an unexpected one: the conversion of the missionary from alienated stranger to a native-speaker whose former native tongue had grown foreign to him. Aaron Buzacott recalled his bafflement as he struggled to learn the language during the early days of the LMS mission to Rarotonga. Consonant substitution meant that the young missionary listened in vain for words that he had first learned at Tahiti: "The spoken dialect seemed such a chaos of noises, musical and discordant, that the new missionary began to fear he should never acquire the barbarian speech so as to proclaim with freedom and clearness the wonderful story of redeeming love."[82] In the end, however, the so-called barbarian speech acquired the missionary. In England years later to see his translation work through the press, Buzacott found it difficult "to preach or speak in the English language, which seemed now almost a foreign tongue to his lips; his mind being prone to thinking according to the habits and ideas of the Rarotongans."[83]

80. *ABM Review* (February 1914): 188.

81. *ABM Review* (February 1914): 188–89.

82. Aaron Buzacott, *Mission Life in the Islands of the Pacific* (London: John Snow & Co, 1866), 29.

83. Buzacott, *Mission Life*, 198.

The theological demands of othering and brothering inclined missionaries to prefer certain scientific theories over others to explain the origins and relationships of Oceanic languages. Jaroslav Pelikan has traced the origin of this "sacred philology" to the Renaissance study of classical Greek and Latin texts.[84] Christianity had embraced the translation of its Scriptures from the earliest days: Jesus of Nazareth spoke Aramaic, but the earliest available accounts of his teachings and the activities of his disciples were written down in Greek. Expanding beyond the Greek-speaking world, Christian communities translated these Greek documents (and the Hebrew of the Jewish scriptures) into their own local languages, and the process of biblical translation continues today. In stark contrast, Islam reveres the original language of the Qur'an as normative. Interpretations are widely available in other languages, but however scholarly these versions might be, the sacred text cannot be translated. Only in Arabic does one truly read the Qur'an.

For our missionary translators the opposite was true: the act of translation was an affirmation of unity between readers of Christian Scripture in all times and places. It is therefore no surprise to find that missionaries clung to the tradition of sacred philology long after it became discredited in metropolitan scientific circles. A highly critical article by Sidney Ray, the British linguist, made this time lag explicit. Ray had been working closely with western Pacific missionaries in order to gather material, and his article on "The Study of Melanesian Languages" appeared in the Anglican *Southern Cross Log* in 1908. Ray must have hoped that by publishing his views in a mission periodical they would have greater influence on missionary scholarship. He was ruthless in his condemnation of the traditional philology still used by so many missionaries to explore the origins and relationship of Pacific languages. "These students [of Melanesian languages] are content to take the languages, as far as they are known, and base upon comparisons various theories of origin. These theories are wrong, both in direction and method, and are also premature."[85] The method was wrong because similarities were assumed to indicate relationship; theories were premature because relatively little was known of interior districts in Indonesia and Melanesia. The direction was wrong because, as we have seen, various writers had argued that Melanesian languages were related, variously, to Aryan, Semitic, American Indian, Japanese, Inuit, Ural-Altaic, Dravidian, and Australian Aboriginal. "Unless all these linguistic families be regarded as

84. Jaroslav Pelikan, *Jesus through the Centuries: His Place in the History of Culture* (New Haven: Yale University Press, 1985), 152.

85. Sidney H. Ray, "The Study of Melanesian Languages," *Southern Cross Log* (May 1908): 176–78.

related," observed Ray, "the arguments in favor of any one of them is destroyed by the arguments in favor of the others."[86]

As a scientist Ray knew that no universal linguistic relationship existed, but for missionary researchers there was a wider relationship to consider. Theirs was a universalist anthropology demanded by faith. Long after metropolitan scientists had embraced modern linguistics, missionaries continued to publish theories about the Semitic roots of Polynesian languages, or they proclaimed the discovery of Sanskrit terms. Possibly the most persistent of these sacred philologists was Daniel Macdonald of the Presbyterian New Hebrides Mission. He published dozens of articles into the early twentieth century, finding a UK publisher for a lengthy book on Semitic Polynesian languages as late as 1907.[87] Such missionary scholars believed that they were tracing the shape of universal human nature and destiny, and they refused to be distracted by metropolitan scientific debate.

As for Ray, he remained dependent on the work of missionary translators and researchers whether he liked it or not. In a letter to E. E. V. Collocott, Methodist missionary to Tonga, Ray confessed that in his forthcoming book on Polynesian languages he would "have to draw all my examples of Tonga construction from the Bible Translation." Apart from the Tongan Bible there was "only Moulton's History of the World, and *Mariner*!"[88] Eager to assist, Collocott and his mission friends sent to Ray their Tongan translations of Aesop's fables and *Pilgrim's Progress*. Ray must have been a supporter of missionary work, or at least a supporter of accuracy in their scriptural translations: in 1927 he reported to Collocott that he was editing "four Gospels in the Kiwai Language" after "reading the proofs of the New Testament in the Sa's Language of Malaita, and am reading also the NT proofs in the Ulawa Language."[89] He disapproved of mission philology, yet, at the same time, he was involved with mission projects and dependent on missionary informants.

In addition to filling out scientific questionnaires and corresponding with metropolitan theorists, the globalizing networks of British imperial science enabled Pacific-based missionaries to engage with current debates about Indian languages. Although geographically distant, India was intellectually present through theories about Aryan language and culture, as we saw in the last chap-

86. Ray, "Study of Melanesian Languages," 177.

87. Daniel Macdonald, *The Oceanic Languages: Their Grammatical Structure, Vocabulary and Origin* (London: Henry Frowde, 1907).

88. S. H. Ray to E. E. V. Collocott, 20 January 1921, Rev. Dr. E. E. V. Collocott, Correspondence, PMB MS 28.

89. S. H. Ray to E. E. V. Collocott, 2 March 1927, Rev. Dr. E. E. V. Collocott, Correspondence, PMB MS 28.

ter. Tony Ballantyne has noted that "New Zealand was charted, described and settled in a world that was fundamentally shaped by the 'Oriental renaissance' and this powerful thread in the intellectual life of the young colony moulded understandings of Maori language and history."[90] Missionaries beyond New Zealand shared a similar interest, effectively orientalizing the whole Pacific world. Samuel Ella of the LMS Samoan mission supplied linguist Sidney Ray with information on Samoan languages and orthography, helping him to obtain the works of an older generation of missionary translators in Samoa as well as his own current research.[91] In return, Ray sent offprints of articles on Oceanic language relationships to Ella, warning the missionary of his opposition to Aryan theories: "I do not agree with Dr. Fraser's [*sic*] attempts to connect those [Samoan] myths with Aryan ones of the Sun &c. I maintain that we are not yet in a position to attempt the comparison of the Oceanic languages with those of other linguistic families. . . ."[92]

Meanwhile, Ella was also exchanging research data and publications with the New Zealand surveyor and ethnologist S. Percy Smith, whose diffusionist theories were more congenial than Ray's skepticism. Smith wrote to Ella in 1898, "I have long come to the conclusion that we must look for the home of the Polynesians in inland India."[93] He thanked the missionary for the research he had done to support this theory, declaring that Ella's article "Relationship of the Polynesian Languages with the Malay" would "shew comprehensively *what the Malays have borrowed from the Polynesians*, for I agree with Dr. Fraser [*sic*] that this appears to be the correct view, not vice versa."[94] Ella's paper was not published in the *Journal of the Polynesian Society* as they had hoped, so he read part of it at the Australasian Association for the Advancement of Science (AAAS) meeting in 1898. To Ella's delight, he met there the well-known missionary ethnographers George Brown and Lorimer Fison who "most warmly commended" him on his paper.[95] Fison was already a prominent member of the anthropology section of the AAAS and Ella became section president in 1893. He later published another paper that makes his debt to oriental diffusionism clear. His work on comparative Polyne-

90. Ballantyne, *Orientalism and Race*, 57.

91. Sidney Ray to Samuel Ella, 12 September 1895, 17 December 1895, and 16 June 1896, Samuel Ella Correspondence 1895–1899, ML A211, Mitchell Library, Sydney, Australia.

92. Sidney Ray to Samuel Ella, 27 December 1895, Samuel Ella Correspondence 1895–1899, ML A211, Mitchell Library, Sydney, Australia.

93. Percy Smith to Samuel Ella, 17 March 1898, Samuel Ella Correspondence 1895–1899, ML A211, Mitchell Library, Sydney, Australia.

94. Smith to Ella, 17 March 1898. Original emphasis.

95. Samuel Ella to Sidney Ray, 26 September 1898, Samuel Ella Correspondence 1895–1899, ML A211, Mitchell Library, Sydney, Australia.

sian grammar demonstrated "a close affinity and agreement between the several dialects of these people, spread over a very extensive portion of the Pacific" that, despite local variations, "point distinctly to a common origin."[96] Despite this tone of confidence, Ella revealed a consciousness of the widening gap between fieldworkers like himself and the academics at home, assuring his audience: "I have cautiously abstained from putting forth any theory founded upon mere conjecture, or weak premises, and I earnestly solicit close and searching investigation from all available sources; and that the facts and evidences obtained may be placed before competent philologues and ethnologists."[97]

The Presbyterian missionary John Mathew also demonstrated a longstanding commitment to diffusionist theory that shaped his contributions to the study of Aboriginal Australian languages. This was a commitment that cost him scientific respect even as it underlined his missionary vocation. Using terminology from the old Aryan debates, Mathew concluded that Dravidian influence was clear in the Aboriginal languages he studied. He was "taking it for granted that the cradle of the human race was in Asia whence all the nations have radiated like successive swarms from a parent hive."[98] But much had changed in the sciences of linguistics and ethnology since the heyday of Aryan diffusion theories. A lively debate ensued in the prominent British journal *Nature* where Mathew's work was reviewed at length by Professor A. C. Haddon of Cambridge. After a critique of Mathew's diffusionism, especially his use of linguistic evidence for a Dravidian presence in Aboriginal Australian ancestry, Haddon (like Ray and others) denounced the "absurd and misleading" use of comparative linguistics as a philological methodology. The gulf was widening between professionals like Haddon and amateurs like Mathew: "Mr. Mathew belongs to that school of Australian pseudo-philologists who believe that a likeness of words in sound and meaning is a proof of common origin."[99] His review concluded with a metropolitan sneer:

> The present writer has endeavored to give a fair summary of the views held by Mr. Mathew, but it appears to him that the author has not fully appreciated the complexity of the problem which he has set himself to solve. It is also evident that Mr. Mathew has not had access to a number

96. Samuel Ella, "Dialect Changes in the Polynesian Languages," *Journal of the Anthropological Institute of Great Britain and Ireland* 29, no. 1/2 (1899): 165.

97. Ella, "Dialect Changes," 166.

98. Mathew, "Australian Aborigines," 382.

99. Alfred C. Haddon, Review of John Mathew, *Eaglehawk and Crow: A Study of the Australian Aborigines, including an Inquiry into their Origin and a Survey of Australian Languages* (1899), in *Nature* 61, no. 1574 (29 December 1899): 194.

> of works that bear upon his subject; some excuse in this respect must, however, be granted to students who reside in the Colonies.[100]

In a letter to the editor of *Nature*, Mathew defended his argument by focusing on the terminology "Papuan" and "Melanesian," claiming that his linguistic definitions had been misunderstood by Haddon. Apart from that, he declared, there was "little more in [Haddon's] notice that needs to be referred to, as he concedes my main positions."[101] A similar critique by Ray in the *Journal of the Royal Anthropological Institute* hit a more sensitive nerve, and Mathew referred to it in his letter in *Nature* as "unnecessarily caustic" and based on "gross misrepresentation of my statements." He countered that Ray

> uses language, and language alone, as a basis of classification for proving racial distinctions and affinities and movements. I do not say that this was an improper use of the linguistic argument, but it differs from mine in this, that I rarely rely upon language alone. I back up the linguistic evidence by that of other ethnological characters.[102]

Unlike Ella, Mathew was refusing to recognize the hardening boundary between professional and amateur ethnographers, arguing instead that detailed scientific observations were what mattered. He compared his use of diffusionist theory to that of "one of the most competent authorities on the Oceanic languages," namely the Reverend Dr. Macdonald of the New Hebrides Mission. As we know, Macdonald was convinced that Malay, Melanesian, and Polynesian languages had a common origin in ancient Hebrew, and he too had been pointedly critiqued by Ray and others. Both of these missionaries objected strongly to having their scientific credentials questioned, yet both were working to obvious theological priorities in a changing scientific climate. As for Mathew, he concluded his impassioned response to Haddon by quoting another unnamed reviewer of his book in the *Saturday Review*: "If Mr. Mathew has not proved his theories to the satisfaction of all his readers, it is not from lack of knowledge or scientific methods, but from the imperfection of his materials."[103] Mathew, delighted to have his scientific reputation affirmed, was convinced that time and further research would bear his theory out.

A different approach to sacred philology can be found in the work of

100. Haddon, Review of Mathew, 195.
101. John Mathew, Letter to the Editor, *Nature* 62, no. 1614 (4 October 1900): 549.
102. Mathew, Letter to the Editor, 549.
103. Mathew, Letter to the Editor, 550.

Anglican missionary Charles Fox, a member of the younger generation at the Melanesian Mission who took Ray's work as their starting point. In a paper read to the Auckland Institute in 1906, Fox used Ray's "The Common Origin of the Oceanic Languages" to sketch out the current linguistic division of Oceanic languages—namely, Indonesian, Micronesian, Melanesian, and Polynesian. Ray had argued, successfully in Fox's view, that Oceanic languages had developed in stages of which Polynesian was the latest. Fox, however, wished to take up the point about their common origin. He included a sophisticated critique of the question of borrowing, using the example of Copland King's dictionary of the Oceanic language spoken on the northeastern coast of British New Guinea at Wedau, Wamira, and Divari. To speak of the words common also to the Banks Islands as elements or borrowing would be wrong, Fox warned, since the words were simply drawn from the common stock. He was equally careful concerning the traditional extension of philology to ethnology, drawing in part on Robert Codrington's skepticism on the subject:

> Whether the Polynesians of the Eastern Pacific are a race resulting from the mixture of a dark Melanesian people with traders from the mainland—a race who spoke the language of their Melanesian mothers rather than that of their foreign fathers—or whether the two races are distinct and one has imposed its language on the other (if this be credible), is really not a question for the student of languages. How it happens that people so different in physical features speak languages which are branches from a common stock he cannot tell.[104]

Although Fox had clearly found Ray's work convincing, he had his own theological priorities. Fox was a diffusionist and his scientific skepticism about too much readiness to talk of linguistic borrowing did not rule out his own quest for a common origin of Pacific peoples. He believed that the linguistic patterns in much of the western Pacific "point to ancient settlement and long isolation" whereas the eastern Pacific had been more recently settled. He drew on the research of New Zealand scholar Edward Tregear to conclude that

> vocabularies which at first sight appear to differ are found to show real agreement. The discovery of a fair number of common words might be explained by trade intercourse, but it is difficult to see how the same word

104. Fox, "Comparison of Oceanic Languages," *Transactions of the Royal Society of New Zealand* 39 (1906): 466. Fox was citing Robert Codrington, *The Melanesian Languages* (Oxford: Clarendon Press, 1885), 33.

occurring at different levels of language in different islands can mean anything but origin from a common stock.[105]

In a paper read in 1909 to the Wellington Philosophical Society on Oceanic Comparatives, Fox concluded that "some comparisons made at first without hesitation are seen to be wrong ones, while many comparisons formerly unthought-of can now be safely made." Phonetic change was particularly vexing:

> no comparison should be made of words whose forms are different unless the difference can be explained according to well-known phonetic laws. One might suppose this caution hardly needed, but it is, in fact, generally ignored. One need only quote a sentence from "Maori and Polynesian": "The Aryan ra (to rest, to be delighted, to love) . . . [i]s not far off in origin from the root la (to yearn for or desire), which appears in Sanskrit lash (to desire). . . . It seems much the same as the Maori reka (pleasant), and, in the other sense of 'calm,' as in the Maori whakaruru (sheltered from the wind)." Such comparisons may easily be a source of confusion.[106]

Fox concluded by saying that only a careful study of both Pacific languages and Pacific social anthropology would be able to convince skeptics that "there were true Aryan and Semitic words in the original Oceanic language."[107] As long as this theory was proclaimed through sloppy research and analysis, he warned, it would continue to be ridiculed by scientists.

For some researchers, no stretch was too great to prove the ultimate unity of trans-Pacific languages. At the close of the nineteenth century the Canadian ethnographer Charles Hill-Tout was laboring to prove linguistic connections between Polynesian and coastal Indian (First Nations) languages. Originally trained in theology in England, Hill-Tout had migrated to British Columbia as a schoolteacher. An article in the Australian journal *Science of Man* reveals the traces of sacred philology in Hill-Tout's determination to make the broadest possible linguistic connections between geographically separated groups. He provided plenty of detailed grammatical analysis to demonstrate affinity, such

105. Fox, "Comparison of Oceanic Languages," 472. Tregear published wide-ranging research on the New Zealand Maori, but Fox would have been particularly interested in *The Aryan Maori* (Wellington: Government Printer, 1885).

106. C. E. Fox, "Oceanic Comparatives," *Transactions of the New Zealand Institute* (1909): 1. He was referring to J. Macmillan Brown's *Maori and Polynesian: Their Origin, History and Culture* (London: Hutchinson and Co., 1907), a classic example of "Aryan" linguistic theory extended to ethnology in general.

107. Fox, "Oceanic Comparatives," 8.

as a common use of prefixes and verbal particles, declaring that this "takes the question of an Oceanic origin for the Salish beyond the bounds of conjecture and renders the explanation of 'accidental coincidence' impossible."[108] In a much longer paper, presented to the Royal Society of Canada, Hill-Tout lamented the "disfavor with which this view is held by some of our eastern Americanists," noting the astonishing navigational achievements of the Polynesians and wondering: "Might not [they] or some of [their] companions have visited our shores"?[109] Both Hill-Tout and his linguistic theory have vanished from academic sight, although the question of where Polynesian explorers might have landed would become a major scholarly preoccupation later in the twentieth century.

Meanwhile, sacred philologists were convinced that time would prove them right. In one of his articles for *Science of Man*, the Presbyterian missionary Daniel Macdonald declared that "it is to be expected that the Semitic relationship of the Oceanic family of languages will be fully established in the opening years of the 20th century, just as the inter-relationship of the Indo-European languages was established in the opening years of the 19th."[110] This confident statement turned the usual narrative of progress on its head. Instead of an early sacred philology being replaced by secular professional linguistics, Macdonald was convinced that rising secular interest in his subject would eventually vindicate his views. Missionaries were proud of what they believed to be the ongoing scientific importance of their work. From Fiji, Thomas Williams had praised the dictionary and grammar compiled by his colleague David Hazlewood, "upon which the Bopps and Grimms of Germany will look with respect, for its philosophical accuracy and completeness, at the same time that they eagerly drink up its precious philology," and he compared this accomplishment with that of the Methodist mission in southern Africa, especially the work of John Appleyard on Kafir grammar published in the same year as Hazlewood's.[111] The networks of empire helped Pacific missionaries to feel connected to an

108. Charles Hill-Tout, "A Comparison of the Polynesian, or Oceanic Languages, with Those of British Columbia," *Science of Man* 1, no. 7 (22 August 1898): 159.

109. Charles Hill-Tout, "Oceanic Origin of the Kwakiutl-Nootka and Salish Stocks of British Columbia and Fundamental Unity of Same with Additional Notes on the Dene," *Transactions of the Royal Society of Canada* 4, no. 2 (1898–99): 188–89.

110. Daniel Macdonald, "Grammatical Relationship of the Oceanic Family of Languages: Their Formative Terminations," *Science of Man* 5, no. 3 (1902): 54.

111. Thomas Williams, *The Islands and their Inhabitants*, ed. George Stringer Rowe, vol. 1 of *Fiji and the Fijians* (London: Alexander Heylin, 1858). Williams was referring to John Whittle Appleyard, *The Kafir language: comprising a sketch of its history; which includes a general classification of South African dialects, ethnographical and geographical: remarks upon its nature: and a grammar* (King William's Town: Printed for the Wesleyan Missionary Society, 1850).

international world of comparative science. For Lorimer Fison, one of the next generation of missionaries to Fiji, the task was to combine scientific and religious priorities. He defended missions from a scientific point of view, praising "they who give an alphabet to a savage tribe, who make a spoken language a written one, who ascertain its grammatical construction & the rules wh. govern its combinations."[112] However, this utilitarian contribution was not the most important aspect of missionary anthropology. Fison emphasized that through their research missionaries "add link after link to the chain of evidence, now possibly approaching completion, which form[s] the truth of that grand Bible Proposition 'God hath made of one blood all nations of man to dwell on all the face of the earth.'"[113]

A complex symbiosis of othering and brothering was at the heart of these scientific projects, demanded by theological anthropology. In his work on biblical translation, Lamin Sanneh has emphasized its ancient imperative: "the destigmatization of Gentile culture by adopting that culture as a natural extension of the life of the new religion."[114] The quest for human unity remained an enduring priority for missionaries, a quest that could not have proceeded without indigenous partners. This partnership generated a matrix of translation activity with multiple motives and tangled legacies, but what was clear, even to their sternest critics, was that missionaries were the most strongly motivated linguistic researchers in the early twentieth century. Sidney Ray realized that scientific debate depended on encouraging their research output, calling for more money to subsidize the work and publish the results: "There is a great danger of this accumulation being lost," he lamented, "as neither in Australia nor in England is the importance of its preservation realized."[115] Here the salvage approach to anthropology was supporting missionary scientific activity: a marriage of convenience by which the urgency of brothering, expressed by sacred philology, kept diffusionist theories under debate for an extended period of time.

112. Lorimer Fison, "Press copy book: Sermons, articles and letters, 1867–1873," f. 365, Lorimer Fison Papers, ML B591, CY Reel 1360, Mitchell Library, Sydney, Australia.

113. Lorimer Fison, "Press copy book: Sermons, articles and letters, 1867–1873."

114. Lamin Sanneh, *Translating the Message: The Missionary Impact on Culture*, 2nd ed. (Maryknoll, NY: Orbis Books, 2009), 1.

115. Sidney Ray, "The Past, Present and Future Study of the Languages of the Pacific Islanders," *Proceedings of the Pan-Pacific Science Congress* (Melbourne: Government Printer, 1923), 219.

CHAPTER 5

Contemporary Ancestors?

In a small mission schoolhouse in Fiji, a Methodist teacher was leading the children through a Fijian version of the well-known hymn "I Have a Father in the Promised Land" when he ran into unexpected difficulties. All was well until the children reached the verse beginning with "I have a brother in the Promised Land." At that point all the girls fell silent and hung their heads with evident shame. The girls sang the next verse with gusto—"I have a sister in the Promised Land"—while the boys looked embarrassed and refused to sing.[1]

Recalling this incident years later, Methodist missionary Lorimer Fison explained that the teacher had not known about the traditional prohibition on sisters speaking about brothers and vice versa. Fison's own theory was that the incident pointed "to a time when intercourse between brother & sister, which had been commonly practiced, was forbidden by some authority powerful enough to enforce the most stringent regulations to put down the practise."[2] By Fison's day, social evolutionary theories were prompting the study of contemporary "savages" in order to gain supposed insight into prehistoric humanity. But missionaries had their own practical reasons for needing to understand local kinship systems, as Fison's story of the mission school choir demonstrates. Missionaries helped to invent the modern study of social anthropology, but they engaged with scientific debates on their own terms. They needed to acknowl-

1. Lorimer Fison, "The Kinship System," Rev. Lorimer Fison, "Press copy book: Sermons, articles and letters, 1867–1873," ff. 478–79, Lorimer Fison Papers, ML B591, CY Reel 1360, Mitchell Library, Sydney, Australia.

2. Fison, "The Kinship System," ff. 478–79.

edge both the alterity of non-European social systems and also their place in an ultimate human kinship.

By the later nineteenth century, missionaries were engaging in scientific debates about a stage of "promiscuous" sexual intercourse in prehistoric human societies. Lewis Henry Morgan, who would collaborate so extensively with Lorimer Fison and other missionary ethnographers, had proposed an evolutionary scheme beginning with promiscuity; then a communal family (incestuous in modern terms); the barbarian family, in which brother-sister intermarriage was no longer officially approved; the patriarchal family, featuring polygyny; and finally the civilized family, with its roots in property law and the associated need for primogeniture.[3] Other anthropologists were debating the various stages and terminologies of kinship, and rival classification systems dominated the literature into the early twentieth century. Not all anthropologists agreed that kinship terms reflected actual social relations. For example, Morgan's approach was criticized by British theorist John McLennan who believed that classificatory terms were merely forms of address: titles or salutations that revealed nothing about either current or prehistoric marriage and family relations.[4]

Missionary ethnographers received requests for field data to support various theories on the subject. In 1881 Edward Tylor, the Cambridge anthropologist, wrote to George Brown at his mission in New Britain to seek information on marriage regulations. "It would be interesting to know if in New Britain there are festivals where the young people see one another," Tylor wrote, "and whether there are any traces of a more promiscuous state of things having once prevailed before it was limited by marriage laws."[5] Some anthropologists began using the term "group marriage" to describe an intermediate state between promiscuity and monogamous marriage as understood by modern Europeans, and Brown published his observations on this subject in *Melanesians and Polynesians*, noting that on New Britain, Duke of York, and New Ireland there were two exogamous classes. Intermarriage banns, cannibalism restrictions, matrilineal class descent, and other features might suggest group marriage, but Brown warned that he had never found any evidence of its current practice.[6] In his

3. George Stocking, *After Tylor: British Social Anthropology 1888–1951* (Madison: University of Wisconsin Press, 1995), 18–19.

4. John McLennan, *Studies in Ancient History: comprising a reprint of Primitive Marriage* (London: Macmillan, 1886), 269–76.

5. Edward B. Tylor to George Brown, 23 September 1881, Rev. George Brown, "Scientific and Ethnological Papers, 1877–1917," ML A1686–22, CY Reel 2765, Mitchell Library, Sydney, Australia.

6. George Brown, *Melanesians and Polynesians: Their Life-Histories Described and Compared* (London: Macmillan and Co., 1910), 28.

section of *Kamilaroi and Kurnai*, the work on Australian social anthropology that he coauthored with A. W. Howitt, Brown's Methodist colleague Lorimer Fison noted that

> it is very difficult for the men of our times to understand marriage in the group, which is something new, even in ethnology. Marriage among civilized races is so entirely different from this, that it is not easy for us to recognize marriage in the group as a form of the marriage relation.[7]

This lack of recognition had prompted some early explorers in Australia to make much of what they perceived to be indiscriminate sexual intercourse among Aboriginal people. Edward John Eyre's *Expeditions of Discovery into Central Australia* (1845) was a widely published example. So alarmed was Eyre by what he observed that he described it in Latin to keep its lurid details from reaching beyond academic circles:

> Cui foemina sit eam amicis libenter proebet. Si in itinere sit, uxori in castris maneti aliquis supplet illi vires. Adversis ex longinquo accedentibus foeminas ad tempus dare hospitis esse boni judicatur. . . . Senioribus mos est, si forte gentium plurium castra appropinquant, viros noctu hinc inde transeuntes, uxoribus alienis uti, et in sua castra ex utraque parte mane redire.[8]

"Women prostitute themselves throughout the course of almost their entire lives," Eyre had written, "he who has a wife readily offers her to his friends, and when he's on a journey, somebody makes good the absence of his virile strength for his wife, who stays in the camp. When outsiders arrive from far off, it's considered the mark of a good host to give women on a temporary basis."[9] There was more: "Young girls starting from the age of nine and boys from the age of twelve or thirteen have sex with each other" after a special signal was given to the group for this purpose. "It can easily be understood that the love between spouses can hardly be great when everything pertaining to women is arranged at the discretion of the men and there's such laxity in the relations of the sexes,

7. Fison and Howitt, *Kamilaroi and Kurnai* (Oosterhout, NB: Anthropological Publications, 1967), 10.

8. Edward John Eyre, *Journals of Expeditions of Discovery into Central Australia* (London: T. and W. Boone, 1845), n. 76; Project Gutenberg <Gutenberg.net.cau/ebooks/e00048.html>, accessed 30 December 2013.

9. Christopher S. Mackay, "Translation of excerpt from E. J. Eyre" (unpublished MS, 2014). I am grateful to my colleague Professor Mackay for translating this passage for me.

and that young men, being given so many opportunities to satisfy their lust, won't have much desire for wives except as slaves."[10]

Scientifically informed ethnographers, argued Fison and Howitt, knew "that the freely-granted favors, which were naturally looked upon by [Eyre] as mere promiscuous intercourse, are strictly regulated by the laws of the class divisions."[11] They explained how group marriage resulted from this classification system: exogamous groups whose *potential* marriage relations were extended to the whole other group. If a man from group A could marry any woman from group B, all women from group B might be referred to as his wives. Missionaries had misunderstood the situation as often as explorers. Referring to the early period of British mission activity in the South Pacific, Fison observed that

> The missionaries who first went among the Polynesians were highly shocked at their immorality; but we know that a woman who was living with one man one day, and with another man the next day, was only following out the "Turanian," or even perhaps the "Malayan," family system which obtained with them.[12]

Fison emphasized that there was nothing promiscuous about this situation, warning his readers that

> we must dismiss from our minds our own notions of relationship. We are accustomed to think of it as a relation between individual and individual: but we must bear in mind the well-established fact that to the savage *the group is the individual*. Where we have any one person in our mind in considering relationship, he has in mind a number of persons, who collectively make up the group the relationship of which he has under consideration; and every one of those persons bears to all other persons in the tribe the relationship which his, or her, group bears to their respective groups.[13]

Because of his reflexive awareness of Eurocentric bias, Fison was particularly keen to show that some ancient European marriage regulations contained similar features. Such a connection would underline the unity of human family relations even as it called attention to the distance between ancient Europe and the contemporary South Pacific. Fison cited the ancient Greek historian

10. Mackay, "Translation of excerpt from E. J. Eyre."
11. Fison and Howitt, *Kamilaroi and Kurnai*, 53.
12. Fison and Howitt, *Kamilaroi and Kurnai*, 258.
13. Fison and Howitt, *Kamilaroi and Kurnai*, 90.

Herodotus's "Legend of the Minyae" in which the Minyae people came to Sparta from the island of Lemnos and "exchanged wives" with the Spartans.[14] Fison explained that the admission of the Minyae as a new clan among the Spartans required a ban on intermarriage among the Minyae. Spartan clans were exogamous; Minyae women had to marry members of a different clan, and vice versa.[15] He also noted the practice of tracing family descent through the female line in the Australian groups he had studied. As George Stocking has noted, of the two research partners, Fison and Howitt, "it was the mathematically inclined Fison who (despite his religious reservations) played the primary role of evolutionary theoretician."[16] The underlying motive was, as usual, the contradictory demands of othering and brothering in missionary ethnography. For Fison, evolutionary theory underlined human unity, at least to some extent. The language of cultural survivals or cases of arrested development could accommodate both the alterity of non-European societies and also the links between them and all humanity across time and space. Aboriginal Australians were contemporary ancestors whose social systems contained survivals from early stages of organization that Europeans had once shared.

This was why Fison was so disgusted by the racism that deterred some anthropologists from even considering the idea that Aboriginal Australians (or any other "savages") might have societies capable of generating insight into European history:

> There will always be a difficulty in our way if we persist in measuring the group with descent through females, as it is found among the lower savages, by that with which we are familiar among the Athenians and the Romans, or even by the group as it existed among our own forefathers. As reasonably might we measure the larva by the perfect insect, and refuse to acknowledge their identity because their forms are different.[17]

From the term "lower savages" to the assumption that historical European societies contained perfect forms of marriage, the othering in this extract is clear. Nevertheless, Fison's main purpose in making these comparisons was "to

14. Fison and Howitt, *Kamilaroi and Kurnai*, 70. Fison was working with a misleading translation, aggravating the problem. A current edition of Herodotus reads "The Minyans immediately set about marrying local women and arranging marriages between Lacedaemonians and the women they had brought from Lemnos." Herodotus, *The Histories*, ed. Carolyn Dewald, trans. Robin Waterfield (Oxford: Oxford University Press, 1998), 283.

15. Fison and Howitt, *Kamilaroi and Kurnai*, note on 70.

16. Stocking, *After Tylor*, 20.

17. Fison and Howitt, *Kamilaroi and Kurnai*, 158.

trace, by its uniformity, the operations of the human mind, in its upward progress from savagery to civilization . . . ."[18] A stress on the uniformity of humanity was motivating his search for forms of formal kinship across time and space in human history. As for the theory of an early promiscuous state, fieldwork had failed to provide any evidence of it, demonstrating for Fison "a type of that moral sense which binds together the elements of civilized society, and refutes the fallacious proposition stereotyped in the phrase, 'the thoughtless brain of a savage.'"[19] Once again, human unity was being underlined by mission anthropology.

A particular challenge for brothering concerned what Europeans considered to be incestuous sexual relations. For them, incest was defined by sexual activity, within marriage or not, between people who shared a forbidden degree of blood relationship. Legal prohibitions differed concerning cousin marriages in Europe and North America, but the bans on marriage (and therefore sex) between parents and children, or brothers and sisters, were ancient and consistent. Confusion arose when these terms and concepts were brought to bear on Pacific peoples. Did they condone incest, or were brothers and sisters defined in ways very different from Europe's emphasis on biological relationship?

This chapter opened with the story of a Methodist teacher in Fiji whose students were obviously reluctant to speak (or even to sing) the terms "brother" or "sister." For Lorimer Fison, this reluctance had reflected the cultural memory of a remote time when incest between biological brothers and sisters was prohibited: "a moral obligation, to break which would be the most shameful crime a man could possibly commit."[20] This initial prohibition, he assumed, had generated the exogamous social structures which fascinated him and so many other missionaries. On New Britain in the western Pacific, Fison's fellow Methodist Benjamin Danks observed the strict avoidance of incest as defined by membership in one or other of the two exogamous classes of the island:

> No man may marry a woman of his own class. To do so would in the old times bring instant destruction upon the woman, and, if not immediate death to the man, his life would always be in jeopardy . . . . The relatives of the woman especially would be so ashamed that only her death would satisfy them.[21]

18. Fison and Howitt, *Kamilaroi and Kurnai*, 7.

19. Fison and Howitt, *Kamilaroi and Kurnai*, 12.

20. Lorimer Fison, "The Kinship System," Rev. Lorimer Fison, "Press copy book: Sermons, articles and letters, 1867–1873," ff. 478–79, Lorimer Fison Papers, ML B591, CY Reel 1360, Mitchell Library, Sydney, Australia.

21. Benjamin Danks, "Women and Marriage Customs in New Britain," ed. Wallace Deane, CY Reel 3465, Mitchell Library, Sydney, Australia.

In more recent times, if a man was accused of sexual relations with a member of his own class "he would at once be acquitted by the public voice" because she belonged to his own group, and this fact "was reckoned sufficient to preclude the possibility of any liaison between them."[22] In other words, the idea of inter-class sexual relations was so abhorrent that nobody would ever violate the ban, and allegations to the contrary must necessarily be false. Danks also noted an inner regulation that prevented close blood relations from marrying even if the exogamy rules technically allowed it. He gave the example of two brothers of one class who married women from the other group. Their children would take their class membership from their mother, making it technically possible for one of the brothers to marry his niece:

> But there is a great repugnance to such unions among the natives of New Britain, and in one case where such a marriage was brought about the natives with whom I conversed upon the subject utterly condemned it. This public feeling against such marriages is the inner regulation to which I have referred.[23]

This was all very well, but early LMS missionaries had recorded examples of biological brother-sister marriage in Hawaii and it was clear that no such concept of inner regulation was involved. William Ellis had observed that "among the higher ranks, marriage seems to be conducted on principles of political expediency, with a view to strengthen alliances and family influence,"[24] a readily understood principle for Europeans like himself. The Hawaiians, however, permitted brothers and sisters to marry, a practice "so revolting to every idea of moral propriety, that the mind is shocked at the thought of its existence."[25] Ellis was surely aware of examples of brother-sister marriage from the ancient Mediterranean world, notably ancient Egypt, but his point here was to emphasize distance between modern European morality and that of the yet-unconverted Hawaiians. Ellis and his colleagues were invited to advise the council of chiefs concerning a betrothal recently approved on Maui. The chiefs argued that "being the highest chiefs in the islands, they could not marry any others who were their equals," in other words, no-one else of sufficiently high rank was available other than a sibling. The resulting marriage would ensure that the highest possible rank was passed down to the next

22. Danks, "Women and Marriage Customs in New Britain."

23. Danks, "Women and Marriage Customs in New Britain."

24. William Ellis, *Polynesian Researches, during a residence of nearly eight years in the Society and Sandwich Islands*, 2nd ed., vol. 4 (New York: Henry G. Bohn, 1859), 435.

25. Ellis, *Polynesian Researches*, 435.

generation.[26] The missionaries countered on three fronts: "that such marriages were forbidden in the word of God"; second, that they "were held in abhorrence by all civilized and Christian nations"; and finally that they "had seldom been known to leave any descendants to wear the honor or sustain the rank the contracting parties desired thus to perpetuate."[27] The Christian and pagan chiefs alike found this pragmatic third point to be decisive, having observed themselves that few living or healthy children had ever been born to brother-sister spouses. The Maui marriage was postponed, and Ellis believed that this would "produce moral feelings highly advantageous,"[28] although it seems likelier that political expediency was the guiding principle at work.

Decades later, Lorimer Fison cited Ellis's account to support his theory that, for most Pacific peoples, the creation of exogamous classes had originated as a form of opposition to marriage between biological siblings. Instead of articulating this opposition in the biological terms of blood relationship, however, it was expressed through forbidden relations between classes of kindred. Confused Europeans had talked of promiscuous or "mindless" relationships in the Pacific world because they failed to understand that indigenous prohibitions on incest could be just as real as western ones:

> To accuse savages of immorality because they are not moral according to our code of morality is both unreasonable and unjust. We can judge the quality of an action only by bringing it to the standard with which we are acquainted; and no more can be expected of any man than that he regulate his conduct by the law of right which is within his knowledge. As far, at least, as the inter-sexual regulations are concerned, this is done with all strictness by the Australian tribes, excepting those who have become demoralized by their contact with a civilization which, while teaching them to disregard their own moral code, neglected to teach them a better one.[29]

Reluctance to speak about brothers or sisters, and other forms of social avoidance, had arisen out of the strength of these indigenous moral codes. In an essay on the Aoba people of the northern New Hebrides, Arthur Webb of the Melanesian Mission noted that brother-sister avoidance was enforced with particular strictness after marriage: "They must not meet under any circumstances after the relationship is realized, but also the sister may not eat any food

26. Ellis, *Polynesian Researches*, 435–36.
27. Ellis, *Polynesian Researches*, 436.
28. Ellis, *Polynesian Researches*, 436.
29. Fison and Howitt, *Kamilaroi and Kurnai*, 102.

which bears her brother's name (a very real disability), nor may her husband risk taking home any food cooked by her brother."[30] For a married man even to mention his sister's name "is to insult her in a most atrocious way." Webb concluded that

> This rule [of brother-sister avoidance] was imposed, so it was alleged, because of cases of incest between brother and sister, and the name of one offender was given me. Later I shall mention a relaxation of this rule in connection with a secret society called Naqatu; and sometimes determined evil-doers will deliberately break the rule, to accomplish which involves a visit to the spot where a most notorious case of incest had taken place.[31]

Webb also explained the importance of clan group membership and its origin:

> There were two exogamous clans on Aoba, the Tagaro and the Merabuto, and local legend told of a wise old man who had created this dual system in the distant past, explaining that "provided every marriage was interclan all would be well." Any breach of this simplified rule is regarded with abhorrence, and the marriage is spoken of as a marriage that stinks.[32]

Some missionaries singled out the British anthropologist Sir John Lubbock for particular criticism with respect to the idea of incest or promiscuity through communal marriage in Pacific societies. Daniel Macdonald of the Presbyterian New Hebrides Mission noted that "to ascertain whether a man called 'father' is really the man's father, you have to ask if this is the father who begot him."[33] In his view, the notion "of a disgusting primaeval state of 'communal marriage' or beastliness" could not account for the obvious abhorrence of incest among Pacific peoples. Like Fison and others, he believed that indigenous prohibitions had originally been intended to *prevent* biological incest. Macdonald denounced Lubbock's claim "that after this supposed brutal herding system arose marriage by capture, and that this system of capture accounts for the restriction of intercourse between a mother-in-law and her son-in-law . . . the 'capture' hypothesis, like the human-brute communal hypothesis, is a mere imagination. . . . "[34] He

30. A. S. Webb, "The People of Aoba, New Hebrides," *Mankind* 2, no. 4 (1937): 76.
31. Webb, "The People of Aoba," 76.
32. Webb, "The People of Aoba," 75.
33. Macdonald, *Oceania*, 188.
34. Macdonald, *Oceania*, 189.

also denounced Lubbock's methodology, especially his use of travelers' narratives as data, and his tendency to string together bits of ethnography from around the world without providing appropriate context.

Lubbock was a pointed critic, among others, of Lewis Henry Morgan's scheme of human social development, meaning that Morgan's supporters were particularly vigorous in their mentor's defense. Howitt gave a valuable bird's-eye view of the current debate about incest and marriage relations in a paper to the Royal Society of Victoria in 1890. He dismissed the matriarchal theory of the German scholar Johann Jokob Bachofen who, "working altogether from a classical standpoint, elaborated a strange and somewhat grotesque hypothesis of a former universal gynecocracy." This theory had been based on the familiar theory of primitive promiscuity where rape was commonplace. Bachofen had "held that of old mankind was found in a condition of universal hetarism [*sic*], from which it was raised by the establishment of gynecocracy by women, as a continuous protest against the degradation to which man's superior physical powers had reduced her."[35] The British theorist John Ferguson McLennan had done little better in Howitt's opinion, having proposed polyandry as a development from an original state of marriage by rape. He noted that Sir Henry Maine had said that polygamy, not promiscuity, was the earliest state of social organization.

Howitt's colleague Fison blamed sloppy research methodology for Lubbock's erroneous theories, claiming that Lubbock's most influential book, *The Origin of Civilisation*, could have been "compiled by anybody who could afford to give an ordinary clerk a pound a week to make extracts from works on Savage Tribes in any good library."[36] Equally disturbing were statements about marriage (or its absence) made by Lubbock to question the moral capacity of some of the world's peoples. His notion of marriage by capture (i.e., rape) was bolstered by claims that "the lowest races have no institution of marriage."[37] As we have seen with regard to parenting and music, missionary ethnographers were always keen to underline human universals. Although non-European social organization and marital regulations might seem alien to European eyes, the complexity of such systems suggested a powerful grasp of morality, and therefore the ability to comprehend the gospel message.

Both Howitt and Fison emphasized the importance of taking indigenous informants seriously and of being prepared to question previously held assumptions. In a delightful anecdote Fison told how, during his research in Australia,

35. A. W. Howitt, "Anthropology in Australia," *Proceedings of the Royal Society of Victoria*, new series 3 (1890): 17.

36. Cited in Stocking, *After Tylor*, 25.

37. John Lubbock, *The Origin of Civilisation* (London: Longmans, Green, and Co., 1870), 50.

he struggled to understand how some marriages had been permitted despite appearing to break the exogamy rules. The answer lay in subdivisions within each of the exogamous groups, but meanwhile Fison was reproached for his ignorance by an Aboriginal woman he was questioning. "What for you stupid?" she exclaimed. She resented his insinuation that her own marriage was a forbidden one. Subdivisions linked to particular animals made it possible for marriages to take place between some members of the same class. After he had grasped the general concept, Fison had expected it to play havoc with the genealogies, creating a host of different descent lines, "but in point of fact it is not affected at all, the confusion being avoided by a very simple arrangement . . . since, in every case, the child takes its mother's totem, not that of its father."[38]

The European and North American theorists with whom missionaries were engaging were also drawing on the Christian Scripture, especially the Old Testament, for information about social anthropology in ancient Israel. At the New Hebrides Mission, Daniel Macdonald welcomed this anthropologizing of Scripture, and, given his abiding interest in Semitic diffusionist theories, this is no surprise. Macdonald noted that according to the Old Testament, Abraham had married his half-sister, Nahor married his niece, and Amram married his father's sister. "This was permitted, because they were not regarded as relations" according to the elaborate local kinship system, Macdonald explained, and this demonstrated "that there is reason to believe, apart from and along with what we find in Oceania, that in the ancient Semitic-speaking world (as, probably, in the ancient world very generally) children of the same mother were considered as more closely related than children of the same father but different mothers."[39] As usual, the main point was to emphasize human unity and the universal human potential for spiritual enlightenment:

> Our system—the monogamous system of Christendom—is not a development from the polygamous system, but a continuation of, or, under the light of divine truth and law and enlightened reason, a reverting to the primitive system; and, therefore, a more ancient than the polygamous system.[40]

Ancient truths about correct marital relations, as in the Garden of Eden before the arrival of sin, could be recovered in any part of the world, having

38. Lorimer Fison, "The Kinship System," "Press copy book: Sermons, articles and letters, 1867–1873," f. 449, Lorimer Fison Papers, ML B529, CY Reel 1360, Mitchell Library, Sydney, Australia.

39. Fison, "The Kinship System," 192.

40. Fison, "The Kinship System," 193.

originally been a shared part of the goodness of creation. These truths had nothing to fear from modern science; on the contrary, the development of historical-critical approaches to biblical study in the nineteenth century allowed theologians, ethnographers, linguists, and others to place biblical texts into their historical context, producing intense interest in the social world of biblical characters. Renewed interest in this subject in the 1970s "was heir to this long tradition rather than a radical break with past scholarship," despite loud claims to the contrary by twentieth-century scholars apparently unable to believe that the Victorians had reached such critical scholarly ground before them.[41]

For missionary ethnographers, the anthropologizing of Scripture simply created new and richer opportunities for exploring human universals. But for many Victorian Christians this enthusiasm for modern scientific methods was worrying. Prominent trials for heresy took place during this period. The Anglican bishop John Colenso, taking seriously the puzzlement of his Zulu translation team, published exegesis questioning the literal truth of population statistics and other assumed facts in the Old Testament.[42] In the Free Church of Scotland, William Robertson Smith's study trips to Germany, and later to the Middle East, armed him with the latest tools of higher criticism in order to explore the sociology of contemporary Semitic peoples, and he hoped to shed light on biblical times this way. Acquainted with the biblical research of McLennan and other British anthropologists, Smith was convicted of heresy in 1877 and ousted from his teaching post. His goal had been to get behind the often-baffling biblical texts in order "to get at the fundamental grounds of religion—in which had been planted the 'living seed of the Divine word,' preserved until 'the fullness of the time when He was manifested who transformed the religion of Israel into a religion for all mankind.'"[43] This was precisely the appeal of such work for missionary ethnographers, but anthropologizing Scripture remained risky and controversial in some Christian denominations. Some readers of Lorimer Fison's work were alarmed by the degree to which modern

41. Keith W. Whitelam, "The Social World of the Bible," in *The Cambridge Companion to Biblical Interpretation*, ed. John Barton (Cambridge: Cambridge University Press, 2006), 35.

42. Early parts of Colenso's seven-volume study, *The Pentateuch and book of Joshua critically examined* (London: Longman, Green, Longman, Roberts & Green, 1862–79), set off a firestorm of protest, and would bring worldwide Anglican bishops together at the first Lambeth Conference in 1867 to decide what to do with him. He was eventually acquitted of heresy. For context, see John Rogerson, "Social Anthropology and the Old Testament—Present, Past and Future," *Journal of the Anthropological Society of Oxford* 4, no. 1 (1973): 42–50, and Robert R. Wilson, "Anthropology and the Study of the Old Testament," *Union Seminary Quarterly Review* 34, no. 3 (1979): 175–81.

43. Cited in Stocking, *After Tylor*, 68. For more on Smith, see Gillian M. Bediako, *Primal Religion and the Bible: William Robertson Smith and His Heritage*, Journal for the Study of the Old Testament Supplement Series 246 (Sheffield: Sheffield Academic Press, 1997).

science informed his reasoning. Fison wrote to Howitt that a fellow Methodist missionary had told him that his mind "was 'greatly exercised on my behalf': he castigated me for 'using the language of the skeptical philosophers of our day.'" This unnamed missionary had his own theories, believing that indigenous kinship terms did not necessarily imply relationship:

> "Calling my brother's son *my son*," he wrote, "is merely raising him to the rank of my own son as a mark of respect to my brother." I should not like to hurt the poor man's feelings by publishing this & indeed it would be wrong to do so because he took some trouble to furnish me with information but I am strongly tempted to print it as a worthy companion to McLennan's System of Addresses.[44]

Both Fison and Howitt championed Morgan's theories against McLennan's; like their mentor, they took seriously the kinship terms and relationships explained to them by their indigenous informants rather than explaining them away as something else. For them, the peoples of the Bible could illuminate the study of contemporary non-Europeans, and vice versa.

Like Daniel Macdonald and others, Fison had discovered the relativity of incest in the context of exogamous clan organization and the tracing of descent through the mother in some Australian contexts. He also recognized its exegetical implications, noting that "the marriage of Abram with Sarai was of this class & even as late as David's time we note its influence still prevailing, though [incest] was distinctly forbidden by the Mosaic Law."[45] The matrilineal system he observed in Australia was perfectly logical on its own terms, as was that of Abram's day. Fison had discovered subdivisions in the exogamous classes he had identified among the Kamilaroi by consulting the work of Presbyterian missionary William Ridley, who had published linguistic work on the same group. Max Müller, one of Europe's best-known ethnologists, had sent a questionnaire to the governor of New South Wales asking for information about kinship systems and marriage regulations among Aboriginal Australians. The governor had sent the questionnaire to Ridley and, at Fison's suggestion, Ridley added detailed questions about class subdivisions. "His success was beyond my hopes," Fison reported, "he found that the four classes were subdivided with six others, each of which bore a totem as its distinguishing mark."[46] Without letting the con-

44. Lorimer Fison to A. W. Howitt, 10 August 1878, Lorimer Fison Project, Letterbook No. 6, PMB 1039/reel 4.

45. Fison, "The Kinship System," 451.

46. Fison, "The Kinship System," 452.

troversial question of totems detain us here, the most important aspect of this discovery was the way that it affected marriage but not descent. Marriages between forbidden classes could be permitted if the totem was different; children always took their mother's totem, leaving lines of descent unaffected. This was what permitted Fison to identify Abram's marriage with Sarai, as recorded in the Old Testament, as an example of the same type of system. The book of Genesis describes Abram (later Abraham) as the son of Terah and brother of Nahor and Haran. Sarai (later Sarah), Abram's wife, was his half-sister, the daughter of Terah by a different mother (Gen. 11:27). Abram lied at least twice about Sarai's status, claiming she was his sister but not his wife, and only when his deception was discovered did he admit that she was his half-sister. His motive seems to have been to exploit Sarai's sexual relationships with powerful local rulers including the Egyptian Pharaoh (Gen. 12:13, 17). Marriage with a half-sister was forbidden in the Britain of Fison's day,[47] but if one looked at the situation with Aboriginal eyes, no incest was involved. Because Abram and Sarai had different mothers, they were not kindred. As Abram himself explained, she was "not of my mother" (Gen. 20:12). "And so," Fison concluded, "here [in Australia] as elsewhere, that which seemed to be disorder falls into its place among the marshaled forces which have been working together in the accomplishment of one Great Design."[48]

This statement, and his observations about arrested development, remind us of the combination of horizontal and vertical engagement with Pacific cultures in the work of Fison and his fellow missionary ethnographers. The benefit of their adoption of Morgan's evolutionary scheme was clear: great horizontal trajectories could be traced across time and space to link human societies together around a concern for organized kinship and appropriate marriage partners. Nevertheless, connecting Old Testament times with contemporary Aboriginal Australian societies inevitably created a temporal axiology as well. Because it resembled those of the ancient Holy Land, the Kamilaroi system "appear[ed] to be an arrested development."[49] The Kamilaroi had failed to progress up the vertical evolutionary scale. If they were brethren, they were also backward ones.

Fison's analysis of the biblical account of Abram and Sarai's marriage provides a powerful example of this double exposure. To connect Aboriginal Australian practices with the great ancestral figure of Judaism was to proclaim a

47. See, for example, the "Table of Kindred and Affinity" in the Book of Common Prayer, <prayerbook.ca/resources/bcponline/kindred-and-affinity/>, accessed 6 January 2014.

48. Fison and Howitt, *Kamilaroi and Kurnai*, 314.

49. Fison, "The Kinship System," 453.

fundamental connection between the world's peoples while his diagnosis of arrested development indicated the distance between contemporary cultures.

Fison was a leading advocate for connecting anthropologically informed exegesis with similar studies of the classical world. In a letter to his fellow missionary anthropologist, Robert Codrington of the Melanesian Mission, Fison struggled to explain references to certain ancient Jewish institutions in terms of a matrilineal social structure; one that predated the current patriarchal system in place at the time the Scriptures were written down. The book of Joshua made reference to the establishment of "cities of refuge" to which someone who had killed another person by mistake could flee from "the avenger of blood" (Josh. 20:1–6).[50] References to these places of refuge were also found in an account of God's instructions to Moses, and they were further explained in Moses' instructions to the Israelites (Num. 35:9–15 and Deut. 19:1–13). Of interest to Fison was the "avenger of blood" who, Fison believed, was "no awful public functionary, but simply the next of kin, on whom primarily the duty of the blood feud fell" as was the case in Aboriginal societies he had studied.[51] Once he had begun to think anthropologically about the Old Testament, Fison found that it also contained (for example) a number of references to daughters marrying their father's brother's sons; arrangements similar to those found in Solon's ancient Greek law code and also in some contemporary Aboriginal Australian societies. We will explore more of Fison's work on classical Greece shortly. Meanwhile, the point here is not to argue that Fison's analysis was correct, but instead to underline his commitment to scientific scholarship in the cause of brothering. Far from mistrusting current trends in exegesis, Fison welcomed them as a means of illustrating the unity of the human family, even if the expressions of that unity were scattered across time and space, and analyzed within an evolutionary scheme of lower and higher civilizations.

During the early nineteenth century, the German philosopher Goethe revived an earlier debate about the nature of color perception in ancient Greece in which the works of Homer and others were scrutinized for the presence or absence of words for the color "blue."[52] Debate about this matter persists today: "Developmental accounts of Greek color categorization—based on ideas of progression from a more primitive, incomplete or pre-modern system—are still at the core of contemporary approaches to the questions first raised by

50. Lorimer Fison to Robert Codrington, 7 January 1879; Lorimer Fison Project, Letterbook No. 6, PMB 1039/reel 4.

51. Fison to Codrington, 7 January 1879.

52. Selina Stewart, "The 'Blues' of Aratus," in *Beyond the Canon*, ed. M. A. Harder, R. F. Regtuit, and G. C. Wakker (Leuven: Peeters, 2006), 319–44.

Goethe."[53] Strikingly neglected, however, have been the contributions made by missionary linguists, especially in the work of CMS missionary William Colenso of New Zealand. Historians have been interested mainly in the late nineteenth- and early twentieth-century work of professional anthropologists with respect to connections between ancient Greece and contemporary "savages," neglecting the contributions of earlier linguists and ethnographers.[54] Like many missionaries, Colenso's work engaged with contemporary anthropological theories directly, and the results revealed the usual tension between othering and brothering.

By 1877, the former (and future) British Prime Minister William Gladstone had weighed into the debate about ancient Greek color perception. Gladstone argued that color adjectives and descriptions in Homer were "not only imperfect but highly ambiguous and confused," proposing an evolutionary theory by which human societies progressed through several stages from the perception of red and black to a stage that Gladstone believed Homeric times had reached when reds, oranges, and yellows could be distinguished, but not greens or blues.[55] This evolutionary scheme was disputed in the science journal *Nature* by William Pole, who thought instead that "it was impossible not to see . . . how exactly" Homer's color perception "corresponds with what might be expected from the color-blind."[56]

One year later in New Zealand, at the September meeting of the Philosophical Institute of Canterbury in 1879, the Reverend James W. Stack had taken up the debate. The child of CMS missionaries, Stack was an Anglican priest, an ardent promoter of a distinctive Maori Anglicanism, and a defender of Maori land rights. Gladstone's article and Pole's counter-argument had already reached New Zealand, and antipodean scientists were keen to engage with the metropolitan debate. Stack approved of Gladstone's evolutionary thesis, using examples of Maori vocabulary to claim that, in the Maori language before European con-

53. Barbara A. C. Saunders, "Linguistic Anthropology," *American Anthropologist* 101, no. 3 (1999): 658.

54. See Henrika Kuklick's work on W. H. R. Rivers and the Cambridge Expedition to Torres Straits in 1898; see Henrika Kuklick, "Islands in the Pacific: Darwinian Biogeography and British Anthropology," *American Ethnologist* 23, no. 3 (1996): 611–38. For a more detailed analysis, see Jane Samson, "Do Savages Get the Blues? William Colenso and the Nineteenth-Century Colour Debate," in *Webs of Words: New Studies in Historical Lexicology*, ed. John Considine (Newcastle: Cambridge Scholars Publishing, 2010), 65–76.

55. W. E. Gladstone, "The Colour-Sense," *The Nineteenth Century* (October 1877): 366. For more on Gladstone's fascination with Homer see David W. Bebbington, *The Mind of Gladstone: Religion, Homer, and Politics* (Oxford: Oxford University Press, 2004).

56. William Pole, "Colour Blindness in Relation to the Homeric Expressions for Colour," *Nature* (24 October 1878): 677.

tact, "blue was not formerly recognized, as no word exists to represent it." Stack concluded that Maori "appear to have reached the third stage of color-sense development, when all at once the arrival of Europeans revealed to them the entire scale of colors possessed by the highest races of mankind."[57] In other words, pre-contact Maori had been at the same level of color perception as the ancient Greeks of Homer's day. This outraged CMS missionary William Colenso: how dare Stack claim that contemporary Maori were at a more primitive stage of color perception than contemporary Europeans? In a booklet he wrote to accompany the New Zealand Exhibition of 1865, Colenso had already commented on Maori color vocabulary. "Their colors, it is true, were mainly divided into three distinctive classes—ma, pango, and whero, (white, black, and red,—or, light, dark, and reddish)—but they were never at a loss with these three words clearly to express all colors" by referring to them in various combinations and employing a range of adjectives. Additionally,

> if a New Zealander wished to convey to another a very exact idea of any color intended, he would mention that of some natural object which was of the same shade of color;—for greens, the karaka leaf, or the blue-green of the sea, or the light-green of the young grass or the yellow glancing green of the plumage of the little parroquet;—for blues, the differing blues of the day, and of the night sky, or of the pukepoto mineral, or of the neck of the red-billed swamp bird Pukura, (Porphyrio melanotus).[58]

There was no question, then, of an inability to perceive either green or blue; the Maori simply described these colors in ways different from European norms. Perhaps they were ahead of Homer. Following Stack's publication, Colenso wanted "to do the old Maoris justice" by offering a paper of his own to the Hawke's Bay Philosophical Institute (of which he was president) in October 1881. Having lived in New Zealand since the 1830s, traveling extensively and living for prolonged periods with Maori (the usual basis of missionary claims to anthropological expertise), Colenso claimed a unique knowledge of the language of the "old Maoris." He recalled how "each tint or shade of color bore its own peculiar name plainly and naturally, or figuratively, and sometimes both," giving a range of examples.[59] The expressiveness of the Maori language, and the Maori appreciation of the beauty of the natural world, had produced a

57. James W. Stack, "Notes on the Colour-Sense of the Maori," *Transactions and Proceedings of the Royal Society of New Zealand* 12 (1879): 156, 158.

58. William Colenso, "On the fine Perception of Colours possessed by the ancient Maoris," *Transactions and Proceedings of the Royal Society of New Zealand* 1 (1868): 36–37.

59. Colenso, "Perception of Colours," 49, 51.

sophisticated color palette. "The principal proper terms for colors were often compounded ingeniously and beautifully," he noted, and "certain colors took their own proper intensives, etc., which could not be used with other colors."[60] He reminded his audience that in his published work on Maori astronomy, he had been the first European scholar to publish the Maori "proper name for the intense blue sky—*kikorangi*."[61]

Maori had developed new words to describe the different shades of blue they encountered for the first time in European cloth, and Colenso had also observed the anglicization process that had introduced the term *puuru* (the Maori pronunciation of the English "blue"), "which (. . .) inevitably became fixed, and drove the pure Maori equivalents—figurative and comparative—out of the philological field."[62] Long lists of terms for colors and hues were included to support his claims. In an addendum to his paper, Colenso provided a detailed critique of Stack's claim that Europeans were a higher race because they possessed a more specific vocabulary for the color blue. Grist to Colenso's mill was Stack's table of color terms drawn from the Old Testament. As we know, anthropologically minded missionaries were enthusiastic about mining Scripture for ethnographic data. Stack had referred to the Greek *Septuagint*: a translation of the Hebrew scriptures created for the use of Greek-speaking Jews dispersed around the ancient Mediterranean. In Exodus 25:4, for example, the word *uakinthon* was translated by Stack as blue.[63] Colenso countered that a range of classical Greek sources used this term to indicate other dark colors as well; scholars were uncertain whether or not the original Hebrew could readily be translated as blue. He quoted from the work of the German philologist Max Müller:

> As no conception is [alleged to be] possible without a name, I shall probably be asked to produce from the dictionaries of Veddas and Papuas any word to express the infinite; and the absence of such a word, even among more highly civilized races, will be considered a sufficient answer to my theory. Let me, therefore, say once more that I entirely reject such an opinion. . . . The infinite was present from the very beginning in all finite perceptions, just as the blue color was, though we find no name for it in

60. Colenso, "Perception of Colours," 56.

61. Colenso, "Perception of Colours," 67. It is not yet clear to which publication Colenso was referring. No other paper by him published by the Royal Society of New Zealand contains this term. It cannot be his *Maori-English Lexicon* because this was not published until 1898. Specimen pages of the *Lexicon* were presented to the New Zealand Parliament as early as 1880, but this does not answer Colenso's claim to have brought the term "into early notice."

62. Colenso, "Perception of Colours," 69.

63. Stack, "Notes," 157.

> the dictionaries of Veddas and Papuas. The sky was blue in the days of the Vedic poets . . . but though they saw it they knew it not by name; they had no name for that which is the sky's own peculiar tint, the sky-blue.[64]

In Colenso's opinion, Stack had no right to speak of "the highest races" having "the entire scale of colors" in contrast to non-Europeans.

Stack's rather crude argument had led the debate away from the sophistication of Gladstone's original argument: Europeans had *not* possessed a full color perception in the past, developing it only relatively recently. Colenso also made another point that later anthropologists would ignore to their cost. Stack, following the conventional opinion of the day, had believed that "the Maoris have never shown any real appreciation of floral charms," citing this as further evidence of their defective color perception. Europeans had often accused "savages" of lacking an aesthetic appreciation for nature. Why, Colenso demanded, did both Maori men and women wear wildflowers in their ears or hair? Why did they plant and train shrubs and vines? Rather than cutting down the trees near their settlements, they chose to travel miles to collect timber. They might have been astonished at the first European flower gardens, planted in New Zealand with imported seeds, but not because they were incapable of comprehending their colors or appreciating their aesthetic charms. Instead, argued Colenso, "being a practical people, a true race of hard-working agriculturalists, they were astonished at such waste of labor, good ground and fences, in non-productive plants."[65]

Colenso was highlighting a significant methodological problem: the conflation of contemporary Maori language and culture—naturally influenced by contact with *pakeha*—with the state of things in pre-contact times. He contested Stack's claim that the Maori terms for color could be readily ascertained, and here we encounter some typical missionary sensitivities: resentment about claims made concerning their indigenous flock, and internecine conflicts among the missionaries themselves about whose translation work or lexicography was definitive. Colenso argued that the reference works used by Stack were inadequate and his knowledge of them confused. Archdeacon Maunsell had not translated the Bible into Maori, as Stack had claimed. The New Testament was translated before he arrived by William Williams, later Bishop of Waiapu, as were the Psalms and other parts of the Old Testament. Maunsell added to and coordinated existing work under Bishop George Selwyn's direction. Stack had claimed that Maunsell was forced to invent Maori terms for green and

64. Cited in William Colenso, "Addendum," *Transactions and Proceedings of the Royal Society of New Zealand* 14 (1881): 480–81.

65. Colenso, "Addendum," 483.

blue because the Maori were "in a state of progression" too primitive to possess appropriate color vocabulary.[66] On the contrary, said Colenso, the quickness with which Maori adopted new terms for colors and hues confirmed the ability to distinguish, appreciate, and name unfamiliar colors brought to New Zealand from Europe. Stack had been misled by his sources. Now he was misleading others. Colenso called for accurate research to be conducted by those (like himself) who were critical and scientific in their methodology

> in the interests of our English and European philological and physiological writers (as Max Müller, Herbert Spencer, Darwin, Tylor, Lubbock, etc.), who, in the prosecution of their studies and researches, naturally look to such a volume as our New Zealand Institute "Transactions" for correct information re the Maoris: and to allow such erroneous notions and statements, however innocently made, to remain unchecked, would never do.[67]

Colenso's main motive for entering the debate was to demand respect for the integrity and sophistication of the Maori culture and people. In an earlier chapter, we have already considered the reflexivity of his methodology of *kenosis* (self-emptying) as a means of understanding the Other. Any such approach is inevitably incomplete, but it was in the context of the color debate that Colenso most clearly articulated his scientific methodology, telling how

> the Maoris of my early days in New Zealand (following out the long-established habits and customs of their forefathers) could receive and communicate knowledge among themselves; and happy was that missionary or teacher who could empty himself, as it were, of his foreign ideas and ways, and thus go with them after their manner in seeking to impart truth: all such always found willing hearers. Ideas must be given through something; and the old Maoris could only receive teaching in and through modes of thought that were natural to them. For it is not the mere use of terms, but the sense in which they are used and received that must be considered. It is a fallacy, though both a natural and a common one (and one into which Mr. Stack in his paper has fallen) to confuse the image with the things signified, like mistaking the color of a substance for its true nature; but the old Maoris always steered clear of this.[68]

66. Colenso, "Addendum," 478.
67. Colenso, "Addendum," 484.
68. Colenso, "Perception of Colours," 70.

In his pioneering 1969 study of missionary linguists in New France, Victor Hanzeli warned that "most scholars, in making their often tangential and undocumented comments upon the linguistic labors of the early missionaries, simply repeated the critical commonplaces which have customarily been directed against all pre-nineteenth-century linguistic research."[69] These critical commonplaces continue to be powerful. In a contribution to *Missionary Linguistics*, Hilary Carey presented a sophisticated, nuanced study of the linguistic research of Lancelot Threlkeld, an early nineteenth-century LMS missionary to Australia. She notes the academic neglect of missionary linguistics in general, highlighting the myth of "long-running hostility between those who have sought out the peoples from all ends of the earth in order to bring them to Christ, and those who have sought to increase scientific knowledge. The scientific and the religious projects have, inevitably, clashed."[70] However, as we have seen, far from clashing with scientific projects, missionary anthropologists engaged with them enthusiastically, often considering themselves superior to the distant academic theorists of Europe or America.

Amid the New Zealand color debate, we can glimpse a process of occlusion that—deliberately or not—allowed the rising profession of anthropology to believe that its work was unprecedented. The Cambridge Anthropological Expedition to Torres Strait was led by A. C. Haddon, Cambridge University's first full-time anthropologist. Other members of the team included psychologist W. H. R. Rivers. Rivers had been studying color vision in the UK and along with his metropolitan equipment, Rivers also brought a metropolitan prejudice against antipodean science in general, and missionary science in particular. In the introduction to his essay "Colour Vision" in the expedition *Reports*, he noted the Gladstonian debate about Homer, and he cited the work of other European philologists and linguists, but he failed to mention the most relevant Pacific-based research.[71] Rivers believed that an article by Adolf Bastian in 1869 had been "the first to call attention to the color language of savage or barbarous races in its bearing on the controversy," yet Colenso's first contribution to this debate was made in 1868, a year before Bastian's article was published in Europe. It seems inexplicable that by 1898 Rivers had also remained unaware of Colenso's lengthy articles on color perception in *Transactions and Proceedings*,

69. Victor Egon Hanzeli, *Missionary Linguistics in New France* (Paris: Mouton, 1969), 16.

70. Hilary Carey, "Lancelot Threlkeld and Missionary Linguistics in Australia to 1850," in *Missionary Linguistics*, ed. Otto Zwarties and Even Hovdhaugen (Amsterdam: John Benjamins, 2004), 261.

71. W. H. R. Rivers, "Colour Vision," in *Reports of the Cambridge Anthropological Expedition to Torres Straits*, vol. 2, *Physiology and Psychology*, ed. A. C. Haddon (Cambridge: Cambridge University Press, 1901), 48.

to say nothing of the earlier article by Stack to which Colenso had responded. Having neglected important contributions to the debate made by these antipodean scholars, Rivers repeated Stack's mistake of fifty years before by using older dictionaries to argue that the use of an anglicized word for blue (*puru*) proved the absence of any indigenous alternative.[72] This lacuna suggests a metropolitan bias so strong that it occluded Pacific-based research: a tradition of academic neglect that would obscure the scientific contributions of Pacific missionaries for generations.

In addition to scrutinizing Homer, both metropolitan classicists and missionary ethnographers were re-evaluating classical Greek drama in light of current anthropological debates.[73] John Lubbock's acclaimed work *The Origin of Civilisation* was into its third edition by the 1870s when Lorimer Fison challenged its conclusions concerning ancient Greek and Roman kinship systems and their place in the history of the family. He agreed with Lubbock that fruitful comparisons could be made between the ancient Mediterranean and current non-European societies, but deplored Lubbock's use of undocumented sources and unsustainable generalizations. Fison was sure that data from Australia could shed light on a particularly controversial aspect of the plays of Aeschylus and Sophocles: tragedians of Athens in the fifth century BCE whose works were iconic members of the classical canon. Significant logistical challenges hampered Fison's work: he had left England with a good stock of books, but the ship's captain had left his cases standing in water, and the precious volumes had all been destroyed. Fiji in 1878 had no bookstores or libraries, and its small European population featured few persons of classical education. Fison was sure that it was the plays of Aeschylus that he needed and he "sent 25 miles to Levuka [the capital of Fiji] for a copy," he told his friend and mentor Lewis Henry Morgan, "but Aeschylus dwelleth not in our metropolis. Our Colonial Secretary, to whom I applied, wrote back, 'From His Excellency down, not one of us has a copy.'"[74] Determined to produce a proper scholarly analysis, Fison began a

72. Rivers, "Colour Vision," 67, n. 8. Graham Richards's study of Rivers accepts uncritically Rivers's claims about the radical novelty of his color study, privileging the use of the latest British technological apparatus rather than looking deeper into the Pacific-based research already available; see Graham Richards, "Getting a Result: The Expedition's Psychological Research 1898–1913," in *Cambridge and the Torres Strait. Centenary Essays on the 1898 Anthropological Expedition*, ed. Anita Herle and Sandra Rouse (Cambridge: Cambridge University Press, 1998), 136–57.

73. For general background see John Edwin Sandys, *A History of Classical Scholarship*, vol. 3, *The Eighteenth Century in Germany, and the Nineteenth Century in Europe and the United States of America* (Cambridge: Cambridge University Press, 1908).

74. Lorimer Fison to Lewis Henry Morgan, 7 November 1878, Letterbook No. 6, Lorimer Fison Project, PMB 1039, reel 4. For an extended analysis of Fison's insights into classical Greek drama, see Jane Samson, "Cracking the 'Antigone Nut': Lorimer Fison, Social Anthropology, and

project that would help to reorient scholarly understanding of the classics, even if his particular contribution was occluded by most of the scholars who built on his work. He "had always looked upon the Greek & Roman organizations as outside of my special line of inquiry—or rather as too modern though in the same line," he confessed; "savages of the present day are more archaic than they."[75] Nevertheless, he wanted to try to solve the mystery of puzzling kinship terms in Aeschylus's cycle of plays *The Oresteia*, and eventually his mentor and friend Lewis Henry Morgan sent him a copy via Sydney. The age of steam was now making its own contribution to the debate, enabling Fison to check his formidable memory against the published text.[76]

Fison was interested in one of the best-known episodes in classical Greek drama: the trial of Orestes for the killing of his mother Clytemnestra. After his victory at Troy, the Greek commander Agamemnon had returned home to discover that his wife Clytemnestra was having an affair. Clytemnestra and her lover murdered Agamemnon, leaving Orestes obliged in law to avenge his father's death. He did so, but was pursued by the Erinyes, the "Furies" who pursued those who shed kindred blood. This blood relationship was shared between mothers and children as expressed by Aeschylus through the word *homaimos*.[77] The Erinyes had no quarrel with Clytemnestra because her husband was of a different clan (*haima*) and there was therefore no blood relationship between them. To quote Fison: "The whole gens was the body corporate, in whose veins flowed the common blood," and "the shedding of that blood by a member of the gens was something more than man-slaying. It was impious homicide—a vital injury inflicted on the body corporate by the one who was a part of that body."[78] Orestes

---

Classical Scholarship," in "Before the Field," ed. Helen Gardner and Robert Kenney, special issue of *Oceania* 86, no. 3 (2016): 278–93. Fison's delight in finding connections between Aboriginal Australian social organization and that of the Greek "cradle of civilization" should be set alongside the more familiar fear, as explained by Tom Griffiths in *Hunters and Collectors: The Antiquarian Imagination in Australia* (Cambridge: Cambridge University Press, 1996), 12, that Australia's living fossils, both animal and human, might degenerate Australia's European settlers.

75. Lorimer Fison to A. W. Howitt, 6 December 1878, Letterbook No. 6, Lorimer Fison Project, PMB 1039, reel 4.

76. Fison referred to the "Cambridge Texts," probably a reference to the "Cambridge Greek and Latin Texts" series. The distinguished Cambridge classicist Frederick Paley edited its 1858 and 1874 editions of the *Oresteia*, and one of these was likely consulted by Fison. References in this chapter are to Paley's translation as published by George Bell in the "Bibliotheca Classica" series: F. A. Paley, trans., *The Tragedies of Aeschylus* (London: George Bell, 1855). This edition provides notes in English on the text, allowing us to view Paley's commentary on the passages that Fison found particularly interesting.

77. F. Paley, *The Tragedies of Aeschylus* (London: Whittaker, G. Bell, 1879), 653.

78. Fison and Howitt, *Kamilaroi and Kurnai*, 123.

had claimed that a son's relationship to his father took precedence over other relationships. Under the goddess Athene's supervision, his case was heard by the Areopagus court, and its decision was rendered in favor of Orestes. Extended passages outlined the supremacy of patrilineal descent, outlining a theory of human conception that would endure for centuries in Europe. This view, championed by Apollo, claimed that mothers played no active role in engendering a child, merely incubating the father's semen instead.

Using the contemporary theory of anthropological survivals, Fison's remarkable contribution was to suggest that the trial of Orestes provided evidence of a time long before the fifth century BCE when descent had been reckoned through the mother rather than the father. He explained that the struggle of Lubbock and others to understand this was fundamentally flawed because their viewpoint was too Eurocentric. Fison believed that scholars needed to "set aside our own idea of 'blood relationship'" because in modern European thinking this relationship applied to both parents of a child. This had less to do with lines of descent than with marriage. Fison rejected the Eurocentric notions of theorists like Lubbock whose "views appear to be based upon our own idea of marriage as a contract between the parties" rather than as a link between kinship groups.[79] Lubbock and other metropolitan theorists had tended to privilege patrilineal lines of descent, failing to consider that European families might not always have taken this particular form. The Erinyes' fury made sense only if their authority came from a different assumption, namely that it was the mother, not the father, who shared blood kinship with offspring.

The standard lexicographical reference of Fison's day was Liddell and Scott's *Greek-English Lexicon*, and when we consider this in conjunction with Frederick Paley's comments on the text of the *Oresteia*, we can better understand Fison's radical insight. In the second (1845) edition, Liddel and Scott translated *homaimos* as "of the same blood, related by blood, Lat. consanguineus": a splendid example of the Eurocentric preoccupation with biological "blood relationship" that had confused generations of classicists.[80] Likewise, their translation of *haima* was "one of the blood or race."[81] This had misled even Paley, one of the greatest classicists of his generation, who found the declarations of the Erinyes to be so baffling that he dismissed them as mere "sophistry."[82] For Paley, the

79. Fison and Howitt, *Kamilaroi and Kurnai*, 127.

80. Henry George Liddell and Robert Scott, *Greek-English Lexicon*, 2nd ed. (Oxford: Oxford University Press, 1845), n/p. Fison was probably using either the fifth or sixth edition of this work, neither of which I could consult, but it makes no difference; the 1996 edition retains the same definitions!

81. Liddell and Scott, *Greek-English Lexicon*, n/p.

82. Paley, *Aeschylus*, 535.

dispute between Apollo and the Erinyes was nothing more than "a temporal and accidental disagreement."[83] For Fison there was nothing accidental about it: the disagreement revealed an alternative reckoning of kinship that was closer to some contemporary Aboriginal understandings than it was to current European ones, and when he sent his findings to Lewis Henry Morgan, the American anthropologist went "into a seventh heaven of rapture."[84]

Morgan's rapture increased when Fison turned his attention to another baffling passage in Greek tragedy, this time in Sophocles' *Antigone*. Persecuted for an incestuous marriage to his mother Jocasta, Oedipus of Thebes left his throne to his two sons. The brothers quarreled and were found dead. Oedipus's brother-in-law, Creon, ascended the throne, decreeing that only one of the brothers was to be buried with full honors. Their sister Antigone defied Creon by properly burying the other brother, Polynices, herself. Creon condemned her to death and she killed herself before learning that Creon had changed his mind. Meanwhile, Creon's wife and son (Antigone's fiancé) had also committed suicide. Creon's impiety had destroyed his family.

Fison was intrigued by the terminology explaining Antigone's relationship to Creon; a relationship that Creon described as *homaimonestera*, a term that had puzzled generations of classicists. It is unclear exactly which edition of *Antigone* Fison was working with, but R. C. Jebb's authoritative Cambridge edition of 1888 demonstrates the state of commentary shortly after Fison's discovery. The relevant passage at lines 486–489 reads "No! Be she sister's child, or nearer to me in blood (*homaimonestera*) than any that worships Zeus at the altar of our house,—she and her kinsfolk shall not avoid a doom most dire. . . ."[85] Jebb's note on the word *homaimonestera* illustrates his puzzlement: "She could be the child of no one nearer than a sister, unless it were of a mother or of a daughter. . . . All that [Creon] means is, 'my niece,—aye, or the nearest relation possible.'"[86] He admitted freely that this reading was unsatisfactory, adding that Creon's statement might simply be "a rhetorical hyperbole" and "the point is a nice one."[87] In a line of patrilineal descent, Antigone would not have been part of Creon's kinship: he was only her father's brother-in-law. Even matrilineal descent, if confined to biological blood relationship only, would not make her uniquely "nearer by blood." Convinced that his Pacific fieldwork could shed light on this

83. Paley, *Aeschylus*, xvi.

84. Lorimer Fison to A. W. Howitt, 5 June 1879, Lorimer Fison Project, Letterbook No. 6, PMB 1039, reel 4.

85. R. C. Jebb, *Sophocles: the plays and fragments with critical notes, commentary, and translation in English prose* (Cambridge: Cambridge University Press, 1883–96), 95–96.

86. Jebb, *Sophocles*, 95.

87. Jebb, *Sophocles*, 95–96.

mystery, Fison once again found himself without the original text to consult. He had no copy of Sophocles' plays and, as before, the Governor's library was no help. In a letter to his old friend Howitt, Fison confessed, "I have not a copy of the Antigone & cannot consult the context. This is a nut for you to crack as you journey on your lakes & have no Bishop to talk with, if you will be kind enough to exercise your wits upon it."[88]

In the end, Fison himself would crack the *Antigone* nut. The answer to the puzzle lay in a combination of biological matrilineal descent within a broader kinship system. Jocasta and Oedipus had been mother and son, but they were also members of the same *haima*. Based on what he had learned from Aboriginal Australians, Fison understood how the potential marriage partners of members of exogamous classes were determined from birth. If Sophocles' play was read with an Aboriginal understanding of kindred, the puzzle immediately resolved itself. Antigone was both the daughter of Creon's sister, and also his sister's son's daughter. Antigone therefore inherited a double strain of Creon's kinship: an aberration possible only through incest and relationship as understood in the Aboriginal sense. Adding another layer to this rich anthropological analysis, Fison explained the relevance of the Fijian *vasu* relationship between a man and his sister's descendants. Fijian noble titles could be inherited only through the mother and (as elsewhere in the Pacific) sisters had a special prominence in family relationships. A man's sister's son was *vasu*: a concept much more complex than the biological English relationship term "nephew." Fison explained that

> It [*vasu*] is a title of office, not a term of relationship. . . . The *vasu* has extraordinary privileges with regard to his uncle—i.e., his mother's brother and can make free with his property to an extent which would be unaccountable if we did not know the *vasu*-right to be a survival of inheritance through the mother, under which a man's sister's son becomes the heir, to the exclusion of his own son.[89]

This was the cracking of the *Antigone* nut: the idea that ancient Greek tragedians were presenting matrilineal and exogamous clan-based survivals in their plays. After all, incestuous royal relationships were hardly unknown in the ancient world, in the sense of biological brother-sister marriages as defined by European kinship terms. What was intolerable in *Antigone* was the fact that Oedipus and Jocasta were also kindred of the same clan. Their marriage was

88. Lorimer Fison to A. W. Howitt, 5 June 1878, Lorimer Fison Project, Letterbook No. 6, PMB 1039, reel 4.

89. Fison and Howitt, *Kamilaroi and Kurnai*, 12.

therefore an abomination in senses that the English word "incest" did not adequately describe.

Morgan was in raptures about all of this because his evolutionary theory of human social development had already enraged scholars offended by the application of Latin kinship terms like *gens* and *gentes* to non-European social organizations. In Fison's opinion, Sir Edward Tylor and the other indignant critics were "so full of the idea of the gens as it was when it became a political institution" in Europe that they were incapable of recognizing it in other forms. Likewise, they were blind to the insights available from non-European societies that, working in reverse, could shed light on classical scholarship. Fison invoked the authority of the field researcher: "those who have been able to take savage life as it is & to observe its organization" would be able to see at once why *gens* was more widely useful as an analytical term. Broadly comparative research across time and space would challenge European complacency: "To say that 'gens' is improperly applied to the [North American] Iroquois subdivisions because they are not precisely what the Roman gentes came to be, is to say that our 'family' is incorrect because it is not exactly what the Roman familia was."[90] Morgan himself was happy to confirm that the full implications for classical scholarship had never occurred to him before Fison's discoveries. In his Preface to *Kamilaroi and Kurnai*, the book on Australian kinship published jointly by Fison and Howitt, Morgan declared that the theory "of Mr. Fison seems to be as conclusive as it is original and complete."[91]

Fison himself relished the idea of a link to the European classical era from Fiji and Aboriginal Australia, but in a way that might surprise scholars such as Christopher Hagerman, who interprets similar links with British India as providing "a sense of control and mastery" that "supported notions of British superiority."[92] His approval of Aryan diffusionist theory was directly related to this quest for anthropological connections. "I am quite satisfied that the Fijians & other islanders in these Seas, will yet be acknowledged as kinsfolk of our Aryan ancestors," he told Howitt, concluding that "what mixture of blood [what]soever they may have taken in on their journeyings, they once dwelt in the same land with the Aryans, spoke the same language & had the same institutions. This is a fixed belief with me; & I believe they emigrated before descent through males became the law."[93]

90. Lorimer Fison to A. W. Howitt, 5 June 1878, Lorimer Fison Project, Letterbook No. 6, PMB 1039, reel 4.

91. Lewis Henry Morgan, "A Prefatory Note," in Fison and Howitt, *Kamilaroi and Kurnai*, 13.

92. Christopher Hagerman, *Britain's Imperial Muse: The Classics, Imperialism, and the Indian Empire* (Houndsmills, UK: Palgrave Macmillan, 2013), 3.

93. Lorimer Fison to A. W. Howitt, 10 October 1879, Lorimer Fison Project, Letterbook No. 6, PMB 1039, reel 4.

In a different letter he put it this way: "I am persuaded that we can trace the development of the intersexual relations from the Aryan Household upstream to the [Australian] Kamilaroi classes."[94] This talk of headwaters and streams reminds us of the othering present in Fison's work. Some cultures were flowing downstream while others had not moved much beyond the headwaters. Talk of survivals conveyed a similar impression of stagnation. Nevertheless, Fison enjoyed the offense taken "by those who cannot endure the thought that civilized men are the descendants of savage ancestors, whose experience was in all probability similar to that of the savages in our own day."[95] As he admitted to Howitt, "it never occurred to me that a question concerning Australian kinship would turn on a passage in a Greek play."[96] We can draw out the irony even more pointedly: European classical scholarship might turn on the insights provided by Aboriginal Australians. Fison told Howitt that his Australian fieldwork had forced him to look at his research in a new way. "When I was living here previous to my return to Australia & after Goldwin Smith first brought Morgan's work under my notice, I was always among 'descent-through-the-father' tribes [of Fijians]" and "supposed that what I had found was the general rule. I now find that its exception is far wider than I supposed it to be."[97] The offense caused to some scholars by comparisons between the classical European and contemporary non-European worlds underlines the radicalism of Fison's work, but, as ever, this radicalism was qualified by the other implications of evolutionary analysis. Sir James Frazer, the British folklorist and anthropologist of religion, wrote to Fison in 1904 about a colleague of his at Cambridge. Outraged after reading Fison's work on the *Oresteia*, Frazer's colleague had asked him to admonish Fison, urging him to remember "that the Greeks of Solon's day were 'not savages.'"[98] Fison was most indignant that anyone could think such a "monstrously absurd notion," explaining his point in a deliberately provocative way amid escalating Anglo-German tensions before the First World War:

94. Lorimer Fison to A. W. Howitt, 17 January 1879, Letterbook No. 6, PMB 1039, reel 4.

95. Lorimer Fison to Lewis Henry Morgan, 26 December 1878, Letterbook No. 6, PMB 1039, reel 4.

96. Lorimer Fison to A. W. Howitt, 6 December 1878, Letterbook No. 6, PMB 1039, reel 4.

97. Lorimer Fison to A. W. Howitt, 17 January 1879, Letterbook No. 6, PMB 1039, reel 4. For more on the importance of Aboriginal Australians to the development of social anthropology see L. R. Hiatt, *Arguments about Aborigines: Australia and the Evolution of Social Anthropology* (Cambridge: Cambridge University Press, 1996), and for a detailed examination of the role played by Fison and Howitt's work see Helen Bethea Gardner and Patrick McConvell, *Southern Anthropology—a History of Fison and Howitt's* Kamilaroi and Kurnai (London: Palgrave, 2015).

98. Lorimer Fison to James Frazer, 6 December 1904, "Rev. Lorimer Fison: Articles, letters & Misc. papers, 1873–1907," Lorimer Fison Project, PMB 1042.

> What we contend for, & what we still believe, is that there were in Attic society survivals in culture of the lower order from which advances had been made through many ages. We find similar survivals among ourselves at the present day. For instance, what is the attitude of the Kaiser & his nobles toward the men who are not [well] "born," but a survival in culture like that of the old S. Sea island chiefs towards the common folk?[99]

Here was Fison at his mischievous best, building provocative connections between "savages" and hallowed European traditions. His contributions, fully credited by Morgan, came at a time when even Oxford and Cambridge were beginning to acknowledge the validity of German historicism in classical studies. The classical world was being located "immanently in its own time and denied [its traditionally] transcendental status."[100] Johann Jakob Bachofen, for example, was also exploring the implications of matrilineal descent for the classics; an ardent Romantic, he hoped to enter the thought-world of ancient Greece by embracing the power of its mythology and "he was mercilessly massacred, consequently, in the academic journals."[101] Rarely read by classicists of his generation, Bachofen's work was unknown to Fison when the latter made his breakthrough discovery. Instead, even Morgan had acknowledged that the full implications for classical scholarship had never occurred to him, and Fison's discovery was "as conclusive as it is original and complete."[102] The debt to Fison was also acknowledged by Friedrich Engels who said that "the most essential contribution to our knowledge of the group marriage we owe to the English missionary, Lorimer Fison, who studied this form of the family for years on its classical ground, Australia."[103]

Meanwhile, the rise of new anthropological theories was challenging earlier evolutionary conceptions, to the regret of W. H. R. Rivers who admired the universalist approach of evolutionary social theory.[104] At the end of the nine-

99. Fison to Frazer, 6 December 1904.

100. Christopher Stray, *Classics Transformed: Schools, Universities, and Society in England, 1830–1960* (Oxford: Oxford University Press, 1998), 118–19.

101. Joseph Campbell, introduction to *Myth, Religion, and Mother Right: Selected Writings of J. J. Bachofen,* trans. Ralph Manheim (Princeton: Princeton University Press for the Bollingen Foundation, 1973), xl.

102. Lewis Henry Morgan, "A Prefatory Note," in Fison and Howitt, *Kamilaroi and Kurnai*, 13.

103. Frederick Engels, *The Origin of the Family, Private Property, and the State*, trans. Ernest Untermann (Chicago: Charles H. Kerr & Company Co-operative, 1902), 51. For a detailed analysis of the use of Australian ethnography by Engels see Helen Bethea Gardner, "From Site to Text: Australian Aborigines and *The Origin of the Family*," *Itinerario* 34, no. 3 (2011): 25–38.

104. W. H. R. Rivers, "On the Origin of the Classificatory System of Relationships," in *Anthro-*

teenth century, one of Fison's protégés, Baldwin Spencer, wrote scathingly about a piece of recent research on Aboriginal Australian social systems: "The [kinship] terms which he has invented are simply hideous," Spencer fumed, "and he writes as if Howitt & Fison & others had never done any work on classificatory system[s] in Australia."[105] By the mid-twentieth century even Marxist classicists like George Thomson (who knew his Engels) were lamenting the end of an era. The significance of classificatory systems, wrote Thomson, was "of considerable importance for the cultural history of the Indo-European-speaking peoples, because it shows that their tribal institutions were of the same character as those of other branches of the human race."[106] Fison would have been the first to agree, but, as Thomson noted, that whole area of research "has been so far neglected by recent historians, especially in [the USA], that most of them are not even acquainted with the results already obtained."[107] Out of fashion and out of mind, Fison and his contributions were forgotten until the history of anthropology began to be reassessed in the later twentieth century by George Stocking and others. Ironically, questions of evolution in social anthropology have resurfaced since the later twentieth century and "it is exhilarating to see that brilliant ideas such as those of Morgan, Fison and Howitt can rise from the grave, overcome long-held prejudice against historical reconstruction and evolutionary modeling, and take their place again in scholarly debate."[108]

---

pological Essays presented to Edward Burnett Tylor in Honour of his 75th Birthday Oct. 2 1907 (Oxford: Clarendon Press, 1907), 309.

105. Baldwin Spencer to Henry Balfour, 18 August 1898, Sir Baldwin Spencer MSS, AJCP Reel M2424.

106. George D. Thomson, *Aeschylus and Athens: A Study in the Social Origins of Drama*, 2nd ed. (New York: Haskell House, 1967), 27.

107. Thomson, *Aeschylus and Athens*, 3.

108. Garner and McConvell, *Southern Anthropology*, 275.

CHAPTER 6

Religion

The *Occasional Paper* of the Anglican diocese of New Guinea, celebrating the success of the mission in its 1920 issue, noted that "the Bishop objects to them [Papuans] now being classified as savages because so many of them are Saints."[1] Australia, Germany, and the Netherlands had competed for imperial territory in New Guinea, and by 1920 Australia had gained control of the former German colony under a League of Nations mandate. By that time western racial science was placing Papuans among the "lowest" of peoples in the scale of humanity, a view shared by most colonial administrators and settlers. Fear of the Papuan Other grew so toxic in the early twentieth century that, despite the infrequency of sexual assaults by Papuan men on white women, a *White Women's Protection Ordinance* was passed in 1926 to impose the death penalty not only for rape but also for attempted rape.[2] The point for missionary anthropologists, however, was always that "savages" were fully human and therefore (potentially) fully Christian. There could be no special alterity reserved for Papuans or any other indigenous group.

In his celebratory address, Bishop Gerald Sharp was pushing the theology of othering and brothering to its logical conclusion that Papuans could be saints: Christian exemplars across time, space, and race. No one else except indigenous Christians could enrich the Christian Church; imitation Europeans would lessen its richness:

1. Diocese of New Guinea, *Occasional Paper: News and Notes on the Work of the Church on the N.E. Coast of Papua* 63 (October 1920): 5.

2. Amirah Inglis, *Not a White Woman Safe: Sexual Anxiety and Politics in Port Moresby, 1920–1934* (Canberra: ANU Press, 1974); Chilla Bulbeck, *Australian Women in Papua New Guinea: Colonial Passages, 1920–1960* (Cambridge: Cambridge University Press, 1992).

> [Papuans] took things into their own hands as soon as they had the opportunity; and the priests of the Mission wanted to develop [the] native genius of race. Of course they did not know what that was going to be until they had seen it for several Christian generations. The Mission priests did not want the Papuan Christians to be Europeanized. They wanted them to develop on the lines for which God had made them.[3]

Twelve years later an event occurred that revealed the seriousness with which the Papuan contribution to being church was taken in the early twentieth century. When Dr. Cecil Gill, a white man, was ordained in 1932 it marked the first time "on which a Papuan priest—Stephen Maiorot—joined in the laying on of hands at the ordination of a priest of another race."[4] For variously colored hands to share in the transmission of the apostolic blessing was a sign of the willingness of white Christians to receive sacraments at Other hands and for the universal church to be shaped by non-westerners. There could be no more central expression of brotherhood. As usual, however, there could be no conception of brotherhood without an Other to embrace, and in their encounters with Pacific alterities, missionaries struggled to identify and therefore to contain the more flamboyant culture features they observed.

For example, when identifying some Pacific peoples as idolaters, missionary ethnographers were attempting to create both distance and kinship. Idol-worshipers were clearly religious Others, appropriate targets for mission work, yet firmly located within the familiar cultural geography of the Bible. Idolatry appears frequently in both the Hebrew and Christian scriptures, locating non-Jews in a narrative of potential redemption. Raised on Scripture, generations of mission ethnographers sought links between Pacific societies and those of the ancient Mediterranean world. Bishop M. Russell, whose popular book on Polynesia went through several editions during the nineteenth century, declared that "it requires no ingenuity to discover in the religious usages of the Polynesians such a resemblance to those of the other Asiatic nations as to afford the greatest probability that they sprung from the same source."[5] We will explore this alleged Asiatic connection in greater detail later. For now, it is important to note Russell's sources of information about Polynesian religious usages, namely the widely publicized adventures of LMS missionary pioneer the Reverend John Williams, the more detailed and nuanced ethnographic publications of Williams's colleague William Ellis, and the observations of other early mission-

3. New Guinea Mission, *Occasional Paper* 63 (October 1920): 5–6.

4. New Guinea Mission, *Occasional Paper* 93 (June 1932): 2.

5. Quoted in Gunson, *Messengers of Grace*, 207.

aries to Polynesian islands. Williams's popular account of early missions to the Society Islands reports the capture of "idols" as trophies. Based at Raiatea, Williams observed the mission boat returning from a preliminary expedition to Rurutu in 1821 "laden with the trophies of victory, the gods of the heathen taken in this bloodless war" and the subsequent service of celebration at which "the rejected idols were publicly exhibited from the pulpit."[6] Returning from a later expedition to Rarotonga in the Cook Islands, "as other warriors feel a pride in displaying the trophies of their victories," Williams and his shipmates "hung the rejected idols of Aitutaki to the yard-arms and other parts of the vessel" as they sailed into the harbor.[7]

This material culture of conquest, and the associated hoards of idols in missionary museums and other collections in Britain, seems to speak only of a silencing of the religious indigenous voice, but such scenes did not speak only of hegemonic colonial power. Nicholas Thomas has shown how such objects can be seen as "converted artifacts" that were "abstracted from their context in native worship and destroyed or displayed" while retaining a significance—even in their absence—that missionary observers did not necessarily understand.[8] They were sometimes discarded deliberately because they appeared powerless or, on other occasions, because they were believed to retain a power now considered to be dangerous. In the New Hebrides, Presbyterian missionaries James Gordon and H. A. Robertson described how they encouraged "the removal of 'idols'" from Christianized villages in the New Hebrides, and approved "when *navilah* [sacred stones] were abandoned by their owners."[9] When George Brown bought spears tipped with human bone in New Ireland, he was collecting evidence of savagery, but he was also accommodating himself to indigenous views of prestige and shame: to have refused to buy generously would have caused offense.[10]

Meanwhile, wider entanglements were revealed by missionary attempts to locate Pacific "idolatry" in the context of the ancient world. Too much alterity might question the effectiveness of preaching, and one way to embrace intellectually the significance of indigenous deities was to suggest their kinship with those of familiar ancient civilizations. For example, by seeing Pacific peoples as contemporary ancestors, missionaries could explain and control their otherness while, at the same time, affirming a universal human nature. The Methodist

6. John Williams, *A Narrative of Missionary Enterprises in the South Sea Islands* (London: John Snow, 1841), 12.

7. Williams, *Missionary Enterprises*, 28.

8. Thomas, *Entangled Objects*, 153.

9. Barbara Lawson, *Collected Curios: Missionary Tales from the South Seas* (Montreal: McGill University Libraries, 1994), 138.

10. Gardner, *Gathering for God*, 131.

missionary Reverend Arthur J. Webb recalled visiting a Fijian mountain village whose people had recently converted to Christianity. He obtained their collection of large conch shells: "the voices of the god and goddess of the place who were deities of war," apparently disarming their power by referring to their acquisition as a transaction: "I was able to purchase these curiosities and took them with me down the Waidina [River]."[11] Fijians had allowed Webb to buy these objects for reasons of their own. What happened next for Webb served a familiar ethnographic purpose:

> My lads amused themselves with sounding the gods when we came near to a village, and the people turned out in excitement to look at these dread powers, for the report of our bearing the shells preceded us. It was like the Egyptians running along the banks of the Nile to view their old Pharaohs floated down in charge of the archaeologists who had exhumed the mummy-cases.[12]

Webb's sarcastic use of the words "gods" and "dread powers" must not obscure for us the danger of his situation; the inland people were famously hostile to outsiders, and Europeans, including fellow Methodist missionary the Reverend Thomas Baker, had been killed in the interior. Webb needed protection badly if he and his lads were to amuse themselves in this way without joining their less fortunate predecessors. Webb disdained the "dread powers" while simultaneously counting on their influence to protect his landing party. Meanwhile, his Egyptian simile conveyed the power of imperial science, with its insatiable appetite for exotic artifacts, and its condescension about indigenous context. After all, contemporary Egyptians "running along the banks of the Nile" were unable to stop the ongoing flow of treasures to the museums of Europe. From his superior perspective, surrounded by the co-opted power of Fijian deities, the missionary collector presumed to interpret their story.

However, this did not necessarily produce "a generalized evangelical discourse that effaces difference by way of habitual moral condemnation."[13] Difference was essential, but so was brothering, and that involved much more than condemnation. Another Methodist, Benjamin Danks, compared New Britain islanders' reverence for banyan trees with the sacredness of certain trees in current Hindu spirituality and beyond:

11. Arthur J. Webb, "Observations on the Hill Tribes of Navitilevu, Fiji," *Report of the Second Meeting of the Australasian Association for the Advancement of Science* (Sydney: AAAS, 1890), 625.

12. Webb, "Observations on the Hill Tribes," 625.

13. Anna Johnston, "The Strange Career of William Ellis," *Victorian Studies* 49, no. 3 (2007): 492.

> in this tree-worship the New Britain man is liked to the savages of the whole world, also to the ancient civilisations, as revealed on the cylinders of Chaldes, some of which date back to 4,000 B.C., and in the folk-lore of many peoples, and still linger among us, as some assert, in our maypole and Christmas tree.[14]

By connecting "savages" with both an ancient civilization and current European folklore, Danks was simultaneously reinforcing both alterity and deep kinship. There are obvious othering strategies at work in his generalization about "savages of the whole world," but much more time is spent on connection-building. Danks's ethnography even included references to contemporary European spiritualism, giving the same name to some of the New Britain practices he observed. "There are no more faithful and ardent spiritualists in the world than the New Britain savage," he declared, after attending what he called a "séance" where "there was deep feeling and great expectancy on the part of the crowd, so much so that the murky atmosphere was charged with it, and under such circumstances one is not surprised that the devotees think they actually see what they came to see."[15] So might a skeptical observer have described a middle class drawing-room séance in late Victorian Britain.

The Presbyterian missionary Daniel Macdonald, one of the most persistent supporters of the Semitic Polynesian theory, was particularly eager to find idolatry in the western Pacific, where so many other missionaries claimed that no recognizable system of worship could be identified. The idea was not to efface difference by condemning idolatry everywhere; instead, Macdonald's goal, as usual, was to connect Pacific peoples with Mediterranean civilizations. His eye was clearly focused on the ancient Holy Land, as when he described an "idol" of the Efatese, "a pillar-like rock in the sea," whose shape was "that of the Anc[ient] Baal pillars."[16] Macdonald also identified as idols the carved wooden pillars erected in commemoration of powerful village men. These pillars featured faces and were "called narai nawot, the face of Wot, lit. 'of the Lord.' This, as far as the word Wot is concerned, might mean either the face of the chief (of the village), meaning the deceased chief, or the face of Wot—that is, the idol Wot. Most probably it originally meant that of the idol," concluded Macdonald.[17] He had to work hard to make these observations fit his theory, continuing: "The

14. Benjamin Danks, "Burial Customs—Mythology—And After Life in New Britain and Duke of York Island," ed. Wallace Deane, MOM 238, CY Reel 3465, folder 3, 7, Mitchell Library, Sydney, Australia.

15. Danks, "Burial Customs," 20.

16. Macdonald, *Oceania*, 168.

17. Macdonald, *Oceania*, 170.

Efatese bali ki Wota, fasted for, or to obtain the favor of Wota, made offerings or sacrifices to Wot, and worshipped Wot and other idols in a most elaborate manner by lectisternia."[18]

This technical term attempts to make a connection between the ancient Mediterranean and the contemporary Pacific even clearer. *Lectisternium* was the Roman version of an ancient Greek ritual whereby gods and goddesses, represented by busts or statues on divans, were honored at a public banquet.[19] Early Christians had adapted it as a feast for martyrs and other honored dead, creating an inviting connection for the brothering necessary to missionary work. Macdonald was particularly interested in what he believed to be parallels with the widespread cult of Baal. "The Ancient idea of Baal seems to have been as of the male principle of nature, and connected with the sun as the vivifying influence of the world," he declared, announcing that "there are distinct traces of sun and moon worship in the New Hebrides" as at Aneityum where he viewed a rock carving of the sun "represented by a rayed circle as in the ancient Semitic (Assyrian and Phoenician) monuments, and the moon by a half circle."[20] At Havannah Harbour he saw "a rayed circle easily recognized as the same as the sun circles on Aneityum, and it is called narai nawot the face of Wot—that is, the face of Baal, the sun-god."[21] With a few strokes of the pen, the chronological and cultural distance between the South Pacific and the ancient Near East was dissolved. This served to occlude differences between widely disparate cultures, to be sure, but it also created a trajectory of kinship that underlined human equality and dignity. If these Victorian missionaries failed to pursue what we would consider to be equality and dignity, that judgment must stand alongside a recognition of the dual imperatives of their theological anthropology.

Another missionary ethnographer keen to connect the Pacific world to biblical lands was William Ellis, one of the most sophisticated early ethnographers of the LMS. Speaking of Polynesian accounts of an ancient deluge, which he compared with the Old Testament story of Noah and the flood, Ellis noted that the stories resembled "not only the Mosaic" or scriptural story but also "those preserved by the earliest families of the postdiluvian world." This similarity "supports the presumption that their religious system has descended from the Arkite idolatry, the basis of the mythology of the gentile nations."[22] Contem-

18. Macdonald, *Oceania*, 171.

19. John Warrington, *Everyman's Classical Dictionary* (London: J. M. Dent & Sons, 1970), 313. Also see Matthew Leigh, "Ovid and the Lectisternium," *The Classical Quarterly* 52, no. 2 (2002): 625–27.

20. Macdonald, *Oceania*, 171.

21. Macdonald, *Oceania*, 172.

22. William Ellis, *Polynesian Researches, during a residence of nearly eight years in the Society and Sandwich Islands*, 2nd ed., vol. 2 (New York: Henry G. Bohn, 1859), 62.

porary readers familiar with the Old Testament would have recognized at once the importance of this: after the biblical flood, God had made an indissoluble covenant with Noah, promising never again to destroy the world. God then made Noah's sons into ancestors of the different human races. The diagnosis of idolatry is operating here both as a distancing and a kinship strategy. Ellis's phrase "Arkite idolatry" referred to the contemporary search for variations on the biblical flood story; as explained by contemporary scholars of mythology, "Arkites" could be found from the ancient Middle East to classical Greece and even among the British Druids.[23]

Here again is the "oriental Pacific" connected with the ancient Middle East and Asia. The published work of Richard Taylor of the CMS demonstrates the impact of the work of Max Müller and others on missionary ethnography about Pacific "Aryans." Comparisons with India were especially sought. "What *caste* is in India, the *tapu* was in New Zealand," declared Taylor:

> it held unlimited sway over their minds, and compelled obedience to its requirements. But it could not exist with Christianity. . . . No sooner had the Gospel obtained root in the land, than the power of the *tapu* was destroyed; the native mind became as completely emancipated from its thraldom as if it never had existence.[24]

By the 1860s, Taylor was working fully within the methodology of comparative philology, building on the classic orientalist scholarship of Sanskrit conducted by Müller and his predecessors. The idea of India as a transnational homeland was particularly well articulated by Müller who told British candidates for the Indian Civil Service that they were simply returning to their "old home," a home "full of memories" that proper anthropological training would enable them to understand.[25] The imperialism of such comments is clear: those seeking their "old home" were "returning" as colonizers. Nevertheless, there was no monolithic, all-powerful Aryan theory at work: debate raged into the twentieth century about exactly what linguistic, physical, and cultural connections

23. Jacob Bryant, *A New System, Or, An Analysis of Ancient Mythology* (London: Payne, White and Walter, 1774–76); William Holwell, *A Mythological, Etymological, and Historical Dictionary* (London: Fox C. Dilly, 1793); and Edward Davies, *The Mythology and Rites of the British Druids* (London: J. Booth, 1809).

24. Richard Taylor, *Te Ika A Maui: New Zealand and its Inhabitants* (Auckland: A. H. & A. W. Reed, 1974; first published 1850), 288.

25. Quoted in Christopher Pinney, "Colonial Anthropology in the 'Laboratory of Mankind,'" in *The Raj: India and the British 1600–1947*, ed. C. A. Bayly (London: Pearson, for the National Portrait Gallery, 1990), 253.

could be made between ancient India and the wider world. In New Zealand, some Maori scholars continued to favor a Semitic "lost tribe of Israel" ethnology while others, such as Sir Peter Buck, favored the idea of an Aryan Maori. The point for missionary ethnography was the benefit of both in connecting the Pacific world to the cradles of human civilization. Taylor found the Aryan theory compelling, but was interested in making all possible connections between the Maori and the peoples of the Bible. Like Macdonald he was fascinated by what he believed to be practices related to the ancient Hebrews. He noted one particular ritual in which a man, bound by a fern stalk, jumped into a river, untied the stalk, and let it float down to the sea along with the transgressions of the tribe. "Here again is another fragment of Scripture seen," concluded Taylor, "an evident allusion to the scape goat."[26]

Central to all of this was theological anthropology. Reading in the Book of Acts, missionaries noted Paul and Barnabas's words to the people of Lystra: "Nevertheless he left not himself without witness, in that he did good, and gave us rain from heaven, and fruitful seasons, filling our hearts with food and gladness" (Acts 14:17). Modern missionaries interpreted this to mean that all human beings were naturally capable of knowing God. The mission encounter with other cultures encouraged what later became known as fulfillment theology. Despite what the skull-measuring anthropologists and missing link theorists might be saying by the later nineteenth century, human unity and universal human spirituality remained essential articles of faith for missionary ethnographers.

In the Melanesian Mission, for example, Bishop Patteson was heavily influenced by the early modern Anglican divines and their emphasis on the universality of natural law, opening the door to accommodation tactics that would encourage the mission to adapt Christianity to Melanesian culture. David Hilliard has helpfully described this approach as a "reverent agnosticism" toward existing Melanesian beliefs.[27] Among the resulting features were the early ordination of Melanesian men to the diaconate and priesthood because, as Patteson wrote, "We must hope to see native self-supporting Melanesian Churches, not weak indolent Melanesians dependent always on an English missionary."[28] The voices of these early Melanesian clergy tell their own story of othering and brothering. George Sarawia, ordained deacon by Patteson

26. Richard Taylor, *Te Ika A Maui: New Zealand and its Inhabitants*, 2nd ed. (London: William Macintosh, 1870), 101.

27. Hilliard, "The God of the Melanesian Mission," 224, and see Sara Sohmer, "Christianity without Civilization: Anglican Sources for an Alternative Nineteenth-Century Mission Methodology," *Journal of Religious History* 18, no. 2 (1994): 174–97.

28. Cited in Delavan L. Pierson, *The Pacific Islanders. From Savages to Saints* (New York: Funk & Wagnalls, 1906), 181.

himself in 1868 and priest in 1873, was the first of a proud new generation of indigenous missionaries.

We have a small number of surviving letters by Sarawia, along with a translated autobiography, and a grubby envelope at Lambeth Palace Library in London featuring a few scribbled lines by Sarawia concerning the significance of confirmation. An explanatory note written by Sarawia's friend and mentor Robert Codrington states that Sarawia had been asked for his thoughts for the benefit of the current confirmation class of young Melanesian boys. Sarawia was already a deacon but, always self-deprecating, he titled his notes "From the Head Cook," a joking reference to the organization of students at the mission school into messes. Paper was in short supply in the islands, so a used envelope came in handy. Sarawia began with a tribute to Patteson, noting that of the fourteen boys who went back with the bishop to the first mission school in New Zealand, "seven of us have been baptized, six of us confirmed, and one not yet."[29] The main point Sarawia wanted to make, however, is a rich source of postcolonial theological analysis. "Bishop Patteson confirmed us," continued Sarawia. "We thought that this was good" because "We thought about the apostles of old, Peter & John, who laid hands [lit. 'touched'] on the people at Samaria who then received grace when the two of them put their hands on them. It was good to do thus."[30] Touching the head was a powerful gesture in this particular cultural context, but Sarawia's reference to the Book of Acts is also of deep significance. He was referring to the story in chapter 8 concerning the apostles at Jerusalem who "heard that Samaria had received the word of God" and sent two of their number, Peter and John, "who, when they were come down, prayed for them, that they might receive the Holy Ghost: (For as yet he was fallen upon none of them: only they were baptized in the name of the Lord Jesus.) Then laid they their hands on them, and they received the Holy Ghost" (Acts 8:14–17). The rite of confirmation involves the bishop laying hands on the head of each candidate and invoking the Holy Spirit, so this particular text is often read at confirmation services.

That, however, is not its main significance here. Later, in Acts 10, Peter is

29. George Sarawia to Robert Codrington, 21 November 1868, "From the Head Cook," Keble 8/7 (original Mota text). The papers contain several documents which provide partial or complete English translations of the text and in some versions the text appears to be a letter to Codrington rather than notes for confirmands. My current research project includes a fresh translation of the Mota original and an editing and comparison of the other texts. Meanwhile, the English quotations provided in the analysis above come from the 1991 translation made by Bishop Derek Rawcliffe, former bishop of the New Hebrides, in an unnumbered, undated note at the end of the Keble 8 file, Lambeth Palace Library, London.

30. Sarawia to Codrington, 21 November 1868.

preaching to the friends and family of the Roman centurion Cornelius and "while Peter was still speaking, the Holy Spirit fell upon all who heard the word. The [Jewish] believers who had come with Peter were astounded that the gift of the Holy Spirit had been poured out even on the Gentiles" (Acts 10:44–45). Here is the postcolonial gist of the text. There was considerable debate in the very early days of Christianity concerning whether or not Jewishness was an exclusive requirement. Peter, Paul, and other apostles began baptizing non-Jews, but not all Christians agreed with their approach. For Jewish Christians the inclusion of Samaritans was a particularly difficult question. Samaritans were despised as lapsed or defective Jews described variously in Scripture and other ancient sources as foreign colonists planted in Samaria by the Assyrian empire, or as traitors who betrayed and murdered "real" Jews, becoming the target of Judaean reprisals.[31] The New Testament reveals a range of attitudes toward Samaritans, but the account in Acts 8 is both one of the earliest and one of the most positive. Uniquely Other, even Samaritans were welcomed into full membership of the new Christian faith. Boundaries between communities were dissolving and those communities were being transformed.

While Sarawia was writing his reflections on this story, his fellow Melanesians were being recruited for work on plantations in Australia and Fiji, belonging to a race deemed inferior by contemporary imperial science. By 1901 the presence of Melanesians in Australia was so disturbing that legislation was passed by the new Commonwealth of Australia to expel them. The Melanesian Mission was proud of its role in bringing labor trade atrocities to light, often citing Acts 17:26 and one blood theology as its justification for challenging the racisms of the day. Sarawia himself wanted to remind other Melanesian youth about brothering: he (and they) had been touched, both in baptism and in confirmation, just as the Samaritan Other had been embraced by the early apostles despite a toxic history of mutual hatred. Patteson had hoped that the living witness of Melanesians would challenge similar boundaries in the world of nineteenth-century racism: "I notice gladly what different notions of a Melanesian lad people take away with them after only half an hour's visit to Kohimarama: and in Auckland very many persons have forgotten all about Papuans and wooly hair and black teeth, and think of the deep human feelings and sympathies which belong to us all alike."[32]

In Australia, European observers of Aboriginal peoples had also been ques-

31. See 2 Kings 17 and John J. Pilch, *A Cultural Handbook to the Bible* (Grand Rapids: Eerdmans, 2012), 73–75.

32. John Coleridge Patteson to [name redacted on original], 11 November 1862, Keble 8/5, Lambeth Palace Library, London, UK.

tioning human universals. Some, like David Collins the deputy judge-advocate, declared their opposition to standard religious opinion back in Britain, disagreeing "that no country has yet been discovered where some trace of religion was not to be found."[33] Broadly speaking, "the battle line was drawn initially and most sharply between Christians who supported missionary work and certain 'natural historians' or 'philosophers.'"[34] In the early Australian context, however, the line was drawn somewhat differently. For example, colonial chaplain the Reverend Samuel Marsden was famously skeptical about the possibility of evangelizing Aboriginal Australians, and instead spent his energies founding a CMS mission to New Zealand.

Even missionaries more enthusiastic about the Australian field could experience a profound intellectual and spiritual struggle before deciding that human universals still applied there. After his first six months near Perth in western Australia, Methodist missionary John Smithies announced that the local Aboriginal people were "universally ignorant of the true God, of their accountability, and consequent rewards and punishment, and as to false Gods and idols they have none at all and of course worship none."[35] He struggled to explain the "vague idea of immortality and transmigration," which he believed the local Aboriginal people to have,[36] but was more enthusiastic about their intellectual capacities. He could not "possibly perceive any physical or mental defect" despite the fact that "judging from the outward appearance we may be tempted to think that they are not of our race."[37] Smithies was adamant "that their mental abilities are good and equal in general to any children I have ever seen";[38] necessary optimism in a mission schoolmaster, of course, but also a sign of the demands of brothering. Religious beliefs might be difficult to discern by Europeans unfamiliar with Aboriginal languages and cultures. This underlined their alterity, but endorsements of their intellectual capacity affirmed the possibility of preaching the gospel to them effectively.

J. B. Gribble, an Anglican missionary in Australia, was particularly critical of those who regarded Aboriginal Australians as too spiritually primitive to absorb the Christian message. His manuscript autobiography refers to a sermon preached at Westminster Abbey claiming that *only* Aboriginal Australians lacked any concept of divinity. If the hapless Westminster preacher had bothered to visit Australia, Gribble fumed, he might have been "the first and

33. Cited in Gardner, "The 'Faculty of Faith,'" 261.
34. Gardener, "The 'Faculty of Faith,'" 261.
35. McNair and Rumley, *Pioneer Aboriginal Mission,* 159.
36. McNair and Rumley, *Pioneer Aboriginal Mission*, 159.
37. McNair and Rumley, *Pioneer Aboriginal Mission*, 159.
38. McNair and Rumley, *Pioneer Aboriginal Mission*, 159.

foremost to declare that the blacks of Australia are not destitute of religious ideas and that they, like all the other fallen children of Adam, are capable of redemption."[39] Gribble made a fundraising tour of England in 1884 during which he enjoyed standing ovations at Exeter Hall by preaching on this theme.[40] He insisted that Aboriginal cultures in South Australia featured a "pretty distinct conception of a supreme being," and "there is no doubt but that they are believers in a future [life]." This was essential for missionary work as

> I have proved again and again. Now the missionary goes amongst these people and finds existing amongst them certain religious ideas. . . . These to the missionary are so to speak foundation stone[s] upon which he may begin to erect his superstructure. The aboriginal mind entertains the idea that Bahami is an arbitrary being only delighting to annoy and punish mankind. This misconception of the Great Spirit the missionary seeks at once to remove and he does remove it by simply disclosing the loving character and purpose of the Almighty.[41]

Gribble added a fascinating comparative statement about missionary praxis: "it is far easier to convert an Australian aboriginal to Christianity than a Mahommedan, Hindo Buddist [*sic*]" because in those cases "they are prepossessed by religious ideas antagonistic to Christianity."[42] Aboriginal Australians were a different case. "The few religious ideas they have, though crude, are favorable to true religion," containing "nothing antagonistic." Gribble believed they were more easily converted than members of Asian religious faiths: "Their faith is that of little children. They simply believe the blessed story and are saved."[43] An Aboriginal Other that was childlike and credulous would indeed have made conversion easy, but Gribble's declarations were profoundly at odds with the statistics in his formal reports to the ABM. Converts were few, and expenses high. What Gribble was revealing in his statements about a receptive, childlike Other was his faith in Aboriginal humanity, wrapped up in colonial paternalism.

In his edition of LMS missionary Launcelot Threlkeld's papers, Niel Gunson noted that Threlkeld "was conditioned by the Calvinist belief in natural depravity and its corollory that all heathen religions were a debased form of the

39. J. B. Gribble, Box G2, folder 4/2, "Autobiography," 42, ABM, "Further Records, 1873–1978," ML MSS 4503, Add-on 1822, Mitchell Library, Sydney, Australia.

40. Christine Halse, *A Terribly Wild Man* (Crows Nest: Allen & Unwin, 2002), 11.

41. Gribble, "Autobiography," 34.

42. Gribble, "Autobiography," 35.

43. Gribble, "Autobiography," 35.

original patriarchal religion practiced before Moses received the Law."[44] This type of degeneration theory influenced a number of missionary ethnographers, including William Ellis and his diagnosis of Arkite idolatry in the Society Islands. Gunson also observed that Threlkeld's interpretation was "founded on a literal acceptance of everything in the Old Testament," including a firm belief "that some tribes lay outside the scheme of salvation."[45] This downplays the brothering present in Threlkeld's ethnography. Diffusionist theories linked ancient civilizations with contemporary indigenous peoples in order to create lines of kinship across time and space. After describing local reverence for two large, upright rock pillars, Threlkeld explained that the pillars were believed to be the transformed remains of two women who were beaten to death by an angry man. He wondered, "Has this tradition any reference to the transformation of Lot's wife into a pillar of salt, and which tradition like all other traditions when merely committed to memory, from generation to generation, become fabulous, like the silly traditions of the 'Roman Papacy'?"[46] There is plenty of Calvinism in these observations, but little evidence of an Aboriginal exceptionalism. By linking contemporary Aboriginal practices with the "fabulous" excesses of Roman Catholic ecclesiology, Threlkeld is embracing, as well as distancing, the Aboriginal Other. Threlkeld's anti-Catholic prejudice allowed him to argue that, however defective were their superstitions, both Europeans and Aboriginal Australians shared a common, human capacity for spirituality. Gunson is quite right to indicate that Threlkeld's views fall well short of today's cultural relativism: "The highest compliment which he could pay to Aboriginal religious beliefs was to compare them to 'Roman superstitions.'" Even this, he concludes, "was elevating them to a higher level of rationality than one would expect from him."[47] On the contrary: this kind of elevation is *exactly* what we should expect.[48]

Writing of the New Zealand Maori, Richard Taylor of the evangelical CMS believed that "in the universal existence of religious rites, there is also a strong evidence of the unity of the human race."[49] For him, ethnology *was* missiology:

44. Launcelot Threlkeld, *Australian Reminiscences and Papers of L. E. Threlkeld, Missionary to the Aborigines, 1824–1859*, ed. Niel Gunson (Canberra: Australian Institute of Aboriginal Studies, 1974), 8.

45. Threlkeld, *Reminiscences*, 9.

46. Threlkeld, *Reminiscences*, 64.

47. Threlkeld, *Reminiscences*, 8.

48. Also see Hilary Carey, "Death, God and Linguistics: Conversations with Missionaries on the Australian Frontier, 1824–1845," *Australian Historical Studies* 40 (2009): esp. 161–69.

49. Taylor, *Te Ika A Maui* (1870), 97.

> The fragmentary remains of Scriptural knowledge to be found amongst the different sections of our race in the most remote and distant parts of our globe, are satisfactory evidences of the same, and were missionaries carefully to collect and record them, they would render essential service to the establishment of truth.[50]

From Fiji, Wesleyan Methodist missionary David Cargill declared of indigenous religion that "like every other heathen mythology, it is absurd, contradictory, and deteriorating in its influence."[51] Things could not be left there, even though it proved incredibly difficult for Cargill and his colleagues to discern brotherhood with Fijians. His colleague Richard Lyth wrote that "the people here certainly carry their religion into every thing. O that it were a better religion. Alas, it sanctions all their vices, even the worst like Cannibalism."[52] But Lyth was also compelled to search for kinship and he did not believe that Fijians were outside the scope of salvation:

> It is well known that the Feejeeans have a tradition of a flood in which the tribe of carpenters were saved by floating on the water in a canoe. Mesake Kara says that he has heard of a tradition about Joseph & Mary. The old folks used to speak about it before Christianity was introduced amongst them, but he does not remember the tradition.[53]

Lyth was clearly aware of the question of contamination, or why take such care to locate the Joseph and Mary tradition before Christianization? Brothering was a priority, especially if it could establish links between Fiji and the biblical Holy Land. Lyth even used Scripture to contextualize Fijian cannibalism:

> Offering human sacrifices. Such are their Baolas, or human bodies for food. Before eaten they are presented to their gods. Tuiilaila [Tui K'ila'ila?] said 'Our god is an angry god, if we do not give him the Baola to eat he will kill us.' See Deut. XII 31 & note in Bagster [*Bagster's Comprehensive Bible*]. Cutting themselves & making themselves bald for the dead. This is a constant practice & also shaving off their beards which otherwise they wear long. This practice is forbidden in Scripture Deut: XIV.1. Eating

50. Taylor, *Te Ika A Maiu* (1870), 100.

51. *The Wesleyan Missionary Notices Relating Principally to the Foreign Missions*, new series 1, no. 30/31 (1841): 535.

52. Richard Burdsall Lyth, "Reminiscences," 49, MS B548, CY Reel 207, Mitchell Library, Sydney, Australia.

53. Lyth, "Reminiscences," 14.

> the blood of animals. The blood of no animal is poured out. The pigs are clubbed & even fowls are knocked on the head. This practice is a plain violation of Scripture Deut: XII.23.24 &c.[54]

This elaborate discussion of how Fijians did or did not keep kosher might seem laughable, but a serious point underlines it. The assumption was that Fijians were somehow connected to Torah and therefore to God's covenant with the Israelites: a recovery discourse that highlights both the Fijian as other—"heathen"—and as lost kindred who can be welcomed back to the family once reminded of their proper heritage. "Innumerable cases of this kind occur in Feejee noticed even by the heathens themselves," wrote Lyth, "for among them God has not left himself without witness."[55]

The ethnography of early CMS missionary Thomas Kendall identified Maori as "formerly acquainted" with the Semitic Middle East, and he observed their religious beliefs with an eye to diffusion theory:

> The longer I live here, and the more I go amongst the natives the more I am convinced that our track is neither more obscure nor less frequented than the track of the servants of God in other heathen lands: the religious superstitions in this country being in many instances similar to those which have been formerly in repute, if they are not now, in other parts of the world. May it not be supposed that the natives of New Zealand in their ideas concerning religion agree in many points with the ancient Egyptians? The circumstance of their acknowledging that every thing below, and all the . . . luminaries in the firmament above are the offspring of *Heena*, and that the stars are [parts] of departed souls puts one in mind of the "Queen of the Host of Heaven." Should it please God to restore my mind to a state of tranquillity [*sic*] as I trust he will, I perhaps shall be enabled in my account of the religious customs & manners of the people to give more substantial proof of the probability of the above remark.[56]

Kendall's convictions about Maori spirituality prompted him to search their vocabulary for an indigenous name for God. Believing that he had found it in the Maori divine name *Atua*, Kendall became the first missionary to publish a Maori vocabulary list in a religious primer, solidifying the identification of *Atua*

54. Lyth, "Reminiscences," 16–17.

55. Lyth, "Reminiscences," 83.

56. Thomas Kendall to Fraser Hall, 31 July 1822, "Thomas Kendall Letters, etc.," MS-0071, ARC 0031, Hocken Library, Dunedin, NZ.

with God. His list translated *Atua nue* as "the Supreme Being."[57] The practice sentences in the primer indicate that no attempt was being made to encourage Maori to use "Jehovah" or "God" even in their English-language work. Instead, they were invited to use *Atua* in every case, as in "good is the word of the great Atua to me" or "Iesus [*sic*] Christ is the Son of the great Atua" and "God is the name of the Great Atua."[58] In a complex process of cultural exchange, Kendall and his fellow missionaries were imposing their own interpretations on Maori words and concepts, a process clearly linked to unequal power relations. We cannot forget, however, that these British Christians were embracing a Maori name for God in preference to the names familiar from their childhoods.

Daniel Macdonald of the New Hebrides mission, that tireless promoter of the Semitic Pacific, published a paper a decade after Kendall's primer. It shows us how far the original decision to use the word *Atua* had become naturalized. Gone were doubts about the translation of this word, let alone doubts about whether it had ever been a word for God in the Christian sense. Macdonald took all of that for granted, seeking instead to prove that *Atua* was originally of Semitic origin; in other words, that Pacific peoples already knew the name of God from its original source in the Middle East. After comparing various words in Arabic, Hebrew, and other languages with Polynesian variations of *Atua*, he pronounced that there was an identification between *Atua* (originally *alua*) and the Arabic word *aluhat* (plural of *ilah*, or god). Macdonald concluded "that the Oceanic mother-tongue was an ancient Semitic dialect; [and] that its speakers had the same mythology and religion as the speakers of the other ancient contemporary Semitic dialects of the Semitic mainland. . . ."[59] By implication, English names such as Jehovah or God were less authentic, turning the usual axiology on its head. Indigenous vocabularies and mythologies might be more directly related to the original source than their European counterparts.

One of the Melanesian Mission's finest anthropologists, Walter Ivens, advised caution when generalizing about *Atua* as a term for God. His insights help to explain why his mission, next door to Macdonald's in what is now Vanuatu, made the choice to use the English word "God" in its Mota-language Scriptures and liturgy, even though Mota is an Austronesian language. Ivens argued that *Atua* was originally the combination of a personal article ("a") with the root word *tua* ("old" or "ancestor").[60] *Atua* held a range of meanings that Ivens sur-

57. Thomas Kendall, *A Korao no New Zealand; or the New Zealander's First Book; being an Attempt to compose some Lessons for the Instruction of the Natives* (Sydney: G. Howe, 1815), 9.

58. Kendall, *A Korao no New Zealand*, 23.

59. Daniel Macdonald, "The Polynesian Word for God and its Anthropological Implications," in *Proceedings of the Pan-Pacific Scientific Congress 1923* (Melbourne: Government Printer, [1924]), 263.

60. Walter G. Ivens, "The Polynesian Word Atua: Its Derivation and Use," *Man* 24 (1924): 133.

veyed across the available linguistic and anthropological research, concluding that "in etymology we must [be afraid] of allowing the applied meaning of a word to blind our eyes as to its radical meaning, and superimposed ideas or presuppositions must not be brought into the question."[61] The English word "God" leaps from the pages of Mota text generated by the Melanesian Mission, but its presence there was as much a decision of principle as was the attempt by Macdonald and his colleagues at the New Hebrides Mission to introduce *Atua*. Although some Melanesian islanders speak Austronesian languages, many do not, and in the early days of the Melanesian Mission Bishop Patteson, a noted linguist, decided against forcing any particular indigenous word out of context.[62] He also advised caution concerning tales about Qat, a figure honored with a special dance and head-dress on the island of Mota. At times islanders spoke of Qat as of a *vui*, or spirit, but at other times his activities suggest an incarnate human being. Rather than looking at Qat as a survival of some sort, he concluded that Qat had been a person, or group of people, who immigrated to Mota in the distant past.[63] Patteson reluctantly concluded that introducing the English word "God" was the best solution: "It is difficult to convey by description the ideas which ought to attach to the new word, but at least nothing erroneous is connoted by it."[64]

Even secular observers, such as the linguist and ethnographer Horatio Hale, could become captivated by the universalist implications of certain Polynesian words. Hale was part of the US Exploring Expedition to the South Pacific in 1838–1842, and he published a large volume of ethnography that Macdonald later used to bolster his own position: "Hale considers Maui as perhaps a name, originally, of God as Preserver and Sustainer of men."[65] Hale himself actually went further than this, declaring that religion in Polynesia

> is not the mere grossness of idolatry, for many of them have no images, and those who have, look upon them simply as representations of their deities, but it is a constant, profound, absorbing sense of the ever-present activity of divine agency, which constitutes the peculiarity of this element in the moral organization of this people.[66]

61. Ivens, "The Polynesian Word Atua," 136.

62. See discussion in Codrington, *The Melanesians*, 121.

63. Walter G. Ivens, "Place of Vui and Tamate in Religion of Mota," *Journal of the Royal Anthropological Institute of Great Britain and Ireland* 61 (1931): 159.

64. Quoted in Codrington, *The Melanesians*, n. to p. 122.

65. Macdonald, "The Polynesian Word for God," 263.

66. Horatio Hale, *Ethnography and Philology* (Ridgewood: Gregg Press, 1968; first published 1846), 17.

Macdonald agreed, describing Mariner's interpretation of "Moooi" as the divinity "that supports the earth, the earth lying on him, he being prostrate," noting that Mariner gives the Tongan verb "to live" as "mooi."[67] He then declared that

> Moooi or Maui is probably the Anc. Verbal noun Eth. Mahyawi, Arb. Mohyi, Arm. Mahe preserving alive, preserver sustainer, literally 'causing to live.' Hence the word might be used either as a name of God or of men. In Arabic it was one of the names of God, and is so used in the Koran.[68]

We have already heard from Macdonald's academic critics, and the liberal use of "probably" and "might be" in his analysis highlights concerns about his scientific rigor. Nevertheless, his quest for a fundamental connection between Tongan, Ethiopian, Arabic, and Armenian is evidence of the strength of his belief in human universals. For Macdonald, the Christian scriptures remained the foundation of science. It was more important to find human brotherhood by that means than it was to take account of the latest developments in linguistics. The value of universalism for mission work was clear:

> The people have practically lost the knowledge of the Supreme Being which their ancestors—the Oceanic fathers—possessed, along with a superstitious reverence for, amounting to worship of, the dead. As the knowledge and the name of God gradually disappeared, the ideas associated with that name became gradually transferred to the prevailing objects of worship.[69]

The task therefore was to restore to the people of Oceania the religious heritage that had always been theirs. This discourse of recovery and return remained alive and well long after the nineteenth century.[70] In a pamphlet designed to raise awareness of the plight of Aboriginal Australians after the Second World War, the Reverend W. G. Thomas summed up the mission's current view of Aboriginal spirituality:

> While possessing no system of religion as we understand it, and having no theistic belief, life for [Aboriginal Australians] had a real spiritual back-

67. Macdonald, *Oceania*, 172.
68. Macdonald, *Oceania*, 172.
69. Macdonald, *Oceania*, 202.
70. K. R. Howe, *The Quest for Origins*, 146–50.

> ground, or more properly perhaps, counterpart. The Rev. T. T. Webb says of the natives of Arnheim Land, "as (for him) all created things possess non-material form, which is always engaged in some spiritual activity, the spiritual or non-material world is ever present to the aborigine, and is as real to him as the physical world which is evident to his sense."[71]

For Lyth and other early missionaries, the quest had been to make connections with religious biblical practices through philology, diffusionism, or other scientific techniques. By the twentieth century the expanding popularity of the word "spirituality" was enabling observers like Thomas to acknowledge a common humanity even when formal religious features seemed absent and when diffusionist theories about Pacific-Semitic connection had been discredited. Nevertheless, the familiar demands of othering and brothering persisted, and missionaries continued to make whatever use they could of available theories and vocabularies.

Anglican missionary Robert Codrington was fond of taking swipes at visitors to the Melanesian Mission's territory, especially with regard to their views of Melanesian religion. He deplored the generalized moral disapproval that viewed every aspect of Melanesian culture as somehow steeped in a depraved spirituality: "It may be confidently asserted that in the Melanesian islands here in view dances have absolutely no religious or superstitious character," he declared, "although visitors find 'devil dances' and 'devil grounds' enough."[72] Codrington was reflexive about his own biases, conceding that there was no such thing as a neutral observer, but he also believed that many years of experience and fluency in various languages gave him insights that others lacked. For example, he stressed the profound spirituality of Melanesian medicine: "All serious diseases are ascribed either to charms such as are above described or to the direct malignant action of tamate. The gismana, or doctors, treated them with counter charms and incantations."[73] He added:

> The gismana were not those who made charms to cause disease. They sincerely believed in their power, though they practiced deceit. They sucked the part of the body where the pain lay, and then spat out something which was supposed to have been causing the pain. For a toothache they

71. W. G. Thomas, "*These My Brethren.*" *Studies in the Problem of the Aborigines of Australia and on Christian Responsibility and Action in regard thereto* (Sydney: Australian Board of Missions, 1946), 7.

72. Codrington, *The Melanesians*, 332.

73. R. H. Codrington, "Notes on the Customs of Mota, Banks Islands, with remarks by the Rev. Lorimer Fison, Fiji," *Transactions and Proceedings of the Royal Society of Victoria* 16 (1879): 132.

> would apply a small roll of leaves with a grup concealed in it, which, when the toothache passed away, was shown as having been drawn out of the tooth. They would stroke the afflicted part, singing songs the while, or blow upon it after chewing certain leaves. Some things, also, they did with the notion of healing qualities in the leaves or poultices applied.[74]

Othering and brothering come together under considerable tension in this extract. Codrington referred to the *gismana* by their indigenous title rather than calling them sorcerers or witchdoctors. Nevertheless, he concludes that "they practiced deceit" because of their use of ritualized actions and symbols rather than medicine as defined by modern science. This was certainly ironic, coming from a high church Anglican whose catholic sacramental theology included the practice of anointing the mortally ill with oil blessed by the bishop. During a lengthy stay on the island of Mota in 1872, he and the islanders practiced an exchange of patient mutual accommodation. Visiting a man wounded by an arrow, Codrington urged the family to take down the shells hung in a nearby tree to ward off ghosts. A large number of these were hung together on a long string, rattling constantly in the breeze or when anyone pulled the string. Once it was clear that the man would recover, Codrington got one of the younger boys to take the shells down, hoping to prove a point about the unnecessary fear of ghosts. But he knew the islanders well enough to be aware that even though they agreed with his statements to his face, agreeing that many of the old practices were "no good," they "then pulled away at the string when I was well out of hearing."[75]

Indigenous leadership (religious or otherwise) often posed problems for missionaries. Niel Gunson has concluded that

> in order to combat utter depravity and the 'religion of false gods' the missionaries had to launch a full-scale attack which meant not only war to the death with priestcraft and immorality . . . but also serious encroachments on the powers of the chiefs and prevailing notions of order and allegiance.[76]

Sometimes there was a clearly identifiable target, as when the *arioi* society was described as a Satanic organization by early missionaries to Tahiti. After

74. Codrington, "Notes on the Customs of Mota," 132.

75. Journal entry, 2 October 1872, f. 18, Melanesian Mission MSS 2/2, School of Oriental and African Studies, UK.

76. Gunson, *Messengers of Grace*, 479.

relating origin stories concerning this group, including one provided by Auna, one of the first indigenous deacons in the Society Islands, William Ellis dismissed as "fabulous" the idea that the society was divinely ordained. Instead it was "a master-piece of satantic delusion."[77] If local deities were false gods, and their worship idolatrous, nothing legitimate could be derived from them. In Ellis's opinion the *arioi* were merely "a sort of strolling players" who performed throughout the islands "spreading a moral contagion throughout society."[78] The Shakespearean image of strolling players, whom Ellis also described as libertines, recalls the early modern era of English theatre. Fraught with moral controversy, the stage was regarded with deep suspicion by Christians of various denominations, and the theater was banned, or permitted only under strict censorship, at various times in English history. Traveling players and their performances were transgressive. Itinerant theater companies raised questions about sexual permissiveness and the absence of stable family ties. The moral inversion of plays in which criminals could be heroes, or where women portrayed boys (and vice versa), appeared to question the moral order of real life.[79]

Arioi performances were accompanied by religious rituals, sacrifices, and offerings to the god Oro and to Orotetefa and Urutelefa, the founders of the society; they were also accompanied by "often obscene exhibitions."[80] *Arioi* could marry, and Ellis noted that female *arioi* were expected to be faithful, but the couple must be childless, meaning that existing children were killed and either abortion or infanticide practiced afterward.[81] Still drawing upon early modern English cultural references, Ellis quoted from Milton's famous poem *Paradise Lost* to underline the Satanic nature of the *arioi* institution, noting its "perverse, all monstrous, all prodigious things."[82] As in hell under the reign of the Great Adversary, so in the Society Islands did indigenous religion use a "delusive system of superstition" and "satanic delusion" to sanction evil rites, a combination that the strongly anti-Catholic Ellis could not resist comparing with "certain portions of the degrading rites performed on the person of a here-

77. William Ellis, *Polynesian Researches, during a residence of nearly eight years in the Society and Sandwich Islands*, 2nd ed., vol. 1 (New York: Henry G. Bohn, 1859), 328.

78. Ellis, *Polynesian Researches*, 1:312.

79. Rory Loughnane, "Introduction: Stages of Transgression," in *Staged Transgression in Shakespeare's England*, ed. Rory Loughnane and Edel Semple (Basingstoke, UK: Palgrave Macmillan, 2013).

80. Ellis, *Polynesian Researches*, 1:319.

81. Ellis, *Polynesian Researches*, 1:322.

82. Ellis, *Polynesian Researches*, 1:325. The full two verses read: "Where all life dies, death lives, and Nature breeds,/ Perverse, all monstrous, all prodigious things"; John Milton, *Paradise Lost* (Waiheke Island: Floating Press, 2008), 57; http://login.ezproxy.library.ualberta.ca/login?url=http://search.ebscohost.com/login.aspx?direct=true&db=nlebk&AN=314149&site=ehost-live&scope=site (accessed 31 January 2014).

tic, in connexion with an auto de fé, in the Romish church."[83] The sting lies here in the tail. For all the othering in Ellis's interpretation of the *arioi* society and its rituals, this final comparison draws them into the Christian and European family. Ellis and others noted that *arioi* converts made particularly dedicated missionaries. Finally, reflecting the notions of natural affection that we considered earlier, Ellis notes that "there were times, when a mother's love, a mother's feelings, overcame the iron force of pagan custom" and the lives of children were spared.[84] Missionaries could not afford to believe in the irredeemability of any indigenous group.

A wide-ranging and durable analysis of Melanesian religion was provided by Robert Codrington of the Melanesian Mission, whose theories on the subject became standard reading for anthropologists well into the twentieth century. An important goal for Codrington, as we know from his views on "devil dances," was to criticize the totalizing generalizations of visitors to the western Pacific and to substitute in their place a nuanced analysis that attempted to understand indigenous beliefs and practices on their own terms. He used the vocabulary of his times, noting that "in close connexion with religious observances come the various practices of magic and witchcraft," a statement that makes a very European distinction between religion and other, presumably non-religious things such as magic or witchcraft. Nevertheless, he undercut his own distinction immediately by noting that such "doctoring and weather-doctoring" was naturally linked with spirituality, "for all is done by the aid of ghosts and spirits." Reporting on magic charms from Mota in the Banks Islands, Codrington discussed three principal types of charms "as distinct from incantations and fetishes": *talamatai*, "a bit of a dead man's bone wrapped in certain leaves while a song was chanted. This being placed in the path, the first who stepped over it was supposed to be afflicted with an ulcer"; *garata*, "a fragment of a man's food, hair, or finger nail, worked up with incantations to bring disease upon him,"; and *tamatetiqa* or "ghost-shot," bones and leaves enclosed in a piece of bamboo with charms. The owner fasted, to generate power for the charms, then pointed the bamboo at an enemy while covering one end of the tube with his thumb. When he lifted his thumb, his enemy would receive the magically charged shot. For Melanesians, the important thing was finding out what worked, not worrying about what was spiritual rather than material and so, as Codrington observed, "Tamatetiqa is the word now used for a gun."[85]

83. Ellis, *Polynesian Researches*, 1:327.

84. Ellis, *Polynesian Researches*, 1:338. For more on the *arioi* see Jørgen Prytzjohansen, "Religious Aspects of the Arioi of Tahiti," *Temenos* 25 (1989): 69–78, and Douglas D. Tzan, "Arioi for Christ: an exploration of early missions by Society Islanders," *Missiology* 37, no. 2 (2009): 221–35.

85. Codrington, "Notes on the Customs of Mota," 131.

Codrington himself took great care to distinguish ghosts from spirits and deities but the multiplicity of western Pacific languages made research difficult. So did the relative lack of access to interviews with those still practicing indigenous rituals (or at least those prepared to admit it). Codrington relied heavily on converts to Christianity who he knew were "disposed to blacken generally and indiscriminately their own former state, and with greater zeal the present practices of others," while "natives who are still heathen still speak with reserve of what still retains with them a sacred character, and a considerate missionary will respect such reserve; if he should not respect it the native may very likely fail in his respect for him, and amuse himself at his expense."[86] Too many missionaries and other visitors had tended to make hasty judgments about indigenous religion, Codrington believed, and then they spent "the whole of their after-career [to] make whatever they observe fit into their early scheme of the native religion."[87] Phrases such as "devil stones" and "devil sticks" included a huge range of artifacts, yet Codrington declared "that a belief in a devil, that is of an evil spirit, has no place whatever in the native Melanesian mind."[88] He reflected ruefully on his own initial naivety with regard to demons when he first encountered Melanesian spirituality. Among other drawings shown to him by San Cristoval islanders he recalled one illustration in particular, in which a canoe was being attacked "as I supposed when I first saw it, by demons. It was not till long afterwards that I found out my supposed demons were only ghosts."[89] He had also noted the funeral drums from the New Hebrides with their "fantastic faces cut upon them, and these remain as in a manner images of the deceased, taken by visitors for idols or devil-drums."[90] Writing from New Guinea a generation after Codrington, William Saville of the LMS, steeped in the anthropological training of R. R. Marett and Bronislaw Malinowski, described Melanesian religion as "a tone," a word he borrowed from Ernest Crawley's book *The Tree of Life: A Study of Religion* (1905). For Saville, this Melanesian tone was a mode of thought and action, permeating all of society, by which islanders tried "to blend the normal with the abnormal for the perpetuation of the good or the best known to them that shall work for the maintenance of life and the well-being of the community."[91]

It was difficult to find English vocabulary adequate to describe a situation so rich and strange. Writing about Fiji, Lorimer Fison wanted to sort out the

86. Codrington, *The Melanesians*, 117.
87. Codrington, *The Melanesians*, 117.
88. Codrington, *The Melanesians*, 117.
89. Codrington, "Notes on the Customs of Mota," 128.
90. Codrington, *The Melanesians*, 175.
91. Saville, *Unknown New Guinea*, 294.

difference between charms, which he defined as objects with a physical power based on magic, and incantations, whose power was purely spiritual:

> Similar charms were commonly used in Fiji, and, indeed, by savages everywhere. In Fiji, however, I think the charm is supposed to have a certain inherent baneful influence of its own—for instance, the method of charging with dropsy, leprosy, &c. The sausau, or disease-bearing reed, does not seem to me to amount to an incantation proper. The Maori spells, on the other hand, are true incantations. They are real 'words of power,' and compel the spirits. (See a weird account of Maori enchantments in Sir George Grey's *Polynesian Mythology*, p. 168).[92]

The "weird account" was Grey's description of the story of Rata's vengeance on his father's murderer, Matukutakotako. Rata went to Matukutakotako's home and a man in the courtyard told him that Matukutakotako actually lived under the earth. Only if invoked correctly by the watcher in the courtyard, right after the new moon, would Matukutakotako appear. Since the new moon was in the sky, the watcher performed the incantation, and Rata killed Matukutakotako.[93] It remains unclear what was weird about this story for Fison, but the point was that an incantation alone had exerted a real, non-material power. Islanders believed that both words and charms had real supernatural power and so did the Christian converts who acted as missionaries to their own people. Fison explained that "the Fijians are terribly afraid of the garats" but so were "some of our mission-agents who faced boldly enough spears and clubs in the hands of angry men" but "quailed" before the power of charmed objects and curses. He was "convinced that natives frequently die of fear when they think themselves thus bewitched." As we know, this was the real power of "poisoned" arrows.

It was Codrington who first formulated a comprehensive theory of Melanesian religion in response to what seemed to be a bewildering array of beliefs and rituals. He believed "that among Melanesians there is a universal belief in the existence of personal intelligent beings of power superior to that of men."[94] He deplored the tendency to confuse spirits with ghosts and criticized the metropolitan theorists (or casual visitors) who presumed that "any personal object of worship" is "a spirit or a god, or a devil." The missiological challenge was clear:

92. Cited in Codrington, "Notes on the Customs of Mota," 131.

93. George Grey, *Polynesian Mythology and Ancient Traditional History of the New Zealand Race* (London: John Murray, 1855), 108.

94. Codrington, *The Melanesians*, 248.

> A man therefore who is approaching with some rite his dead father, whose spirit he believes to be existing and pleased with his pious action, is thought to be worshipping a false god or deceiving spirit, and very probably is told that the being he worships does not exist. The perplexed native hears with one ear that there is no such thing as that departed spirit of a man which he venerates as a ghost but his instructor takes to be a god, and with the other that the soul never dies, and that his own spiritual interests are paramount.[95]

For all Codrington's disparagement of the demonic discourse of more evangelical missionaries, his main point was echoed by Presbyterian missionary Daniel Macdonald about the southern New Hebrides:

> When the Efatese become Christian they continue the same way of thinking, and have constantly to be corrected for attributing every calamity of a man to some particular sin, like those Jews who supposed the tower of Siloam fell upon certain persons and killed them because they were the greatest sinners in Jerusalem. Here are a people among the lowest cannibal savages in the world who are nevertheless a very religious people, for whom the whole world is filled with innumerable spiritual beings that walk unseen, to offend whom is calamity and death, to please whom is life. . . . There is no people under the sun more obedient to what they regard as the mandates of deity than these "savages."[96]

Macdonald's explanation was diffusionism: "There was among the Romans and Greeks, and perhaps generally in the ancient heathen world, a similar confounding of the divine with the human." As for islanders encountered by the New Hebrides Mission:

> the transition from the ancient state to the present was easy. In the ancient state the name and attributes of the Supreme Being were known, but nearly the whole of the religious activity of the people was absorbed in the worship of idols and at the tombs of dead men. Gradually the latter increased at the expense of the former, until the present state was reached in such places as Efate.[97]

95. Codrington, *The Melanesians*, 121.
96. Macdonald, *Oceania*, 201.
97. Macdonald, *Oceania*, 203.

For Macdonald, Christian missionary work was a recovery operation: the resurrection of an original cultural orientation rather than the discarding of one discrete cultural system in favor of another. The name of God had once been universally known (Macdonald's labors concerning *Atua* had served their purpose). Linking "the ancient state to the present" served to explain away cultural difference as a function of time and space; not of some terminal alterity. Near the end of his book, Macdonald declared that

> A fair consideration of the facts that meet us in examining the religious system of the Oceanic speakers leads to the conclusion that it is a corruption of the system of their forefathers, whose system itself was a corruption of the primitive religion in which there was but one object of worship, the Supreme Being, Creator of the world and of man. . . . It is only in certain atmospheres that certain plants will take root and flourish: only in such a poisoned atmosphere as this could such monstrous insanity as the putting of these ghosts in the seat of the Supreme prevail. . . . And how truly it may be said of such of them as have embraced Christianity, that they are "now," after millenniums of unparalleled wanderings over trackless seas, the world's great ocean wildernesses, "RETURNED unto the Shepherd and Bishop of their souls."[98]

Both Macdonald and Fison used current anthropological vocabulary to describe survivals of earlier religious systems not only in Pacific cultures but also in a more familiar Other: the Roman Catholic Church. "I have seen somewhere a long list of demons who are to be called by name in cases of possession at the present day among Roman Catholics," wrote Fison. "This method of exorcism was used, I believe, as late as 1861, during the prevalence of the strange phenomena which appeared at Morzine. This is a very curious instance of the survival of a savage custom in civilisation."[99] Presbyterian missionary Daniel Macdonald also made comparisons between "savage" practices and Roman Catholicism. Speaking of Roman Catholic reverence for saints as worship, a common feature of anti-Catholic polemic, he concluded that "the ideas that are thus manifested are substantially the same as are manifested in the Efatese natemate worship, in the Maraes of the central Pacific, and in the mysterious structures of Easter Island."[100]

98. Macdonald, *Oceania*, 212.

99. R. H. Codrington, "Notes on the Customs of Mota, Banks Islands" with remarks by Rev. Lorimer Fison, *Transactions and Proceedings of the Royal Society of Victoria* 16 (1879): 128.

100. Macdonald, *Oceania*, 205.

Codrington's theory, by contrast, was a unique one, based on what he considered to be the distinctiveness and integrity of Melanesian cultures. With Macdonald, Fison, and others Codrington believed in a universal human spiritual impulse, but he also believed that a Pacific-centered theory was needed. The starting point had to be a more precise vocabulary. Melanesians found it difficult to explain their religious beliefs, but so did "people very much more advanced than themselves" when asked to explain Christian doctrine:

> The civilized observer is always ready to assume that the savage takes a childish view and has absurd beliefs, when all the while, if the savage could put him to a close examination, his own conceptions would be found very indistinct and his expressions mainly figurative.[101]

Codrington noted the observations of the early Methodist missionary ethnographer in Fiji, Thomas Williams, whose account had confused the Fijian word for soul, *yalo*, and the word for shadow, *yaloyalo*. Williams's comments about Fijian beliefs in two spirits must therefore be treated with caution, and Codrington joked that "many a voyager, not an observer, carries away as a sort of joke the story that the natives think their shadows are their souls." Instead, indigenous religion should be taken seriously on its own terms.

Codrington's approach was to use the Polynesian word *mana* as the basis for a theory that would demonstrate the religiosity of Melanesian beliefs and practices. In a letter to Professor Friedrich Max Müller, Oxford professor of modern languages and prominent orientalist, Codrington explained that "the notion of a Supreme Being is altogether foreign to [Melanesians]," but they had "a belief in a force altogether distinct from physical power, which acts in all kinds of ways for good and evil, and which it is of the greatest advantage to possess or control."[102] This "force altogether distinct from physical power" he named *mana*: a term in widespread use in the South Pacific. He believed that "all Melanesian religion consists . . . in getting this Mana for one's self, or getting it used for one's benefit—all religion, that is, as far as religious practices go, prayers and sacrifices."[103] This power, "though itself impersonal, is always connected with some person who directs it; all spirits have it, ghosts generally, some men."[104] Objects had *mana* because of their association with spirits; men

101. Macdonald, *Oceania*, 248.
102. Codrington, *The Melanesians*, 118.
103. Cited in Hilliard, *God's Gentlemen*, 37.
104. Codrington, *The Melanesians*, 119.

demonstrated *mana* by success in warfare, prosperity, and a range of other signs of power and influence.

For Codrington, this distinctively Melanesian belief system revealed the universality of human spirituality, not by demonstrating a debased survival, but by being a thriving religion in its own right. "No missionary who knows and loves his people," wrote Codrington, "will ever fail to find this foundation, even among the lowest races of mankind, or find himself utterly unable to say to them: 'Whom ye ignorantly worship, Him I declare unto you.'"[105] This was a scriptural reference to the Book of Acts where the apostle Paul, visiting Athens, found an altar dedicated to "the unknown god." The story concludes with familiar passages concerning one blood anthropology, and the supposedly universal nature of human spirituality:

> Then Paul stood in the midst of Mars' hill, and said, Ye men of Athens, I perceive that in all things ye are too superstitious. For as I passed by, and beheld your devotions, I found an altar with this inscription, TO THE UNKNOWN GOD. Whom therefore ye ignorantly worship, him declare I unto you. God that made the world and all things therein, seeing that he is Lord of heaven and earth, dwelleth not in temples made with hands; Neither is worshipped with men's hands, as though he needed any thing, seeing he giveth to all life, and breath, and all things; And hath made of one blood all nations of men for to dwell on all the face of the earth, and hath determined the times before appointed, and the bounds of their habitation; That they should seek the Lord, if haply they might feel after him, and find him, though he be not far from every one of us. (Acts 17:22–27)

By naming "the unknown god" to be the divine father of Jesus Christ, Paul reconfigured the entire pantheon at the heart of ancient Greek religion. It was no longer merely heathen or pagan, but contained within itself the Christian revelation. We have seen how challenging it was for missionaries to remember the scriptural declaration that God had never left himself without witness throughout the world. For Codrington, the task was "to search for and recognize what is true and good among wild and foul superstitions; to find the common foundation, if such there be, which lies in human nature itself, ready for the superstructure of the Gospel."[106] Some of Codrington's younger colleagues

105. Cited in Sohmer, "The Melanesian Mission," 330–31.

106. Robert Codrington, "Religious Beliefs and Practices in Melanesia," *Journal of the Anthropological Institute* 10 (1881): 312. For a deeper analysis of Codrington's notion of a "fulcrum" and "superstructure," see Sohmer, "The Melanesian Mission," 330–31.

refined his findings; Walter Ivens noted that *mana* as an impersonal force was rarely found in Melanesia, whereas it was much more common for the word "to express the virtue imminent [*sic*] in certain human beings, and in the souls of the dead, particularly the greater dead."[107]

Max Müller, one of Codrington's academic admirers at Oxford, cited his research in the Hibbert Lectures of 1878, and it was Codrington's *mana* theory that won out over the rival theories of Tylor, Frazer, and others. Younger British anthropologists like R. R. Marett (also at Oxford) investigated the "pre-animistic" principle of *mana*, drawing directly on Codrington to challenge Tylor's theory of animism.[108] Codrington's principal work *The Melanesians* was reprinted into the 1950s as a working anthropology textbook. By 1983 Darrell Whiteman could declare that "Codrington's description of *mana* is still the classic definition used today."[109] Codrington's ethnography of Melanesian religion was "firmly rooted in, and new transplanted from, the pre-evolutionary tradition of linguistic ethnology," in contrast to the firmer evolutionism of Codrington's friend and anthropological colleague Lorimer Fison.[110] As we know, there was no missionary position on evolution. Although he accepted evolutionary explanations for other things, Codrington was uncomfortable with the increasingly popular idea that human religiosity developed by degrees. Acutely aware of the European tendency to pass judgment on non-European cultures, Codrington was anxious to challenge the notion that "primitive" Melanesians necessarily had little or no "real" religion. On the contrary, as we have seen, he argued that Melanesian beliefs provided evidence of a "common foundation" for human spirituality. As Stocking notes, Codrington's work called "into question the very category of 'savagery' upon which so much of evolutionary reconstruction was founded."[111] Stocking links him with a paradigm shift, exemplified by the later work of W. H. R. Rivers and Franz Boas, that led to the discrediting of evolutionary models in early twentieth-century anthropology.[112] For Codrington, "a

107. Walter Ivens, "The Diversity of Culture in Melanesia," *Journal of the Royal Anthropological Institute of Great Britain and Ireland* 64 (1934): 52.

108. Stocking, *Victorian Anthropology*, 237, 319; also see R. R. Marett, *The Threshold of Religion* (London: Methuen & Co., 1909); Arthur Cappell, "The Word Mana: A Linguistic Study," *Oceania* 9 (1938): 89–96; Raymond Firth, "The Analysis of Mana: An Empirical Approach," *Journal of the Polynesian Society* 49 (1940): 483–510; Ernst Cassirer, *Language and Myth* (New York: Harper, 1946); and Alan Tippett, *Solomon Islands Christianity: A Study in Growth and Obstruction* (London: Lutterworth, 1967).

109. Darrell L. Whiteman, *Melanesians and Missionaries: An Ethnohistorical Study of Social and Religious Change in the Southwest Pacific* (Pasadena: William Carey Library, 1983), 96, n. 138.

110. Whiteman, *Melanesians and Missionaries*, 38.

111. Stocking, *After Tylor*, 45.

112. Stocking, *After Tylor*, 46.

savage people, if such are to be found," who had no conception of spirituality, "would fail to supply a missionary a fulcrum by which, when it exists, they may be raised to a higher level."[113]

Could missionaries experience a full or partial engagement with indigenous religion or spirituality? The reflexivity prompted by brothering could lead to a process of reverse conversion in some cases. Thomas Kendall, new to the CMS mission in New Zealand in 1822, wrote confidently that the Maori

> are so puffed up with their own notions of independence and strength, that it will be some time before they are brought so low as to entertain correct views of their dependance [*sic*], wretchedness, and insignificance, and the value of the blessings which are intended for them.[114]

Nevertheless, it would be Kendall himself who was brought low as he became better acquainted with the reasons for Maori pride and confidence. As we know, Kendall's translation work and his adoption of the diffusionist theories allowed him to connect Maori language and culture with the ancient eastern Mediterranean and Asia. What we find in his ethnography of religion is the same pattern of othering and brothering. For example, he was upset by the curses rained down on ailing family members by their nearest and dearest. Observing such a scene when one of the mission students was ill, Kendall asked the boy's father to explain his actions. The man replied that it was

> to frighten the *Atua* away who would otherwise, very probably have destroyed his son. The boy had been out in the rain a whole day, and had caught a severe cold, but the natives will not allow that excessive heat or cold, or being long out in the wet can hurt a man. They ascribe every pain they feel to the *Atua* who they say is preying upon them.[115]

Kendall concluded that "here 'Satan reigns with destructive sway,'"[116] apparently placing these Maori firmly on the Other side of Christian cosmography. This was required by the total depravity theology of evangelical Anglicans, and of many Protestant missionaries as well, with its emphasis on the utter

113. Codrington, "Notes on the Customs of Mota," 312–13.

114. Thomas Kendall to Samuel Marsden, 1 August 1822, "Letters etc. 1816–1827," Thomas Kendall MSS, Hocken Library, Dunedin, NZ.

115. Thomas Kendall to Joshua Mann, 4 July 1817, "Samuel Marsden MSS," MS 56A, Hocken Library, Dunedin, NZ.

116. Thomas Kendall to Joshua Mann, 4 July 1817, "Samuel Marsden MSS," MS 56A, Hocken Library, Dunedin, NZ.

dependency of all human beings on the grace of God. Nevertheless, Kendall added at once that "when the natives are sick they are impatient and angry. . . . How similar is the language they use on this most solemn occasion to that recommended to Job namely to 'curse God and die.'"[117] The young Kendall was linking Maori practices across time and space to the Holy Land, in this case to the Old Testament story of the temptations of Job. There, the tempters had been fellow Jews, something occluded by Kendall's use of the passive voice when he talks of the language recommended to Job. His account of this episode underlines both alterity and kinship, as we would expect. Satan might reign in New Zealand at the moment, but Kendall found similarities—not alienating distance—between Maori and God's chosen people.

We have seen how hard Kendall struggled to find a Maori word for God, and his early ethnography reveals an awareness of cultural contamination. Convenient as it might have been for him to say that Maori worshiped the devil, he preferred a more nuanced analysis:

> Those natives who have been amongst Englishmen and are acquainted with our Language tell me that "their Atua is the Devil." It is not possible to ascertain how far this idea might be correct, but it appears they have no notion of the Supreme Being as a God of love & mercy.[118]

Kendall the scholar was careful to note the lack of evidence for devil worship; Kendall the missionary feels obliged to note that the belief in a supreme being was present, even if it took a form he considered to be misguided. He therefore attempted a conversion of the meaning of the word "Atua." At the bedside of an ailing Maori man, Kendall explained "that there was one Great Atua who made the Universe. I could tell him in his own Language that all men had offended this Great Atua and therefore all men died," but through Christ their souls would live forever.[119]

Having learned the language quickly, Kendall was eager to study Maori religion more deeply. Conscious of his educational shortcomings and motivated by missionary hope, he had a genuine desire to understand. It was this intellectual zeal that invited him to study Maori beliefs thoroughly, a process that began to convert him to Maori perspectives. There were other

117. Thomas Kendall to Joshua Mann, 4 July 1817, "Samuel Marsden MSS," MS 56A, Hocken Library, Dunedin, NZ.

118. Thomas Kendall to Samuel Marsden, 11 March 1815, "Samuel Marsden MSS," MS 56A, Hocken Library, Dunedin, NZ.

119. Thomas Kendall to Samuel Marsden, 11 March 1815, "Samuel Marsden MSS," MS 56A, Hocken Library, Dunedin, NZ.

considerations too. In 1822 he left his wife and lived for a time as a member of a Maori family, incorporated as their kin by a sexual relationship with a Maori woman. Later, Kendall explained the intellectual and spiritual impact of his conversion:

> I am now after a long, anxious and painful study, arriving at the very foundation and Ground work of the Cannibalism & Superstitions of these Islanders. All their notions are metaphysical and I have been so poisoned with the apparent sublimity of their ideas, that I have been almost completely turned from a Christian to a Heathen. All their carnal representations have a spiritual signification, hence, they are much more deeply rooted in their Superstitions than either Mr. Marsden or myself supposed them. They have this idea of the Trinity: The first person—Divine presence; the second person—Divine likeness; the third person—Divine Shadow or that principle of reflection by means of *water* which shews a man's image to himself when he looks over it. I trust I shall be enabled in a little time to give a clear and systematic view of the origin of the language, religious superstitions &c. of the New Zealanders.[120]

This extract is rich in othering and brothering, revealing a genuine attempt to understand the world of Maori spirituality in a way that was both exhilarating and painful. He wanted to be clear about how compelling he had found this system to be in spiritual terms. His "fall" was about far more than sexual indiscretion. After the CMS expelled him from the mission, he wrote to the society's leadership in repentance:

> After long and sore temptation I *myself* fell. From December 1821 until April 1822 I was completely under the influence of Satan. I was reduced to such a dreadful state of mind that I had no thought whatever as to what might happen to me in this world. I was both a fool and a madman.[121]

Nevertheless, Kendall had remained in New Zealand. He reconciled with his wife, although many of the other missionaries (and certainly the settlers) never let him forget his disgrace.[122] He wanted to visit England again for scholarly

120. Thomas Kendall to J. Eyre, 27 December 1822, "Letters etc. 1816–1827," Thomas Kendall MSS, Hocken Library, Dunedin, NZ.

121. Kendall to Pratt and Bickersteth, 13 August 1823, "Letters etc. 1816–1827," Thomas Kendall MSS, Hocken Library, Dunedin, NZ.

122. Sexual transgressions could be handled with surprising tolerance as long as there was no open scandal; see Rhonda Semple, "Missionary Manhood: Professionalism, Belief and Masculinity

reasons, "specially as I cannot communicate all I want to say respecting the religion &c of the New Zealanders in writing, but must undergo an examination in the presence of competent judges."[123] This is one of the most fascinating aspects of the Kendall correspondence: the legacy of his conversion experience. He was keenly aware of how difficult it would be to explain what he had learned, given his lack of formal education, and was pleading for a debriefing by scholars trained in metaphysics. They could make sense of what he wanted to describe. He also sent a shipment of Maori carvings to England, hoping that material artifacts would speak more clearly than the notes he had made about them.[124] Tragically, these precious carvings went down in a shipwreck, a poignant metaphor for all that was lost in translation between New Zealand and the distant metropolis.

This story indicates the urgent need to move beyond the familiar argument that missionary collections were overdetermined by "the colonial context in which the material was acquired."[125] Such discussions of visual ideology must be nuanced by considering the theological entanglement of unity and alterity in the collection and use of material artifacts. From this perspective, objects can act as envoys "to create and maintain relationship and to represent, both internally and externally, something of the complex identities of the island's diverse peoples."[126] What was of the greatest importance for Kendall was the way "that the language, idolatry, theology, mythology, tradition &c of the New Zealanders are inseperably [*sic*] blended together, and if I am correct in my judgment to study their ideas in the above respects is to study the Science of Metaphysics from nature itself."[127] He had relied on the Maori themselves to train him: "This is a very difficult task for me who am entirely unacquainted with such intricate and obtuse notions only as I

---

in the Nineteenth-Century British Imperial Field," *Journal of Imperial and Commonwealth History* 36, no. 3 (2008): 397–415.

123. Kendall to Hall, 23 January 1832, "Letters etc. 1816–1827," Thomas Kendall MSS, Hocken Library, Dunedin, NZ.

124. Thomas Kendall to CMS Secretary, 5 April 1823, "Letters etc. 1816–1827," Thomas Kendall MSS, Hocken Library, Dunedin, NZ.

125. Jeanne Cannizzo, "Gathering Souls and Objects: Missionary Collections," in *Colonialism and the Object: Empire, Material Culture and the Museum*, ed. Tim Barringer and Tom Flynn (London: Routledge, 1998), 153–66.

126. Christine Mullen Kreamer and Sarah Fee, eds., *Objects as Envoys: Cloth, Imagery, and Diplomacy in Madagascar* (Washington: Smithsonian Institution, 2002), 17. The pioneering Pacific example is Thomas, *Entangled Objects*.

127. Thomas Kendall to Thomas Hassall, 9 April 1823, "Letters etc. 1816–1827," Thomas Kendall MSS, Hocken Library, Dunedin, NZ.

require a knowledge of them from the Natives themselves to perform."[128] It had taken a long time to work out how to do justice to Maori ideas in English

> and it now plainly appears to me that what I have been so many years acquiring a knowledge of by incessant application and research, in the course of which I have spent many sleepless nights, some of the Native Children who are not more than six or seven years of age can explain to me with ease so early are they made acquainted with the mysteries of their own System.[129]

To be sure, the holistic Maori attitude toward spirituality and sexuality had also attracted Kendall. He does not duck the issue, but he insists that it be considered in context:

> There is also another inconvenience attached to the study of the ideas of the New Zealanders which combined with the workings of my own corrupt nature has almost overpowered and overwhelmed me . . . namely that as they in all respects draw their Spiritual and Metaphysical notions & conclusions from the study of Nature they are of course generally obtained from very impure sources.[130]

He explained that "with them to study the different members and appendages of the human body, with their uses, and the origin, progress and end of Nature, is to study the Supreme Being. . . . It is in fact to study the Universe."[131] As a result, both he and the CMS must overstep the bounds of decency for the sake of conveying accurate ethnography. This was othering and brothering up at the sharp end. Kendall explained that

> It is my intention to write to the Society with as much decency of sentiment and expression as possible, but should I in the course of my observation occasionally or necessarily deviate from this rule, I must nevertheless speak the truth, trusting that such a deviation will not be imputed to any other motive than an earnest desire to represent and expose the Mysterious System of the Natives with all its horrors & to point out the secret lurking place of the subtle deceiver of Mankind; and to do this not

128. Kendall to Hassall, 9 April 1823.
129. Kendall to Hassall, 9 April 1823.
130. Kendall to Hassall, 9 April 1823.
131. Kendall to Hassall, 9 April 1823.

> so much with the view of exciting the wonder, as the compassion of the Christian World.[132]

Here the man of science—"I must nevertheless speak the truth"—was also confident that his research would reinforce a theological and missiological position—"the Mysterious System of the Natives with all its horrors." His was an ethnographical account intended both to incite horror and to invite engagement.

It was important, therefore, not to present Maori religion as completely Other. Kendall's belief in an indigenous Maori trinity was crucial here. He elaborated at great length on the "*three* States or *modes* of Existence" of the Maori "Supreme Being" in several very long letters to the CMS. He remained determined to convey information about Maori religion even though the scandal concerning his adultery was already well known. "Although I am exceedingly doubtful that a letter from me will at present be acceptable to you," he wrote to CMS secretary Josiah Pratt, "yet the importance of the subject on which I write constrains me once more to address you."[133] By 1824 Kendall was under orders from the CMS to relocate to New South Wales, but he wrote another long letter relating his research findings, now paying special attention to the importance given to the concept of "the first and the last" in Maori theology. He was reflexive about his use of Christian metaphors and vocabulary to explain Maori concepts, noting that "I have made use of the words *Eternal Word* in order to denote the First and Last, because in all my studying of the New Zealand Language, I cannot find any other word so suitable to express the native meaning."[134] This was not merely a case of pragmatism; the concept of the Eternal Word was as central to Christian theology as it was (Kendall believed) to Maori religion. "I have taken the above word from 'St. John,'" explained Kendall, because

> his writings particularly the Apocalypse [have] a most striking allusion to those Pagan Superstitions which are still preserved at New Zealand. It is remarkable indeed that the sound of the vowel *o* from whence originates the idea of the wisdom of the First and Last, exactly agrees with the revolving of the *Tongue*, or the act of *speaking*.[135]

132. Kendall to Hassall, 9 April 1823.

133. Thomas Kendall to Josiah Pratt, 11 April 1823, "Letters etc. 1816–1827," Thomas Kendall MSS, Hocken Library, Dunedin, NZ.

134. Thomas Kendall to Josiah Pratt, 27 July 1824, "Letters etc. 1816–1827," Thomas Kendall MSS, Hocken Library, Dunedin, NZ.

135. Kendall to Pratt, 27 July 1824, "Letters etc. 1816–1827," Thomas Kendall MSS, Hocken Library, Dunedin, NZ.

In a classic brothering strategy, Kendall was locating Maori religion within the eschatological context of the gospel of John and the book of Revelation, claiming that it had preserved features of classical pagan religion from the ancient Mediterranean. He took seriously the integrated nature of Maori theology, connecting abstract concepts with the sound of the Maori vowel involved and the physiology of speech. He was also keenly aware of the permanent problem of understanding metaphysical words and concepts in Maori terms. "The Missionaries can make themselves understood by the Natives in matters of commerce and in the ordinary Subjects of conversation," he wrote to Professor Lee at Cambridge, the man who had helped him during his visit there with the Maori chiefs,

> but I do not think they are yet acquainted with one of their 'songs' or themes. The New Zealand Language is very imperfectly understood. A man may be tempted to *make* the Language to correspond with his own idea of it, but time will convince him in such a case of his error.[136]

In her pioneering biography of Kendall, Judith Binney underlined his Calvinist and millennial theology, both aspects of evangelical Anglican CMS missiology.[137] This missiology needs to be understood in the broader context of Victorian missionary anthropology, however, or the tensions revealed by Kendall's complex ethnography cannot be fully explored. A Calvinist theology of total depravity referred to humanity's total dependency on the grace of God: a concept drawn from the Protestant Reformation's rejection of the mediation role played by the Roman Catholic Church. It does not necessarily involve a judgment of total depravity concerning the cultural practices of non-European peoples (although it often did). It was a theological principle rather than an anthropological theory. For Kendall, Maori culture could not be utterly depraved, whatever the state of Maori souls might be. Points of connection and communication were necessary if the saving gospel was to be preached and understood. Kendall sought those points of connection assiduously both before and after his brief conversion to Maori manhood. In a letter to a secular friend, Captain Currie of HMS *Satellite*, he explained his motives in much greater detail than he had to his religious superiors. The original letter appears to have been lost, but its contents were related later by Sir Thomas Brisbane, governor of New South Wales. Kendall had confided that he lived with a Maori woman not only

136. Thomas Kendall to Samuel Lee, 7 January 1825, Thomas Kendall MSS, "Letters etc. 1816–1827," MS-0071, Hocken Library, Dunedin, NZ.

137. Judith Binney, *Legacy of Guilt*, 6–7.

out of sinful temptation, but also "in order to obtain accurate information as to their religious opinions and tenets, which he could in no other way have obtained; but that he was fully aware of the impression his conduct would produce amongst his friends in England."[138]

This might look like special pleading ("I did it for anthropology"), but the complexities here deserve to be taken seriously. Kendall's conversion was a direct result of the tension between othering and brothering in which sexual attraction played only one role of many. This is the explanation of what Judith Binney identified as a contradiction in Kendall:

> The essence of Kendall's tragedy was not only his capacity to react with sympathy to the alien society all around him, which reaction contradicted what he believed to be the whole purpose of his being, but also his failure to transcend that part of his mind which cried that this knowledge was sin, and this understanding that he sought and even the very culture itself was damned.[139]

But Kendall had not failed to transcend his Christian moral judgment. He had transcended it all too well, as he admitted to the CMS and others. There is also no evidence that his desire for sympathetic engagement with Maori culture was somehow in contradiction to his whole purpose as a missionary. On the contrary, it was required by it. By seeing both othering and brothering as inevitably entangled, the two can be examined not as a contradiction, but as a symbiosis. As Angela Wanhalla has noted: "Intimate relationships entered into by missionaries, whether they involved the absence of a wife, a difficult relationship with a partner, or sexual encounters across racial and moral boundaries, suggest affection and intimacy were implicated in the success or failure of a mission."[140]

In a very early letter from 1817 Kendall made generalized statements about "pride and ignorance, cruelty and licentiousness" as characteristics of Maori religion: generalized characteristics often found in missionary othering regardless of geographical location or cultural context. Nevertheless, he also noted that

> Those customs the description of which would be most painful to the tender feelings, are consistent with the natives' ideas of the properties of

138. Thomas Brisbane to Josiah Pratt, 29 April 1823, CN/M2, Mission Book 1823, Hocken Special Collections Library, Dunedin, NZ.

139. Binney, *Legacy of Guilt*, 97.

140. Angela Wanhalla, "'The Natives Uncivilize Me': Missionaries and Interracial Intimacy in Early New Zealand," in *Missionaries, Indigenous Peoples and Cultural Exchange*, ed. Patricia Grimshaw and Andrew May (Brighton, UK: Sussex Academic Press, 2011), 33.

> the Supreme Being. They describe Him as an invisible anthropophagus, and regard Him with a mixture of fear and hatred. They vex themselves, as I have before told you, when He thinks good to afflict them or call any of them away, for having lost sight of Him so long, how can they think of Him as a God of Love and Mercy?[141]

Kendall capitalizes references to the Maori "supreme being," linking their faith with his belief in the Judaeo-Christian God. The connection was dim; the Maori had "lost sight" of the universal faith once shared by all humanity. Satanic influence had misled them further. Nevertheless, the original faith was as much their own patrimony as it was Kendall's, or any other Christian's. The most painful aspects of Maori culture were also the best, reflecting as they did the notion of a Supreme Being. As we have seen so often, the missionary task was neither to inscribe on a blank slate, nor to replace a totally depraved culture in favor of a completely new creation. The task was to remind Pacific peoples of the road to a faith obscured by time and distance, yet still authentically their own.

141. Thomas Kendall to Joshua Mann, 4 July 1817, MS 56A, "Samuel Marsden MSS," Hocken Library, Dunedin, NZ.

CHAPTER 7

Engendering Difference

During his long service in the Solomon Islands, the Anglican missionary Charles Elliot Fox wished to live as one of the islanders, realizing that he could never really understand them except on their own terms. His deep commitment to radical engagement led to a *haimarahuda*—an exchange of names—with Martin Taki of San Cristoval. In January of 1920, Fox walked away from his house, leaving behind his books (and his even more precious stock of tobacco), and entered his new home village as Martin Taki. "You have no idea how great a difference it made," Fox recalled, because "I got to know the *women* for the first time, to find out how they chaff the men continually. I was treated entirely differently, with less respect but with infinitely greater friendliness."[1]

Missionary ethnographers had a great deal to say about gender relations and sexuality, yet during this period almost all of them were men, and although they could be strikingly reflexive about other cultural factors, they rarely were about these ones. Fox's comment is practically unique in this respect, and he went to exceptional lengths to achieve the insight he obtained. Although we still find the familiar theological anthropology of othering and brothering in missionary ethnography about gender and sexuality, it is here that the exclusive term "brothering" points most strongly to unfinished business in the radical universalism preached by missionaries. Women had to be affirmed as fully human and capable of salvation, but there was no question of equality in terms of church leadership. Missionaries who delighted in racially transgressive ordina-

1. C. E. Fox to [W. J. Durrad], 8 July 1920, transcribed by Durrad in his introduction to Charles Elliot Fox, "A Missionary in Melanesia," 16, MS-Papers-1171–02, Alexander Turnbull Library, Wellington, NZ.

tions in order to welcome indigenous brothers to the clergy did not even discuss the question of ordaining female bodies, and when considering male same-sex relationships of various kinds they treated supposedly effeminate men more harshly than those perceived to be performing more masculine roles. Finally, with regard to oral sexuality or in cases of what anthropologists would later call ritualized homosexuality, especially when it involved children, missionaries could find no ground for brothering and abandoned the usual language of theological anthropology by naming such practices as bestial.

During the time period covered by this book, modern conceptions and vocabularies of sexuality were in considerable flux, along with judgments about what constituted an acceptable geography of sexual expression. For example, modern middle and upper-class westerners tended to assume that for members of the opposite sex to share a bed was to have sex, to the point that the phrase "to sleep with" became synonymous with sexual intimacy. By the nineteenth century, most missionaries came from households prosperous enough to feature separate sleeping arrangements (however crowded by today's standards) for adults and children. Thus John Orsmond of the LMS, in a letter to friends in England, complained in 1849 that after a generation of Christianization in the Society Islands "the people generally herd as brutes, all ages and sexes under one covering, on the same mat, without a single parting in the house." Orsmond presumed that illicit intercourse might be taking place or that children were witnessing their parents' sexual intimacy. He therefore invoked images of extreme alterity, using bestial metaphors rather than brothering these practices, however imperiously, by connecting them with the ancient world or with scriptural references. Consciously or not, Orsmond's reaction reflected discourse about sleeping arrangements in impoverished households back in Britain. By the 1840s urban statistical societies, staffed by middle class volunteers bent on good works, were conducting social surveys of working-class neighborhoods. The surveys focused on nocturnal household geography, especially the number of rooms and beds.[2] Numerous surveyors reported marked hostility toward these inquiries but they persisted, adding "questions about the ratio of people to beds, which provoked equal resistance."[3] At home and abroad, earnest Victorians were struggling to reform domestic geography in order to force it to reflect middle-class views of social and sexual norms.

Some Pacific missionaries took a more sophisticated approach to understanding indigenous sleeping arrangements, especially with regard to questions of sex-

2. Eileen Yeo, "Social Surveys in the Eighteenth and Nineteenth Centuries," in *The Cambridge History of Science*, vol. 7, *The Modern Social Sciences* (Cambridge: Cambridge University Press, 2003), 89.

3. Manchester Statistical Society, *Report . . . on the Conditions of the Working Classes* (London: James Ridgway, 1838) cited in Yeo, "Social Surveys," 90, n. 21.

uality. Methodist William Bromilow explained that among the 'Edugaula people of Dobu island off the SE coast of New Guinea "a man proposes to a woman by first getting the woman's consent to his sleeping with her in her usual sleeping place [usually shared by mother and sister/s]; then repeating his visits for several consecutive nights." If the woman was still interested in marrying the man, she spoke formally to her mother about him and he was permitted to work in her mother's garden. Bromilow made it clear that

> The betrothed boy or man is expected to sleep with his betrothed in her mother's house, but only as brother and sister. Should the man go further than the compact allows, and the woman become pregnant, her relatives will reproach him . . . and angrily hand the woman over to him without further ceremonies—an act which will be a constant disgrace to the woman in the future.[4]

Although this description is Eurocentric, it does not support Michael Young's condemnation of Bromilow's "inflexible denigration of 'the essential vileness' of Dobuan culture."[5] Instead, Bromilow's ethnography had to do the usual double duty. All humanity was sinful, dependent on divine grace, but humanity was also linked by its common creation in the image of God. Inflexible denigration would have rendered the missionary project useless; instead, as Young's own analysis brilliantly demonstrates, Dobuans came to love Bromilow and re-enacted his arrival among them in a cherished annual festival. This trans-generational affection and respect surprised Young, but, as he notes elsewhere in the article, "Bromilow would have been influenced by Papuan imagery just as half a century or more of regular church-going had exposed local mythologers to the powerful tropes of the mission."[6] Influence was a two-way street; necessarily so if missionaries were to achieve effective engagement with a people whose culture was so unlike their own. But there is no doubt that missionaries could be insensitive to cultural context, particularly when indigenous converts were concerned. The Anglican New Guinea Mission's report from 1901 included the complaint that

> To make people Christians and then let them to pack and herd together in houses where several families live together, where the sexes are not

4. W. E. Bromilow, "Some Manners and Customs of the Dobuans of S. E. Papua," *Report of the Meeting of the Australasian Association for the Advancement of Science* 12 (1909), 480.

5. Michael W. Young, "Commemorating Missionary Heroes: Local Christianity and Narratives of Nationalism," in *Narratives of Nation in the South Pacific*, ed. Ton Otto and Nicholas Thomas (Amsterdam: Harwood Academic Publishers, 1997), 101.

6. Young, "Missionary Heroes," 103.

divided nor the married separated from the unmarried, not to mention a plentiful supply of pigs, seems purposeless, not to say irreverent.[7]

The postcolonial eye will notice at once the unspoken link with contemporary discourse about Ireland where "the pig in the parlor" was currently under assault by Roman Catholic, Anglican, and Protestant churches in "an ideological battle between the forces of tradition and modernity . . . a tussle for dominion over domestic space."[8] Within that space, adults, children, married couples, and animals should be appropriately separated.

Nevertheless, missionaries were critical of Eurocentric theories about primitive promiscuity and some of them proposed new theories in order to demonstrate the social order behind allegations made by explorers and other transient observers. Aware of the public fascination with indigenous sexual practices, Lorimer Fison declared to his mentor Lewis Henry Morgan that

> These [practices] certainly appear grossly immoral to us; but it is now fully ascertained that they are in strict accordance with ancient law. This is notably the case with regard to the Australian aborigines whose practice is referred to more than once in proof of the absence of "moral feeling." The nature of the subject makes it impossible for me to go into particulars; & it must suffice to say that their practice is governed by established rules founded upon their social organization, & that any infringement of those rules is looked upon as an offence against morality, & is very severely punished. This at least is the case among tribes which have not been demoralized by their contact with civilization.[9]

Fison's research, combined with that of others, had established that Aboriginal Australians used the same four class names across the continent and

> we have ascertained that their marital rights extend over all the tribes who have [these names]—e.g. that one man's claim to the women who are free to him in his own tribe would be recognized in a tribe 1000 miles

7. New Guinea Mission, *Report of the New Guinea Mission for the year ending 31st March, 1901* (Sydney: W. A. Pepperday & Co., 1901), 8.

8. Joseph Nugent, "The Human Snout: Pigs, Priests and Peasants in the Parlor," *Senses and Society* 4, no. 3 (2009): 285. See also Brian P. Kennedy, "The Traditional Irish Thatched House: Imagery and Reality, 1793–1993," in *Visualizing Ireland: National Identity and the Pictorial Tradition*, ed. Adele Dalsimer (Boston: Faber and Faber, 1993).

9. Lorimer Fison, "Note-book Leaflets, No. iii. Morality among Savages," Lorimer Fison Project, Letterbook No. 6, PMB 1039.

> distant from his own if he were to visit them, though the languages are as widely apart as is French from English. It is the most astounding system of communion that the world has ever known.[10]

By the time Fison gave a paper on the subject to the Australasian Association for the Advancement of Science in 1892, he had noted the recent publication of Edward Westermarck's *History of Human Marriage* and its denunciation of the concept of communal marriage. Fison said that he and his collaborator Howitt had already dropped this phrase in favor of "group marriage," noting that the whole concept of Aboriginal marriage must be rethought because "it does not mean in this connection all that it means in our own society." Europeans presumed that marriage involved sex, or at least cohabitation, but in Aboriginal society the term was much broader, including "a marital right, or rather a marital qualification, which comes by birth."[11] In a letter to the Australian anthropologist W. Baldwin Spencer, Fison reminded the younger man that

> By the way Group-marriage is not Morgan's theory—it is mine. I corresponded with him for several years before he published his Ancient Society, & sent him three papers of which my Chapters on Group Marriage & Relationship in K & K are simply an elaboration. He had these published in some American magazine—I forget its name—& I am thankful to say that its editor paid me six guineas for them. Morgan did not perceive that the Classificatory Terms are the outcome of exogamous intermarrying divisions, & when I pointed it out to him he was wild with delight.[12]

He added that Morgan "grew perfectly rampant & called me names. He actually called me 'a genius.'" The main point here is Fison's emphasis on the integrity and coherence of the classification system, and his desire to quash attempts to sensationalize its implications for "promiscuity." A second point, however, was the defense of his achievements as a scientific theorist in his own right: accomplishments that were acknowledged by Morgan himself.

In their struggle to emphasize a universal human nature, missionaries criticized popular theories about Aboriginal ignorance concerning the biological process of conception. Patrick Wolfe has noted that this alleged ignorance, which he has termed "nescience," was key to Victorian debates about the in-

10. Lorimer Fison to Lewis Henry Morgan, [10] August 1878, Lormer Fison Project, Letterbook No. 6, PMB 1039/reel 4.

11. Lorimer Fison, "Group Marriage and Relationship," in *Proceedings of Section G, Anthropology* (Hobart: Government Printer for the AAAS, 1892), 3.

12. Lorimer Fison to Baldwin Spencer [1890], Baldwin Spencer MSS, AJCP Reel M2424.

feriority of Aboriginal Australians and their cultures. Wolfe's careful analysis demonstrates how nescience was used to counterpose Aboriginal Australians against the universal empiricism of western science. Presuming that anthropologists Spencer and Gillen's theory of nescience quickly became universalized, Wolfe regarded it as a "convergence of ethnography and imperialism since it replicates the opposing territorial interests at stake in the context of settler colonialism," namely the interests of science and geopolitics.[13] Without setting the work of Spencer and Gillen into the context of contemporary mission ethnography, however, nescience can appear to be a colonizing monolith.

We have already noted Lorimer Fison's extensive correspondence with Baldwin Spencer, and in a letter to Frazer at Cambridge he mentioned Spencer's findings concerning Aboriginal conception stories:

> The people have a curious belief that the country is full of little unborn children—not spirits exactly, but incorporeal. They follow the married women about until they get their chance; when they suddenly enter them, & the women conceive—or perhaps this may take place when the foetus quickens. I am not sure about the time. I have great pleasure in telling you of these things, but the facts are Spencer's property & nothing should be written about them for the public until his work appears.[14]

Fison's interest in Spencer's observations shows his acceptance of a complex network of physical and spiritual causes for conception in this particular Aboriginal context. A physical conception might already have taken place before a spirit-child "quickened" the pregnancy. Fison does not mention this, but we need to be aware that for centuries Europeans themselves had believed that quickening—the mother's awareness of movement in her womb—was a crucial stage of fetal development, and debates about the precise circumstances and timing of human ensoulment went back at least as far as Aristotle.[15] Increased knowledge about the precise biological role of sperm and egg had not yet entirely displaced this older picture, and by Fison's day there was as yet no understanding, for example, of exactly what determined the biological sex of the fetus. Meanwhile, in the same letter to Fraser, Fison reported that Gillen's finding of "descent through males" was hardly evidence of allegations of ignorance about the male role in reproduction.[16]

13. Wolfe, *Settler Colonialism*, 10.

14. Lorimer Fison to James Fraser [*sic*], 24 December 1896, "Rev. Lorimer Fison: Articles, letters & misc. papers, 1873–1907," Lorimer Fison Project, PMB reel 1042.

15. Norman M. Ford, *When Did I Begin? Conception of the Human Individual in History, Philosophy and Science* (Cambridge: Cambridge University Press, 1988), 19–43.

16. For a critique of early anthropology's preoccupation with conception stories, see Gilbert H.

Perhaps unaware of the vast Fison archive, Wolfe quotes Fison's book on the implication of group marriage as evidence of his endorsement of nescience, namely, "when a woman is married to a thousand miles of husbands, then paternity must be, to say the least of it, somewhat doubtful." For Wolfe, nescience "could spring from the same promiscuous factors as those underlying mother-right,"[17] but missionaries strongly rejected anthropological theories about promiscuity, and they knew that matrilineal cultures were not necessarily ignorant of the male role in conception. We need to consider more carefully what Fison meant by paternity. In Britain or in Australia, a woman might for various reasons be unsure exactly who was the individual father of her child, while nevertheless understanding perfectly well the male role in conception.

The Presbyterian missionary John Mathew was also critical of the idea "that the Australian natives *do not connect the knowledge of conception with intercourse between the sexes*" [original emphasis]. Instead, he explained, "There is a spiritual and a material part. *Sexuality is the stimulus of the corporeal reproduction, but the spirit quantity is derived through mystic, abstract influences controlled by a 'totem' spirit* or Knainja." Spencer and Gillen had "been at great pains to show that conception was regarded by certain tribes as independent of sexual intercourse. Supposing that that were true, while they must see that animal procreation is dependent on sexual intercourse, it surely is inconceivable that they should conclude the opposite to be the case in human beings."[18] Mathew therefore insisted that Aboriginal Australians were simply distinguishing between fertilization and conception. Missionaries outside Australia also contested allegations of nescience.

From the New Hebrides Mission, A. S. Webb reported that that on Aoba, descent was matrilineal and child betrothals were common, but betrothal protocol featured strict avoidance before the marriage actually took place. Before the final ceremonies the bride was carefully watched by near relatives who also slept with her at night "to make sure that the groom can bring no accusation of pre-marital unchastity against the bride. This is an important matter affecting greatly the price paid for a wife." Webb explained that it was usually several years before the first child was born, due either to natural or artificial forms of birth control, but that

> pregnancy, though the essentials to it are well understood, is said to be due to external influences, as, for example, the fact that a lizard crossed the

---

Herdt, *Ritualized Homosexuality in Melanesia* (Berkeley: University of California Press, 1984), 200–202.

17. Wolfe, *Settler Colonialism*, 15.

18. John Mathew, "The Religious Cults of the Australian Aborigines," *Report of the Australasian Association for the Advancement of Science* 18 (Sydney: AAAS, 1926), 526.

path of the mother; or she may have gone on a definite quest to a sacred cave or rock near which she will see some sign that all is well. The father of the child has his part to play as the mother's pregnancy advances; he must not climb trees or do heavy work lest some harm befall the child; and if when labor comes there is any delay, he is expected to perform certain rites which will help the mother. A woman desiring to avoid pregnancy will be most careful to keep well away from the sacred places which are sought eagerly by those who desire children.[19]

Rather than a monolithic, colonizing dismissal of indigenous understandings of conception, this was a quarrel between missionary ethnographers and professional academics, a quarrel carried out very publicly in the proceedings of the AAAS and other scientific venues. It was the academics who seemed keen to promote a theory of nescience. As so often, mission priorities involved underlining a common response to the human condition in every way they could.

Even as they were exploring and defending the integrity of indigenous sexual morality and marriage systems, however, missionaries were also endeavoring to change the situation. Whatever the indigenous tradition had been, monogamous Christian marriage was to be the norm among Christian converts, at considerable cost to anthropology as Bishop Stone-Wigg of the Anglican New Guinea Mission observed:

> there is reason to believe that men whose wives were suckling their children had access for the time to the wives of all those of their own generation; yet native customs never failed to forbid men having intercourse with women of their own sept or clan. Christian teaching has practically killed this practice of group marriage, even though its widespread existence was only discovered after its extinction.[20]

There was far more than group marriage that missionaries wished to change. Even in an era vastly less sensitive to pedophilia than our own, they were particularly disturbed by the early sexualization of children in some parts of the Pacific. "Tahiti is a vortex of iniquity," thundered John Davies of the LMS,

> the Sodom of the Pacific and gazing stock to the world, a thorn in the eyes of the just. . . . If our children, by the turgency of their breasts, shew

19. Webb, "The People of Aoba," 188.

20. Montagu John Stone-Wigg, *The Papuans: A People of the South Pacific* (Melbourne: The Shipping Newspapers Ltd., 1912), 33–34.

> signs of puberty, it is immediately asked who was her man, or was it the father. For it is maintained that no one can menstruate till she has been ruptured by coition. By 7 or 9 years of age all are ruptured. They say, 'Oh, let them alone, they are only children, and will grow the faster for it.' Be not shocked, the half has not been told you.[21]

The missing "half" was sex between children, including homosexual sex; hence the reference to the biblical city of Sodom and its fate.

The condemnation of child marriage was familiar from missions around the world in this period, especially India. As Mrinalini Sinha's pioneering study has shown, British opinion was surprisingly ambivalent about the *Consent Act* brought before the Indian Legislative Council in 1891. Intended to raise the age of consent for girls from 10 to 12 years of age, the bill was a compromise, affirming the legality of child marriage while objecting only to its underage sexual consummation. This was too great a concession to upper caste Hindu men in the eyes of some British critics, and Indian nationalists objected to its interference with the traditional marital rights of husbands.[22]

Any missionary discussion of childhood sexuality in the Pacific can usefully be read in light of what Sinha calls an "overdetermined context for colonial masculinity."[23] Davies's main objection in Tahiti was to the early "rupture" of girls who would therefore not be virgins when they married: a preoccupation of European men that he transposes onto Tahitians. A secondary concern was homosexual activity between boys, the Sodom of which the half had not yet been told. We will discuss homosexuality at greater length shortly. For now, we need to recognize what a significant challenge to traditional theological anthropology was posed by apparently shameless sexual activity involving Tahitian children. John Wesley himself, the father of British Methodism, refused to believe Captain Cook's account of sex at Tahiti between an adult man and a young girl "10 or 12 years of age publickly before several of our people and a number of the Natives."[24] Scripture stated clearly that after Adam and Eve disobeyed God in the Garden of Eden, they became aware for the first time of their nakedness. Shame about genitalia and sexual activity was presumed to be an essential part

21. John Davies, "Epilogue: Extracts from the 'Old Orsmond MS, 1849,'" in *The History of the Tahitian Mission 1799–1830*, ed. Colin Newbury (Cambridge: Cambridge University Press, 1961), 358.

22. Mrinalini Sinha, *Colonial Masculinity: The 'Manly Englishman' and the 'Effeminate Bengali' in the Late Nineteenth Century* (Manchester: Manchester University Press, 1995), 138–80.

23. Sinha, *Colonial Masculinity*, 172.

24. Cited in Neil Rennie, "The Point Venus 'Scene,'" in *Science and Exploration in the Pacific*, ed. Margarette Lincoln (Woodbridge, UK: Boydell Press, 1998), 135.

of human consciousness: a universal consequence of sin. As we know, Pacific peoples had to be Other to a certain extent in order to underline their need for the gospel, but not so alien that they seemed outside the universal biblical story. Theological anthropology therefore required universal evidence of sexual shame. When this evidence was not revealed by Captain Cook's story, Wesley rejected the story: "Men and women coupling together in the face of the sun, and in the sight of scores of people! Hume or Voltaire might believe this, but I cannot."[25] The reference to Hume and Voltaire indicated that to believe a story about shameless sex was to reject Christian orthodoxy.

It is intriguing, therefore, to find no attempt to resolve this enormous theological difficulty in early mission accounts from Tahiti. One way of avoiding it was to keep the reader's eye focused on the presence or absence of virginity in girls: "It is most distressing to the feelings to see so much degeneracy among the children of these people," wrote Richard Osmond. "There is I firmly believe *No* girl of 7 years old who has not been deprived of her virginity at her own request."[26] Osmond later noted that it was usually other children who shared this first sexual experience, and not necessarily with the opposite sex: "Little children hardly ever live to the age of Seven ere they are deflowered. Children with children, often boys with boys. They are often on the mountains playing in wickedness together all the day long."[27] Perhaps he did not know of the objections by Wesley and others to Captain Cook's account, or perhaps he was simply not a particularly deep thinker. Early missionaries to Tahiti were chosen more for their practical abilities than their theological acumen. Whatever the reason, Osmond and his colleagues usually chose to dodge the question in favor of ongoing mission outreach.

The main reason for this was the overwhelming need for brothering in the mission field. Back in Britain, Wesley could afford to point to the quandary posed by Cook's observations, and rejected the observations in order to maintain his theological position. Missionaries in the field, however, were forced to make observations of their own, and when these underlined the plausibility of Cook's account, they could have simply rejected an Other too alien to be part of the universal biblical story. But that would be no way to run a mission, especially when shameless sexual activity was so commonplace, and so the theologically indigestible elements were noted, and then ignored or transposed. Same-sex activities among children were linked with anal sex between adult

25. Cited in Rennie, "The Point Venus 'Scene,'" 140.

26. Richard Osmond Journal, 9 March 1827, South Sea Journals, Box 6, Council of World Mission Archives, School of Oriental and African Studies, London, UK.

27. Richard Osmond Journal, 24 October 1827, South Sea Journals, Box 6, Council of World Mission Archives, School of Oriental and African Studies, London, UK.

males condemned at Sodom, creating an apparent connection with biblical cultures. The possibility of brothering could remain precariously intact.

In some cases involving adult sexuality, missionaries denounced particular practices as bestial: a sign that transposition was not enough and brothering was being abandoned, but without any apparent awareness that a foundational theological principle was being abandoned with it. Watching a display of Samoan dancing, John Williams of the LMS found himself in some conflict of mind. He confided in his journal in clumsy English that was much more candid than his heavily edited book would be. Begged to attend a dance to be performed by noblewomen in his honor, he declined "not knowing the exact nature of their dances & whether or no they would be allowable on Christian principles." But then he sat in the front door of his guest house, looking into the assembly hall where the dance was taking place. "I must confess I did not hear or see any thing immoral or indecent in the whole performance," he recorded, having obviously watched closely! Later he asked the women to give him the words of the songs to which they had been dancing because he had recognized his name in the lyrics. "I cannot find an indecent word or phrase in either of them," he wrote, almost in disappointment, providing the reader with the lyrics in both Samoan and English.[28]

Nevertheless, he felt compelled to state, "That they [the Samoans] have songs & dances of the most disgusting & filthy nature is known so much so that I fear the most modest & chaste description of them could scarcely be read in England," yet at the same time admitting: "I did not see or hear neither did I think it well to enquire into them, but speak of them with disgust."[29] It is clear, however, that he did enquire into them. In an appendix to his journal, possibly never intended for publication, the dances in question are described in great detail. They "exceed in obscenity any thing I ever read or heard of," Williams declared, mainly because the dancing women taunted the watching men until they approached them "& with their tongues perform what one beast does to another." The women then demanded that the men strip naked. The goal seemed to be for either the men or the women to embarrass the other group into leaving the dancing house, but "the Samoa ladies not possessing a great degree of the grace that adorns the female sex the efforts of the gentlemen generally prove fruitless, for there is nothing like shame in the dancing house."[30] The lack of shame, which Williams assumed that women should possess in greater

28. John Williams, *The Samoan Journals of John Williams 1830 and 1832*, ed. Richard M. Moyle (Canberra: Australian National University Press, 1984), 152.

29. Williams, *Samoan Journals of John Williams*, 152.

30. Williams, *Samoan Journals of John Williams*, 247–48.

quantities than men, made scenes like this even more transgressive in his eyes. A whole scheme of gendered theology was at stake, but like others, Williams preferred not take up the implications of his choice of bestial language. How could sexual behavior—cunnilingus in this case—be both bestial and unnatural? Sexual behavior among animals was inevitably both natural and sinless. Similar behavior among humans might be deemed sinful, but it could not be unnatural. If there was no shame in the dancing house, did this not disprove the biblical story of humanity's expulsion from the Garden of Eden? Like his colleagues in Tahiti, Williams in Samoa was observing behavior that called many assumptions of traditional theological anthropology into question. Here was an apparently irreducible Other, yet the mission continued. Missionaries simply chose to ignore the contradiction between the radical universalism of their faith and the gendered and sexualized boundaries they drew to place some practices beyond the pale of humanity.

The perceived status of women in indigenous society was commonly used by European observers to locate various peoples on a scale of civilization, and this process was fraught with difficulty for missionary ethnographers. In some cases they made a simple equation between women's clothing, their moral consciousness, and their people's ripeness for the gospel. George Brown described visiting islands near his new Methodist mission station on New Britain, deciding that the inhabitants of one were considerably in advance of the other. The first piece of evidence he supplied for this judgment concerned female clothing: "Every woman & girl on Meoko wears a girdle or dried Banana Leaf," he wrote, "whilst in all the other places here clothing or covering of any kind is quite unknown." These observations led to an aesthetic judgment—"I quite liked the appearance both of place and people"—and to an immediate decision "to put down Meoko on the first list of Stations."[31] But indigenous clothing might not mean what missionaries assumed it to mean and, in other cases, the adoption of European clothing might not necessarily reflect a European understanding of gender roles. These unsettling moments were sometimes controlled by mockery, as when the New Hebrides Mission's local magazine declared, "Their ideas of dress are more influenced by display than decency. A man will appropriate a lady's night-dress and leave his wife to tie a pair of trousers round her neck; or will parade along the beach in a 'bell-topper' and a fresh coat of paint."[32] Homi Bhabha's "baboo" mimic comes to mind.[33] The sort of savage who would wear

31. George Brown Journal, 25 September 1875, Rev. George Brown, "Letterbook, 1870–1876," ML A 1868–2, CY Reel 2767, Mitchell Library, Sydney, Australia.

32. "Island Humour," *New Hebrides Magazine* 25 (1907): 9.

33. Homi Bhabha, "Of Mimicry and Man: The Ambivalence of Colonial Discourse," *October* 28 (1984): 125–33.

a top hat with his body-paint was also incapable of realizing that he should not wear his wife's nightie.

Of equal interest here, however, is the use made of clothing in missionary arguments underlining unity as well as difference. We have already seen how often diffusion theory was invoked by missionaries in order to underline common human ancestry and culture; William Bromilow remarked from Papua that "it was pleasing to find, also, that the women's dress, the grass skirt, was seemly—and, it may be remarked incidentally, capable of being worn with distinctive style and effect—upon which there was no need to innovate. This, too, is a vestige, probably, of better days."[34] Talk of vestiges or survivals were tell-tale signs of a classic othering and brothering strategy that went much further than endorsing new European standards. Indigenous clothing, scientifically interpreted, could indicate a kinship with a universalized human morality. Local forms therefore had their own integrity. Environmental conditions in the South Pacific were very different from those in northwestern Europe. Although some missions insisted on the adoption of European clothing, others realized that this could be harmful. E. R. Gribble wrote of Australia:

> in the tropics clothing for warmth is generally unnecessary and in their native state aborigines do not need it. Moreover, it can be a grave danger to health. Natives have not the same facilities as Europeans for washing and drying clothes and not only will they continue to wear garments that have never been washed and should have long since been discarded, but drenched in the tropical rains they will contract disease through wearing wet clothing. In Papua natives are forbidden, except under special circumstances, to wear any clothes on the upper part of their bodies on account of the danger to health and it is generally agreed that the prohibition is a wide one. Clothing is no part of Christianity and the native can be benefited, civilized, and Christianized without having to adopt the clothes of the whites.[35]

Missionaries also reflected on the contingency of their own cultural norms. Shortly after arriving at Duke of York Island, George Brown wrote to his wife that the islanders did not "seem to have any shame or to be in any way conscious of any impropriety in standing stark naked before us." Even more interesting

34. William Bromilow, *Twenty Years among Primitive Papuans* (London: Epworth Press, 1929), 114.

35. E. R. Gribble, *A Despised Race: The Vanishing Aboriginals of Australia* (Sydney: Australian Board of Missions, 1923), 27–28.

were reflexive remarks about his own reaction: “Still it is astonishing how soon you get used to it all. I scarcely ever notice now that the folks have no lavalavas on.”[36] In his own way, Brown was reflecting Gribble’s view that “clothing is no part of Christianity,” but the lack of shame in nakedness left open a theological question that missionaries usually preferred neither to ask nor to answer.

Their ethnography about women and female gender roles was thus fraught with tension. In 1855 the CMS periodical *The Church Missionary Gleaner* published an article entitled “Condition of Women in Heathen and Mahommedan Countries.” Its theological anthropology reflected traditional European Christian interpretations of Genesis, blaming women for their own social subordination: “When we cast our eye over the yet unevangelized portions of the earth, we are constantly reminded of the punishment which God pronounced on Eve, namely, that hers should be a state of subjection and of servitude.” The task was not to question gender relations that were believed to be divinely ordained, but instead to assess whether or not women were being unduly oppressed. The *Gleaner* therefore asserted that the gospel was “raising the daughters of Eve from the state of degradation and utter worthlessness in which, in heathen countries, it finds them, and placing them in a position to glorify God, and with patience and humility to endeavor to advance the cause of that Saviour to whom they owe so much.” Although the article quoted the radical universalism of the Letter to the Galatians—“In Christ there is neither Jew nor Greek, bond nor free, male nor female”—it was careful to specify that women were to express this spiritual liberation in terms of “patience and humility.” As for non-Christians: “Whether in Asia, Africa, America, or Australia, wherever heathenism prevails, we find woman equally degraded.”[37]

From Fiji, Richard Burdsall Lyth made similar sweeping statements: “The degraded state of slavery in which the Feejeean women are held is like that of other heathen countries though in some respects much more revolting & oppressive.” Lyth was particularly incensed by their inability to refuse the sexual advances of high-ranking men: “No Bau lady can be a church member for the disgraceful reason that though a married woman she has no way of escape from forced adultery.” One woman, Adi Tagici, “has had to produce abortion again & again as I have been informed lest the discovery shd [*sic*] lead to the club of her husband or his employers as the punishment for her infidelity.” He gave other examples, the most interesting of which concerned the clash between indig-

36. Brown to Brown, 22 August 1875, “Rev. George Brown, Letterbook 1870–1876,” ML A1686-2, CY Reel 2767, Mitchell Library, Sydney, Australia.

37. “Condition of Women in Heathen and Mahommedan Countries,” *The Church Missionary Gleaner*, new series 5 (1855): 90.

enous and Christian constructions of women's status. The mission was by no means the winner of these contests. A chief, Tuinayi, converted to Christianity, and his two junior wives "being desirous of saving their souls, were allowed to meet in class on trial on condition that they were no longer concubines. The king heard of this & said 'I'll see whose [*sic*] master. I or the lotu' and obliged them to be the slaves of his will." In another case

> a young woman the daughter of one of the first chiefs of the land, a papist, was allowed to meet in class on trial, though the nominal wife of a polygamist chief (Mara) as he was & had been for a long time living in another land. But he has come again to Lakemba. For some time she kept out of his way & objected to go to him *though against the remonstrances of her father who said he was ashamed of her*. But at length he (Mara) went and took her by force: there was no redress, power was on the one side, abject slavery on the other.[38]

Like their counterparts in India and elsewhere, Pacific missionaries denounced the marriage of young girls to older men. "I have seen a fine healthy girl of eleven or twelve years of age married to a man of twenty-five or thirty," wrote Lyth, and "the result of such an early union has been dreadful. To judge of her sufferings by her altered appearance within a few years, they must have been acute."

At Samoa, John Williams met the chief Malietoa on the day he took a new wife. "Strange to tell the old man had bought a young wife with part of the present made him yesterday [gifts of western goods, including a gun, brought by the missionaries]." The new wife "was better looking than any female we had seen on the Island but the Chief was not only aged but far from handsome. We hope the day is not far distant when the light of the glorious gospel will chase away all such works of Darkness." He added:

> We were informed that young women designed for sale are carefully watched during their youth to prevent improper liberty being taken with them and even after a girl is sold and falls into the hands of a new master he appoints one or two young men to take care of her, and particularly to prevent eloping again to her relations for in that case he would have to repurchase her or fight for her.[39]

38. Richard Burdsall Lyth, "Reminiscences," 110–11, ML B548, CY Reel 207, Mitchell Library, Sydney, Australia (original emphasis).

39. Williams, *Journals of John Williams*, 76–77.

Despite his sarcastic tone, Williams never claimed that Samoans lacked sexual morality. Adultery was severely punished and he told of the killing of a powerful and much-hated chief whose body was mutilated after death. Among other things, the chief's killers "cut off his parts for having connection with other men's wives."[40] Williams also noted that social rank complicated his own picture of "young women designed for sale." The chief Vavasa had once captured one of Malietoa's daughters, but since Malietoa outranked Vavasa, so did Malietoa's daughter. "The young girl would not accede to his wishes & all the people raised their voices against Vavasa saying it was a base thing in him to take so great a lady to wife."[41] Vavasa killed the woman instead, to Malietoa's grief.

In some cases the missionaries intervened in such situations by acceding to local cultural norms in order to interrupt the "sale." The Methodist missionary Benjamin Danks at New Britain contributed his own observations of the "enslavement" of women. He told the story of Ia Wawaluk, a young woman who worked at the mission as a maid:

> One day we were dismayed to hear that she had been sold, and that she must go to her husband on a fixed day. She stamped her foot and indignantly said she would not go, a determination in which I encouraged her. Her purchaser was a very old leading man from a place called Tokirebera. He had seen the girl a day or two before, admired her youthful beauty, and being rich had offered a price hard to resist. He was a toothless, failing old man of a very debased type. We encouraged the girl in her refusal as we considered that our mission house, rightly or wrongly, was a place of refuge.[42]

Her family eventually captured her, taking her back to her village for a beating and public humiliation "by having her clothes torn from her while the men stood round making ribald remarks."[43] Ia eventually escaped and Danks fended off her spear-wielding brother by agreeing to pay a ransom for the girl.

Pacific missionaries did not only denounce the enslavement of women by indigenous men; they were even more vocal about white men purchasing island women by manipulating local custom. Their anti-slavery campaign on the subject won them the sympathy of key Royal Navy officers and colonial

40. Williams, *Journals of John Williams*, 131.

41. Williams, *Journals of John Williams*, 138.

42. Benjamin Danks, "Women and Marriage Customs in New Britain," ed. Wallace Deane, CY Reel 3465, Mitchell Library, Sydney, Australia.

43. Danks, "Women and Marriage Customs in New Britain."

officials, resulting in a high-profile campaign for legislation and sanctions.[44] Missionaries thought they were seeing evidence of a universal tendency toward the oppression of women that, they believed, could be countered only by the adoption of modern western gender relations. When western men preferred indigenous practices, missionaries felt betrayed. Richard Lyth told of a young woman named Mereane Vale who eloped with a married American man. She returned after three months but the man "knew with whom he had to deal, so made friends with the chiefs by means of gifts in the form of powder, shot & axes." Lyth concluded that "the girl to all intents was sold & all appeal was in vain." The girl's mother reproached Lyth and the other missionaries: "Ah said she, the chiefs formerly ruled our children, but this is the age of the lotu, she thought the age of oppression was over but not so."[45]

The othering in these accounts concerns inappropriate age disparities, bride-payments, and the lack of individual agency by women who (the missionaries assumed) would naturally rather marry for love. We must be careful not to dismiss these assumptions out of hand, however, simply because direct evidence of women's own views is so scarce. During one of his lengthy stays at the island of Mota, Robert Codrington of the Melanesian Mission was paying a visit to one of his closest Melanesian friends, a high-ranking man named Merina. Merina's son was soon to be married and he had asked Codrington to visit the prospective bride and to give his opinion of her. Later, he asked "what we gave for a wife in England. He thought us rather mean I think for giving nothing, but my description of the estate of matrimony as with us, & with [the Melanesians] who live with us, met with ejaculations of approval from his wife."[46] There was also a special concern about widows, especially in Fiji where a widow of high rank might be strangled after her husband's death. As they sometimes did with women purchased from their families by white men, missionaries offered to buy the lives of widows to save them from strangulation. There was not much time in some cases; William Moore at Bua "caught hold of one of the men who held the fatal cord and dragged him away" before offering to purchase the woman. "They became very angry but we persisted and got the woman who is still alive."[47] As colleague Thomas Williams explained, the *loloku* was not religiously motivated; instead, its purpose was to honor the dead chief by providing him with appropriate attendants into the world of spirits. He added that "Christianity is disliked because it rigorously

44. Jane Samson, "Rescuing Fijian Women? The British Anti-Slavery Proclamation of 1852," *Journal of Pacific History* 30, no. 1 (1995): 22–38.

45. Lyth, "Reminiscences," 111–12.

46. Journal entry, 4 October 1872, n/p, Melanesian Mission MSS 2/2, School of Oriental and African Studies, UK.

47. Cited in Thornley, *Exodus of the I Taukei.*

discountenances the cherished custom."[48] The *loloku*, like *sati* in India, was interpreted by British observers as evidence of women's degradation to the point of death.[49] Benjamin Danks reported a different problem from the western islands of Melanesia: "The fate of a widow, on Duke of York, at least, was a cruel one, for she becomes common property." An elderly widow had sought baptism at the Kinawanua mission station, but Danks "was advised to delay, chiefly because of the above custom . . . it was the regular thing for men to claim all widows."[50] This widowed woman, despite her desire to be baptized and received into the Christian community, was unable to defend her chastity, and Danks's use of the passive voice might indicate that he was required by his superiors to refuse baptism accordingly.

Assumptions about the alleged enslavement of Pacific women were based not only on assumptions about sexual morality, bride price, or the fate of widows, but also on labor practices that missionaries were endeavoring to change.[51] From Fiji, the Methodist missionary Arthur J. Webb reported from the interior of Viti Levu that men "gave their wives a hard time of it by making them beasts of burden, on Petruchio's maxim, that 'women are made to bear.'"[52] He reported having "seen a procession of women going in single file through the woods, bent double under heavy loads, while the lord and husband of the lot marched with stately masculine dignity behind, carrying a spear."[53] Reports of a bestial degree of female labor were common in the Pacific mission field, and the language here alerts us to the borderlines of human universalism. Like observations of "bestial" sexual behavior, however, a closer look at these observations reveals complexity and contradiction. Webb, for example, seemed preoccupied mainly by the impact of heavy labor on Fijian women's physical attractiveness. Women aged quickly in the interior district, he reported, and lacked "the comeliness of their better-treated sisters in the other parts of Fiji." His concerns reveal a

48. Williams, *Islands and Their Inhabitants*, 188–89.

49. See Lata Mani, *Contentious Traditions: The Debate on Sati in Colonial India* (Berkeley: University of California Press, 1998), and Andrea Major, *Sovereignty and Social Reform in India: British Colonialism and the Campaign against Sati, 1830–60* (Abingdon, UK: Routledge, 2010).

50. Danks, "Women and Marriage Customs in New Britain."

51. For studies of the responses of indigenous women to Christianity see Margaret Jolly and Martha Macintyre, eds., *Family and Gender in the Pacific: Domestic Contradictions and the Colonial Impact* (Cambridge: Cambridge University Press, 1989), and Margaret Jolly, "'To Save the Girls for Brighter and Better Lives': Presbyterian Missions and Women in the South of Vanuatu: 1848–1870," *Journal of Pacific History* 26, no. 1 (1991): 27–48.

52. Arthur J. Webb, "Observations on the Hill Tribes of Navitilevu, Fiji," *Report of the Second Meeting of the Australasian Association for the Advancement of Science* (Sydney: AAAS, 1890). This was a significant misinterpretation of Shakespeare's *Taming of the Shrew*, Act II, scene i, where Petruchio is clearly referring to the bearing of children.

53. Webb, "Observations on the Hill Tribes of Navitilevu, Fiji," 625.

class-related conception of female beauty in which the signs of physical labor were deplored, just as they would be at home in England among middle- and upper-class Britons. Webb was assuming that Fijian women could be more universally attractive if "bestial" cultural practices were eliminated. Likewise, LMS missionary W. Wyatt Gill reported from Mangaia that "woman is the slave of man in heathen society," but the reason for this conclusion was a division of labor that would have been familiar to most working-class British women. On Mangaia the woman "plants, carries home the food, collects the firewood and succulent oven-leaves, cooks her lord's meal, spreads out supper on hibiscus leaves (in lieu of plates, and of the same size), never omitting the sea-water, used as sauce and salt." He also complained that

> Torch-fishing is woman's occupation only. Whenever she gets home, often in the small hours of the morning, a special oven for these dainties must be prepared by her for husband and children. The wife is expected not only to feed but to clothe her husband. . . . *His* duty is to defend land and life, to plant and weed, and to fish with hook or net or spear.[54]

But this is a division of labor rather than a picture of slavery, and Gill's critique reflected the British middle-class paternalism that had led to the banning of women from mining and other physically demanding trades earlier in the nineteenth century.

Other missionaries reflected more carefully on indigenous divisions of labor, including James Chalmers's account from New Guinea that among the Toaripi "women do all the cooking, and a great part of the fishing. Husband and wife plant, fetch wood, make sago, &c. As a rule the women are well treated; not many beat their wives. A husband beating his wife would have to bear the wrath of all her relatives." This point is an interesting one. Although some missionaries were quick to diagnose slavery, linking the South Pacific to western Africa in a globalized scheme of imperial benevolence, others revealed information that countered suppositions about a lack of female agency. The situation differed widely between cultures, contrary to the universalized statement with which this chapter began. For his part, Chalmers believed that married life was "a hard one for women," not least because their husbands might beat them, but

> it is possible for her to complain of ill-usage and run away to her friends who may or may not protect her. If they decided to take up the cudgels

54. W. Wyatt Gill, "Mangaia (Hervey Islands)," in *Report of the Second Meeting of the Australasian Association for the Advancement of Science* (Sydney: AAAS, 1890), 332.

> on her behalf, then the husband, however much he may wish to regain possession of his spouse, cannot use any violence to carry out what is in his mind. In the end he may demand that the bride-price which he advanced to them at the time of his wedding shall be refunded. If they think sufficiently well of her, they may do this. I have come across a few cases where the money has been repaid, and the wife went free.[55]

Bromilow reported that among the matrilineal 'Edugaula of New Guinea, wives could divorce their husbands for a variety of reasons including adultery, insulting behavior, or laziness. The reverse was also true, but betrothal gifts given to the wife's family were not returned, making divorce a very expensive business for men. In this connection it is worth noting that escaping an abusive marriage was much easier for some Pacific women than it was for their English counterparts.

Patty O'Brien has suggested that European observers saw men, especially men's bodies, as the primary site of customary culture in the Pacific world,[56] but the opposite is true in missionary accounts. From Malekula, T. Watt Leggatt deplored the sensationalized nature of many reports about the abuse of "heathen women," but warned against going to the other extreme to

> imagine that the condition of women in heathen islands is at all comfortable or happy. Their lot is one of inferiority and degradation, and if in course of generations they have reconciled themselves to the inevitable, and so fitted their necks to the yoke that it is really less galling than it seems to us, their condition is no less pitiable.[57]

Talk of "the yoke" evokes images of farm animals hauling cultivation equipment, or of the peasant women who sometimes had to take their place. It also suggested cultural imprisonment, an imprisonment unique to women.

Newly arrived at Aniwa in the New Hebrides Mission, Maggie Paton, wife of the Reverend Dr. John G. Paton, was very pleased to note that unlike the situation in other parts of the Pacific "there are *Widows* here." Women were quite well treated on the whole, she believed, and she offered a mischievous observation in evidence: "I was quite delighted to hear one of them scold a man most energetically for some offence, two or three days after arriving;

55. Danks, "Women and Marriage Customs in New Britain."

56. Patty O'Brien, *The Pacific Muse: Exotic Femininity and the Colonial Pacific* (Seattle: University of Washington Press, 2006), 99.

57. T. Watt Leggatt, "The Position of Heathen Women in the New Hebrides," *The New Hebrides Magazine* (October 1910): 22–23.

not that I think it Woman's most beautiful function to be always attempting to bring the lords of creation into subjection, but the fact that she even dared to speak her mind so revealed a great deal."[58] Mrs. Paton's ambivalent reference to "the lords of creation" points us once more to the unexamined borderlands of gender where a British woman, however ironically, endorses the idea that women were not beautiful if they too often attempted to bring men "into subjection."

From New Guinea, LMS missionary James Chalmers's report of the Koiari noted that "some husbands are wife-beaters," assuming that this would be the first question on his readers' minds, but he went on to explain that the division of labor was actually fairly equitable: "She is supposed to care for the house, fetch and cook food; she assists in planting, but the husband does all the heavy work."[59] Later, William James Viritahitemauvai Saville, also writing of New Guinea, provided a more deterministic analysis, linking the perpetuation of custom with women rather than men:

> In marriage the girl emerges from the individual state and becomes an integral part of a clumsy unwieldy machine, little suspecting that by her entrance into it she is helping to keep up its motion. The flywheel of custom forbids her getting beyond its own circumference or connecting up its power for the accomplishment of anything new. It is an endless revolution about one axis.[60]

He explained that:

> In such matters [continuing to use ever-scarcer cone shells to exchange for pigs] the women are the conservative element. They are vitally concerned, for a great part of the effect of these trips is to satisfy marriage customs. Unknown to them, healthy life demands the expenditure of energy to maintain the standard. Much that the savage does is, unconsciously to him, the doing of a dictation lesson, and nature, in its fullest sense, is the dictator. Much that he does, so little understood by us, is the outlet for energy that the struggle for existence demands.[61]

58. Maggie Whitecross Paton, *Letters and Sketches from the New Hebrides*, 3rd ed. (London: Hodder and Stoughton, 1865), 38.

59. James Chalmers, "New Guinea. Toaripi and Koiari Tribes," *Report of the Second Meeting of the Australasian Association for the Advancement of Science* (Sydney: AAAS, 1890), 320.

60. William James Viritahitemauvai Saville, *In Unknown New Guinea* (London: Seeley Service & Co., 1926), 85.

61. Saville, *Unknown New Guinea*, 165.

The conventions of contemporary English required Saville to use the masculine third person to make an argument about the agency of women, something that tells its own story of the occlusion of female agency in the English language itself. Like Chalmers, he seems to anticipate trouble, generalizes about it, but then makes his own detailed observations to undercut it. Saville admitted that "to a casual observer it might appear that the woman carries all the heavy burdens," such as large loads of garden produce or wood, "while her lord walks in front, carrying his garden knife. Sometimes he may carry the child, but very often, when the husband is not with her, she seats the child on the topmost load, with his legs dangling round her neck. Custom has apportioned her load and her way of carrying it."[62] So far, Saville's account has typical features: reference to burdens and loads, to the weight of custom, and sarcastic reference to husbands as lords. But he tried to delve beneath these typical impressions to discover more:

> 1. She will brook no interference from the man. 2. The load is prepared in such a way that he would appear ludicrous in *her* eyes were he to carry it. 3. She looks to him to carry burdens for house or canoe building, which she would not think of tackling. 4. She expects him to shoulder the big nets and the fish, while she will carry the garden stuff if he will make canoes in which he can travel to augment her garden supply. 5. She is the slave not of tyrant man but of tyrant custom, from which she would be the very last to wish any departure.[63]

However, even this nuanced account did not lead Saville to abandon the language of slavery. The idea that women colluded in their own oppression has reappeared here, as has the portrayal of indigenous custom as a static, conservative force. Heathenism must generate enslavement.

Other Melanesian cultures displayed very different social structures and gender relations, as among the 'Edugaula people of the island of Dobu. "The women are by no means slaves," wrote William Bromilow of the Methodist mission, acknowledging that this was the usual view held by Europeans. Instead, 'Edugaula women had a voice in all the family and village concerns. "In many duties the women have a distinct sphere from the men, but in general matters they have an equal voice," Bromilow wrote. "They have ownership in land, and frequently prevent the men from selling native wealth."[64] There were caveats:

62. Saville, *Unknown New Guinea*, 73.

63. Saville, *Unknown New Guinea*, 73.

64. W. E. Bromilow, *Some Manners and Customs of the Dobuans of S. E. Papua* (Brisbane: James Cumming, 1910), 471.

"The men seem generally content to let the women have their own way in domestic and general affairs, as long as they are themselves allowed to rule in war, and carry out trade expeditions."[65] Men were the primary agents; they simply "let the women have their own way" at times. Saville, cited above concerning the tyranny of custom, also struggled to generalize when he learned of the situation on Mailu Island where women owned all land: "the man is dependent on the woman for his living, and she is aware of it, and will have her say on any question."[66] He cannot bring himself, however, to conclude that men were enslaved by women on Mailu.

Descriptions of women enslaved by custom, but (it was hoped) soon to be liberated by the gospel, are deeply ironic when we consider the deeply traditional roles that Christianized island women were expected to play. At the Melanesian Mission school on Norfolk Island, even as late as the early twentieth century, girls were taught no English and were prepared exclusively for domestic service in support of a better-educated husband. In this case the husbands were mostly destined for mission work, and the whole business was drenched in Anglo-Catholic nostalgia. Group weddings were held in the Norfolk chapel, with its pre-Raphaelite windows by Burne-Jones, and its splendid organ donated by the famous Victorian author Charlotte Yonge. After the ceremonies and the evening celebrations (segregated by sex, following Melanesian practice), each bride went to one of the small houses on the grounds to await the arrival of the bridegroom escorted by his male friends. "It is a pretty and romantic picture, and reminds one somehow of the way things were done in history-days," sighed mission teacher Florence Coombe, who was possibly thinking of the ancient tradition of "bedding."[67]

As for the ambiguous role of female agency in missionary stories about "beasts of burden," Charles Fox of the Melanesian Mission was able to provide uniquely personal insights. As we know, he exchanged names with a Melanesian man and was therefore able to experience the fullness of life in a Melanesian family and village community. "People are always sorry for women in the Solomon Islands because they think that women do most of the work," Fox wrote:

> They certainly do a great deal of the heavy work. . . . When you see a man and woman going along the path, it is the woman that is carrying things and the man striding along with nothing in his hands. One reason for the man carrying nothing is that not so very long ago the thing that the man carried was his weapons, to defend the woman. . . . Then the time came

65. Bromilow, *Some Manners and Customs*, 473.

66. Saville, *Unknown New Guinea*, 47.

67. Florence Coombe, *School Days in Norfolk Island* (London: SPCK, 1909), 62.

> when the need for this ceased, but he had got into the custom of letting the woman do the carrying, and the custom went on. It never occurred to the man that it was now the time for him to take his share in carrying the burdens.[68]

Men's roles were changing on the mission stations and beyond, but men were not necessarily keen to see women's roles change. Fox explained that on the island of Gela the woman was "the Lord of the Garden" while the man was "the Lord of the Reef." Since men no longer had to fight, women did more everyday work than men: year-round cultivation was very demanding in comparison with sporadic fishing expeditions. Nevertheless, no generalizations should be made about enslavement, Fox warned:

> The men are supposed to rule the villages, but very often it is the women who actually do rule, while the men think they rule. The wife often persuades her husband to the course that she wants him to take, very often after they are both in bed she talks to him, persuading him to what she wants. After a time the man agrees—he wants to go to sleep.[69]

This pillow diplomacy was hardly evidence of bestial enslavement, but neither was it evidence of open political power. Even as sensitive an ethnographer as Fox did not critique the privileged position of men.

One who did—and the reflexivity of his critique of gender roles is practically unique in missionary ethnography—was T. Watt Leggatt of the New Hebrides Mission. He did not equate Christianity with the "high" position enjoyed by women in modern western countries. "In early Christian times, to say nothing of Old Testament days, the condition of women was very different indeed. . . . The injunctions of the early Fathers would provoke indignant remonstrance from ladies nowadays; and rightly so."[70] Unlike almost any of his missionary brethren, Leggatt believed that the process of female emancipation remained incomplete, even in Britain, where "even among ourselves there are survivals of a similar way of thinking," he wrote, referring to some Pacific practices of female seclusion. Leggatt had in mind "the 'grille' in the Houses of Parliament and the seclusion of women from the chancels of ritualistic, i.e. medieval, churches and many other instances [that] will occur to the reader

68. Charles Elliot Fox, "A Missionary in Melanesia," 114, MS-Papers-1171–03, Alexander Turnbull Library, Wellington, NZ.

69. Fox, "A Missionary in Melanesia," 114–15.

70. T. Watt Leggatt, "The Position of Heathen Women in the New Hebrides," *The New Hebrides Magazine* (October 1910): 23.

at once."[71] Of Melanesian women he emphasized "that her position is not one of *utter* degradation," explaining that "in many instances a woman holds her own property, sometimes very tenaciously, and her children inherit through her." He agreed that "she is the burden bearer and the toiler" but explained that this left her man free to handle his weapons for her protection."[72]

In addition to contesting the concept of women as "beasts of burden," Leggatt also wanted to mitigate the charge of enslavement:

> The custom, too, of disposal in marriage for a certain number of tusked pigs is not quite such utter slavery as it looks at first sight. It is really a kind of hostage or ransom to the tribe that the other tribe will give a woman in return at a future period, and then the property will be returned. If the husband should die, her own tribe claims the right of redeeming her. So far from resenting this purchase, we hear of the women in the Santa Cruz Islands going on strike and refusing to marry because the men were not ready to pay a high enough price for them. But all the same, the idea of purchase, which regards woman as a chattel, is repugnant alike to modern ideas and the Christian mind. It is a work of time and patience to elevate woman, but we are convinced that it is the gospel of Christ alone that can do so.[73]

He seemed unaware of undermining the argument he had just been making concerning the tenuous connection between Christianity and the position of women in contemporary Britain.

Missionary accounts of polygamy were equally complex. George Brown of the Methodist mission on New Britain declared that "polygamy is extensively practiced," but in the same sentence added: "As a rule, however, comparatively few had more than two wives whilst the great majority were content with one," concluding that "the relation of husband and wife was on the whole harmonious."[74] These ambiguous conclusions were borne out by Benjamin Danks, who succeeded Brown at the Methodist mission on New Britain. "Polygamy obtained," Danks declared, and then immediately contradicted himself:

> while the majority of men had only one wife, all men might have as many as they could purchase, and polygamous family life is anything but ideal.

71. Leggatt, "The Position of Heathen Women," 23–24.
72. Leggatt, "The Position of Heathen Women," 24.
73. Leggatt, "The Position of Heathen Women," 24.
74. Brown, *Melanesians and Polynesians*, 32.

> There was usually a favorite wife of whom all the other wives were jealous, and whom they annoyed and traduced in every possible way, in the hope of supplanting her in their husband's regard.[75]

He told the story of a local man who had five wives, one of whom was particularly jealous of the alleged favorite. But given Danks's own observations, a man with five wives must have been a great rarity, making it unclear how polygamy could have obtained in the area. From his station on New Guinea, LMS missionary James Chalmers completed an anthropological questionnaire issued by the anthropology committee of the Australasian Association for the Advancement of Science, an organization eager for documentation of polygamy. Chalmers reported of the Toaripi people that few men had more than one wife even though polygamy was not restricted to those of high rank. There seemed to be a determination among Europeans to highlight polygamy, but fieldwork suggested that it was rare: a picture similar to that of women allegedly enslaved as beasts of burden.

Where polygamy did exist, missionaries often sought to probe beneath the surface to discover its social benefits. There was debate, rather than certainty, about what mission policy should be concerning members of polygamous families who converted to Christianity. As ever, missionaries were simultaneously promoting the alterity of Pacific peoples while underlining their humanity. Too much beastliness would undermine the point of mission work. In New Zealand, William Colenso observed that polygamy was commonplace in families of chiefly rank, and more constructive than destructive. "All chiefs had several wives; which increased their power and influence considerably," he wrote, an observation frequently made by missionaries in the South Pacific. Much rarer, however, was Colenso's conviction that

> Polygamy was not the cause of disagreement or jealousy among the wives, who lived together in great harmony. Nor did it cause a disproportion of marriageable women, as many males were being continually killed in their frequent battles. The *sudden* bringing home of a new wife, which sometimes happened (perhaps a slave, or from a distance), as a matter of course made quite a sensation among the old wives, but it was only temporary. Often the old wives themselves encouraged their husband to take another, and aided efficiently in doing so.[76]

75. Danks, "Women and Marriage Customs in New Britain."

76. William Colenso, "On the Maori Races of New Zealand," *Transactions and Proceedings of the New Zealand Institute* 1 (1868): 357.

His explanation for this state of affairs was "their injudicious early betrothals, (marriages of policy, not love), which *must* take place; their great desire of offspring; their belief that barrenness always proceeded from the female; and their rule of a brother always taking the widow of his deceased brother. . . ." He then made an extraordinary claim: "Politically speaking, had polygamy and divorce not been too early and rudely ecclesiastically interfered with and prohibited, the New Zealanders as a nation would, in all probability, have now been very much more numerous and better off."[77] Colenso was an evangelical Anglican hostile to the high notion of episcopal power exhibited by George Selwyn, New Zealand's first bishop. The reference to ecclesiastical interference is typical of his lament that bishops failed to defer to the superior knowledge and experience of missionaries on the spot. Nevertheless, the main point of Colenso's critique was to draw attention to the cultural integrity of polygamy, when understood in context.

Policy decisions were complicated by these cultural insights. At Samoa in 1830, LMS missionary John Williams mused over the problem: "Some have two, others as many as six" wives, he noted, revealing (perhaps unconsciously) that most married men had only one wife, and only some had two or more. Still, "we resolved that it was necessary to state that such a practice was inconsistent with Christianity." Williams reported that some converts "put away all but one wife so that I think the accomplishment of the object will not be found so difficult as at first sight it may appear." For Williams, only male converts possessed agency in these matters; he does not speak of female converts making decisions about their marriages. Nevertheless, he was aware of the emotional and social cost of the shift to monogamy, and he was uncertain about whether or not polygamous families should be forcibly broken up:

> In many instances a man has two wives with whom he has lived for many years & has a family by each[,] feels an attachment to both, & of course is at a loss which to put away. If he is allowed to keep his two others will make it a pretext for keeping half a dozen so that prudence & consideration must be exercised in the management of this affair. I have thought that in some instances perhaps it might be well to allow them to retain their wives & yet admit them into Christian communion. . . .[78]

William Yate of the CMS in New Zealand approved of the LMS policy in Tahiti that had set a precedent for the baptism of men with more than one wife.

77. Colenso, "On the Maori Races," 357–58.
78. Williams, *Samoan Journals of John Williams*, 142–43.

William Ellis had written that polygamous families deserved to be treated with pastoral compassion, and Yate felt that with regard to New Zealand: "I think that the Natives here are so situated that a case may occur in which it would be an act of great injustice for a man to force away one of his wives if he happens to have two." Other members of the mission disagreed with Yate, and he wrote to the leaders of the society in England for advice. He gave the example of a man he knew with two wives, both of whom had been married to him for 8 or 10 years. Both were the mothers of his children and both were

> equally dear to him and he is equally dear to them. They will neither of them consent to be separated and if one is put away it will be by actual force. Do you think that it would be right to refuse the man baptism because he *could* not remove one of his wives? I think it would be decidedly wrong.[79]

Yate's own personal life was deeply complicated, featuring sexual relationships with European and Maori men and boys that would result in his disgrace. As Tony Ballantyne has written, "In the 1990s, where difference, heterogeneity and ambivalence have greater value, Yate can only be seen in shades of grey."[80] Perhaps, as a grey man, he was more willing to acknowledge grey areas in the sexual practices of others.

By the twentieth century similar decisions were being made in the New Guinea Mission. In a history of the Australian Board of Mission in New Guinea, the Anglican missionary Copland King noted the "difficulties connected with the moral relationships of the natives . . . where a man had two wives already, we did not try to disturb the relationship, thinking it best to leave it until the man became a candidate for Baptism."[81] What about after baptism? The official position was that baptized Christians could have only one wife (as usual, it was presumed that the man was the only member of the polygamous family with agency). But debate continued at the highest level. The bishop of New Guinea knew that "a few members of the Staff occasionally had misgivings as to our marriage rules being too strict and rigid. Difficulties arise in a country like this, where the population is a mixture of heathens and Christians, which do not come to the front in so-called Christian countries." As a result, during a

79. William Yate to CMS Secretaries, 1 June 1832, "Correspondence 1808–1840," Hocken Library, Dunedin, NZ.

80. Tony Ballantyne, "William Yate: Mythmaking and Transgression in New Zealand," *Thamyris* 2, no. 1 (1995): 131.

81. Copland King, *A History of the New Guinea Mission 1891–1901* (Sydney: Australian Board of Mission, [1901]), 31.

recent trip to England, he "consulted the Archbishops of Canterbury and York, both of whom expressed the opinion that we are right and ought not to make any alteration."[82] This did not prevent members of the mission from continuing to debate their pastoral responsibilities, but it does cast doubt on some of the allegations of professional anthropologists. By the early twentieth century, Cambridge anthropologist A. C. Haddon, an advocate of academic anthropological training for missionaries, was assisting personally with the creation of appropriate courses. We know his indebtedness to missionaries as partners in anthropological research, yet he also criticized them as cultural bunglers. In a stern letter to the secretary of the Board of Study for the Preparation of Missionaries in 1911, Haddon castigated what he presumed to be a wholesale failure to comprehend the integrity of indigenous social institutions:

> It is not sufficiently recognized that most natives have a very rigid system of ethics which makes for social solidarity, and any weakening of this is liable to entail disastrous results. The wisest course in my judgment is to work through this public opinion and recognized authority and to upset as little as possible the native institutions. The people will gradually adapt themselves to the new ideals as they are ready for them, and an evolution of this kind is much more stable since it proceeds from below upwards.[83]

But this was also the view of many missionaries. A mythology was being born in which missionaries were othered by a new profession anxious to distance itself from its amateur roots. The main difference between the approach of most missions, and that advocated by Haddon, was usually a matter of degree rather than substance.

Lorimer Fison became convinced that patriarchal social organization, not polygamy, was responsible for the lack of female agency in Fijian families (women of high rank were another story). "As long as the old [matrilineal] rule continues, polygamy has no disintegrating influence," he wrote. "But when descent is through the father, & hereditary ideas have become rooted, polygamy is a strong, disintegrating power." This was because

> The wives' interest is no longer a common one. Each desires the best portion for her children & the communal is lost sight of in mutual jealousies & hatreds. I have seen enough of this among the Fijians to understand it

82. *Report of the New Guinea Mission* ([Sydney]: Central Depot, 1915), 17.

83. A. C. Haddon to Canon Weitbrecht, 19 Decmeber 1911, A. C. Haddon MSS, envelope 4067, Cambridge University Library, Cambridge, UK.

> thoroughly, & those who swear at missionaries because they insist upon monogamy for their converts, betray their lack of knowledge, even if we look at the question from this point alone.[84]

If a social system was patriarchal, monogamy gave wives (and their children) clearer rights and diminished conflict, but this did not make polygamy unjust. Fison could not have been clearer about the devastating effects of the shift from matrilineal to patrilineal descent: "Where the community begins to split up under this influence the tendency to further disintegration becomes stronger & stronger until the formerly united community is divided into a number of petty lands fighting & destroying one another, & handing down blood feuds to their children." He continued: "When a people comes to this pass despotism is beneficial & a strong tyranny is a blessing . . . repugnant as this is to our own notions. . . . For such a people the choice lies between despotism & anarchy, & it is no use to argue as to the respective merits of those two things."[85] Gender relations drove social change: between tyranny and anarchy lay the fragmentation and confrontation engendered by patrilineal descent. Nevertheless, as we know from his work on social anthropology, Fison agreed with the mainstream view that matrilineal kinship systems represented a lower stage of development. There was unresolved tension here between the insights generated by his own ethnography, and his support for a narrative of progress that considered matrilineal social systems backward.

Returning to the question of whether indigenous social structures revealed "bestial" behavior, missionary ethnography, as usual, probed behind assumptions concerning the victimization of women in indigenous marriage practices (polygamous or otherwise). James Chalmers reported from New Guinea that among the Toaripi people, where most men had only one wife, "there is no cohabitation until the child is grown and able to crawl about. Only then will the husband have connection with her and eat food cooked by her. A man having connection with his wife before then would injure the child, who would sicken and die." Even more interesting is what he reveals of indigenous imagery concerning misbehavior: "A woman having another child before one is quite grown is spoken of as an animal, a pig, or something else; she would be terribly ashamed."[86] What was "bestial," for the Toaripi, was the relentless childbearing

84. Lorimer Fison to Louis Henry Morgan, [10] August 1878, Lorimer Fison Project, Letterbook No. 6, PMB Reel 4.

85. Lorimer Fison to Louis Henry Morgan, [10] August 1878, Lorimer Fison Project, Letterbook No. 6, PMB Reel 4.

86. James Chalmers, "New Guinea, Toaripi and Koiari Tribes," *Report of the Second Meeting of the Australasian Association for the Advancement of Science* (Sydney: AAAS, 1890), 311.

in Christian families. They found revolting the idea that a Christian husband would treat his wife like an animal by demanding sex before she had sufficient time to recover from the last birth: "An Eastern Polynesian woman had two children within a year, and the natives were horribly disgusted and said she was only a sow."[87] Sometimes missionaries themselves became self-conscious about their reproductive practices. Marriage to a suitably pious British woman quickly became the norm before departure for the islands. Mission masculinity demanded an appropriate sexual outlet; celibacy remained rare, even among High Church Anglicans. William Colenso disapproved of the results. The huge number of children in mission families at Paihia in New Zealand, and the scramble for access to the small number of marriageable white women after the original wife died of disease or exhaustion, all seemed to him to be unseemly distractions.[88] After making an arranged marriage of this type himself, Colenso's own career with the CMS ended after an affair with his Maori housemaid.

By the early twentieth century the myth of the "bad missionary," even in church circles, often featured a critique of mission policy about polygamy. T. Theodore Webb, writing for the Australian Board of Mission in the 1930s on Aboriginal policy in Australia, was critical of earlier mission practice in a way that reveals the developing "bad missionary" stereotype, even in church circles. "Probably the most disturbing and difficult feature in the social life of the aborigines is their practice of Polygamy," he wrote,

> and I am afraid that the Christian Church generally has been gravely remiss in her failure to arrive at a real understanding of, and to adequately deal with this matter. Polygamy may be highly repugnant to us but that does not constitute a sufficient reason for our regarding it as essentially evil, as though it had been deliberately adopted and is but an expression of the inherent evil of human nature.[89]

But rather than condemning what was essentially evil, missionary ethnographers had often struggled to understand polygamy, and to interpret it in a way that would emphasize a shared humanity. Fison and others by no means considered it to have "been deliberately adopted"; instead, they saw it as a logical outcome of particular types of social organization.

Despite recent attention to the transnational history of bodies in interaction

87. Chalmers, "New Guinea," 311.

88. William Colenso to CMS Secretaries, 13 December 1852, "Letters of William Colenso, February 1850-January 1854," MS 63B, Hocken Library, Dunedin, NZ.

89. T. Theodore Webb, "A Suggested Basis for Aboriginal Mission Policy," 5, CY Reel 3465, Mitchell Library, Sydney, Australia.

with colonialism, the traditional neglect of men's bodies remains.[90] Mission ethnography highlighted and interpreted female bodies as the primary site of custom in the Pacific world, but it also recorded observations of male bodies, gender roles, and sexualities. Methodist missionary Benjamin Danks provided an intriguing description of the trials of widowers on New Britain. It was "quite an unpleasant affair," in his opinion, which began when the female relatives of the dead wife took up the weapons of their menfolk and dressed in men's clothing "and in a sort of jocular horse-play take the liberty of daubing any man they can catch with red paint. Men are careful to keep out of their way when the women 'run amok' in this fashion." After a time they would descend on the widower's house and gardens, destroying everything. "The only explanation I have been able to elecit [*sic*] by inquiry is that the women are angry on account of the first wife. The underlying notion is that they resent her labor going to benefit a second wife."[91]

Danks also observed the practices designed to pressure young men into marriage:

> A number of young men having arrived at the age of from fifteen to sixteen years, or even less, a great feast is prepared, and all the relatives of the young men or boys are there. At a certain stage of the feast a rush is made by the men towards the boys. The latter are quickly seized from behind and their arms pinioned, lest they should break loose and attempt to spear their captors. While they are being held a chief or a relative of the lad advances toward him with a coil of shell-money, and throws it over his head on to his shoulders. This, so far as I am able to understand the matter, is simply intended to appease his supposed anger at being forced (!) into matrimony. Yet if he can break away before the money is thrown over his head he may escape his matrimonial destiny, for the time being, at least.[92]

This extract is full of gendered ambivalence. Danks, assuming that men always possessed individual agency, cannot bring himself to describe this situation as "forced marriage," as many missionaries would if youthful female bodies were involved. Indeed, he places a bracketed exclamation mark after the word "forced" in order to create ironic distance from the concept.

90. For example Tony Ballantyne and Antoinette Burton, "Introduction" to *Bodies in Contact: Rethinking Colonial Encounters in World History* (Durham, NC: Duke University Press, 2005), 4, which, despite the presence in the collection of a small number of essays on male bodies, explains that the purpose of the book is "to dramatize how, why, and under what conditions women and gender can be made visible in world history."

91. Danks, "Women and Marriage Customs in New Britain."

92. Danks, "Women and Marriage Customs in New Britain."

A young man of New Britain, if he escaped this first attempt, could not put off marriage for long. "Driven perhaps by shame his parents set about bringing about his marriage," Danks reported. "They may arrange, therefore, with his particular friends or companions to decoy him to a given place, where they meet him. He suspects nothing until he is suddenly seized from the rear and held firmly, while his friends throw the shell-money over his head, and the ceremony is completed."[93] Having compared notes with his colleague George Brown, Danks noted that after being garlanded with shell money, the prospective bridegroom went into the bush to avoid all of his female relatives for three to six months. "I may be permitted here to point out," he wrote, "that this custom is the same as that mentioned above by Dr. Brown as obtaining on New Ireland, except that there the women, not the men, go into hiding."[94] He carried out a rather disrespectful test in order to check the integrity of the isolation period. "Often," said Danks "one in hiding has come to the back door of the Mission House, to beg in a whisper for tobacco. To test the custom I have called out a female relative's name, upon which he would entreat me to desist, and indeed, on my continuing to call, would forget all about his tobacco, and flee into the woods."[95] One wonders why Danks felt compelled to test the custom if he was already familiar with it, and why he risked offending the young men of his neighborhood by deliberately doing what he knew to be forbidden.

Another missionary with an eye to the role of custom in men's lives was Lorimer Fison. During his work on Fijian kinship systems, Fison explored the implications of what he called the Fijian housefather system. Although noble titles in Fiji continued to pass through the maternal line, the head of the household was male. Unlike European norms, however, this headship had intrusive cultural implications where reproduction was concerned. So completely was the father connected with each child that a strict diet was required during the later stages of the mother's pregnancy. "I remember a case," wrote Fison, "in which a father bitterly reproached himself for causing the death of his newborn child by eating a feed of boiled fish some time before its birth." The connection persisted after birth: "Especially when the child is newborn the father must be very careful as to his food. In fact it is the father who lies in, not the mother. She will be up & about within a few hours."[96] For Europeans, "lying in" was the protracted period during which middle and upper-class women recovered from childbirth. It was presumed to be necessary due to the physical weakness

93. Danks, "Women and Marriage Customs in New Britain."

94. Danks, "Women and Marriage Customs in New Britain."

95. Danks, "Women and Marriage Customs in New Britain."

96. Lorimer Fison to James Frazer, 7 December 1899, "Rev. Lorimer Fison: Articles, letters & misc. papers, 1873–1907," Lorimer Fison Papers, Mitchell Library, Sydney, Australia.

of women, although ethnographers around the world observed much faster recovery times among non-European women. Male lying in in Fiji raised questions about the customary (rather than medical) necessity for female lying in in Europe, but Fison did not raise these questions. Instead, he found the Fijian practice to be "a comical aggravation" especially when he was running the mission's seminary for Fijians: "Most of the students were married men & an increase in their families—& they were always increasing—was an exasperating interruption to the course of study."[97]

Fison was also interested in the subject of polyandry, having obtained permission to create a questionnaire to send to the colonial government in India for the purpose of obtaining comparative data: a fine example of imperial networking. Fison and his research partner A. W. Howitt eventually received information from Ceylon as well as a copy of "The Report of the Malabar Marriage Commission" from Madras. "But none of these touch the difficulty we want to clear up, excepting in so far as they go to show that polyandry is not a general system of marriage."[98] The difficulty, for Fison, was obtaining evidence of polyandry in Australian cultures and elsewhere in the Pacific. Some anthropological theorists emphasized polyandry as a stage in human social evolution. If Aboriginal Australians and other Pacific peoples exhibited survivals of other stages in this process, ethnographers hoped that evidence of polyandry could also be found.

Probably unknown to Fison, the early LMS missionary William Pascoe Crook had recorded an account of the cohabitation of women with more than one man, although he does not assume that this was polyandry, and provides a remarkably nuanced account of what he understood to be happening. He begins by stating that the Marquesas islanders were not as "lascivious" as other Polynesians (notably the Arioi of Tahiti) "but, on the other hand . . . the customary cohabitation of one Woman with two Men, which seems to be unknown at the Friendly Islands, & uncommon at Otaheite [Tahiti], is here universal." He explained that

> Every daughter of a family when she arrives at puberty cohabits with some male Servant who is called a Pekkeyo & is considered in a light superior to others not thus privileged. When the Young Woman goes to live statedly [*sic*] with a man of property the Pekkeyo accompanies her to her new habitation & remains in the same connexion with her, or is succeeded in it by another servant. The Pekkeyo of a married Woman is spoken of as

97. Fison to Frazer, 7 December 1899.
98. Fison to Frazer, 7 December 1899.

> belonging equally to the husband's part of the family as to the Wife's & is usually regarded by the former as a confidential friend.[99]

Crook also noted that "men of considerable property sometimes condiscend [*sic*] to this subordinate station & are much respected in it." Most elite European men would never tolerate such a situation, let alone facilitate it; hence the condescension required. As Greg Dening has observed, *pekio* "shocked the sensibilities" of early European visitors to the Marquesas, and later anthropologists struggled to explain their role and its significance.[100] Crook did not seem shocked. Despite the fact that many Marquesan women lived intimately with more than one man, he never concluded that they were sexually promiscuous. He noted a dance during which women "let their cloths hang aside & wholly expose themselves," but added, "This is not considered as tending to lewdness, nor are the lascivious gestures, spoken of at other Islands, known to be practiced at these Koenas [*sic*]." Likewise the commonplace Polynesian practice of sleeping together under the same covering did not lead Crook to diagnose "promiscuous intercourse":

> Every woman having one male bedfellow, if not more, their common covering is the large cloth in which the woman is clothed, when she is up. In consequence of this custom, if a man comes into the house, in the daytime to lie down, which is not unusual, & finds a Woman lying down in the house, he makes no scruple, whoever she may be, to shelter himself under the cloth she has covered herself with. It is not supposed that this familiarity is often made a pretence for lewdness.[101]

With regard to *pekio* Crook did not speak of prostitution, as did his LMS brethren of the Tahitian *mahu*. The heterosexual *pekio* relationship commanded greater respect, at least from Crook, although he observed that all Marquesan women and their male entourages were (like *mahu*) potentially contaminating for *tabu* men. He also noted that if a woman was married to a young boy for dynastic reasons "she takes pekkeyo's, in succession, as often as she pleases; but all the children she bears are considered as belonging to her husband, & inherit either property or dignity from him, as if they were, or possibly might

99. William Pascoe Crook, "Account of Marquesas Islands, 1799," 2, C111, CY Reel 329, Mitchell Library, Sydney, Australia.

100. Greg Dening, *Beach Crossings: Voyaging Across Times, Cultures, and Self* (Melbourne: Miegunyah Press, 2004), 194–95.

101. Crook, "Account of Marquesas Islands," 5.

be, his own."[102] He does not condemn these relationships as unnatural, harmful or bestial: language used of polygamous or homosexual relationships by other missionary observers. This does not mean that Crook approved of what he was seeing, but his reservations were expressed in terms of the absence of romantic love:

> The Nature of their Marriages, & the ways of living of the different Sexes, preclude, in general, the exercise of Conjugal Affections; instances of which are rare in the extreme, partialities toward one man, or one Woman, being chiefly discovered by jealousy. . . . Among the men & women, there are persons who discover much more benevolence of disposition than others do; but real disinterested friendship, or even genuine compassion, is almost utterly unknown.[103]

Crook is reflecting the "love revolution" of the Romantic era, including the assumption that western marriages featured a fullness of union, including romantic love, whereas "eastern" relationships were restricted to social/dynastic and sexual elements.[104] But as Greg Dening explains in the case of Edward Robarts, runaway sailor and unwitting *pekio*, perhaps they could also be a way of coping with the "disordering presence" of a married woman's lover, or of the movement of an unexpected European stranger across the land.[105]

A similar combination of fascination and repulsion prompted keen missionary interest in indigenous circumcision practices. As we know, when talking of male bodies, they did not diagnose an enslavement to custom, revealing substantial fault lines at the limits of othering and brothering. Women's bodies could be the objects of compassion, disgust, and paternalism. Male bodies were credited with agency and respect except, as we will see, in cases of extreme genital mutilation or transgressive gender roles. Meanwhile, when writing about circumcision, missionaries demonstrated little of the prudery that is traditionally attributed to them although, like anyone else at the time, they exercised discretion when writing for popular publication. Their manuscript records and scientific publications were more candid, revealing that, at times, brothering was relatively easy. Crook's account of the Marquesas noted that "Boys of 8 or

102. Crook, "Account of Marquesas Islands," 15.

103. Crook, "Account of Marquesas Islands," 101.

104. See Scott Coltrane and Randall Collins, *Sociology of Marriage and the Family: Gender, Love, and Property* (Belmont, CA: Wadsworth/Thomson Learning, 2001), and William M. Reddy, *The Making of Romantic Love: Longing and Sexuality in Europe, South Asia, and Japan, 900–1200 CE* (Chicago: University of Chicago Press, 2012).

105. Dening, *Beach Crossings*, 290.

9 years old, generally undergo the operation of having the prepuce slit, with the sharp edge of a stone. It never unites again. No compulsion is used on this account. A few, who have refused to conform, are called pea, or nasty."[106] W. Wyatt Gill, another LMS missionary, also noted what he called an "imperfect sort of circumcision" at Mangaia in the Cook Islands, referring his readers to Captain Cook's account of Tahiti for a similar practice. This is a significant comment. If circumcision at Mangaia was "imperfect," where was it perfect? Gill was making an indirect comparison with the Jewish rite of circumcision, as specified in the Old Testament, where the whole foreskin was removed. He explained that "in point of fact, the term 'circum-cision,' as applied to these islanders is a solecism," referring to the fact that the prepuce or foreskin was slit rather than cut all around and removed. He commented approvingly that "the greatest insult that can be offered to a man is to accuse him of being uncircumcized. The contemptuous expressions in the sacred writings, in reference to the uncircumcized Gentiles, seem to the Hervey Islanders to be quite natural." Again, connections were being forged across time and space with the ancient biblical lands.[107] After reading early missionary accounts John Dunmore Lang agreed: "The rite of circumcision—of decidedly Asiatic origin—is practiced in several of the groups of Polynesia . . . not, however, as a religious observance, but as an ancient custom, of the origin of which no account can be given."[108] Unusually, Lang speaks here of male bodies as the site of "custom," perhaps because he lacked more detailed information about the range of motives for circumcision in some parts of Polynesia. Missionaries, who knew more, found it difficult even to begin to understand the alien gender relations involved.

On Tahiti in the early days, missionaries were struck by how their circumstances were "by no means dissimilar" to those of the apostolic age.[109] The New Testament made it clear that circumcision was not required of Christians, a consequence of Paul's extensive missionary work among uncircumcised gentiles. But its texts reveal that there had been considerable debate about this among the earliest converts to Christianity who, like its leadership, were converted Jews. Missionaries in Tahiti therefore considered themselves obliged to admit circumcised Tahitian converts to baptism. Good evangelicals all, they believed that only "a regeneration of the heart" could reveal the sincerity of conversion, not any bodily practice. Spiritual and emotional regeneration was, after all, "designed, by the great Head of the church, to occupy that place in the dispen-

106. Crook, "Account of the Marquesas Islands," 27.

107. W. Wyatt Gill, "Mangaia (Hervey Islands)," 327.

108. John Dunmore Lang, "View of the Origin and Migrations of the Polynesian Nation," *Journal of the Royal Geographical Society of London* 4 (1834): 259.

109. Ellis, *Polynesian Researches*, vol. 2, 251.

sation of the New Testament, which circumcision did in that of the Old."[110] A circumcision of the heart would allow the Other to be embraced.

On Mangaia, on the other hand, the LMS knew that insults concerning the presence or absence of circumcision had led to considerable conflict, so they initially decided to forbid it among their converts. The first indigenous pastors agreed with the ban, and "the entire despotic power of the great warrior chief, who embraced Christianity, was brought to bear upon the extinction of this custom," but without success.[111] So widespread was indigenous resistance to the ban that it had to be rescinded. The reason Gill gives is of particular relevance to our discussion of male bodies under female influence or control. Even Europeans married to native women "submitted to this degrading custom to please their wives."[112] Like Crook's "condescension" of *pekio*, Gill's "submissive" and "degraded" white men have placed their bodies, notably their genitalia and sexuality, under the transgressive power of women. Gill's account of all of this switched between languages, indicating the extent of his discomfort. He described the procedure itself in English:

> a piece of cocoanut [*sic*] shell (scraped smooth and thin) is introduced beneath the upper part of the prepuce, and a longitudinal slit made. The divided prepuce is then drawn underneath into a slight twist. A soothing application heals the wound in a few days. The operator frequently renews the twist, so that eventually a small lump remains underneath the urethra.[113]

When it came to the motivation behind the procedure, however, Gill switched to Latin in order to conceal the information from uneducated (i.e., female) eyes: a commentary on his extreme discomfort with the sexualized female agency revealed by the practice. According to information given to Gill by one of his indigenous clergy, "Hoc facere eo consilio, cum ne album illud (piapia quam vocant), sub praeputio exsistat; tum autem maxime, quo magis feminae venerea voluptate fruantur."[114] The goal of circumcision was "the greater sexual pleasure of women" (my translation), and Gill added in English: "Polynesian women are far more lascivious than their Melanesian sisters in the Western Pacific, where this curious practice was originally unknown."[115] This observa-

110. Ellis, *Polynesian Researches*, vol. 2, 252.
111. Gill, "Mangaia (Hervey Islands)," 328.
112. Gill, "Mangaia (Hervey Islands)," 328.
113. Gill, "Mangaia (Hervey Islands)," 329.
114. Gill, "Mangaia (Hervey Islands)," 329.
115. Gill, "Mangaia (Hervey Islands)," 329.

tion sits awkwardly alongside missionary generalizations about the degraded position of women in the Pacific world. Gill disapproves of lasciviousness, but cannot avoid an even more uncomfortable truth: Mangaian men (and some Europeans too) were willing to undergo genital modification in order to enhance female sexual pleasure.

In northern Australia, lengthy and agonizing initiation ceremonies for young men created great difficulty for European observers. What became known as "Sturt's terrible rite," as described in the explorer Charles Sturt's published narrative, seemed to defy explanation. Most circumcision practices involved the foreskin but, in this case, the penis itself was sliced open along the length of the urethra. The Australian anthropologist Baldwin Spencer described to Lorimer Fison a ceremony that he had witnessed:

> The night was spent by them dancing & yelling & singing round their fire and performing sacred ceremonies for the benefit of the novices. Just before sunrise they performed one and then at the base of the [murtunja] (which will henceforth reside in the Museum) they performed the operation of subincision. It was a ghastly sight which I shall not trouble to see again. If only one could get to the bottom of the meaning of this initiation one could find the key to a good deal but it seems hopeless for us to do so. I am afraid that it is buried in the far away misty days of the Alcheringa.[116]

Fison agreed: "All we can do is to go on collecting and collating facts. Perhaps the key to them will turn up some day. If it is never found, it doesn't matter much as long as men keep from trying to manufacture the master key out of their inner consciousness." He added that in some parts of Fiji subincision was performed as a remedy for wasting sickness while on other islands the inhabitants denied that this had ever been an indigenous practice.[117] By the end of the nineteenth century in Australia, subincision was being extensively studied by anthropologists, so much so that one thinks of Roagia Abusharaf classification of a new genre of ethnography: "ethno-porn."[118] Meanwhile, missionaries failed to integrate subincision into a universalized scheme of brothering because it failed to correspond with ancient circumcision's significance as a social or religious identity marker. John Mathew, for example, simply declared himself in

116. Baldwin Spencer to Lorimer Fison, 26 April 1901, Sir Baldwin Spencer MSS, AJCP M2424.

117. Lorimer Fison to Baldwin Spencer, 18 May 1901.

118. Rogaia Abusharaf, "'We Have Supped So Deep in Horrors': Understanding Colonialist Emotionality," *History and Anthropology* 17, no. 3 (2006): 209–28. Also see Andrew P. Lyons and Harriet Lyons, *Irregular Connections: A History of Anthropology and Sexuality* (Lincoln, NE: University of Nebraska Press, 2004), 1–19.

support of Westermark's theory "that the object is ornamentation and increased virility of appearance."[119]

Male homosexual practices, on the other hand, were all too readily connected with ancient Mediterranean cultures, and with Judaeo-Christian scriptural prohibitions.[120] During the early years of the LMS mission to the Society Islands, John Jefferson and his colleague William Henry witnessed a sexual encounter that they immediately deplored. During a language lesson in Henry's house, the chief they were consulting became tired (or quite possibly bored) and lay down on a piece of cloth belonging to one of his male attendants, as though preparing for a nap. Not wishing to disturb him, Jefferson and Henry finished the lesson and left the room. Returning later, Henry found the chief and his attendant enjoying fellatio on the floor of the missionary's own bedroom.[121]

It is worth noting how freely missionaries could write about homosexual practices, at least in their private papers. Some scholars have endorsed the traditional stereotype of the repressed Victorian missionary incapable of discussing sexuality. Gilbert H. Herdt, in his pioneering work on ritualized homosexuality in Melanesia, declared that missionary accounts reveal "seemingly common censorship practice vis-a-vix ethnographic reports on sexuality, at least until recently."[122] A glance at the footnotes for the essays in Herdt's anthology, however, reveals a wealth of ethnographic information on this subject in missionary records, if only on the subject of male same-sex behavior.

Once the Tahitian mission settled down enough to produce regular journals, the issue of homosexuality was highlighted fairly regularly. There was plenty of moral judgment, but little prudery about the details. In fact it took the missionaries time to work out exactly what was happening. In 1803 James Elder and Charles Wilson went on a preaching circuit under the protection

119. Mathew, *Eaglehawk and Crow*, 121.

120. Appropriate terminology for pre-modern or non-western sexual identies and practices has always been elusive, and debate about this important point continues without apparent resolution. This section of the chapter follows scholarly convention while recognizing that its inevitably modern and Eurocentric vocabulary is not only inadequate, but misleading. There still appears to be no viable alternative to phrases such as "ritualized homosexuality." For a more detailed discussion of this important problem see Bruce Knauft, *South Coast New Guinea Culture: History, Comparison, Dialectic* (Cambridge: Cambridge University Press, 1993), 55–59.

121. "John Jefferson: Tahiti 1801," South Sea Journals, Box 1, Council of World Mission Archives, School of Oriental and African Studies, London, UK.

122. Gilbert H. Herdt, "Ritualized Homosexual Behaviour in the Male Cults of Melanesia, 1862–1983: An Introduction," in *Ritualized Homosexuality in Melanesia*, ed. Gilbert H. Herdt (Berkeley: University of California Press, 1984), 19. As Herdt notes, male anthropologists were not interested in lesbianism or female bisexuality, and therefore we lack ethnography about them from our period.

of the Tahitian chief Pomare and "took lodgings in the house of another of Pomare's matooa's," a man they named "Oray." He was not at home, but his son took care of the mission guests and they gave him the present of a comb.[123] They also encountered the *matooa* of another chief, Tu, whom they described as a woman with a strikingly masculine voice. These early observations contain no denunciations; it seems that neither Elder nor Wilson realized that a *mahu* (variously spelled in these early accounts) was a male sexual partner attendant on a particular chief. Ironically, three years earlier, their colleague John Jefferson had recorded the detailed description of a person traveling with a group of women from Raiatea:

> Among them was a man, not otherwise to be distinguished from the women but by a little coarser features & rougher voice: this man keeps himself for the abominable sin of sodomy. We have lately learnt [that] it is usual for some persons from their youths to set themselves apart for this base purpose. They go among women, observe all their customs, eat & drink & sleep with them & do all the offices of females in making cloth &c. and prostitute their bodies to men for the above sin. They never cohabit with women, but only with men. They are not paid by men, but pay men for sinning with them. Some of them are so effeminated as not to be distinguished by their countenances, voices or manners from the women. They are, when spoken to, called by the same name of endearment that men use to women, & women to women, Pattaa.[124]

Elder and Wilson might not have been aware of Jefferson's account or, more likely, they did not realize that the person they identified as a woman with a masculine voice was probably one of Tu's *mahu* (a word they used without seeming to understand what it meant). Jefferson, however, thought that he knew exactly what was going on. "Something that was seen among the people today shews us these heathens, like the heathens of old, are given up to vile affections. . . ." Jefferson had biblical references in mind: "the heathens of old" whom the ancient Israelites encountered (and to whose cultural practices they sometimes succumbed). He had no interest in the sexual practices of women, focusing instead on the men who "leaving the natural use of the woman, burn in their lusts one towards another, men with men working that which is unseemly.

123. "Brs Elder & Wilson's Journal round Tyearrabboo, 1803," 38 July 1803, South Sea Journals, Box 1, Council of World Mission Archives, School of Oriental and African Studies, London, UK.

124. Cited in Stephen O. Murray, *Oceanic Homosexualities* (New York: Garland Publishing, 1992), 153–54.

Indeed it is said that Otoo never cohabits with his wife, but has a number of boys with whom he satiates his passion."[125]

We should be wary of the passive "it is said," which obscures the source of Jefferson's information. We should also treat the allegation of pedophilia with caution: as the mission increased its acquaintance with Tu it became clear that his retinue did include *mahu*, and Jefferson's own story from 1801 (quoted earlier) refers to an adult *mahu* rather than to one of "a number of boys." At best, Jefferson was collapsing together different types of sexual activity in his eagerness to connect what he thought was happening in Tahiti with the "abominable sin of sodomy" as described with reference to the cities of Sodom and Gomorrah in the Old Testament and in the New Testament prohibitions found in the letters of the apostle Paul.

As Elder and Wilson's mis-identification shows, sometimes missionaries did not understand what they were seeing, or were incapable of incorporating it into the universalized construction of human sexuality found in the Bible. Brothering had exceeded its limits. Missionaries who so vigorously denied that Pacific peoples lived in a bestial state of non-spirituality were quick to employ bestial metaphors when discussing male homosexual practices or transgressive male identities, especially those outside the biblical frame of reference. Here they pushed alterity to the extreme. In Henry's bedroom "the chief . . . was detected committing an act of bestiality with another man, which perhaps had no existence even in Sodom and Gomorrha." In recounting Henry's observations, Jefferson concluded that "a most singular and horrible species of bestiality" was being committed, "the chief having in his mouth the other's penis." He added that "the most unnatural lusts are indulged by the Otaheiteans perhaps to as great an excess as in any nation under the sun."[126] Oral sex is denounced here not only as bestiality, but as "a most singular and horrible species of bestiality." This word brings the text into tension with another of its adjectives: "unnatural." After all, what was bestial would surely be natural (if sinful) rather than its opposite. Jefferson's account allows the contradiction to stand in a doubled discourse of othering. "Even in Sodom and Gomorrha" behavior had not been this bad, suggesting that, for Jefferson, fellatio was somehow more morally reprehensible than homosexual anal intercourse.

There is no room here for a discussion of Regency and Victorian attitudes toward sexual practices, but two points are of particular relevance. First was

125. John Jefferson and others, "A Journal of the Missionaries proceedings on Otaheite, 1799," 8 June 1799, South Sea Journals, Box 1, Council of World Mission Archives, School of Oriental and African Studies, London, UK.

126. "John Jefferson: Tahiti 1801," 12 February 1801, South Sea Journals, Box 1, School of Oriental and African Studies, London, UK.

the traditional European hostility toward male anal intercourse, based in the scriptural story of Sodom and Gomorrah, but also in Paul's prohibitions in the New Testament that were (and are) variously interpreted: "For this reason [idolatry] God gave them up to degrading passions. Their women exchanged natural intercourse for unnatural, and in the same way also the men, giving up natural intercourse with women, were consumed with passion for one another" (Rom. 1:16–27). It is important to understand that for most of the time period covered by this book, western understandings and vocabularies of human sexuality were in considerable flux. Today's view of sexual orientation as a personal matter, arising from an individual's own nature, was developing alongside much older notions of sexuality as defined by what one did, rather than who one was. This preoccupation with acts rather than identities helps to explain why biblical injunctions were translated into legal structures prohibiting (for example) anal sex between men, while ignoring whole other areas of homosexual intimacy including sexual relationships between women. The point was not to prohibit being gay, but rather to prohibit particular forms of behavior.[127]

The second factor involves the biblical reference to the "natural use of women." For Pacific missionaries and many others, both gender roles and sexuality were defined in terms of who was penetrating whom, and in homosexual anal intercourse, one of the men was "unnaturally" playing a role traditionally gendered as female. This is very familiar to historians of gender and sexuality, and it helps to explain the very different reaction of missionaries to Christian converts involved in *mahu* relationships. When debating whether or not to admit *mahu* converts to church leadership, they revealed much higher levels of disapproval and discomfort than they did about converted chiefs whose role was perceived to be the masculine one. A special anxiety was created for missionaries by men who betrayed their manhood by playing "feminine" sexual roles. It is worth quoting John Davies's journal for January 1818 at some length in order to understand this point:

> Evening meeting as usual, the most interesting question was about a man of Papeuriri in Tahiti, who has made a profession for some years, has attended school, can read well and write, but has been formerly a *mahu*, that is a man assuming the garb and manner of a woman, and prostituting himself for most vile and abominable purposes, the question was proposed by the man himself, whether it would be proper for him to take

127. For useful background see James Neill, *The Origins and Role of Same-Sex Relations in Human Societies* (Jefferson, NC: McFarland, 2008), and Kim M. Phillips and Barry Reay, *Sex Before Sexuality: A Premodern History* (Cambridge: Polity, 2011).

> the lead, or engage in any part of public worship, such as reading and praying in the Tahitian prayer meetings as it was generally known what his character had been. I found difficulty and knew not well what to say, but answered to the following effect; that tho' our God doth often magnify his mercy and grace in the salvation of the vilest and greatest of sinners, and make some that had been distinguished for wickedness, afterwards distinguished as promoters of his cause and the good of others; and tho' in the present case I would not say that there would be anything unlawful or criminal in the man engaging in prayer &c. in public, yet upon the whole, thought it not expedient, or well in every respect for him to do so, because it was probably the people in general did not approve of it, and there might be such sensations raised in their minds as were not at all congenial with the purposes of religious worship. And as the man had been noted for vile, abominable practices, so there ought to be also especial marks of humiliation and deep repentance in him before his engaging in public worship could be likely to produce good effect.[128]

Davies noted that earlier in January he had announced that "for the first time a reading of a portion of the Scriptures in Tahitian" would be included in the public services because Tahitians themselves had been "reading what they had obtained of the Scriptures in their family worship." The mission gave prominence in these new leadership roles to high-ranking converts regardless of whether or not they previously had relationships with *mahu*. An embittered John Orsmond blamed several of his fellow missionaries for encouraging that "beastly sot," King Pomare. "He was a beastly creature, there had been no *one* who could call him *father*," Orsmond said meaningfully, "and a few weeks before his baptism he had to dismiss several of his great, ugly male wives. The Missionaries dared not to baptize anyone before the King had passed under that ceremony. To remove his guilt, Mr Bicknell urged on him the penance of planting in Taravao a large grove of cocanut trees."[129] But could the alleged guilt of a *mahu* be so easily absolved?

Davies's journal had presumed that "a man assuming the garb and manner of a woman, and prostituting himself" was more "vile and abominable" than the man or men with whom he had sex. This double standard is a familiar one in

128. John Davies, "Voyage from Moorea to Huahine; Settlement at Huahine: June 21–July 2," 12 January 1818, South Sea Journals, Box 4, Council for World Mission Archives, School of Oriental and African Studies, London, UK.

129. John Davies, "Epilogue: Extracts from the 'Old Orsmond MS, 1849,'" in *The History of the Tahitian Mission 1799–1830*, ed. Colin Newbury (Cambridge: Cambridge University Press, 1961), 150.

discussions of prostitution today when, more often than not, law enforcement focuses on the prostitute rather than the customers. The early missionaries to Tahiti enforced a triple standard, privileging not only the male "customer" in a perceived relationship of "prostitution," but also by privileging the male penetrative role in sexual intercourse between men. The ultimate Other here was neither a woman nor a homosexual man per se. It was a particular man who performed what was perceived to be a transgressively feminine sexual role. Davies's discourse of bestiality alerts us to his high level of discomfort with the subject, a discomfort that threatened his usual interest in integrating indigenous behavior with a universalized human nature. This accords with Lee Wallace's findings concerning the *fa'afafine* of Samoa. Their gender liminality "overdetermines" their identity in their relationships with other men whereas "a discretionary privilege extends to the nonliminal men to voluntarily engage in sexual acts with *fa'afafine* or *fakaleiti*."[130]

The double and triple standards do not stop there. When we consider the sexuality of missionaries themselves it becomes clear that a spectrum of relationships and behavior prevailed among them too. As Tony Ballantyne points out, the CMS missionary William Yate, disciplined for homosexual relationships with European and Maori men and boys in New Zealand, was spoken of as unnatural and bestial, language never applied to the heterosexual adulterer William Colenso.[131] However, this language was not as well "contained" as Ballantyne suggests by the mission's emphasis on restricting sex to heterosexual marriage. Rhonda Semple has proposed that the real problem with missionaries caught in adultery with other women was just that: they got caught. The importance of maintaining a reputation for vigor on the fringes of the British Empire led even missions to treat male heterosexual transgressions with surprising leniency because such acts reinforced the masculinity of mission work.[132] Limits had to be set when such transgressions became public knowledge, and the leaders of the Melanesian Mission were disappointed to find that a number of their leading indigenous clergy were carrying on adulterous affairs. However, as David Hilliard notes,

> their moralism had a double standard, for the dismissal of three [European] missionaries within eight years after horrified discovery of their

130. Lee Wallace, "*Fa'afine: Queens of Samoa* and the Elision of Homosexuality," *GLQ: A Journal of Lesbian and Gay Studies* 5, no. 1 (1999): 26. Also see Stephen O. Murray, *Oceanic Homosexualities*, xxi–xxiii, and Caroline E. Robertson, "The Mahu of Hawai'i," in *Pacific Diaspora: Island Peoples in the United States and Across the Pacific*, ed. Paul Spickard, Joanne L. Rondilla, Debbie Hippolite Wright (Honolulu: University of Hawai'i Press, 2002), 263.

131. Ballantyne, "Mythmaking and Transgression," 120–23.

132. Semple, "Missionary Manhood," 408–9.

> homosexual friendships with Melanesian schoolboys—adolescent homosexuality having been 'rampant' at St. Barnabas' during the 1890s—was not taken to invalidate the call for an increased white staff.[133]

When we turn to the indigenous cultures themselves in the western Pacific, we sometimes find "ritualized homosexuality" as it is described (with the usual caveats) by modern anthropologists. Douglas Oliver warned that the existence of such behavior and roles must not detract from the importance, in Tahiti for example, of very sharply defined roles for *te huru tane* ("human maleness") and *te huru vahine* ("human femaleness").[134] If missionaries in Polynesia needed time to comprehend the alternative sexualities they encountered, this was even more true in Melanesia where the secrecy surrounding some men's societies and their practices created an intriguing lacuna in mission ethnography. Members of the Presbyterian New Hebrides Mission, for example, can hardly have been expected to describe homosexuality directly in the pages of the popular *New Hebrides Magazine*, a periodical intended for British residents in the islands. However, the apparent absence of any reference to it in private journals and letters, even to "unspeakable" practices, is intriguing. The island of Malekula in the New Hebrides would become famous among modern anthropologists for its highly structured male homosexual interactions; the pioneering work of A. B. Deacon took place during the time of the New Hebrides Mission, and with its support.

As we have seen in LMS ethnography from the Society Islands, missionaries sometimes made observations whose significance they did not understand. The same was true of some of their western Pacific counterparts. T. Watt Leggatt published an illustrated piece on "Malekulan Images" for the *New Hebrides Magazine* in 1906. In it he noted that Malekulan carved statuary was meant to represent the spirits of the different ranks into which Malekulan men were divided: "These are separated from each other by many barriers, the most striking of which is, that no man of rank can eat food prepared on the fire of one lower."[135] He reflected ruefully on "the ignorance of the present generation, as well as the reticence of the older men in discussing such subjects" and was unable to understand the cultural significance of the anatomical details on the male carved figures he studied. "Every part is carefully put in," he noted. "Some parts, indeed, whose absence or seclusion we could willingly excuse, are much exaggerated. . . ."[136] Classically educated like most missionaries of his day, he

133. Hilliard, *God's Gentlemen*, 180.

134. Douglas L. Oliver, *Ancient Tahitian Society*, vol. 2, *Social Relations* (Honolulu: University of Hawaii Press, 1974), 597.

135. T. Watt Leggatt, "Malekulan Images," *New Hebrides Magazine*, October 1906, 20.

136. Leggatt, "Malekulan Images," 23.

wondered why there were no fertility figures, assuming that these would have to be female: "There are no figures like the Ephesian Diana, denoting the nourishment of men and animals from many-breasted Nature."[137] The material culture he was observing was speaking a language he did not understand. As we will see, the exaggerated male genitalia he observed were expressions of just that sort of nourishment, but in a differently gendered context. He could only confess that "I feel that I have only touched the fringe of this mysterious and fascinating subject . . . but I earnestly hope that others will pursue it."[138]

Anthropologist Arthur Bernard Deacon was among the first to do so, beginning extensive fieldwork on Malekula in 1925 at the urging of his mentor A. C. Haddon. He died of fever only two years later, aged only 24, and his papers were subsequently published by Camilla Wedgwood, another of Haddon's students. Deacon was befriended at South-West Bay, Malekula, by the Reverend R. Boyd of the New Hebrides Mission and his family. Though friendly to Deacon personally, Haddon tells us that "he felt very acutely their entire lack of appreciation of the kind of work he was doing, which fortunately is not the attitude of more enlightened missionaries."[139] Haddon added that Deacon was careful not to hinder Boyd's mission work in any way. Deacon was frustrated by the toll taken by alcohol and disease on the local population, noting the indigenous view that at certain villages every eight years a particularly important fertility ceremony was held by the clan magicians who alone knew how to supervise and perform the necessary rituals. One such site was Iumoran in the southwest, Deacon's terrain, but he could not afford the price (in alcohol) charged by those who could have taken him there. He wrote only that

> In the sacred place are said to be the largest specimens of the sacred pottery and on the continuation of the performance of fertility magic here the life of the whole district is apparently supposed in some way to have depended. The descent group of Iumoran has only one survivor, the village has fallen into ruin, and the line of clan-magicians came to an end some years ago; hence, according to the natives, the present appalling depopulation.[140]

137. Leggatt, "Malekulan Images," 23.

138. Leggatt, "Malekulan Images," 23.

139. A. Bernard Deacon, *Malekula: A Vanishing People in the New Hebrides* (London: George Routledge & Sons, 1934), xvii. Early fieldwork on Malekula has generated its own ethnography: see Haidy Geismar, "*Stone Men of Malekula* on Malekula: An Ethnography of an Ethnography," *Ethnos* 74, no. 2 (2009): 199–228.

140. Deacon, *Malekula*, 640.

Annual harvest ceremonies and commemorations of the dead were still held in various places, but Deacon notes a ceremony to "make man" for the prosperity of the district, including "the ceremonial sexual intercourse between the *nemughut nogho* [a group consisting of a head-man from each clan house] and the women from all villages in the district."[141] Each man had intercourse with each woman, "a practice which necessarily violates all rules of clan exogamy and results in incest with even close blood relatives. The only explanation given for this ceremony is that it is done 'to make men as Kabat had done.'"[142] The source of strength for men and fertility for women was semen. In the village of Lembelag there was another clan fertility rite, the *Nogaro Nömur*, for "making man" and invigorating the district. In this case, however, the two surviving clan magicians refused to answer Deacon's questions: "The rites of the *Nogaro Nömur* may, I think, be said to be the most impenetrable secret of Malekulan culture. No money can buy it or patience extract it."[143] The point here is not to draw conclusions from this fragmentary information, but simply to point out that missionary ethnography like Leggatt's can shed further light on what happened during the months of male seclusion in the *Nogaro Nömur*, and related rituals for making men and giving life to land, people, and crops. The material culture Leggatt observed is a key piece of evidence.

The southern coast of New Guinea has also been of great interest to anthropologists working on Melanesian homosexual practices. Few Europeans lived in Papuan south New Guinea until the twentieth century: economic resources seemed scarce and the coastal people were reputedly hostile. Most mission societies first became active on the northern and eastern coasts of New Guinea, but a notable exception was the establishment run by missionary-explorer James Chalmers of the LMS. The society had been in New Guinea since 1874, but only in 1896 did they establish a station, under Chalmers's leadership, far enough to the west to encounter societies featuring extensive ritualized homosexuality.

At Saguane near the mouth of the Fly River, Chalmers and his wife spent most of their time trying to persuade the local boys and girls to stay in school. They mentioned one reason in particular in letters published by the Religious Tract Society. "There is a yearly snake-worship (*Kina*) here," wrote Chalmers in 1896. "The worship is indescribably filthy, beats anything I know

141. Deacon, *Malekula*, 651.

142. Deacon, *Malekula*, 652. Kabat was both a mythological hero and the title of each clan house leader.

143. Deacon, *Malekula*, 655. For an example of later analysis of Deacon's findings, see the discussion of male initiation rites in John Layard, *Stone Men of Malekula* (London: Chatto & Windus, 1942), 473–528.

of or have ever read of."[144] Mrs. Chalmers's observations were equally revealing. "I told you how well the school was doing," she wrote to a friend. "Well, now there are only a very few children left. All have gone to the great *muguru*, and they go for from four to six months. . . . This vile *muguru*, with its dancing, feasting, and abomination. Most of the boys are going in for all the excitement of their first initiation ceremony . . . terribly evil practices, impossible to write about."[145]

These remarks were republished in a new edition of Chalmers's popular autobiography.

Readers familiar with Victorian and Edwardian literary conventions will recognize this statement as the opposite of what it appears to mean: far from being "impossible to write about," the information Mrs. Chalmers wished to convey is revealed clearly by the word "abomination." This was shorthand, drawn from the Bible, for homosexual intercourse. Those familiar with Scripture since childhood would recognize at once the wealth of information being conveyed under the rubric "impossible to write about." They would also know that the mention of boys attending "terribly evil practices" suggested sex with or between male children. The killing of Chalmers and his colleague the Reverend Oliver Tomkins in 1901 would discourage further western contact for many years, making these early missionary observations all the more valuable for future scholarship.

Bruce Knauft warns that "even apart from the problems of labeling whole societies as 'homosexual' in the ethnographic present on the basis of precolonial male sexual practices, the notion that lowland south New Guinea was generally associated with ritual homosexuality is empirically erroneous."[146] The further study of missionary ethnography should be included to pursue these generalizations; they contain less presumed censorship than Knauft assumed. The LMS missionary William James Viritahitemauvai Saville, trained in anthropology by Malinowski himself at the University of London, made no overt mention of homosexuality in his detailed study of Mailu initiation. Like most missionaries in the early twentieth century, Saville was operating to the eastward of lowland south New Guinea. He noted that many traditional initiation rituals for boys were no longer conducted in his area: "Boys in the Mailu district who go through any initiation at all, now undergo it on the canoes during one of the big trips east or west, but its main impetus has disappeared."[147] Nevertheless, he

144. Richard Lovett, *James Chalmers: His Autobiography and Letters* (London: The Religious Tract Society, 1902), 431.

145. Lovett, *James Chalmers*, 447.

146. Knauft, *South Coast New Guinea Cultures*, 51.

147. Saville, *In Unknown New Guinea*, 109.

observed a "calling" ritual practiced by the Dimuga people whose villages extended into the central mountain range of New Guinea. "The male voices of the Dimuga are very good, and the calls from mountain to mountain or to valley-garden are as thrilling as they are impossible to describe," he wrote, noting the special cadences and enunciation of this male-only, long distance communication. He could not also help noticing that "every muscle and apparently every part of the man's anatomy contributes" to the call.[148] This might have indicated a sexual dimension either to the calling itself, or to the now-neglected rituals to which it once summoned men and boys. Chalmers, as we have seen, had obtained much more detailed information on the southern coast and Knauft makes reference to it, noting among other things Chalmers's statement that "the lads are prostituted by the men for quite a long time and soon become so diseased that they never recover."[149] I cannot agree that accounts like this are evidence of censorship; on the contrary, they are remarkably candid. A better acquaintance with missionary observations and interpretations of same-sex relationships in the Pacific world can clear up Knauft's puzzlement about the statement by Chalmers concerning the Bugilai people of the left bank of the Fly River: "'At the initiation of young men, they practice sodomy, but not bestiality as some other tribes do.' (No further explanation!)."[150] No further explanation was needed. As we have seen in John Williams's journal, missionaries in various parts of the Pacific distinguished between homosexual anal intercourse, which could be linked with biblical history and injunctions, and oral sex, which seemed so alien as to be bestial. Brothering had been pushed beyond its limits.

A Tahitian chief and his *mahu* could suggest the decadence of ancient Greece, or could be linked to biblical accounts of Sodom and Gomorrah. Missionaries disapproved of what was happening, but were able to locate it in a universalized context and therefore in the theological anthropology of othering and brothering. They showed particularly sharp disapproval of the men who (in their opinion) played feminine roles in homosexual relationships, subjecting them to sanctions not imposed on the supposedly masculine partner. However, they were at a loss about practices such as oral sex, which they could not connect either with classical societies or the Bible. Even cannibalism had not overstretched the capacity of othering and brothering, but unduly transgressive gender or sexual roles and behaviors were uniquely problematic. There is much work still to be done on alternative sexualities in Pacific ethnography, beyond

148. Saville, *In Unknown New Guinea*, 311.

149. Cited in Herdt, "Ritualized Homosexual Behaviour in the Male Cults of Melanesia, 1862–1983: An Introduction," in *Ritualized Homosexuality in Melanesia*, ed. Herdt, 19.

150. Cited in Herdt, *Ritualized Homosexuality*, 18.

the familiar debate concerning anthropologist Margaret Mead's discredited work on Samoa. What about "Jacobus X" and his *L'Amour aux colonies* (1893), translated into English as *Untrodden fields of anthropology* in 1898?[151] A close review of this work, written by a French army surgeon, could be compared with neglected missionary sources to better effect than what Robert Aldrich has called "specious anthropology."[152]

Meanwhile, the double and triple standards of missionary attitudes exhibited in these cases help us to understand why the question of female religious leadership was rendered invisible. The female Other was too alien for anything beyond membership and carefully regulated, gender-appropriate tasks in support of missionary efforts. The brothering of *mahu* and *fa'afafine* was also incomplete, and the leadership position of converts from these groups was also an inevitably compromised one. In other cases, as in some parts of Melanesia where later anthropologists identified ritualized homosexuality, missionaries could not fully comprehend what they were observing. The otherness here was at times too alien to be embraced. The missionary ethnographies that had transcended race and rank, however paternalistically, consistently privileged matters of gender and sexuality as barriers to full equality and leadership in Christian communities. Here was an Other too irreducible, too alien, and here lies the unfinished business of Christian theological anthropology in the Pacific world and beyond.

151. Jacobus X, *Untrodden fields of anthropology: observations on the esoteric manners and customs of semi-civilized peoples*, ed. Charles Carrington (Paris: Librarie de medicine, folklore et anthropologie, 1898).

152. Robert Aldrich, *Colonialism and Homosexuality* (London: Routledge, 2003), 17.

Conclusions

Some missionaries arrived at their posts open to listening and learning, while others did not. For example, two missionaries arrived within two years of each other at the Swan River colony in Australia, but with very different approaches to their work. The Reverend William Mitchell of the Society for the Propagation of the Gospel arrived from India in 1838 expecting to find compliant natives ready for teaching and domestic service. He was unable to cope with the difference between Indian and Aboriginal cultures, and his time in Swan River was brief. One observer commented that Mitchell "seems to have been discouraged by the discovery that Australian blacks were at such a low stage."[1] The Reverend John Smithies, a Methodist, arrived in 1840 and waited six months before attempting to describe the local Aboriginal people in detail. His first report reflected humility and candor. "Not having been connected with any aborigines before, in our work," he wrote, they were "strange and affecting and yet encouraging in the Lord."[2]

Missionaries as dismissive as Mitchell did not last long. Those who grasped the necessity of understanding indigenous cultures drew upon the anthropology of Christian tradition: a diagnosis of otherness to which the gospel mission was the response, and the simultaneous need for profound connection-building if the gospel was to be preached and understood. The combination of strangeness and affect in Smithies' comment is a superb illustration of this symbiosis of othering and brothering and the creative tensions it generated. By considering a broad range of missionary ethnography, including linguistics and philology,

1. McNair and Rumley, *Pioneer Aboriginal Mission*, 59.
2. McNair and Rumley, *Pioneer Aboriginal Mission*, 154.

across the Pacific world from the late eighteenth century to the early twentieth, we have seen how profoundly theological anthropology shaped their conceptions of Pacific peoples and cultures.

Sometimes missionaries engaged formally with academic anthropology where they favored some theories over others for theological reasons. At other times they were engaging with popular audiences on questions of vanishing races or indigenous rights. Scholars have known for some time that missionaries could sometimes be found promoting those rights, although this insight sits awkwardly alongside the popular image of the destructive, even genocidal missionaries who staffed residential schools and presided over forced-adoption schemes. One of this book's goals has been to challenge this disconnection by illustrating why brothering had to be as strong a priority as othering, and therefore why contemporary religious figures like Archbishop Desmond Tutu have long histories of the championship of human rights. In Australia, for example, the bishops of the Australian Board of Mission issued a statement in 1903 stating (optimistically, to say the least) that "it will scarcely be questioned that the Aborigines of the soil have a primary claim" to mission resources, not because they were members of inferior races, but "as the owners and inhabitants of the country in which we dwell, whose land we have taken and whose means of subsistence we are daily diminishing."[3] Perhaps surprisingly, the bishops' paternalistic proposals included measures "of justice, or reparation, of plain and obvious duty."[4] These measures are still being worked out over a century later in Australia, South Africa, Canada, and so many other places where the legacy of colonialism is both historically significant and a tragically lived reality.

Nevertheless, the goal here was not to substitute a new "good" missionary for the traditional "bad" one. This book has also been written with an eye to the privileged status of gender identity and sexual orientation in debates about the boundaries of Christian church membership and leadership. The postcolonial turn in historiography has tended to privilege race, perhaps in conjunction with class or gender, in analyzing power relations in the British empire. However, in the case of missionary ethnography, gender and sexuality presented problems out of all proportion to either race or class. In 1914, when Bishop Gerald Sharp of New Guinea reported the happy news of the first ordinations of New Guinea men, his announcement was redolent with brothering. Peter Rautamara and Edwin Nuagoro had joined the leadership of the universal Church, and Bishop Sharp enjoyed presenting racially transgressive images of the interaction of

3. Cited in Noel Loos, *White Christ Black Cross: The Emergence of a Black Church* (Canberra: Aboriginal Studies Press, 2007), 64.

4. Loos, *White Christ Black Cross*, 64.

white and black flesh. His white hands had ordained these men, but it was from their black hands that he and his colleagues would receive the chalice at the next Eucharist. Thinking especially of the mission pioneers King and Tomlinson in New Guinea, the bishop wondered "if they thought they would ever live to have the Chalice in Holy Communion administered to them by the hands of Papuans." He delighted in the knowledge that "New Guinea natives, or Papuans, are associated in many people's minds only with savagery and cannibalism," but "for the first time on earth a Papuan will celebrate the Holy Sacrament, and I shall receive It at his hands."[5] In some ways this brotherly rejoicing was remarkably egalitarian and color-blind. In other ways, however, its exclusive male discourse occluded even the possibility of considering female bodies for ordination. It would also generate anxieties about masculinity that would exclude openly gay men from ministry as well. Debates about these things are prominent today, but remain uniquely problematic when compared, say, with debates about encouraging more indigenous or working-class candidates for ministry. The contemporary situation is outside the scope of this book, but I hope that my contribution has shed light on how and why gender and sexuality have posed such sharp challenges to brothering in mission ethnography, and to theological anthropology up to the present day.

Brian Stanley has proposed that the ultimate purpose of Christian missions was reconciliation: reconciliation between human beings, and between humans and God. This argument has been contested because it does not take sufficient account of the unequal power relations of colonialism in the modern period of missionary expansion, but Stanley wants to challenge the widespread assumption that universalized religious claims are necessarily colonizing.[6] In response, Robert Schreiter has called for forms of engagement that "are willing to critique and be critiqued and, if necessary, change." He adds, "We are still at an early stage of this" and need to get "to know the 'other' at a deeper level." A useful methodology, he suggests, would be *kenosis*: a self-emptying with the goal of creating the conditions for exchange. The result, he believes, would be "disciplined yet generous."[7] William Colenso could not have put it better, writing at his desk in New Zealand in the 1840s. A number of religions today make universalized, exclusive truth claims in a globalized world, creating an urgent need for methodologies of constructive engagement. In our haste to

5. Bishop Gerald Sharp, "The First Native Ordination in New Guinea," *ABM Review* 5, no. 9 (1914): 170–71.

6. Brian Stanley, "Mission and Human Identity in the Light of Edinburgh 1910," *Mission Studies* 26, no. 1 (2009): 80–97.

7. Robert Schreiter, "Mission and Human Identity in the Light of Edinburgh 2010. A Response to Brian Stanley," *Mission Studies* 26, no. 1 (2009): 100, 101.

critique religious apologetics, let us not fail to honor the human struggle for understanding, equality, and respect.

This book can make a modest contribution by showing that even at the height of Victorian imperialism, some missionaries were already embracing *kenosis* and self-critique in order to combine brothering with othering. They did so in an incomplete and sometimes inconsistent way, especially where gender and sexuality were concerned. They did so as part of an accelerating western imperialism. Nevertheless, as John Wilken has noted, for millennia Christianity has had "to face the issue of wide cultural differences between peoples and the resulting problems and conflicts," and this matter "has had to be faced" by modern academic scholarship.[8] This is why Christianity has proved to be such an ironic and contested bridge between different voices in current debates about Aboriginal rights in various parts of the world. Rabbi Lord Jonathan Sacks wrote recently that "religion can be a source of discord. It can also be a form of conflict resolution. We are familiar with the former; the second is far too little tried. Yet it is here, if anywhere, that hope must lie if we are to create a human solidarity strong enough to bear the strains that lie ahead."[9] A nuanced mission historiography can contribute to the urgent need for constructive engagement between people of different faiths (or none), especially since classical secularization theory has proved such an unreliable guide to the future. If genuine attempts at engagement have been made before, they can be made again.

8. John Wilken, "A Theological Approach to Reconciliation," in *Reconciling Our Differences: A Christian Approach to Recognizing Aboriginal Land Rights*, ed. Frank Brennan (Brunswick: Aurora Books, 1992), 63–77.

9. Quoted in Stanley, "Mission and Human Identity," 82.

Bibliography

Unpublished Primary Sources

Anthropological Society of Australasia Papers, Mitchell Library, State Library of New South Wales (SLNSW), Sydney, Australia

George Brown Journals and Letterbooks, Mitchell Library, SLNSW, Sydney, Australia

Robert Codrington Papers, Rhodes House Library, Oxford, UK

William Colenso Correspondence, Hocken Library, Dunedin, NZ

E. E. V. Collocott Correspondence, Mitchell Library, SLNSW, Sydney, Australia

Council of World Mission Archives, School of Oriental and African Studies (SOAS), London, UK

Crook, William Pascoe, "Account of Marquesas Islands, 1799," Mitchell Library, SLNSW, Sydney, Australia

Benjamin Danks Papers, Mitchell Library, SLNSW, Sydney, Australia.

Charles Darwin Papers, Cambridge University Library, Cambridge, UK

Samuel Ella Correspondence, Mitchell Library, SLNSW, Sydney, Australia

Lorimer Fison Papers, Mitchell Library, SLNSW, Sydney, Australia

Lorimer Fison Project, Pacific Manuscripts Bureau (PMB) 1039, 1042

Charles Elliot Fox Papers, Alexander Turnbull Library, State Library of New Zealand, Wellington, NZ

A. C. Haddon Papers, Cambridge University Library, Cambridge, UK

Thomas Kendall MSS, Hocken Library, Dunedin, NZ

"Letters from the Rarotonga Misssionaries," University of Hawai'i at Manoa, USA

Richard Burdsall Lyth Papers, Mitchell Library, SLNSW, Sydney, Australia

Mackay, Christopher S., "Translation of excerpt from E. J. Eyre," in possession of the author

Samuel Marsden MSS, Hocken Library, Dunedin, NZ

Melanesian Mission Papers, Lambeth Palace Library, London, UK

Melanesian Mission Papers, School of Oriental and African Studies, London, UK

Methodist Overseas Mission Papers, Mitchell Library, SLNSW, Sydney, Australia

George Selwyn Papers, Selwyn College, Cambridge, UK
Sir Baldwin Spencer Papers, AJCP M2424
Webb, T. Theodore, "A Suggested Basis for Aboriginal Mission Policy," Mitchell Library, SLNSW, Sydney, Australia
William Yate Correspondence, Hocken Library, Dunedin, NZ

Periodical Primary Sources

The A.B.M. Review
Australasian Anthropological Journal
The Bulletin of Missionary Studies
The Church Missionary Gleaner
The Echo
The Evangelical Magazine
The Home and Foreign Missionary Record
Journal and Proceedings of the Royal Society of New South Wales
Journal of the Anthropological Institute of Great Britain and Ireland
Journal of the Polynesian Society
Journal of the Royal Geographical Society of London
New Hebrides Magazine
New York Times
The Nineteenth Century
Occasional Paper (Diocese of New Guinea)
Oceania
Practical Anthropology
Proceedings of the Australasian Association for the Advancement of Science
Proceedings of the Royal Society of Victoria
Report of the Wesleyan Methodist Missionary Society
Reports of the New Guinea Mission
Science of Man
The Southern Cross Log
Transactions and Proceedings of the New Zealand Institute
Transactions and Proceedings of the Royal Society of Victoria
Transactions of the Royal Society of Canada
The Wesleyan Missionary Notices Relating Principally to the Foreign Missions

Published Primary Sources

Appleyard, John Whittle. *The Kafir language: comprising a sketch of its history; which includes a general classification of South African dialects, ethnographical and geographical: remarks upon its nature: and a grammar.* King William's Town: Printed for the Wesleyan Missionary Society, 1850.

Armstrong, E. S. *The History of the Melanesian Mission.* London: Isbister and Co., 1900.

Boggis, R. J. E. *A History of St. Augustine's College, Canterbury.* Canterbury: Cross & Jackman, 1907.

The Book of Common Prayer.

Bromilow, W. E. "Some Manners and Customs of the Dobuans of S.E. Papua." *Report of the Australasian Association for the Advancement of Science.* Sydney: AAAS, 1909.

———. *Some Manners and Customs of the Dobuans of S.E. Papua.* Brisbane: James Cumming, 1910.

———. *Twenty Years among Primitive Papuans.* London: Epworth Press, 1929.

Brown, George. *Melanesians and Polynesians: Their Life-Histories Described and Compared.* London: Macmillan and Co., 1910.

Brown, J. Macmillan. *Maori and Polynesian: Their Origin, History and Culture.* London: Hutchinson and Co., 1907.

Bryant, Jacob. *A New System, Or, An Analysis of Ancient Mythology.* London: Payne, White and Walter, 1774–76.

Bullock, Charles. *Missionaries and Anthropologists; or, Christian facts versus asophophilosophical 'day-dreams.' The success of missionary enterprise in New Zealand illustrated from the biography of the Rev. Richard Davis.* London: William Macintosh, 1865.

Bunyan, John. *O le Malaga a le maumausolo nai le olga nei I le olaga atali: ua fa'atusaina male miti, na tusia e Ioane Paniani.* Samoa: LMS Press, 1846.

———. *Pilgrim's Progress: Translated into Mukawan, Eastern Papua.* Sydney: Pacific Christian Literature Society, 1950.

Burton, J. W. *A Hundred Years in Fiji.* London: Epworth Press, 1936.

Buzacott, Aaron. *Mission Life in the Islands of the Pacific.* London: John Snow & Co., 1866.

Calendar of the Calvinistic Methodist or Welsh Presbyterian Theological College. Wrexham: Huges & Son, 1897.

Calendar of the Missionary College of St. Augustine, Canterbury. London: H. Ward, 1851.

Calvert, James. *Mission History.* Edited by George Stringer Rowe. Vol. 2 of *Fiji and the Fijians.* Suva: Fiji Museum, 1985; first published 1858 by Alexander Heylin.

Campbell, F. A. *A Year in the New Hebrides, Loyalty Islands, and New Caledonia.* Geelong: George Mercer, 1873.

Chalmers, James. "New Guinea. Toaripi and Koiari Tribes." *Report of the Second Meeting of the Australasian Association for the Advancement of Science.* Sydney: AAAS, 1890.

Codrington, Robert. *The Melanesians.* New Haven, CT: HRAF Press, 1957; first published 1891 by Clarendon Press.

———. *The Melanesian Languages.* Oxford: Clarendon Press, 1885.

Colenso, John. *The Pentateuch and Book of Joshua critically examined.* London: Longman, Green, Longman, Roberts & Green, 1862–79.

Coombe, Florence. *School Days in Norfolk Island.* London: SPCK, 1909.

Crook, William Pascoe. *William Pascoe Crook, An Account of the Marquesas Islands, 1797–1799.* Edited by Greg Dening. Papeete, Tahiti: Haere Po, 2007.

Darwin, Charles. *The Descent of Man.* London: John Murray, 1871.

———. *On the Origin of Species.* London: John Murray, 1859.

Davies, Edward. *The Mythology and Rites of the British Druids.* London: J. Booth, 1809.

Davies, John. *The History of the Tahitian Mission 1799–1830*. Edited by Colin Newbury. Cambridge: Cambridge University Press, 1961.

Deacon, A. Bernard. *Malekula: A Vanishing People in the New Hebrides*. London: George Routledge & Sons, 1934.

Deane, Wallace, ed. *In Wild New Britain: The Story of Benjamin Danks, Pioneer Missionary, from His Diary*. Sydney: Angus and Robertson, 1933.

Ellis, William. *Polynesian Researches, during a residence of nearly eight years in the Society and Sandwich Islands*. 2nd ed. New York: Henry G. Bohn, 1859.

Engels, Frederick. *The Origin of the Family, Private Property, and the State*. Translated by Ernest Untermann. Chicago: Charles H. Kerr & Company Co-operative, 1902.

Epistle of Mathetes to Diognetus. http://www.earlychristianwritings.com/text/diognetus-roberts.html (accessed 31 March 2014).

Eyre, Edward John. *Journals of Expeditions of Discovery into Central Australia*. London: T. and W. Boone, 1845.

Farquhar, J. N. *The Crown of Hinduism*. Oxford: Oxford University Press, 1913.

Fison, Lorimer. "Group Marriage and Relationship." In *Proceedings of Section G, Anthropology*. Hobart: Government printer for the AAAS, 1892.

Fison, Lorimer, and A. W. Howitt. *Kamilaroi and Kurnai*. Oosterhout, NB: Anthropological Publications, 1967; first published 1880 by G. Robertson.

Fox, C. E. *The Threshold of the Pacific. An Account of the Social Organization, Magic and Religion of the People of San Cristoval in the Solomon Islands*. London: Kegan Paul, Trench, Trubner & Co., 1924.

Gill, W. Wyatt. *Cook Islands Customs*. Suva: University of the South Pacific, 1979; first published 1892.

———. *Gems from the Coral Islands*. Philadelphia: Presbyterian Board of Publication, 1855.

———. "Mangaia (Hervey Islands)." In *Report of the Second Meeting of the Australasian Association for the Advancement of Science*. Sydney: AAAS, 1890.

Grey, George. *Polynesian Mythology and Ancient Traditional History of the New Zealand Race*. London: John Murray, 1855.

Gribble, E. R. *A Despised Race: The Vanishing Aboriginals of Australia*. Sydney: Australian Board of Missions, 1933.

Hale, Horatio. *Ethnography and Philology*. Ridgewood: Gregg Press, 1968; first published 1846 by Lea & Blanchard.

Haweis, Thomas. *A View of the Present State of Evangelical Religion throughout the World with a View to Promote Missionary Exertions*. London: Williams & Son, 1812.

Hazlewood, David. *A Compendious Grammar of the Feejeean Language, with Examples of Native Idioms*. Vewa: Wesleyan Mission Press, 1850.

Herodotus. *The Histories*. Edited by Carolyn Dewald. Translated by Robin Waterfield. Oxford: Oxford University Press, 1998.

Hockin, John Pearce. *A Supplement to the Account of the Pelew Islands; compiled from the journals of the Panther and Endeavour, two vessels sent by the Honorable East India Company to those Islands in the Year 1790 and from the Oral Communications of Captain H. Wilson*. London: W. Bulmer and Co., 1803.

Holwell, William. *A Mythological, Etymological, and Historical Dictionary*. London: Fox C. Dilly, 1793.

The Holy Bible. King James (Authorized) Version.

Ivens, Walter G. *Dictionary and Grammar of the Language of Sa'a and Ulawa, Solomon Islands*. Washington: Carnegie Institution, 1918.

———. "The Diversity of Culture in Melanesia," *Journal of the Royal Anthropological Institute of Great Britain and Ireland* 64 (1934): 45–56.

———. "Place of Vui and Tamate in Religion of Mota," *Journal of the Royal Anthropological Institute of Great Britain and Ireland* 61 (1931): 157–66.

———. "The Polynesian Word Atua: Its Derivation and Use," *Man* 24 (1924): 133–36.

Jaggar, Thomas James. *Unto the Perfect Day: The Journal of Thomas James Jaggar, Feejee 1838–1845*. Edited by Esther and William Keesing-Styles. Auckland: Solent Publishing, 1988.

Jebb, R. C. *Sophocles: the plays and fragments with critical notes, commentary, and translation in English prose*. Cambridge: Cambridge University Press, 1883–96.

Keate, George. *An Account of the Pelew Islands, Situated in the Western Part of the Pacific Ocean. Composed from the Journals and Communications of Captain Henry Wilson, and Some of His Officers, who, in August 1783, were there Shipwrecked in the Antelope, a Packet Belonging to the Honourable East India Company*. London: G. Nicol, 1788.

Kendall, Thomas. *A Grammar and Vocabulary of the Language of New Zealand*. London: Church Missionary Society, 1820.

———. *A Korao no New Zealand; or the New Zealander's First Book; being an Attempt to compose some Lessons for the Instruction of the Natives*. Sydney: G. Howe, 1815.

King, Copland. *A History of the New Guinea Mission 1891–1901*. Sydney: Australian Board of Mission, [1901].

Layard, John. *Stone Men of Malekula*. London: Chatto & Windus, 1942.

Liddell, Henry George, and Robert Scott. *Greek-English Lexicon*. 2nd ed. Oxford: Oxford University Press, 1845.

Lovett, Richard. *James Chalmers: His Autobiography and Letters*. London: The Religious Tract Society, 1902.

Lubbock, John. *The Origin of Civilisation*. London: Longmans, Green, and Co., 1870.

Macdonald, Daniel. *Oceania: Linguistic and Anthropological*. Melbourne: M. L. Hutchinson, 1880.

———. *The Oceanic Languages: Their Grammatical Structure, Vocabulary and Origin*. London: Henry Frowde, 1907.

———. "The Polynesian Word for God, Atua, and its Anthropological Implications." *Proceedings of the Pan-Pacific Scientific Congress 1923*. Melbourne: Government Printer, [1924].

Malinowski, Bronislaw. *Argonauts of the Western Pacific: An Account of Native Enterprise and Adventure in the Archipelagoes of Melanesian New Guinea*. Long Grove, IL: Waveland Press, 1922.

Marett, R. R. *The Threshold of Religion*. London: Methuen & Co., 1909.

Mathew, John. *Eaglehawk and Crow: A Study of the Australian Aborigines, Including an Inquiry into their Origin and a Survey of Australian Languages*. London: Nutt, 1899.

———. "The Religious Cults of the Australian Aborigines." *Report of the Australasian Association for the Advancement of Science*. Sydney: AAAS, 1926.

Mathews, Basil. *The Clash of Colour: A Study in the Problem of Race*. London: Wesleyan Methodist Missionary Society, 1925.

McHardy, Emmet. *Blazing the Trail. Letters from the North Solomons*. Edited by Eileen Duggan. Sydney: Dominion Publishing Company, 1935.

McKenzie, Maisie. *Road to Mowanjum*. Sydney: Angus and Robertson, 1969.

McLennan, John F. *Studies in Ancient History: comprising a reprint of Primitive Marriage*. London: Macmillan, 1886.

Messer, A. B. *Continuation of an enquiry into the reputed poisonous nature of the arrows of the South Sea Islanders*. London: Government Printer for the Admiralty, 1876.

Milton, John. *Paradise Lost*. Waiheke Island: Floating Press, 2008.

Ottley, Robert. *The Doctrine of the Incarnation*. London: Methuen & Co., 1896.

Paley, F. A., trans. *The Tragedies of Aeschylus*. London: George Bell, 1855.

Pankhurst, John, ed. *An Hebrew and English Lexicon Without Points*. London: T. Davison, 1807.

Paton, John G. *John G. Paton, Missionary to the New Hebrides*. Edited by James Paton. London: Banner of Truth Trust, 1965; first published 1889.

Paton, Maggie Whitecross. *Letters and Sketches from the New Hebrides*. 3rd ed. London: Hodder and Stoughton, 1865.

Pierson, Delavan L. *The Pacific Islanders. From Savages to Saints*. New York: Funk & Wagnalls, 1906.

Prichard, James Cowles. "Ethnology." In *A manual of scientific enquiry, prepared for the use of Her Majesty's Navy and adapted for travelers*, edited by J. W. Herschel. London: John Murray, 1849.

———. *The Natural History of Man*. London: H. Bailliere, 1855.

Rivers, W. H. R. "Colour Vision." In *Reports of the Cambridge Anthropological Expedition to Torres Straits*. Vol. 2, *Physiology and Psychology*. Edited by A. C. Haddon. Cambridge: Cambridge University Press, 1901.

———. *The History of Melanesian Society*. Vol. 1. Oosterhout, Netherlands: Anthropological Publications, 1968; first published 1914 by Cambridge University Press.

———. "On the Origin of the Classificatory System of Relationships." In *Anthropological Essays presented to Edward Burnett Tylor in Honour of his 75th Birthday Oct. 2 1907*. Oxford: Clarendon Press, 1907.

Sarawia, George. *They Came to My Island*. Siota: St. Peter's College, 1968.

Saville, William James Viritahitemauvai. *In Unknown New Guinea*. London: Seeley Service & Co., 1926.

The Septuagint Version of the Old Testament. London: Samuel Bagster and Sons, 1844.

Smith, Gordon Hedderly. *The Missionary and Anthropology: An Introduction to the Study of Primitive Man for Missionaries*. Chicago: Moody Press, 1945.

Smith, Grafton Elliot. *The Ancient Egyptians and the Origin of Civilization*. London: Harper, 1923.

Stevens, Edward T. *Flint Chips. A Guide to Pre-Historic Archaeology, as Illustrated by the Collection in the Blackmore Museum, Salisbury*. London: Bell and Daldy, 1870.

Stone-Wigg, Montagu. *The Papuans: A People of the South Pacific.* Melbourne: The Shipping Newspapers for the Association for Missionary Services, 1912.

Taylor, Richard. *Te Ika a Maui: New Zealand and its Inhabitants.* Auckland: A. H. & A. W. Reed, 1974; first published 1850.

———. *Te Ika A Maui: New Zealand and Its Inhabitants.* 2nd ed. London: W. Macintosh, 1870.

Thomas, W. G. *"These My Brethren." Studies in the Problem of the Aborigines of Australia and on Christian Responsibility and Action in regard thereto.* Sydney: Australian Board of Missions, 1946.

Threlkeld, Launcelot. *Australian Reminiscences and Papers of L.E. Threlkeld, Missionary to the Aborigines, 1824–1859.* Ed. Niel Gunson. Canberra: Australian Institute of Aboriginal Studies, 1974.

Tregear, Edward. *The Aryan Maori.* Wellington: Government Printer, 1885.

Waterhouse, Joseph. *The King and People of Fiji.* London: Wesleyan Conference Office, 1866.

Webb, Arthur J. "Observations on the Hill Tribes of Navitilevu, Fiji." *Report of the Second Meeting of the Australasian Association for the Advancement of Science.* Sydney: AAAS, 1890.

Williams, John. *A Narrative of Missionary Enterprises in the South Sea Islands.* London: John Snow, 1841.

———. *Samoan Journals of John Williams.* Edited by Richard M. Moyle. Canberra: Australian National University Press, 1984.

Williams, Thomas. *The Islands and their Inhabitants.* Edited by George Stringer Rowe. Vol. 1 of *Fiji and the Fijians.* London: Alexander Heylin, 1858.

World Missionary Conference. *Report of Commission V: The Preparation of Missionaries.* Edinburgh: Oliphant, Anderson & Ferrier, 1910.

World Missionary Conference. *Report of Commission VII: Missions and Governments.* Edinburgh and London: Oliphant, Anderson & Ferrier, 1910.

X., Jacobus. *Untrodden fields of anthropology: observations on the esoteric manners and customs of semi-civilized peoples.* Edited by Charles Carrington. Paris: Librarie de medicine, folklore et anthropologie, 1898.

Secondary Sources

Abusharaf, Rogaia. "'We Have Supped So Deep in Horrors': Understanding Colonialist Emotionality." *History and Anthropology* 17, no. 3 (2006): 209–28.

Agnew, Vanessa. *Enlightenment Orpheus.* Oxford: Oxford University Press, 2008.

Aldrich, Robert. *Colonialism and Homosexuality.* London: Routledge, 2003.

Alter, Stephen G. *Darwinism and the Linguistic Image: Language, Race, and Natural Theology in the Nineteenth Century.* Baltimore: Johns Hopkins University Press, 1999.

Anderson, Warwick. *The Cultivation of Whiteness: Science, Health and Racial Destiny in Australia.* Carleton: Melbourne University Press, 2002.

Arens, W. *The Man-Eating Myth: Anthropology and Anthropophagy.* Oxford: Oxford University Press, 1979.

Armitage, Andrew. *Comparing the Policy of Aboriginal Assimilation: Australia, Canada and New Zealand.* Vancouver: University of British Columbia Press, 1995.

Axtell, James, and William C. Sturtevant. "The Unkindest Cut, or Who Invented Scalping?" *The William and Mary Quarterly* 37, no. 3 (1980): 451–72.

Bagnall, A. G., and G. C. Petersen. *William Colenso, Printer, Missionary, Botanist, Explorer, Politician; His Life and Journeys.* Wellington, NZ: A. H. & A. W. Reed, 1948.

Ballantyne, Tony. "Introduction." In *Science, Empire and the European Exploration of the Pacific,* edited by Tony Ballantyne. Aldershot: Ashgate, 2004.

———. *Orientalism and Race: Aryanism in the British Empire.* New York: Palgrave Macmillan, 2006.

———. "The Reform of the Heathen Body." In *When the Waves Rolled in Upon Us: Essays in Nineteenth-Century Maori History*, edited by Michael Reilly and Jane Thomson. Dunedin, NZ: University of Otago Press, 1999.

———. "William Yate: Mythmaking and Transgression in New Zealand." *Thamyris* 2, no. 1 (1995): 115–33.

Ballantyne, Tony, and Antoinette Burton. "Introduction." In *Bodies in Contact: Rethinking Colonial Encounters in World History*, edited by Tony Ballantyne and Antoinette Burton. Durham, NC: Duke University Press, 2005.

Barker, John. "Christianity in Oceanic Societies." In *Christianity in Oceania,* edited by John Barker. New York: University Press of America, 1990.

———. "Christianity in Western Melanesian Ethnography." In *History and Tradition in Melanesian Anthropology,* edited by James G. Carrier. Berkeley: University of California Press, 1992.

Barnett, Clive. "Impure and Worldly Geography: The Africanist Discourse of the Royal Geographical Society, 1831–73." *Transactions of the Institute of British Geographers* 23, no. 2 (1998): 239–51.

Bayly, C. A. *Empire and Information: Intelligence Gathering and Social Communication in India, 1780–1870.* Cambridge: Cambridge University Press, 1996.

Bebbington, David W. *The Mind of Gladstone: Religion, Homer, and Politics.* Oxford: Oxford University Press, 2004.

Bediako, Gillian M. *Primal Religion and the Bible: William Robertson Smith and His Heritage.* Journal for the Study of the Old Testament Supplement Series 246. Sheffield: Sheffield Academic Press, 1997.

Bell, Catherine. "Modernism and Postmodernism in the Study of Religion." *Religious Studies Review* 22 (1996): 179–90.

Bhabha, Homi. "Of Mimicry and Man: The Ambivalence of Colonial Discourse." *October* 28 (1984): 125–33.

Binney, Judith. *The Legacy of Guilt: A Life of Thomas Kendall.* Auckland: Oxford University Press, 1968.

Birtwhistle, Allen. *In His Armour: The Life of John Hunt of Fiji.* London: Cargate Press, 1954.

Blake, Richard. *Evangelicals in the Royal Navy, 1775–1815: Blue Lights and Psalm-Singers.* Woodbridge, UK: Boydell and Brewer, 2008.

Borsboom, Ad, and Jean Kommers, eds. *Anthropologists and the Missionary Endeavour:*

Experiences and Reflections. Saarbrüken: Verlag für Entwicklungspolitik Saarbrüken GmbH, 2000.

Bowler, P. J. *The Invention of Progress: The Victorians and the Past*. Oxford: Blackwell, 1989.

Bradford, Tolly. *Prophetic Identities: Indigenous Missionaries on British Colonial Frontiers, 1850–75*. Vancouver: University of British Columbia Press, 2012.

Brandwie, E. "Ethnology and Missionaries: The Case of the Anthropos Institute and Wilhelm Schmidt." In *Missionaries, Anthropologists and Cultural Change*, edited by D. L. Shiteman. Williamsburg: College of William and Mary, 1985.

Brantlinger, Patrick. *Taming Cannibals: Race and the Victorians*. Ithaca, NY: Cornell University Press, 2011.

Brennan, Frank, ed. *Reconciling Our Differences: A Christian Approach to Recognising Aboriginal Land Rights*. Brunswick: Aurora Books, 1992.

Brock, Peggy. "Setting the Record Straight: New Christians and Missionary Christianity." In *Indigenous Peoples and Religious Change*, edited by Peggy Brock. Leiden: Brill, 2005.

Brown, Andrew. *The Darwin Wars*. London: Simon & Schuster, 2000.

Brown, Stewart J. *Providence and Empire 1815–1914*. London: Pearson/Longman, 2008.

Bulbeck, Chilla. *Australian Women in Papua New Guinea: Colonial Passages, 1920–1960*. Cambridge: Cambridge University Press, 1992.

Burridge, Kenelm. *In the Way: A Study of Christian Missionary Endeavours*. Vancouver: University of British Columbia Press, 1991.

Calder, Alex. "Temptations of William Pascoe Crook: An Experience of Cultural Difference in the Marquesas, 1796–98." *Journal of Pacific History* 31, no. 2 (1996): 144–61.

Campbell, Joseph. Introduction to *Myth, Religion and Mother Right: Selected Writings of J. J. Bachofen*. Translated by Ralph Manheim. Princeton: Princeton University Press for the Bollingen Foundation, 1973.

Cannizzo, Jeanne. "Gathering Souls and Objects: Missionary Collections." In *Colonialism and the Object: Empire, Material Culture and the Museum*, edited by Tim Barringer and Tom Flynn, 153–66. London: Routledge, 1998.

Cappell, Arthur. "The Word Mana: A Linguistic Study." *Oceania* 9 (1938): 89–96.

Carey, Hilary. "Companions in the Wilderness." *Journal of Religious History* 19, no. 2 (1995): 227–48.

———. "Death, God and Linguistics: Conversations with Missionaries on the Australian Frontier, 1824–1845." *Australian Historical Studies* 40 (2009): 161–77.

———. *God's Empire: Religion and Colonialism in the British World, c. 1801–1908*. Cambridge: Cambridge University Press, 2010.

———. "Lancelot Threlkeld and Missionary Linguistics in Australia to 1850." In *Missionary Linguistics*, edited by Otto Zwarties and Even Hovdhaugen. Amsterdam: John Benjamins, 2004.

Carson, Penny. "The British Raj and the Awakening of the Evangelical Conscience." In *Christian Missions and the Enlightenment*, edited by Brian Stanley. Grand Rapids: Eerdmans, 2001.

Cassirer, Ernst. *Language and Myth*. New York: Harper, 1946.

Chong, Hwa-Young. *In Search of God's Power in Broken Bodies: A Theology of Maum*. New York: Palgrave Macmillan, 2013.

Christensen, Torben, and William R. Hutchison, eds. *Missionary Ideologies in the Imperialist Era: 1880–1920*. Copenhagen: Aros, 1982.

Christophers, Brett. *Positioning the Missionary: John Booth Good and the Confluence of Cultures in Nineteenth-Century British Columbia*. Vancouver: University of British Columbia Press, 1998.

Clay, Brenda Johnson. *Unstable Images: Colonial Discourse on New Ireland, Papua New Guinea, 1875–1935*. Honolulu: University of Hawai'i Press, 2005.

Clifford, James. *Person and Myth: Maurice Leenhardt in the Melanesian World*. Berkeley: University of California Press, 1982.

Cole, Keith. *A History of the Church Missionary Society of Australia*. Melbourne: Church Missionary Historical Publications, 1971.

Colley, Linda. *Captives: Britain, Empire and the World, 1600–1850*. London: Jonathan Cape, 2002.

Coltrane, Scott, and Randall Collins. *Sociology of Marriage and the Family: Gender, Love, and Property*. Belmont, CA: Wadsworth/Thomson Learning, 2001.

Comaroff, Jean, and John Comaroff. *Of Revelation and Revolution*. Chicago: University of Chicago Press, 1991.

Coombes, Annie. *Reinventing Africa: Museums, Material Culture and Popular Imagination in Late Victorian and Edwardian England*. New Haven: Yale University Press, 1994.

Cortez, Marc. *Theological Anthropology: A Guide for the Perplexed*. London: T&T Clark, 2010.

Costo, Rupert, and Jeanette Henry Costo. *The Missions of California: A Legacy of Genocide*. San Francisco: The Indian Historian Press, 1987.

Cove, John J. *What the Bones Say: Tasmanian Aborigines, Science and Domination*. Ottawa: Carleton University Press, 1995.

Cox, Jeffrey. *The British Missionary Enterprise since 1700*. New York: Routledge, 2008.

———. *Imperial Fault Lines: Christianity and Colonial Power in India, 1818–1940*. Stanford, CA: Stanford University Press, 2002.

———. "The Missionary Movement." In *Nineteenth-Century English Religious Traditions*, edited by D. G. Paz. Westport, CT: Greenwood Press, 1995.

Crocombe, R. G., and Marjorie Tuainekore, eds. *The Works of Ta'unga: Records of a Polynesian Traveller in the South Seas, 1833–1896*. Canberra: Australian National University Press, 1968.

Crocombe, Ron, and Marjorie Tuainekore Cracombe, eds. *Polynesian Missions in Melanesia: From Samoa, Cook Islands and Tonga to Papua New Guinea and New Caledonia*. Suva: Institute of Pacific Studies, University of South Pacific, 1982.

Davidson, Allan. "The Legacy of Robert Henry Codrington." *International Bulletin of Missionary Research* 27, no. 4 (2003): 171–72, 174–76.

De Conick, April. *Holy Misogyny: Why the Sex and Gender Conflicts in the Early Church Still Matter*. New York: Continuum, 2011.

Dening, Greg. *Beach Crossings: Voyaging Across Times, Cultures, and Self*. Melbourne: Miegunyah Press, 2004.

———. *Islands and Beaches: Discourse on a Silent Land. Marquesas 1774–1880*. Honolulu: University of Hawai'i Press, 1980.

Diaz, Vicente M. *Repositioning the Missionary: Rewriting the Histories of Colonialism, Native Catholicism, and Indigeneity in Guam.* Honolulu: University of Hawai'i Press, 2010.

Dixon, David N. "The Second Text: Missionary Publishing and Bunyan's Pilgrim's Progress." *International Bulletin of Missionary Research* 36, no. 2 (2012): 86–90.

Dixon, Thomas, Geoffrey Cantor, and Stephen Pumphrey, eds. *Science and Religion: New Historical Perspectives.* Cambridge: Cambridge University Press, 2010.

Douglas, Bronwen. "Climate to Crania: Science and the Racialization of Human Difference." In *Foreign Bodies: Oceania and the Science of Race 1750–1940*, edited by Bronwen Douglas and Chris Ballard. Canberra: ANU e-Press, 2008.

———. "Encounters with the Enemy? Academic Readings of Missionary Narratives on Melanesians." *Comparative Studies in Society and History* 43, no. 1 (2001): 37–64.

———. "'*Novus Orbis Australis*': Oceania in the Science of Race, 1750–1850." In *Foreign Bodies: Oceania and the Science of Race 1750–1940*, edited by Bronwen Douglas and Chris Ballard. Canberra: ANU e-Press, 2008.

———. "Provocative Readings in Intransigent Archives: Finding Aneityumese Women." *Oceania* 70, no. 2 (1999): 111–29.

———. *Sciences, Voyages and Encounters in Oceania 1511–1850.* Houndsmills, UK: Palgrave Macmillan, 2014.

Douglas, Bronwen, and Chris Ballard, eds. *Foreign Bodies: Oceania and the Science of Race 1750–1940.* Canberra: ANU e-Press, 2008.

Driver, Felix. *Geography Militant: Cultures of Exploration and Empire.* Oxford: Blackwell, 2001.

Edmond, Rod. *Representing the South Pacific: Colonial Discourse from Cook to Gauguin.* Cambridge: Cambridge University Press, 1997.

Emerson, Caryl. *The First Hundred Years of Mikhail Bakhtin.* Princeton: Princeton University Press, 2000.

Errington, Frederick, and Deborah Gerwertz. "First Contact with God: Individualism, Agency and Revivalism in the Duke of York Islands." *Cultural Anthropology* 8 (1993): 279–305.

———. "From Darkness to Light in the George Brown Jubilee: The Invention of Nontradition and the Inscription of a National History in East New Britain." *American Ethnologist* 21 (1994): 104–22.

Etherington, Norman. "Introduction." In *Missions and Empire,* edited by Norman Etherington. Oxford: Oxford University Press, 2005.

Eves, Richard. "Commentary: Missionary or Collector? The Case of George Brown." *Museum Anthropology* 22, no. 1 (1998): 49–60.

———. "Dr. Brown's Study: Methodist Missionaries and the Collection of Material Culture in the Pacific." *Museum Anthropology* 24, no. 1 (2000): 26–41.

Firth, Raymond. "The Analysis of Mana: An Empirical Approach." *Journal of the Polynesian Society* 49 (1940): 483–510.

Fletcher, C. Brunsdon. *The Black Knight of the Pacific.* Sydney: Australasian Publishing Company, 1944.

———. "George Brown and the Pacific." *Royal Australian Historical Society, Journal and Proceedings* 7, no. 1 (1921): 1–54.

Ford, Norman M. *When Did I Begin? Conception of the Human Individual in History, Philosophy and Science.* Cambridge: Cambridge University Press, 1988.

Forman, Charles W. "The Legacy of George Brown." *International Bulletin of Missionary Research* 22, no. 1 (1998): 28–33.

Fox, C. E. *Kakamora.* London: Hodder & Stoughton, 1962.

———. *Lord of the Southern Isles.* London: A. R. Mowbray, 1958.

Gardner, Helen Bethea. "'By the Facts We Add to Our Store': Lorimer Fison, Lewis Henry Morgan and the Spread of Kinship Studies." *Oceania* 79, no. 3 (2009): 280–92.

———. "Defending Friends: Robert Codrington, George Sarawia and Edward Wogale." In *The Atlantic World in the Antipodes: Effects and Transformations since the Eighteenth Century,* edited by K. Fullagar. Newcastle, UK: Cambridge Scholars Publishing, 2012.

———. "The 'Faculty of Faith': Evangelical Missionaries, Social Anthropologists, and the Claim for Human Unity in the 19th Century." In *Foreign Bodies: Oceania and the Science of Race 1750–1940*, edited by Bronwen Douglas and Chris Ballard. Canberra: ANU e-Press, 2008.

———. "From Site to Text: Australian Aborigines and *The Origin of the Family.*" *Itinerario* 34, no. 3 (2011): 25–38.

———. *Gathering for God: George Brown in Oceania.* Dunedin: Otago University Press, 2006.

———. "'New Heaven and New Earth': Translation and Conversion on Aneityum." *Journal of Pacific History* 41, no. 3 (2006): 293–311.

———. "The Origin of Kinship in Oceania: Lewis Henry Morgan and Lorimer Fison." *Oceania* 78, no. 2 (2008): 137–50.

Gardner, Helen Bethea, and Patrick McConvell. *Southern Anthropology—a History of Fison and Howitt's* Kamilaroi and Kurnai. London: Palgrave Macmillan, 2015.

Garrett, John. *To Live Amongst the Stars: Christian Origins in Oceania.* Fiji: World Council of Churches, 1982.

Gascoigne, John. *Encountering the Pacific in the Age of the Enlightenment.* Cambridge: Cambridge University Press, 2014.

———. "Introduction: Religion and Empire, an Historiographical Perspective." *Journal of Religious History* 32, no. 2 (2008): 159–78.

Geismar, Haidy. "*Stone Men of Malekula* on Malekula: An Ethnography of an Ethnograpy." *Ethnos* 74, no. 2 (2009): 199–228.

Gibbs, Philip. "Culture and Faith: The Contribution of the Melanesian Institute, Papua New Guinea." In *Anthropology's Debt to Missionaries,* edited by Leonard Plotnicov, Paula Brown, and Vinson Sutlive. Pittsburgh: University of Pittsburgh Press, 2007.

Goldsmith, Michael. "Understanding or Believing? On Researching Christianity in Tuvalu." *Journal of Pacific Studies* 20 (1996): 161–74.

Gonzalez, Michelle A. *Created in God's Image: An Introduction to Feminist Theological Anthropology.* Maryknoll, NY: Orbis Books, 2007.

Goodman, Paul. *Of One Blood: Abolitionism and the Origins of Racial Equality.* Berkeley: University of California Press, 1998.

Gould, Eliga H. "Prelude: The Christianizing of British America." In *Missions and Empire,* edited by Etherington. Oxford: Oxford University Press, 2005.

Griffiths, Tom. *Hunters and Collectors: The Antiquarian Imagination in Australia*. Cambridge: Cambridge University Press, 1996.

Grimshaw, Patricia. *Paths of Duty: American Missionary Wives in Nineteenth-Century Hawai'i*. Honolulu: University of Hawai'i Press, 1989.

Grimshaw, Patricia, and Andrew May, eds. *Missionaries, Indigenous Peoples and Cultural Exchange*. Brighton, UK: Sussex Academic Press, 2010.

Guest, Kristen, ed. *Eating Their Words: Cannibalism and the Boundaries of Cultural Identity*. Albany: State University of New York Press, 2001.

Gunson, Niel. "British Missionaries and the Contribution to Science in the Pacific Islands." In *Darwin's Laboratory: Evolutionary Theory and Natural History in the Pacific*, edited by Roy MacLeod and Philip F. Rehbock. Honolulu: University of Hawai'i Press, 1994.

———. "Brown, George (1835–1917)." *The Australian Dictionary of Biography*. http://adb.anu.edu.au.login.ezproxy.library.ualberta.ca/biography/brown-george-3075 (accessed 7 May 2012).

———. *Messengers of Grace: Evangelical Missionaries in the South Seas, 1797–1860*. Melbourne: Oxford University Press, 1978.

———. "The Theology of Imperialism and the Missionary History of the Pacific." *Journal of Religious History* 5, no. 3 (1969): 255–65.

Gustafson, James M. "Man—In Light of Social Science and Christian Faith." In *Conflicting Images of Man*, edited by William Nicholls. New York: The Seabury Press, 1966.

Hagerman, Christopher. *Britain's Imperial Muse: The Classics, Imperialism, and the Indian Empire*. Houndsmills, UK: Palgrave Macmillan, 2013.

Hall, Catherine. *Civilising Subjects: Metropole and Colony in the English Imagination, 1830–1867*. Chicago: University of Chicago Press, 2002.

Halse, Christine. "Gribble, Ernest Richard Bulmer." In *Australian Dictionary of Biography*. Vol. 14. Melbourne: Melbourne University Press, 1996. http://adb.anu.edu.au.login.ezproxy.library.ualberta.ca/biography/gribble-ernest-richard-bulmer-ernie-10367/text18363 (accessed 15 April 2014).

———. *A Terribly Wild Man*. Crows Nest: Allen & Unwin, 2002.

Hanlon, David. "Converting Pasts and Presents: Reflections on Histories of Missionary Enterprises in the Pacific." In *Pacific Lives, Pacific Places: Bursting Boundaries in Pacific History*, edited by Brij Lal and Peter Hempenstall. Canberra: Journal of Pacific History, 2001.

Hannaford, Ivan. *Race: The History of an Idea in the West*. Baltimore: Johns Hopkins University Press, 1996.

Hanzeli, Victor Egon. *Missionary Linguistics in New France*. Paris: Mouton, 1969.

Harris, John. *One Blood: 200 Years of Aboriginal Encounter with Christianity*. Sydney: Albatross Books, 1990.

Heartfield, James. *The Aborigines' Protection Society: Humanitarian Imperialism in Australia, New Zealand, Fiji, Canada, South Africa, and the Congo, 1836–1909*. London: Hurst & Co., 2011.

Herbert, Christopher. *Culture and Anomie: Ethnographic Imagination in the Nineteenth Century*. Chicago: University of Chicago Press, 1991.

Herdt, Gilbert H. "Ritualized Homosexual Behaviour in the Male Cults of Melanesia,

1862–1983: An Introduction." In *Ritualized Homosexuality in Melanesia,* edited by Gilbert H. Herdt. Berkeley: University of California Press, 1984.

———, ed. *Ritualized Homosexuality in Melanesia.* Berkeley: University of California Press, 1984.

Hiatt, L. R. *Arguments about Aborigines: Australia and the Evolution of Social Anthropology.* Cambridge: Cambridge University Press, 1996.

Hiebert, Paul G. *Anthropological Insights for Missionaries.* Grand Rapids: Baker Book House, 1985.

Hilliard, David. "The God of the Melanesian Mission." In *Vision and Reality in Pacific Religion,* edited by Phyllis Herda, Michael Reilly, and David Hilliard. Christchurch: Macmillan Brown Centre for Pacific Studies, 2005.

———. *God's Gentlemen: A History of the Melanesian Mission, 1849–1942.* St. Lucia: University of Queensland Press, 1978.

Hofmeyr, Isabel. *The Portable Bunyan: A Transnational History of The Pilgrim's Progress.* Princeton: Princeton University Press, 2004.

Horley, William. *The History of Methodism in New Zealand.* Wellington: McKee and Co., 1900.

Howe, K. R. *The Quest for Origins: Who First Discovered and Settled the Pacific Islands?* Auckland: Penguin, 2003.

Huber, Mary Taylor, and Nancy C. Lutkehaus. *Gendered Missions: Women and Men in Missionary Discourse and Practice.* Ann Arbor: University of Michigan Press, 1990.

Hughes, Daniel T. "Mutual Biases of Anthropologists and Missionaries." In *Mission, Church, and Sect in Oceania,* edited by James A. Boutilier, Daniel T. Hughes, and Sharon W. Tiffany. Ann Arbor: University of Michigan Press, 1978.

Inglis, Amirah. *Not a White Woman Safe: Sexual Anxiety and Politics in Port Moresby, 1920–1934.* Canberra: ANU Press, 1974.

James, Kerry, and Akulia Tabaki, eds. *Religious Cooperation in the Pacific Islands.* Suva: Institute of Pacific Studies, University of the South Pacific, 1989.

Jenkins, Richard. *The Victorians and Ancient Greece.* Oxford: Blackwell, 1980.

Johnston, Anna. "The Book Eaters: Textuality, Modernity, and the London Missionary Society." *Semeia* 88 (1999): 13–41.

———. *Missionary Writing and Empire, 1800–1860.* Cambridge: Cambridge University Press, 2003.

———. "The Strange Career of William Ellis." *Victorian Studies* 49, no. 3 (2007): 491–501.

Johnston, Elizabeth. *She Who Is: The Mystery of God in Feminist Theological Discourse.* New York: Crossroad, 1992.

Jolly, Margaret, and Martha Macintyre, eds. *Family and Gender in the Pacific: Domestic Contradictions and the Colonial Impact.* Cambridge: Cambridge University Press, 1989.

Kaeppler, Adrienne L. *"Artificial Curiosities": Being an Exposition of Native Manufactures Collected on the Three Pacific Voyages of Captain James Cook, RN, at the Bernice Pauahi Bishop Museum, January 18, 1978–August 31, 1978, on the Occasion of the Bicentennial of the European Discovery of the Hawaiian Islands by Captain Cook, January 18, 1778.* Honolulu: Bishop Museum Press, 1978.

Kaplan, Steven, ed. *Indigenous Responses to Western Christianity.* New York: New York University Press, 1995.

Kennedy, Brian P. "The Traditional Irish Thatched House: Imagery and Reality, 1793–1993." In *Visualizing Ireland: National Identity and the Pictorial Tradition,* edited by Adele Dalsimer. Boston: Faber and Faber, 1993.

Kidd, Colin. *The Forging of Races: Race and Scripture in the Protestant Atlantic World, 1600–2000.* Cambridge: Cambridge University Press, 2006.

Kiernan, Victor. *The Lords of Human Kind: European Attitudes to Other Cultures in the Imperial Age.* 2nd ed. London: Serif, 1995.

Kilgour, Maggie. *From Communion to Cannibalism: An Anatomy of Metaphors of Incorporation.* Princeton: Princeton University Press, 1990.

Kipp, Rita. *The Early Years of a Dutch Colonial Mission: The Karo Field.* Ann Arbor: University of Michigan Press, 1990.

Kitchen, John. "Going Medieval: Paradigm Shifts and the Phenomenological Tendency in the Contemporary Encounter with Medieval Religion." *Method & theory in the Study of Religion* 14 (2002): 375–414.

Knapman, Gareth. "Race, Empire and Liberalism: Interpreting John Crawfurd's History of the Indian Archipelago." Paper presented to the 17th Biennial Conference of the Asian Studies Association of Australia in Melbourne, July 1–3, 2008. artsonline.monash.edu.au/mai/files/2012/07/garethknapman.pdf (accessed 25 November 2013).

Knauft, Bruce. *South Coast New Guinea Cultures: History, Comparison, Dialectic.* Cambridge: Cambridge University Press, 1993.

Kolshus, Thorgeir S. "House upon Pacific Sand: W. H. R. Rivers and His 1908 Ethnographic 'Survey Work.'" In *The Ethnographic Experiment: A. M. Hocart and W. H. R. Rivers in Island Melanesia, 1908,* edited by Edvard Hviding and Cato Berg. Oxford: Berghahn, 2014.

Kolshus, Thorgeir S., and Even Hovdhaugen. "Reassessing the Death of Bishop John Coleridge Patteson." *Journal of Pacific History* 45, no. 3 (2010): 331–55.

Koskinen, A. A. *Missionary Influence as a Political Factor in the Pacific Islands.* Helsinki: The Finnish Academy of Science and Letters, 1953.

Kraus, C. Norman. *On Being Human: Sexual Orientation and the Image of God.* Eugene, OR: Cascade Books, 2011.

Kreamer, Christine Mullen, and Sarah Fee, eds. *Objects as Envoys: Cloth, Imagery, and Diplomacy in Madagascar.* Washington: Smithsonian Institution, 2002.

Kuklick, Henrika. "Islands in the Pacific: Darwinian Biogeography and British Anthropology." *American Ethnologist* 23, no. 3 (1996): 611–38.

Lange, Raeburn. *Island Ministers: Indigenous Leadership in Nineteenth Century Pacific Islands Christianity.* Canberra: Pandanus Books, 2005.

Langmore, Diane. *Missionary Lives: Papua, 1874–1914.* Honolulu: University of Hawaiʻi Press, 1989.

———. *Tamate, a King: James Chalmers in New Guinea, 1877–1901.* Carlton: University of Melbourne Press, 1974.

Larsen, Timothy. *Crisis of Doubt: Honest Faith in Nineteenth-Century England.* Oxford: Oxford University Press, 2006.

Larson, Edward J., et al. *The History of Science and Religion in the Western Tradition: An Encyclopedia.* New York: Garland Press, 2000.

Lātūkefu, Sione, and Ruta Sinclair. "Pacific Islanders as International Missionaries. Papua

New Guinea and Solomon Islands." In *Polynesian Missions in Melanesia: From Samoa, Cook Islands and Tonga to Papua New Guinea and New Caledonia*, edited by Ron and Marjorie Crocombe. Suva: Institute of Pacific Studies, University of the South Pacific, 1982.

Lawson, Barbara. *Collected Curios: Missionary Tales from the South Seas.* Montreal: McGill University Libraries, 1994.

Leigh, Matthew. "Ovid and the Lectisternium." *The Classical Quarterly* 52, no. 2 (2002): 625–27.

Lestringant, Frank. *Cannibals: The Discovery and Representation of the Cannibal from Columbus to Jules Verne.* Berkeley: University of California Press, 1997.

Livingstone, David N. *Adam's Ancestors: Race, Religion, and the Politics of Human Origins.* Baltimore: Johns Hopkins University Press, 2008.

Loos, Noel. *White Christ Black Cross: The Emergence of a Black Church.* Canberra: Aboriginal Studies Press, 2007.

Lorimer, Douglas. "From Victorian Values to White Virtues: Assimilation and Exclusion in British Racial Discourse, c. 1870–1914." In *Rediscovering the British World,* edited by Phillip Alfred Buckner and R. Douglas Francis. Calgary, AB: University of Calgary Press, 2005.

Loughnane, Rory. "Introduction: Stages of Transgression." In *Staged Transgression in Shakespeare's England,* edited by Rory Loughnane and Edel Semple. Basingstoke, UK: Palgrave Macmillan, 2013.

Love, J. R. B. *The Aborigines Calling! By the Missionaries on the Different Stations.* Malvern, Australia: McKellar Press, 1941.

Lynch, John M., ed. *Creationism and Scriptural Geology, 1817–57.* Bristol, UK: Thoemmes, 2002.

Lyons, Andrew P., and Harriet Lyons. *Irregular Connections: A History of Anthropology and Sexuality.* Lincoln, NE: University of Nebraska Press, 2004.

MacLean, John. *James Evans, inventor of the syllabic system of the Cree language.* Toronto: Methodist Mission Rooms, 1890.

MacLeod, Roy, and Philip F. Rehbock, eds. *Darwin's Laboratory: Evolutionary Theory and Natural History in the Pacific.* Honolulu: University of Hawai'i Press, 1994.

Major, Andrea. *Sovereignty and Social Reform in India: British Colonialism and the Campaign against Sati, 1830–60.* Abingdon, UK: Routledge, 2010.

Mani, Lata. *Contentious Traditions: The Debate on Sati in Colonial India.* Berkeley: University of California Press, 1998.

Mann, Thomas L., ed. *Biographical Dictionary of Anthropologists Born before 1920.* New York and London: Garland Publishing, 1988.

Maretu. *Cannibals and Converts: Radical Change in the Cook Islands.* Edited and translated by Marjorie Crocombe. Suva: Institute of Pacific Studies, University of the South Pacific, 1983.

Markus, Andrew. *Governing Savages.* Sydney: Allen & Unwin, 1990.

Marshall, P. J., and Glydwr Williams. *The Great Map of Mankind: British Perceptions of the World in the Age of Enlightenment.* London: J. M. Dent & Sons, 1982.

Maughan, Steven. "An Archbishop for Greater Britain: Bishop Montgomery, Missionary Imperialism, and the SPG, 1897–1915." In *Three Centuries of Mission: The United Soci-*

ety for the Propagation of the Gospel 1701–2000, edited by Daniel O'Connor. London: Bloomsbury, 2000.

McNair, William, and Hilary Rumley. *Pioneer Aboriginal Mission: The Work of Wesleyan Missionary John Smithies in the Swan River Colony, 1840–1855*. Nedlands, WA: University of Western Australia, 1981.

Michaud, Jean. "French Missionary Expansion in Colonial Upper Tonkin." *Journal of Southeast Asian Studies* 35, no. 2 (2004): 237–310.

Montgomery, Charles. *The Last Heathen: Encounters with Ghosts and Ancestors in Melanesia*. London: HarperCollins, 2004.

Moore, James R. *The Post-Darwinian Controversies: A Study of the Protestant Struggle to Come to Terms with Darwin in Great Britain and America, 1870–1900*. Cambridge: Cambridge University Press, 1979.

Munro, Doug, and Andrew Thornley, eds. *The Covenant Makers: Islander Missionaries in the Pacific*. Suva: Pacific Theological College and the Institute of Pacific Studies at the University of the South Pacific, 1996.

Murray, Stephen O. *Oceanic Homosexualities*. New York: Garland Publishing, 1992.

Muzorewa, Gwinyai Henry. *An African Theology of Mission*. Lewiston, NY: Edwin Mellen Press, 1990.

Neill, James. *The Origins and Role of Same-Sex Relations in Human Societies*. Jefferson, NC: McFarland, 2008.

Neill, Stephen. *Colonialism and Christian Missions*. London: Lutterworth, 1966.

Noll, Mark A. "We Are What We Sing." *Christianity Today* 43, no. 8 (1999): 37–41.

Nugent, Joseph. "The Human Snout: Pigs, Priests and Peasants in the Parlor." *Senses and Society* 4, no. 3 (2009): 283–301.

Numbers, Ronald L., and John Stenhouse, eds. *Disseminating Darwinism*. Cambridge: Cambridge University Press, 1999.

Nutini, Hugh G. "The Contributions of Mendicant Friars to Mesoamerican Ethnography." In *Anthropology's Debt to Missionaries*, edited by Leonard Plotnicov, Paula Brown, and Vinson Sutlive. Pittsburgh: University of Pittsburgh Press, 2007.

Obeyesekere, Gananath. *Cannibal Talk: The Man-eating Myth and Human Sacrifice in the South Seas*. Berkeley: University of California Press, 2005.

O'Brien, Patty. *The Pacific Muse: Exotic Femininity and the Colonial Pacific*. Seattle: University of Washington Press, 2006.

O'Hanlon, Michael. "'Mostly Harmless'? Missionaries, Administrators and Material Culture on the Coast of British New Guinea." *Journal of the Royal Anthropological Institute* 99, no. 5 (1999): 377–95.

Oliver, Douglas L. *Ancient Tahitian Society*. Vol. 2, *Social Relations*. Honolulu: University of Hawai'i Press, 1974.

The Oxford English Dictionary Online.

Peacock, Daniel J. *Lee Boo of Belau: A Prince in London*. Honolulu: University of Hawai'i Press, 2007.

Pearce, Susan M. *Museums, Objects, and Collections: A Cultural Study*. Leicester: Leicester University Press, 1992.

Pelikan, Jaroslav. *Jesus through the Centuries: His Place in the History of Culture*. New Haven: Yale University Press, 1985.

Pels, Peter. "Anthropology and Mission: Towards a Historical Analysis of Professional Identity." In *The Ambiguity of Rapprochement: Reflections of Anthropologists on Their Controversial Relationship with Missionaries*, edited by R. Bonsen, H. Marks, and J. Miedema. Nijmegen: Focaal, 1990.

Phillips, Kim M., and Barry Reay. *Sex before Sexuality: A Premodern History.* Cambridge: Polity, 2011.

Piggin, Stuart. *Making Evangelical Missionaries 1789–1858.* Appleford, UK: Sutton Courtenay Press, 1984.

Pilch, John J. *A Cultural Handbook to the Bible.* Grand Rapids: Eerdmans, 2012.

Pinney, Christopher. "Colonial Anthropology in the 'Laboratory of Mankind.'" In *The Raj: India and the British 1600–1947,* edited by C. A. Bayly. London: Pearson, for the National Portrait Gallery, 1990.

Plotnicov, Leonard, Paula Brown, and Vinson Sutlive. "Introduction." In *Anthropology's Debt to Missionaries,* edited by Leonard Plotnicov, Paula Brown, and Vinson Sutlive. Pittsburgh: University of Pittsburgh Press, 2007.

Podmore, Colin. *The Moravian Church in England, 1728–1760.* Oxford: Clarendon Press, 1998.

Porter, Andrew N. *Religion versus Empire?: British Protestant Missionaries and Overseas Expansion, 1700–1914.* Manchester: Manchester University Press, 2004.

Prentis, Malcolm. *Science, Race & Faith: A Life of John Mathew, 1849–1929.* Sydney: Centre for the Study of Australian Christianity, 1998.

Prytzjohansen, Jørgen. "Religious Aspects of the Arioi of Tahiti." *Temenos* 25 (1989): 69–78.

Quanchi, Max. "The Imaging of Pastors in Papua." In *The Covenant Makers: Islander Missionaries in the Pacific*, edited by Doug Munro and Andrew Thornley. Suva: Pacific Theological College and the Institute of Pacific Studies, 1996.

Rafael, Vicente L. *Contracting Colonialism: Translation and Christian Conversion in Tagalog Society.* Durham: Duke University Press, 1993.

Ranger, Terence. "Christianity and Indigenous Peoples: A Personal Overview." *Journal of Religious History* 27, no. 3 (2003): 255–271.

Reddy, William M. *The Making of Romantic Love: Longing and Sexuality in Europe, South Asia, and Japan, 900–1200 CE.* Chicago: University of Chicago Press, 2012.

Reid, R. E. "John Henry Holmes in Paua, Changing Missionary Perspectives on Indigenous Cultures, 1890–1914." *Journal of Pacific History* 13, no. 3 (1978): 173–87.

Reilly, Michael. "A Political Succession Text from Mangaia." *Journal of Pacific Studies* 102, no. 1 (1993): 70–98.

Rennie, Neil. "The Point Venus 'Scene.'" In *Science and Exploration in the Pacific,* edited by Margarette Lincoln. Woodbridge, UK: Boydell Press, 1998.

Richards, Graham. "Getting a Result: the Expedition's Psychological Research 1898–1913." In *Cambridge and the Torres Strait. Centenary Essays on the 1898 Anthropological Expedition,* edited by Anita Herle and Sandra Rouse. Cambridge: Cambridge University Press, 1998.

Robbins, Keith. "Britain, 1940 and 'Christian Civilization.'" In *History, Society and the Churches: Essays in Honour of Owen Chadwick,* edited by Derek Beales and Geoffrey Best. Cambridge: Cambridge University Press, 1985.

Robertson, Carolina E. "The Mahu of Hawai'i." In *Pacific Diaspora: Island Peoples in the*

United States and Across the Pacific, edited by Paul Spickard, Joanne L. Rondilla, Debbie Hippolite Wright. Honolulu: University of Hawai'i Press, 2002.

Robinson, Michael D. *The Storms of Providence: Navigating the Waters of Calvinism, Arminianism, and Open Theism*. Dallas: University Press of America, 2003.

Rogerson, John. "Social Anthropology and the Old Testament—Present, Past and Future." *Journal of the Anthropological Society of Oxford* 4, no. 1 (1973): 42–50.

Roque, Ricardo. *Headhunting and Colonialism: Anthropology and the Circulation of Human Skulls in the Portuguese Empire, 1870–1930*. New York: Palgrave Macmillan, 2010.

Rubel, Paula G., and Abraham Rosman. "George Brown, Pioneer Missionary and Collector." *Museum Anthropology* 20, no. 1 (1996): 60–63.

Runesson, Anna. *Exegesis in the Making: Postcolonialism and New Testament Studies*. Leiden: Brill, 2010.

Sahlins, Marshall. "Artificially Maintained Controversies: Global Warming and Fijian Cannibalism." *Anthropology Today* 19, no. 3 (2003): 3–5.

Said, Edward W. "The Return to Philology." In *Humanism and Democratic Criticism*, edited by Edward W. Said. New York: Columbia University Press, 2004.

Samson, Jane. "Christianity, Masculinity and Authority in the Life of George Sarawia." *Journal of the Canadian Historical Society* 20, no. 2 (2009): 60–84.

———. "Cracking the 'Antigone Nut': Lorimer Fison, Social Anthropology, and Classical Scholarship." In "Before the Field: Colonial Ethnography's Challenge to British Anthropology," edited by Helen Gardner and Robert Kenney. Special issue of *Oceania* 86, no. 3 (2016): 278–93.

———. "Do Savages Get the Blues? William Colenso and the Nineteenth-Century Colour Debate." In *Webs of Words: New Studies in Historical Lexicology*, edited by John Considine. Newcastle: Cambridge Scholars Publishing, 2010.

———. "Hero, Fool or Martyr? The Many Deaths of Commodore Goodenough." *Journal for Maritime Research* 10, no. 1 (2008): 1–22.

———. *Imperial Benevolence: Making British Authority in the Pacific Islands*. Honolulu: University of Hawai'i Press, 1998.

———. "Poisoned Arrows and Poisoned Ethnographies from Victorian Melanesia." In *The Victorians and the Pacific: Encounters at Home and Abroad*, edited by Amy Woodson-Boulton, Richard Fulton, and Peter Hoffenberg. Forthcoming.

———. "The Problem of Colonialism in the Western Historiography of Christian Missions." *Religious Studies and Theology* 23, no. 2 (2004): 3–25.

———. "Rescuing Fijian Women? The British Anti-Slavery Proclamation of 1852." *Journal of Pacific History* 30, no. 1 (1995): 22–38.

———. "Translation Teams: Missionaries, Islanders, and the Reduction of Language in the Pacific." In *Missionaries, Indigenous Peoples and Cultural Exchange*, edited by Patricia Grimshaw and Andrew May. Brighton: Sussex Academic Press, 2010.

Sandys, John Edwin. *A History of Classical Scholarship of America*. Vol. 3, *The Eighteenth Century in Germany, and the Nineteenth Century in Europe and the United States*. Cambridge: Cambridge University Press, 1908.

Sanneh, Lamin. *Translating the Message: The Missionary Impact on Culture*. 2nd edition. Maryknoll, NY: Orbis Books, 2009.

Saunders, Barbara A. C. "Linguistic Anthropology." *American Anthropologist* 101, no. 3 (1999): 657–59.

Schreiter, Robert. "Mission and Human Identity in the Light of Edinburgh 2010. A Response to Brian Stanley." *Mission Studies* 26, no. 1 (2009): 98–101.

Semple, Rhonda. "Missionary Manhood: Professionalism, Belief and Masculinity in the Nineteenth-Century British Imperial Field." *Journal of Imperial and Commonwealth History* 36, no. 3 (2008): 397–415.

Seo, Bo-Myung. *A Critique of Western Theological Anthropology.* New York: Edwin Mellen Press, 2005.

Seton, Rosemary. "Reconstructing the Museum of the London Missionary Society." *Material Religion* 8, no. 1 (2012): 98–102.

Sharpe, Eric J. *Not to Destroy, But to Fulfil.* Uppsala: Gleerup, 1965.

Sherlock, Peter. "Missions, Colonialism and the Politics of Agency." In *Evangelists of Empire? Missionaries and Colonial History,* edited by Amanda Berry et al. History Conference and Seminar Series 18. Melbourne: eScholarship Research Centre, 2008.

Sinha, Mrinalini. *Colonial Masculinity: The 'Manly Englishman' and the 'Effeminate Bengali' in the Late Nineteenth Century.* Manchester: Manchester University Press, 1995.

Sivasundaram, Sujit. "A Global History of Science and Religion." In *Science and Religion: New Historical Perspectives,* edited by Thomas Dixon, Geoffrey Cantor, and Stephen Pumfrey. Cambridge: Cambridge University Press, 2010.

———. *Nature and Godly Empire: Science and Evangelical Mission in the Pacific, 1795–1850.* Cambridge: Cambridge University Press, 2005.

Smith, Bernard. *European Vision and the South Pacific, 1768–1850: A Study in the History of Art and Ideas.* Oxford: Clarendon Press, 1960.

Smith, Vanessa. "Banks, Tupaia, and Mai: Cross-cultural Exchanges and Friendship in the Pacific." *Parergon* 26, no. 2 (2009): 139–60.

———. *Literary Culture and the Pacific: Nineteenth-Century Textual Encounters.* Cambridge: Cambridge University Press, 1998.

Sohmer, Sarah. "Christianity Without Civilization: Anglican Sources for an Alternative Nineteenth-Century Mission Methodology." *Journal of Religious History* 18, no. 2 (1994): 174–97.

———. "The Melanesian Mission and Victorian Anthropology: A Study in Symbiosis." In *Darwin's Laboratory: Evolutionary Theory and Natural History in the Pacific,* edited by Roy MacLeod and Philip F. Rehbock. Honolulu: University of Hawai'i Press, 1994.

Solheim, Wilhelm G. "Edward Winslow Gifford, 1887–1959." *Journal of the Polynesian Society* 68, no. 3 (1959): 177–80.

Stanley, Brian. "Africa through European Christian Eyes: The World Missionary Conference, Edinburgh 1910." In *African Identities and Global Christianity in the Twentieth Century,* edited by Klaus Korschorke. Wiesbaden: Harrassowitz Verlag, 2005.

———. *The Bible and the Flag: Protestant Missions and British Imperialism in the Nineteenth and Twentieth Centuries.* Leicester: Apollos, 1990.

———. "Mission and Human Identity in the Light of Edinburgh 1910." *Mission Studies* 26, no. 1 (2009): 80–97.

———. *The World Missionary Conference, Edinburgh 1910.* Grand Rapids: Eerdmans, 2009.

Stanley, Brian, ed. *Christian Missions and the Enlightenment*. Grand Rapids: Eerdmans, 2001.

Stewart, Selina. "The 'Blues' of Aratus." In *Beyond the Canon,* edited by M. A. Harder, R. F. Regtuit, and G. C. Wakker. Leuven: Peeters, 2006.

Stipe, Claude E. "Anthropologists versus Missionaries: The Influence of Presuppositions." *Current Anthropology* 21, no. 2 (1980): 165–79.

Stocking, George. *After Tylor: British Social Anthropology 1888–1951*. Madison: University of Wisconsin Press, 1995.

———. *Victorian Anthropology*. New York: The Free Press, 1987.

Strathern, Andrew, and Pamela J. Steward. "Ethnographic Records from the Western Highlands of Papua New Guinea: Missionary-Linguists, Missionary-Ethnographers." In *Anthropology's Debt to Missionaries,* edited by Leonard Plotnicov, Paula Brown, and Vinson Sutlive. Pittsburgh: University of Pittsburgh Press, 2007.

Strauss, W. Patrick. "Paradoxical Cooperation: Sir Joseph Banks and the London Missionary Society." *Historical Studies: Australia and New Zealand* 11 (1964): 246–52.

Stray, Christopher. *Classics Transformed: Schools, Universities, and Society in England, 1830–1960*. Oxford: Oxford University Press, 1998.

Sugirtharajah, R. S. *Exploring Postcolonial Biblical Criticism: History, Method, Practice*. Malden: John Wiley & Sons, 2011.

Swain, T., and D. B. Rose, eds. *Aboriginal Australians and Christian Missions: Ethnographic and Historical Studies*. Adelaide: Australian Association for the Study of Religions, 1988.

Thomas, Nicholas. *Colonialism's Culture: Anthropology, Travel and Government*. Cambridge: Polity Press, 1994.

———. *Entangled Objects: Exchange, Material Culture, and Colonialism in the Pacific*. Cambridge, MA: Harvard University Press, 1991.

———. *Islanders: The Pacific in the Age of Empire*. New Haven: Yale University Press, 2012.

Thomson, George D. *Aeschylus and Athens: A Study in the Social Origins of Drama*. 2nd ed. New York: Haskell House, 1967.

Thorne, Susan. *Congregational Missions and the Making of an Imperial Culture in Nineteenth-Century England*. Stanford: Stanford University Press, 1999.

Thornley, Andrew. *Exodus of the I Taukei: The Wesleyan Church in Fiji*. Suva: Institute of Pacific Studies, University of the South Pacific, 2002.

———. *The Inheritance of Hope: John Hunt, Apostle of Fiji*. Suva: Institute of Pacific Studies, 2000.

———. "On the Edges of Christian History in the Pacific: A Personal Journey." *Journal of Pacific Studies* 20 (1996): 175–87.

Tippett, Alan. *Solomon Islands Christianity: A Study in Growth and Obstruction*. London: Lutterworth, 1967.

Turman, Eboni. *Toward a Womanist Ethic of Incarnation: Black Bodies, the Black Church, and the Council of Chalcedon*. New York: Palgrave Macmillan, 2013.

Turner, Lynette. "Alfred W. Howitt and Lorimer Fison: 'Victorian' ethnography and the gendered 'primitive.'" In *Writing and Race,* edited by Tim Youngs. London: Longman, 1997.

Tzan, Douglas D. "Arioi for Christ: an exploration of early missions by Society Islanders." *Missiology* 37, no. 2 (2009): 221–35.

Urry, James. "'Notes and Queries on Anthropology' and the Development of Field Methods in British Anthropology, 1870–1920." *Proceedings of the Royal Anthropological Institute* (1972): 45–72.

Van der Geest, Sjaak. "Anthropologists and Missionaries: Brothers under the Skin." *Man* 25, no. 4 (1990): 588–601.

Viswanathan, Gauri. *Outside the Fold: Conversion, Modernity, and Belief*. Princeton: Princeton University Press, 1998.

Wallace, Lee. "*Fa'afine: Queens of Samoa* and the Elision of Homosexuality." *GLQ: A Journal of Lesbian and Gay Studies* 5, no. 1 (1999): 25–39.

Wanhalla, Angela. "'The Natives Uncivilize Me': Missionaries and Interracial Intimacy in Early New Zealand." In *Missionaries, Indigenous Peoples and Cultural Exchange,* edited by Patricia Grimshaw and Andrew May. Brighton, UK: Sussex Academic Press, 2011.

Warrington, John. *Everyman's Classical Dictionary*. London: J. M. Dent & Sons, 1970.

Webb, Michael. "Heart, Spirit and Understanding: Protestant Hymnody as an Agent of Transformation in Melanesia, 1840s–1940s." *Journal of Pacific History* 50, no. 3 (2015): 275–303.

Weir, Christine. "'White Man's Burden,' 'White Man's Privilege': Christian humanism and racial determinism in Oceania, 1890–1930." In *Foreign Bodies: Oceania and the Science of Race 1750–1940*, edited by Bronwen Douglas and Chris Ballard. Canberra: ANU e-Press, 2008.

Wench, Ida. *Mission to Melanesia*. London: Elek Books, 1961.

Wetherell, David. *Charles Abel and the Kwato Mission of Papua New Guinea, 1891–1901*. Melbourne: Melbourne University Press, 1996.

———. *Reluctant Mission: The Anglican Church in Papua New Guinea 1891–1942*. St. Lucia: University of Queensland Press, 1977.

Whitelam, Keith W. "The Social World of the Bible." In *The Cambridge Companion to Biblical Interpretation,* edited by John Barton. Cambridge: Cambridge University Press, 2006.

Whiteman, Darrell L. *Melanesians and Missionaries: An Ethnohistorical Study of Social and Religious Change in the Southwest Pacific*. Pasadena: William Carey Library, 1983.

Wilken, John. "A Theological Approach to Reconciliation." In *Reconciling Our Differences: A Christian Approach to Recognizing Aboriginal Land Rights,* edited by Frank Brennan. Brunswick: Aurora Books, 1992.

Wilson, Robert R. "Anthropology and the Study of the Old Testament." *Union Seminary Quarterly Review* 34, no. 3 (1979): 175–81.

Wolf, Eric. *Europe and the People without History.* Berkeley: University of California Press, 1982.

Wolfe, Patrick. *Settler Colonialism and the Transformation of Anthropology: The Politics and Poetics of an Ethnographic Event*. London: Cassell, 1999.

Wood, A. Harold. *Overseas Missions of the Australian Methodist Church*. Melbourne: Aldersgate Press, 1978.

Yeo, Eileen. "Social Surveys in the Eighteenth and Nineteenth Centuries." In *The Cam-*

bridge History of Science, vol. 7, *The Modern Social Sciences*. Cambridge: Cambridge University Press, 2003.

Young, Michael W. "Commemorating Missionary Heroes: Local Christianity and Narratives of Nationalism." In *Narratives of Nation in the South Pacific*, ed. Ton Otto and Nicholas Thomas. Amsterdam: Harwood Academic Publishers, 1997.

Young, Robert J. C. *Colonial Desire: Hybridity in Theory, Culture and Race*. London: Routledge, 1995.

Unpublished Theses

Carolane, Peter. "Instinct for Mission: John Bulmer, Missionary to the Aborigines of Victoria, 1855–1913." PhD thesis, University of Melbourne, 2009.

Close-Barry, Kirstie Louise. "A Mission Divided: Race and Culture in Fiji's Methodist Mission." PhD thesis, Deakin University, 2014.

Hallett, Keith Robert. "The Reverend George Brown and Australasian Methodist Missionary Endeavours in the Pacific, 1860 to 1914." PhD thesis, University of Melbourne, 2011.

Holman, Jeffrey Paparoa. "Best of both worlds: Esldon Best and the metamorphosis of Maori spirituality. Te painga rawa o nga ao tokura: Te Peehi me te putanga ke o te wairua Maori." PhD thesis, University of Canterbury, 2006.

Jensz, Felicity Ann. "Collecting Cultures for God: German Moravian Missionaries and the British Colony of Victoria, Australia, 1848–1908." PhD thesis, University of Melbourne, 2007.

Lousberg, Marjan. "Dr. Edward Shortland and the politics of ethnography." PhD thesis, University of Otago, 2007.

Index